Bat Out of Hell

Bat Out of Hell

by
Granger Korff

Bat Out of Hell

Published in 2019 by
30° South Publishers (Pty) Ltd
16 Ivy Road, Pinetown 3610
South Africa
email: office@30degreessouth.co.za
website: www.30degreessouth.co.za

Copyright © Granger Korff, 2019

Cover by Anthony Cuerden (Flying Ant Designs)
Final Layout Blair Couper
Sketches by Murray Korff

Printed by Pinetown Printers (Pty) Ltd, Pinetown, KwaZulu-Natal

ISBN 978-1-928359-11-1

All rights reserved. No part of this publication may be reproduced, stored, manipulated in any retrieval system, or transmitted in any mechanical, electronic form or by any other means, without the prior written authority of the publishers, except for short extracts in media reviews. Any person who engages in any unauthorised activity in relation to this publication shall be liable to criminal prosecution and claims for civil and criminal damages.

DISCLAIMER:
The statements and opinions contained in the publications of 30 Degrees South are solely those of the individual authors and do not necessarily reflect those of the editors or the publisher.

Dedication

*I dedicate this book to South African soldiers
who served in the Angolan bush war,
whose memories of a time
when we were soldiers
can seem just like yesterday.*

ACKNOWLEDGEMENTS

Writing the sequel to *19 with a Bullet* was not as simple and as straightforward as the story of being a combat paratrooper in Angola during the height of the Border War. The sequel, *Bat Out of Hell*, covers the longer aftermath of fighting on the Angolan border, is spread over a longer period of time, and is divided between two continents, illustrating the fact that no matter where you travel, you take your demons with you. As Virgil said in *The Aeneid*:

> It is easy to go down into Hell;
> Night and day, the gates of dark Death stand wide;
> But to climb back again, to retrace one's steps to the upper air – there's the rub, the task.

I would like to thank some of the people closest to me for their support and for encouraging me to sit down amongst the hustle and bustle of daily life and write this book, *Bat Out of Hell*.

Thank you to my talented brother, Murray Korff, for his endless ideas in form, setting and story and for providing the excellent drawings in the book; my daughter, Natalie Korff, a young writer herself, who has tirelessly listened to my ramblings and offered her inspiration; my long-time partner, Tina Marie Angelone, for listening and pushing me onwards; and especially to my father and my hero, Nicolaas Korff, for endlessly asking me, "How is the writing coming along son?"

Thank you also to Roger Brook, former Rifleman at 1 Parachute Battalion in South Africa, now Roger Brook Ph.D., Professor of Psychology and the Director of Military Psychology at Duquesne University, Pittsburgh, for his valuable input and notes on my writing, and for having granted me the use of his papers and providing reading references and information on Post-Traumatic Stress; to Peter Chapman, also for his input and notes; and to my comrade, John Delaney, for assuring me that this book is necessary.

Acknowledgements

    I am grateful also to Aulette Goliath and other staff associated with my publishers, 30 Degrees South. And, of course, all the readers of *19 with a Bullet* who kept asking, "So what happened next and when is the next book?"

* A belated thank you to Debbie Smith, a South African living in Los Angeles, for having re-ordered the rough format of my first book, *19 with a Bullet,* into an accomplished format.

* Some names have been changed in this book. Some of the time frames have been shortened or extended, to a limited degree, to include certain events within that period.

* This memoir is written as a non-fiction narrative style spread over two parts: the period immediately after my time in the army and then a jump forward to some 14 years later. I have described in detail some violent combat scenes that may be disturbing or which may be perceived as being over the top. After much thought about the matter I have decided to describe these scenes as they occurred, in real life.

* I have written my memories as a paratrooper. There were many other military units within the SADF (as it was then) and the police force, who were in the thick of it.

* Sketches done by Murray Korff

CONTENTS

Prologue 11

Chapter 1 WIN SOME, LOSE SOME 18

Chapter 2 ATLANTIC BREEZE 21

Chapter 3 HANGIN' HARD, STAYIN' TOUGH 40

Chapter 4 TAKING IT TO THE TOP 49

Chapter 5 BACK IN JOHANNESBURG 60

Chapter 6 WAY DOWN INSIDE 68

Chapter 7 MOVIN' ON 80

Chapter 8 JOHNNY 'DUNDEE' HOGG 95

Chapter 9 LEARNING FAST 107

Chapter 10 PASSIVE HOUND 115

Chapter 11 CITY OF ANGELS 135

Chapter 12 KNEE DEEP 148

Chapter 13 PAIN, NOW NOT WASTED 175

Chapter 14 IF I STUMBLE AND FALL 184

Chapter 15 SUCKER PUNCH 204

Chapter 16 HARDER THAN DIAMONDS, TOUGHER THAN STEEL 219

Chapter 17 THE BEST PRICE I CAN GET 234

Chapter 18 ALWAYS FIGHT HARD 251

Chapter 19 FACES LIKE FLINT, EYES LIKE FIRE 260

Chapter 20 RUN ALL YOU CAN 280

Chapter 21 AMBUSH 292

Chapter 22 TEN THOUSAND MILES 302

Chapter 23 RIDE THE SAME TRAIN 315

Chapter 24 A LIGHT CLOAK OF RELIEF 326

Chapter 25 CITY OF ANGELS ON FIRE 345

Chapter 26 FINLANDIA 361

Chapter 27 RICH AS A KING 374

Glossary 379

The might of the Airborne – Exercise Iron Eagle 1988.
Night drop of 600 paratroopers, 34 Tonnes of equipment and 16 vehicles into a rough drop zone

PROLOGUE

Sometimes, sitting alone, I would try to imagine the number of SWAPO, FAPLA and Cuban enemy killed during the South African Bush War ... surely ten thousand or more. I would imagine them dressed in uniform on parade together, brigade after brigade of SWAPO men – we called them 'terrorists' – ten thousand souls standing at ease in open order formation on a huge parade ground somewhere in the African bush. On an opposing parade ground, facing them, the souls of the South African soldiers who had died in our small war, 2,700, black and white together, also in company strengths. On this same parade are our allies in the bush war, UNITA, also in large numbers, all on parade in Valhalla. Heroes to their own, enemies to the opposing armies; men who died fighting for what each one thought of as freedom.

Men who deserve to be remembered by everyone but, sadly, who are mostly remembered only by their comrades who participated in the conflict, and friends and families.

For many South Africans now past middle age, the Bush War of some 40 years ago often seems just like yesterday. Then, we young men, fresh out of high school, heard the shouts of battle and were unquestionably prepared to do our best for our country – steely-nerved and ready to make the ultimate sacrifice for a cause we possibly didn't even fully understand. For this generation, and particularly those at the tip of the spear, there will always be a quiet part, deep within us, that few others will know or understand, other than a comrade or someone who was there, with a similar history.

How difficult it is to forget a time when we were at our finest, young men pushing ourselves so hard, past what we thought physically possible, bonding with strangers who, at home, you might not have given the time of day. Strangers with whom we grew into men, who became comrades and brothers, men to rely on, for whom in a split second you might give up your own life, to save his. Many today still walk with a limp, a bent or missing arm, some have suicided, years later, from living in constant pain. The lives of many other comrades were cut short at this point.

In some ways they may have been the lucky ones, never to grow old, shabby and weary, like the rest of us. They are buried in graves with epitaphs such as "Our ever-loving son and soldier" and "At thy call we will answer", or similar. Many of these graves sit in the red sands of Africa, while their families have moved on, emigrated overseas, leaving their brave young son buried alone in his native land, just another casualty of the country he had died for, in defence of freedom.

And our enemy, SWAPO, who put up a brave fight against such great odds. SWAPO, the great red threat who have been as quiet as mice since the cessation of the Border War. How many shallow SWAPO graves, how many scattered, uncovered bones of these fighters lie in the Angolan bush? And the SWAPO soldiers who survived, who are now the same age as SADF survivors, what aftermath and memories do they live with, from their time fighting against the South African war machine? Is it all also "just like yesterday" for them?

Trying to make sense these days, of our current, turbulent world, filled with terror, horrendous wars in the Middle East, crime in South Africa at an all-time high … it took a lot of thinking on my part to assess whether it was relevant, or even worthwhile, to write about a subject such as the psychological aftermath of the South African Bush War. So what? Who cares?

But, as I chewed over it, it became clear that yes, it is relevant, it is just as pertinent as anything written on any past conflict, about big or small wars. This history is significant, even today. These memories of the Border War are just as real as the memories of any other person in any other war in the past.

I am certain that, to this very day, these legions of men, South Africans, Namibians, Angolans, friends and foes alike, retain deep and vivid memories, and a host of mental scars, with which they have wrestled for decades past, since our own 'small war'.

It seems just like yesterday that we heard the birds erupting out of the trees, like bats out of hell, after the first, early morning, loud reports from a contact, or a bomb drop, when we hunted one another in a small, remote area of southern Africa, an area that most people on earth have never heard of.

It is in this spirit that I have written this book, *Bat Out of Hell*. It is the sequel to my earlier book, *19 with a Bullet*, which described my time in 1 Parachute

Prologue

Battalion in the Bush War. I am one of those young men who walked out of the gates of 1 Parachute Battalion as a civilian. Little did I know that I, as with many others, had just begun my own private battle, one that would last much longer than the time I spent in the dry bush of Angola.

From an aviary close by, the hauntingly shrill cry of the fish eagle, the emblem of 1 Parachute Battalion, shattered the silence of the parade ground. The tall, square-jawed, fearsome Regimental Sergeant Major, a legend and a man amongst men, stood ramrod straight, then he slowly turned his large head and quietly surveyed the six parachute companies on his parade ground. Everything was to his satisfaction. He cracked his jumper boot into the hard gravel and began marching, in long strides, one arm swinging up level with his shoulder, the other holding a pace stick firmly tucked into his armpit. The weak winter sun reflected off his mirror smooth red jumper boots, slamming into the gravel of the famous parade ground.

This Airborne parade ground was the site where the spirits of legions of men had been cracked and ruined. Broken down, after having given their all, having been chased off and sent back, marked 'Return to Unit' – not Paratrooper grade. Others had risen in triumph, overcoming their pain and hardships, to discover on this same parade ground the mettle from which they had been made.

"ONE PARACHUTE BATTALIOOOOOON COME OOOOON PARAAAAAAAADE!"

Six hundred boots cracked as one, as the Parachute Companies came smartly to attention and stood as erect as their formidable sergeant major facing them. They came to open order staring dead ahead, inspected by sharp-eyed officers. Some companies were dressed in new darker uniforms and encompassed younger South African boys, just out of high school, yet to become men on the battle field. The Delta and Hotel companies were half way through their training. We looked on eagerly as our senior 'parabats' stood at attention; this was their last day at Parachute Battalion. Older and seasoned, lean and darkly tanned, their uniforms were faded almost to white. They all had a glint in their eyes that would probably stay there forever. For these men this was their last parade on the hallowed ground of 1 Parachute Battalion before returning to their families. To look for jobs, wives and careers.

These two hundred young men, fresh from high school, had volunteered and served their time at the tip of the spear for their nation, in the well hushed-up Bush War. Having completed their harsh training they had seen swift action in dry African bush, fighting against brave, bloodshot-eyed, Communist-backed insurgents on the Angolan border, equally committed to their cause but not as well trained and supported. They all carried with them memories that would not easily be forgotten. The smell of gunpowder. A blur of movement through the leaves. There! Shoot! Bam bam ... bam bam bam! Rush forward, split up, search the area, shouts of caution. Sounds of silence. Laboured breathing, boots crunching. The wounded moaning for mercy before death in the African sand. Bang! Body count. Stone faces flash to momentary grins of triumph and sighs of relief ... smoke a quick Marlboro. Move on.

These two Senior Paratrooper Companies had proved themselves well in battle in Angola and had left scores of our nation's enemies dead in the bush of Angola and Ovamboland. Their time was now done and the junior Paratrooper Companies of Delta and Hotel would follow in their boots.

They walked out of the gates of Parachute Battalion with their maroon berets set at proud angles on their heads, their polished wings on their chests. These were not the same high school boys who had walked in through these gates, two years ago. It was late 1981 and their war was supposedly over ... but for many of these soldiers, and many others who had passed through the big iron gates of 1 Parachute Battalion before them, walked through those gates with a dull cast to their eyes ... the long silent battle that lay ahead had only just begun.

Within the medieval church anyone and everyone who had shed blood during a war had to do penance. Those who had committed atrocities had to do even more penance. Even non-combatants in the armies had to do penance. Most warrior societies, as well as many not dominated by warfare, have historically engaged in communal rites which provided their returning fighters with purification.

The Bible (Numbers 31: 19–20 and 23–24) (KJV) tells us that God through Moses demanded a seven-day purification process when the Israelite army returned from a revenge attack against the Midianites:

Numbers Chapter 31:
19. And do ye abide without the camp seven days: whosoever hath killed any person, and whosoever hath touched any slain, purify both yourselves and your captives on the third day, and the seventh day.
20. And purify all your raiment and all that is made of skins, and all work of goats' hair, and all things made of wood.
23. Everything that may abide the fire, ye shall make it go through the fire, and it shall be clean: nevertheless it shall be purified with the water of separation: and all that abideth not the fire ye shall make go through the water.
24. And ye shall wash your clothes on the seventh day, and ye shall be clean, and afterward ye shall come into the camp.

In addition to this, in *Odysseus in America: Combat Trauma and the Trials of Homecoming*, Jonathan Shay, a psychiatrist working with Vietnam veterans, writes:

The ancient Athenians had a distinctive therapy of purification, healing and reintegration of returning soldiers that was undertaken as a whole political community. Sacred theatre was one of its primary means of reintegrating the returning veteran into the social sphere as 'citizen'.
The early Romans had a ceremony of purification for returning armies, the details of which we know little. It apparently involved passing under a beam erected across a street, with head covered, as well as other ceremonies, purifications and sacrifices.

In another book, *War and the Soul: Healing Our Nation's Veterans from Post-Traumatic Stress Disorder*, psychotherapist Dr Edward Tick explores how other cultures define and treat the trauma of war. He discovered that:

… for thousands of years, American Indians, like tribal peoples around the world, have been dealing with the problem we now call PTSD, but in a very different way. Suffering warriors were people whose *soul and spirit* had been tainted by what they had done and witnessed; so they were cleansed and purified through rituals. There were other ceremonies intended to transfer the responsibility of a warrior's actions to the entire community, relieving him of the burden of his deeds. Another step was the honouring of veterans by the community, an important rite of passage that put them on a life-long path of service to their people.

All of these different rituals, although merely symbolic, were powerful medicine for returning soldiers. They provided recognition of these men, and acceptance of the actions undertaken during their service to their nation or their tribe.

Roger Brooke, Ph.D., is a veteran of South Africa's 1 and 3 Parachute Battalions. He is now Professor of Psychology and Director of the Military Psychological Services at Duquesne University, Pittsburgh, and President of Soldier's Heart. Roger advises ex-combatants as follows:

A mistake that so many veterans make is to attempt to forget the trauma of the war zone by hurling themselves into civilian life as though they can become merely civilians again. Much of what we call combat post traumatic disorder can be understood as the insistence of memory and of the debt that is owed to a terrible knowledge which will not go away. The veteran cannot undo this knowledge once it is experientially known. It cannot be medicated away, nor obliterated with drugs or alcohol either – at least not forever. The challenge for the veteran returning from war is to find a way to a life that can embrace this knowledge, which is never far from one's mind.

In South Africa, on the last day before leaving 1 Parachute Battalion, after an action-filled two years the 'cleansing rite' for Delta Company 1980/81 was to stand together in a big circle for ten minutes, casually smoking our Marlboro cigarettes, each one taking a turn to tell his comrades what he was going to do back on Civvy Street, now that military service was over. One person said he was going to be a teacher, another said he wanted to study engineering, and so on. When it was my turn I said, "I was going to live life." Whatever that meant, I didn't quite know.

The last day had finally arrived for us. One day we were in Angola on operation, the next we had a quick final parade, smoked a cigarette and walked out of the big iron gates. Our time in the army was over, as quickly as it had begun. And so, without much in the way of purification, the living of life began for me.

Chapter One

WIN SOME LOSE SOME

'Don't Stop Believin' ~ *Journey*

Blood spouted from my nose, spilling down onto my chest ... no surprise after the wild, no-holds-barred, first round. I glared across the ring at my opponent and got up from my stool, ready for the second round. He was already up, standing solid, shaking his head from side to side like a bull, swinging his short muscular arms, his eyes glazed over, lost in the lust for fighting. I balled my fists inside my small amateur boxing gloves and immediately threw out any ideas of the sweet science of boxing – this was going to be a street fight with gloves.

The amateur boxing tournament was taking place in Mitchell's Plain, in an area known as the Cape Flats, southeast of the central business district of Cape Town. My stocky, well-muscled opponent, as I had been warned, was a known street fighter in this gang-infested area, with the scars to prove it. He obviously didn't give a damn about the future of his boxing career, or any boxing rules. My groin still ached from him blatantly lifting his knee into me in the first round, and I was feeling nauseous. The ref seemed equally unconcerned about this; he had given the wild-eyed street fighter a warning but allowed the fight to continue. That suited me fine, I had no problem with that. Let's go! Let's take off the fucking gloves, if you want! Let's take them off and throw them out and do things that way!

The bell was hard to hear above the disco music that played throughout the fight. He came straight at me from across the ring, no technique, no planning, just plain filled with rage to fight. But, instead of using his fighting rage to my advantage, I met him head on in the middle of the ring, just as keen to clash and put an end to this. I had also forgotten all about boxing. This was a street fight behind a party hall, a brawl in a stairway leading up to the disco door. He propelled his stocky body forward, pushed me hard with his left arm, I spun around, using his momentum, and threw untidy, hard punches, the kind you throw in an alley fight. No straight neat boxing punches, as I'd been taught in the gym. These were vicious hooks, and ugly, looping, overhand rights with full power. He turned to follow me, almost at a run, his arms up high, not worried about looking unorthodox. I shifted my weight and sat into my punches, delivering a combination that drove him off.

I followed him into the corner and tried to take advantage of him moving backwards, away from my attack; he stumbled back, tripped untidily over his own feet, but managed to stay upright by catching the ropes with one hand. I was just as off balance but quickly took advantage, slamming him with a hard left and then a right hand, into the side of his head. I felt hit home. Quickly he lifted both hands to cover his face, protecting himself.

"Now!" I shouted to myself, jumping back for space. I hit him hard, left hooks to his exposed but very muscular body. I saw him buckle as my left hook found its mark above his liver. Forgetting all about boxing he charged forward to get out of the corner, his hands still held high.

"What the fuck have I done to you? What's your fucking problem?"

I was unable to avoid his sloppy, unpredictable charge as he tried to grab me with an open left glove, pushing me backwards against the ropes.

"Spin around! Spin around!" I heard my coach shout.

I tried to spin but as I turned his open hands pushed me back into the ropes. The ref was on the other side, unable to see as our bodies clashed together. My opponent's face was five inches from mine and I looked up, staring into his wild, crazed eyes.

Mother fucker!

He had slipped his hand under my left arm and was holding onto the ropes with one hand, locking me in, so that I couldn't escape the ropes. I knew it was coming right then ... I could see the thought in his wild eyes ... but this time I was ready, judging his move as he dropped his head. In full view of the referee he again viciously lifted his knee, with all his might, up towards my groin – but I had judged well and turned my body just in time. His knee dug hard into the inside of my thigh.

Within seconds he lifted his head and glared at me, still five inches from my face. Without hesitation I threw my upper body forward and slammed him with a head butt, catching him high on his forehead; I could hear and feel the solid thump as it connected. The crowd went wild, catcalling and whistling, and the ref finally rushed in from his safe distance, pushing his way in between us to break us apart. I seized the opportunity, spun away from the ropes and walked to the middle of the ring. I thought without a doubt the fight would be stopped and both of us disqualified, but no, this was Mitchells Plain ... the ref turned to the judges, indicated that he had warned both of us, but that the fight would continue. Then he motioned us to box on. The watching crowd, mostly Cape Coloureds, hooted and laughed and jeered over the disco music. My crazed opponent seemed a little confused, his face was contorted with emotion and he looked around him like a disoriented bull trying to find the matador. The ref gestured for us to continue and I didn't waste a second. I flew into him with everything that I had, my fists feeling like rocks inside the small gloves. I felt them connecting and drove him backwards, not stopping until he went sprawling onto the canvas.

In the third round my challenger floored me with a flash knockdown, but at the end of the brutal, untidy, street fight I was judged the winner. The referee quickly raised my hand and then turned to leave the ring. My seemingly possessed opponent glared at me as I left the ring without shaking his hand. I was glad to see a blue knob swelling on his forehead from my head butt.

In the dressing room I sat down, pulled off my hand wraps and handed the small, worn-out horsehair-filled boxing gloves to the kid they had sent to collect them for the next fight. I was unhappy at how the fight had turned out; it had been wild and rough from the first bell when he had rushed out at me like a crazy man. I guess this was a lesson for me to be ready at all times for different opponents. I stuffed my bloodstained boxing pants and vest into my maroon 1 Parachute battalion duffel bag.

Oh well, a win is a win.

Chapter Two
ATLANTIC BREEZE

'Abracadabra' ~ *The Steve Miller Band*

It had been six months since I had finished my two years national service with 1 Parachute Battalion. It had been an honour to be a South African paratrooper. We were trained, chased, kicked, cursed at, humiliated, encouraged, supported, taught, pushed and hammered through mental barriers that we never knew we had. All the time we were being moulded to work together as a tight unit, an all-for-one-and-one-for-all fighting unit, as close as a family, a group within which you could all depend on one another, for your life.

But that was all behind me now. A thing of the past. For a number of reasons I had always thought there was a good chance that I might not live to make it past 21 years old and for the last two years I had put any future planning on hold. But here I was, alive and kicking, and now it looked as though I was not going to get off that easily; I would have to come up with a Plan B.

So I sat in the fair city of Cape Town, watching the cold Atlantic waves crash on the white shore, listening to the wild cries of the seagulls, and wondering what my next move was going to be. I was a civvy again, free to roam, free to do what I wanted. No more sergeant pushing me into line, no more kitting up and racing to the fire force helicopter as the siren wailed. No more tracking the SWAPO enemy through the dry bush.

Tania (my long-time, beautiful girlfriend, with whom I had been involved since high school and who had waited for me all through my time in the army) and I had decided to get away from the Johannesburg East Rand scene and move to Cape Town. We had arrived in windy Cape Town at the end of a sweltering summer, determined to try and live away from families and friends, to give it a go at living on our own. Tania was a doll and I had been taken with her from the moment I first saw her, when I was 16 years old and she only 14. She had brunette hair and a strong face with small freckles and big green eyes.

The rest of her body was equally well put together.

This was our first attempt at living together, becoming independent and entering the work place as adults. But, after seven years of being together, trouble was brewing in paradise. Close to the end of my military service, Tania had met me outside the gates of 1 Parachute Battalion, for one of my weekend passes. She had placed her hands on my shoulders and looked at me as an inspector would assess a system of wheels and cogs, for effective operation. Matter-of-factly she told me, "You've changed." I didn't know it then, but she was right.

Since then, and unbeknown to me, a slow, low intensity battle had been brewing within me, from the time that I walked out of the gates of 1 Parachute Battalion for the 'last' time. I had always been a somewhat reserved but happy-go-lucky type of youngster, and I had not realised there was a cauldron of confliction bubbling inside me, until it surfaced and faced me, head-on, one hot summer afternoon in Cape Town, with the arrival of a guest, a new friend.

My new friend was a tall blond American. He was perched on the wall of the small brick balcony of our flat, dressed casually in jeans and a T-shirt, wearing that ridiculous jarhead haircut worn by most US Marines and a broad smile. Slowly he swallowed a mouthful of white wine, crinkled his brow and gave an approving smile.

"It's good – I had never heard of South African wine before I came out here. Who'd think of wine coming from Africa … it's pretty good though," he said in his slow American twang.

Matt was a good guy. He was a US Marine consigned to a year in South Africa as a guard at the offices of the US Consulate General, in downtown Cape Town. He was much the same as the few Americans I had met up to that point, confident in himself, with a big easy smile and could talk the hind leg off a donkey.

We chatted easily while I spread the coals in the small *braai* we had set up on the balcony.

"Man, I've noticed you guys take your barbecues real seriously over here."

I moved our chairs to create elbow room for flipping the chops and *wors* (sausage) on the *braai*. Summer had arrived and Tania was wearing shorts and a skimpy top that barely covered her enticing figure. I had adopted the casual summer dress worn by the local people of colour in the Western Cape, white slacks with white shoes and a loose Island shirt ... I fancied myself as tropical island shaker and mover.

I loved Cape Town in the summer. The scent of *fynbos* (fine-leaved plants) from huge Table mountain mixed with the salty Atlantic breeze wafting in from the ocean ... Coco Rico rum, the scent of suntan oil ... long concrete steps winding down to small sexy beaches, fine white beach sand that squeaked as you walked on it, big round beach boulders, beautiful girls in short pants and halter neck tops, wild frizzy hair, sexy round backsides in bikini bottoms ... brightly coloured ice cream and foot long cheese hot dogs ... beach traffic and the newly released aquamarine colour Mercedes Benz. Life was good.

I sipped my white wine while bragging to Matt the American about our wonderful country: our well-built South African girls of mixed German, Dutch and French stock; our vineyards that had been around since the days of Jan Van Riebeeck; the upright and easy-going nature of most South Africans – hard working and hard drinking people. Gold mines with shafts that dropped down five miles into the earth, where thousands of black and white miners battled daily to wrestle gold from the earth, for us and the rest of the world. I gave my new American friend a brief history lesson of the early rush for gold and diamonds, drawing on stuff I could remember from school. He was all ears. I told him about the SADF our great defence force.

And then, after a few glasses of wine, I made the big mistake of fetching my military photograph album, to show to Matt. Instinctively, Tania knew this was a bad move. When I returned to the balcony with the album, she caught my eye and discreetly shook her head, a non-verbal 'don't do this' gesture. I ignored her.

This was not a normal photograph album; it was a visual record of the two years I had spent in Parachute Battalion. Matt opened it to see the faces of my friends and comrades grinning at the camera, blackened with camouflage grease, stacked with heavy kit, filthy from months at a time in the Angolan bush. Matt stopped at the pages showing SWAPO insurgent fighters, lifeless in the bush, in bunkers, among sparse foliage, or wherever they had made their last stand. Some had been killed after a long day's chase through the dry bush – their sweat showed on their uniforms, the desperation of the chase was etched on their dead faces; their brains laying split and broken in the sand next to them.

Matt was startled, his eyes wide, "What the hell is this?"

I pointed to the photographs. "These are photos of the Bush War on the Angolan border that I was telling you about. These are SWAPO guerrillas; these are Communist backed insurgents, crossing our border, trying to get independence for South West Africa. But they were backed by the Communists."

Silently Matt flipped through the album, a glazed look in his eyes. Photos of young conscripts, paratroopers, smiling, training, standing with parachutes, then later in the operational area, looking older and grim. South African youngsters who were taking the fight to SWAPO guerrillas and the Angolan army, FAPLA. Sitting beside captured Soviet T55 tanks and BTR-80s, armoured vehicles produced in the USSR. Photos showing tall columns of dirty brown smoke from South African Mirage jets in attack, strafing the air defence units of the Angolan army with 1,000-pound bombs, burning Soviet tanks, villages on fire, helicopters flying at tree level packed with stony faced young paratroopers, heading towards contact.

I was excited, galvanised by talking to a fellow soldier about my experiences in Angola. There was a lot inside me that I wanted to tell. Matt the Marine asked questions about the Border War and our conversation turned to warfare, killing, dawn ambushes and sudden death. I asked him about the Marines. He said he had not seen any action, he was just doing a job at the US embassy.

I poured our cheap Carafino wine with a heavy hand. The flames spurted and Tania ran for a glass of water while I used white wine to tamp them down, still talking. I felt my heart quicken and familiar goose bumps appear as I described various attacks and contacts that I had been part of … I told him how close I had come to being shot while bent over, puking, during a sudden asthma attack after a ten-minute fire fight, right in front of a terrorist concealed in the grass not twenty feet from me, an old AK-47 in his hands. Quick as a blink the two comrades to the left of me in the sweep line, Johnny Fox and Greef, had shot him before he could shoot me – while I was bent over, retching, a few metres in front of his hiding place.

I told Matt about how we had been led by an old Angolan man to take FAPLA soldiers by surprise … about the American made M79 grenade launcher we had used and had he ever seen what happened to someone who had been struck by a 40mm shell? How hard it was to shoot a man running in zigzag to save his life, in front of you. My hands shook as I mouthed off. It was unlike me to jabber away like this, but I carried on, forgetting about the braai. Matt laughed (too loudly?) as he watched me try to save the meat from the flames, but I was too late – the meat was scorched, the evening ruined.

Matt told us that before he had arrived in South Africa he had heard, vaguely, of a bush war in Angola but hadn't known any details. He said he had barely heard of South Africa, before being stationed here as a guard for the US consul general. By now, the bravado I had shown while talking about my time in the army, had evaporated. I felt small and realised I had slipped into a dark and ugly place. I stopped talking. I felt detached from everything around me; now it felt meaningless to be braaiing and trying to have a good time. What's the point?

Matt carried on talking and said that had also never heard of our famous wines. He had never heard of Sun City, Anneline Kriel or even our boxing heavyweight champion, Gerrie Coetzee. Who the hell has not heard of South African wine? I thought SA wine was world famous? Or at least of Gerrie? He continued chatting, crunching on the caramel popcorn that Tania had found, thinking Matt might enjoy it, being an American.

"I don't think most folk at home have even heard of South Africa. How many white people are there in the country, you say?"

"I think about five million white people."

"Only five million white people?"

"Yeah, five million."

"That's all?"

"Ja."

"Not many."

"Not many what?"

"Well, not many people here."

"There are a lot of people in this country."

"Well, your country is small, my man. We have twelve million people in the state of Pennsylvania alone."

He had stopped drinking but I went ahead and poured myself another glass of cheap wine.

Matt chuckled as he told me that my country, although beautiful, with good wine and gorgeous girls, was essentially as important to world affairs as a pimple on a pig's butt.

"And all those photos that you showed me, of when you were in Angola, all those dead bodies, what do you call them … terrorists … no one knows that you are fighting to defend your border. No one even knows about it."

The mood had turned dark and Tania tried her best to lighten it, bustling around with a worried smile, carrying away the burnt meat and the empty wine bottles, bringing out Coke instead. But all the good feelings had fizzled out. I wished I hadn't told him about the fighting in Angola; it seemed that once I started I couldn't stop … and it had all gone downhill from there. But what are you supposed to do, pretend that it never happened, never tell anyone? Like the old veterans from World Wars I and II, whose families say, "Dad never spoke about it, not once in his life, until the day that he died." Is that the way to handle it – silence forever?

But now I felt that the consequences of talking about close enemy contacts and sudden death in the bush were not worth the effort. To Matt it was just a story, to me it had been reality. And I was back in it. I felt as if somebody had plugged me into an electric socket, current running through me, my heart pounding. Suddenly I was aware, for the first time, that I felt somehow separated from other people, that a wall was being built around me, that the first bricks had probably already been set in place the day I had walked out the gates of Parachute Battalion. This process had probably started about a year before, but I had never really noticed it. Here, now, the first sign of a fierce and lonesome conflict was showing itself, from inside me. The shouts of battle, the rifle kicking against my shoulder, gun shots, gun smoke, leaping out of a fire force helicopter, the yelling of orders, pulling the trigger … body count, collateral damage, stacking the captured AK-47s, scratching a notch above the hand grip of my R4 rifle. These memories had become an exhilarating but also soul-crushing part of me, a sound track to almost everything that I would do and they were not going away anytime soon.

I had smashed a few wine glasses during my pantomime of a deadly ambush in Angola and now I felt foolish about it. My hands were shaking, I was not feeling good ... I had slipped into a strange and dark place. I wanted to jump over the balcony, take off my shirt and run all the way to Table Mountain. The Marine and I sipped at our Cokes and I tried to make light conversation. I told Matt that America was responsible for a tradition that had taken hold here in the Western Cape, a minstrel festival known originally as the Coon Carnival, now called the Cape Town Minstrel Festival, with its traditional song of '*Daar Kom Die Alibama*' (Here Comes the Alabama) about the CSS *Alabama*, a Confederate ship that had visited Cape Town in 1863 ... but Matt was a Yankee and didn't find the story funny.

I was disappointed that the average American didn't know much, if anything, about our great country. What about our proteas, Table Mountain, Stellenbosch wines, our brilliant beaches? Surely, they had heard of Anneline Kriel, or Gerrie Coetzee ... but no.

"Well, one thing you guys have in this country that *is* a damn good thing is that sausage – what's that sausage called again?" as he was saying his goodbyes.

"*Boerewors.*"

"Yeah, that's it ... *boerewors* ... damn fine stuff."

§

Quite soon after arriving in Cape Town, I had been lucky enough to score an apprenticeship as a plumber, with a big plumbing firm working on the new 32 storey Southern Suns building in downtown Cape Town. I had been told that there was a long line of wannabe plumbers and that I was lucky to have been offered this apprenticeship. It was my first job after having spent two years in the army. Early one morning I reported for duty on the huge high-rise construction site with a small and useless tool box of household spanners, pliers and a tape measure. I was teamed up with a skinny, cheerful, Cape Coloured plumber (qualified) named Lawrence. He wore a perpetual smile on his face and always had spit in the corners of his mouth. My journeyman tutor would prattle on all day, carrying on about this and that. He found it hilarious when, my first day on the job, a worker fired a Hilti gun (which uses a small cartridge) a few yards from my head and instantly I dropped almost flat, kneeled low on the floor, causing a group of Cape Coloured plumbers to fall about with laughter.

"Ha ha!, *Jy is lekker bos befok my larney* (you are nicely bush crazy my smarty-pants) … don't worry, you not in the army now!"

My appointed journeyman, Lawrence, laughed along with them. It had been four months since I had heard a gunshot fired in anger, but my reflexes were still on edge. Feeling like a goon I had laughed along with them, at myself, but sheepishly.

Now it was the beginning of a cold and rainy winter in Cape Town and being a plumber on a high-rise was losing its appeal. It was tough, for a first job. I rose at 05h00 to catch the train in the dark, together with the hordes of people heading to work in the city. I have only fleeting memories of my grandfather, Theo Ohlsson, whom I met just once; he had been a master plumber on the railways in Cape Town and had probably travelled these very same rails, boarding the train at the Observatory station on his way to work in the morning. Grandfather Theo had been in North Africa during World War II, where he served as an engineer during the rout of Field Marshal Erwin Rommel. Apparently, he had come home a different man after the war … One of the only the handful of stories that I knew about him that I remembered, was my mother telling me that as a child that during the war he had crawled around on his belly, day after day, "poking with a bayonet", trying to locate German land mines.

I drilled holes in the concrete floors above and hammered in anchors to hang pipes in position. I learned to solder copper fittings … and found something familiar about the acrid smoke that rose up while burning solder – to me it smelt just like the gun smoke that hung thick in the air after a fast fire fight in the dry bush of Angola. Also, I was secretly quite proud of my knack for making a smooth, clean solder joint around the copper pipes.

Lawrence fancied himself as something of a crooner and constantly broke into, "She wears my ring … to show the world that she belongs to me," a 1960 song by Elvis Presley, teasing me but also complimenting my copper solder joints.

"That join is as smooth and round as my wedding ring, my bru," he said, his ring finger pointing to the sky.

"Is it good?"

"Ja, it's good, and smooth ... you know, maybe you can become a plumbing contractor one day," and again he broke into the old number, "She wears my ring ... she wears my ring."

I had grown to like Lawrence and his quick wit, and I suppose I would eventually have learned the trade from my comedic plumbing tutor; but after about two months of early morning starts, in the cold, wet winter, I decided that plumbing, after the last two action-packed years in Parachute Battalion, felt like a sad anti-climax. I thought maybe I could find something better to do. Something exciting. Something where I didn't have to lug a tool box around. I phoned in one morning and told the office manager at the plumbing company that I would not be coming in again. Immediately after the call I thought, "You fool! You searched so hard to find that apprentice plumbing position; now you've fucked it up with just one phone call."

§

"To hell with plumbing!" I announced, when Tania asked why I had quit my apprenticeship. But she wasn't happy with my decision; she felt strongly that it was important for me to try and qualify at a trade, and that I was displaying a reckless attitude by quitting my hard-won apprenticeship. She switched on the bright lights in the living room and started cleaning up, signalling the end to the little Friday night party that she and I had been having. I quickly slugged down the last of a glass of cheap wine before it was snatched away and poured down the kitchen sink.

Tania and I had searched for, found and rented a small flat in a yellow brick building in Wynberg, next to a big open field and just down the road from the Wynberg train station. We were proud of our first little home together and had turned it into a love den ... there were big posters all over the walls, of the South Sea Islands with their elegant palm trees, above our cheap living room furniture and in the kitchen, with its new pots and pans.

Now Tania's eyes flashed with anger at the news that I was unemployed.

"Well then, if you are going to find something else to do, you'd better hurry up! I don't want to be the only one working and earning money. I don't enjoy my job either, but you don't see me throwing it in."

Strangely, apart from Tania's response, even though I was now jobless in the windy city of Cape Town, I felt recklessly happy. I would find another job. I enjoyed the Capetonians. I never tired of looking up at magnificent Table Mountain, looming high over Cape Town with its vertical walls and grey crags, changing shape as you looked at it from different angles while moving around the city. This was the tip of Africa, and the point where the warm Indian Ocean crashed together with the cold Atlantic at Cape Agulhas. I could easily see in this place what old Jan Van Riebeeck must have seen in it, all those years ago when he was sent here to establish a supply station for the Dutch East India Company. Coming from Holland with its flat marshes and dykes, he and his crew must have been dazzled by the magnificent Table Mountain rising to 1,085 metres above sea level, with its flat top and almost vertical cliffs flanked by noble Lion's Head to the west and craggy Devil's Peak to the east. I wondered if it had been a clear day when Van Riebeeck had first sailed into Table Bay and gained his first sight of this natural splendour; or had it been a rainy day, with the magnificent mountain invisible, cloaked in mist. He might have come to ground in foul weather, when Table Mountain disappears completely and can be shrouded in mist for weeks on end. Maybe he was there for a whole week before the weather cleared and he woke up one morning to see this glorious mountain in front of him. We will never know. What we do know is that Jan Van Riebeeck and his crew did a fine job. The Cape Colony grew into the biggest European settlement in Africa ... and it stayed that way until the discovery of gold, which led to the gold rush on the Witwatersrand and the development of Johannesburg.

§

I collected Stan from the Wynberg station in my Renault. He was standing on the corner, smoking and looking around with his usual dark stare. He flagged me down and jumped into the car. We were both dressed in our best clothes. Stan was even sporting a tie ... and a serious expression as he started giving me directions for the quickest route down town.

"What's with the tie?" I wasn't used to seeing Stan looking so dapper.

"Hey! We're not going for an interview with the Railway police, this is the fucking South African Secret Police," he responded, disapprovingly. "I thought you were going to dress well?" he said, giving my brown corduroy pants a scornful stare.

"I am dressed well. What's wrong with cords?"

"You look like a fucking hippie peacenik."

"These are corduroy bro' … classic."

"Ja, classic hippie."

Then he proceeded to give me instructions on how to act and what to say if certain questions were asked. I nodded as I manoeuvred the Renault past the huge pine forests on the slopes of Table Mountain and down De Waal Drive, into the city.

Stan was my friend from 1 Parachute Battalion and he lived in Cape Town. He and I had been in the same platoon together during our national service, had been side by side through some tough times, had each earned the right to wear the maroon beret. We had pulled the trigger together in quite a few life changing situations up in Angola on cross border operations. He was a serious guy who had proved himself a good soldier in action. He was also quite a hard case and had survived some of the rougher parts of Cape Town before making his way to Parachute Battalion. Stan had always believed in fighting for a good cause and he wanted to follow in the footsteps of fighting men before him. I had always thought he had missed his calling. He should have been in the Foreign Legion, bringing understanding and compliance to misguided rebels in developing French territories.

I was well aware that Stan did not have a great sense of humour and was not easily enthused about anything, but he had heard that the Bureau of State Security (known as BOSS) was looking to hire 'a few good men' and had called me, showing some real excitement. I was all for exploring the opportunity with him. I was sick of fucking around and loading fish at the city docks. I thought this would be just up my alley. Cloak and dagger stuff. BOSS, the notorious South African secret police. These guys had a good reputation.

"This is our chance, Gungie," said Stan, using my nickname from our army days. "They need guys with our background, and we've just come back from fighting on the Border, defending the country."

"Yip, tell them about the operations in Angola."

"No, don't need to do that, they'll find out by themselves when they investigate our backgrounds."

"They going to investigate us?" I asked, suddenly thinking back to the trouble in which I had landed while in the army.

"Probably, why?"

"Remember, I kicked the crap out of that staff sergeant, the camp sergeant major at Umbalantu who killed our cats. That must be on my record I suppose?"

Stan paused, thinking about it.

"Naw, bro. That shouldn't matter, they not looking for angels...this is the South African security police, they need guys that can make things happen."

I nodded, agreeing with him. It was a great chance for us. BOSS probably, desperately, needed to expand its force in these troubled times for our country. I had read about their tactics and they seemed quite a slick and sophisticated lot, although I guessed they were the ones who were often in the newspapers ... having a 'suspect' try to escape and fall to his death from a window on the thirteenth floor of the police headquarters at John Vorster Square.

When I had told Tania that I was going to join the secret police she looked at me with a wry grin, shaking her head as she sat on the couch, flipping through a magazine.

"That's nice ... Do they know about your police record, as long as your dick?"

"Doesn't matter. They need all sorts."

She chuckled as she stood up. "Well, if they accept you, they will definitely have all sorts."

Stan knew his way around Cape Town and soon we found ourselves riding the elevator up to the fifth floor of an elegant building down town. Both of us wore overly serious expressions as we walked down the hallway and knocked on the unmarked wooden door. The familiar German Waffen SS glare smouldered in Stan's blue eyes as he announced to the Afrikaans-speaking blond man at the front desk that we were here for an eleven o'clock interview. We were told to take a seat, so we sat in the foyer and gazed at the Atlantic

Ocean for about ten minutes, quietly, exchanging looks with one another every now and then. Ten minutes of sitting in the office of the South African Secret Police seemed like ten hours. I could only imagine what this would feel like for someone who was not trying to join them. Then the same blond man arrived, led us to a different room, and sat us down at a desk. He had a pleasant face with alert eyes. He started asking a few questions: where were we brought up? what were we doing at the moment? why were we interested in joining the Bureau of State Security?

I lied and told him that I was still selling security systems (one of the jobs I had held for a month or two since leaving the army) to show a stable work record. We made sure that we mentioned we had both served in Parachute Battalion and had recently spent time fighting in Angola. He raised an eyebrow but nodded as he handed us some lengthy forms and instructed us to fill them in and answer all the questions.

So Stan and I sat there for thirty minutes, answering an assortment of questions. Most of them seemed quite mundane. None of them asked, 'What are your political views, and have you ever been convicted of any crime?' The blond-haired chap was pleasant enough as he took our applications and gave us a second appointment for two weeks later.

I was chuffed. A second appointment. That's a good sign.

When Tania arrived home from work I was shadow boxing in the living room and trying to imagine just what the hell the secret police did for their day-to-day activities. Surely it was more than interrogating banned ANC members or terrorists? And trying to stop them escaping from a window on the thirteenth floor? This was the silent force that worked behind the scenes of our troubled country. Surely they spent long dark nights watching suspected enemies of the state, enemies that conspired and worked against our government? Our small country on the tip of Africa was surrounded by Marxist regimes, in Angola, Mozambique and Zimbabwe. These threats, together with trying to help the government maintain white rule, must mean that there was more than enough work to keep the South African Security Police busy.

I kept on shadow boxing, throwing a boxing combination of punches. In between punches I announced that Stan and I had been told to come back for a second interview.

Tania was busily sorting the items from her shopping bags, but she seemed impressed.

"How much do they pay?"

"I don't know; I didn't ask … probably more than a regular policeman."

"Well, anything is better than nothing. You find any work?"

"I just told you."

"Did you get the job?"

"I was at the interview. What more – "

"Are you starting as a policeman on Monday?"

"Jeez, don't start that crap again."

We were back at it, needling one another. Tania had started resenting me for not having a nine to five job, thought I just grooved around town as I pleased. I didn't blame her; it would have ticked me off had I been in her shoes. I left the flat and headed out for a run.

I had not seen a lot of my Airborne friend, Stan, of late, so we got together the following week over some eggs and bacon, to discuss our chances of being accepted as new members of the BOSS workforce.

"Hey, they've been following me around."

"You saw someone following you?"

"I've seen the same guy three times, parked in a blue Fiat. Must think I'm blind and can't see him."

"Where?"

"Coming out of my place."

"Where else?"

"Yesterday at the gym, parked close to my car."

"I thought you didn't have a car?"

"OK, my chick's car."

"The same guy?"

"Yes, same guy, blue Fiat with a fucked-up light; thinks I'm blind, thinks I can't see him."

Stan had always been one to pick up on the details.

"Does he know you saw him?"

"Ja, he saw me bust him."

It would be hard for anyone to miss Stan's intense glare, even if he was looking at you in friendship. His glowering gaze could bore a hole through a car door.

I wondered why I hadn't seen anyone following me. Not that I had been on the lookout. Maybe I just hadn't seen the guy?

"I didn't see anyone following me."

"Maybe you ought to wake up then," Stan hissed.

I thought Stan was losing it. I hadn't seen anyone following me.

Stan levelled his unnerving stare at me.

"I don't care anyway; they can follow us all they want. We're not just wankers off the street; they need guys like us. We had the best training in the country bru. Look at all the shit we went through on the Border, that's what they are looking for, guys that can do the thing."

I looked up from my breakfast platter at the Golden Egg and out the big plate glass window, searching for any suspicious characters looking like the secret police. I thought about it. If they were watching me, they would have seen me hanging around with the long-haired liberal crowd from Cape Town University. I would be toast, would have no chance. Well, we'll see.

"Look, it doesn't matter what the hell the job pays, it's a good career and we can carry on fighting these communist fucks. The country's in trouble brother, we need to step up and be counted."

Stan glared at the African waiter delivering more coffee to our table.

"You know all these bombs going off?" He adopted a loud whisper as he looked around the busy restaurant. "It's almost every week now that you hear about some bomb going off somewhere. That's what we'd be involved in, with BOSS, catching these fucks that plant bombs at bus stations and restaurants like this. These guys that you were talking about … these guys jumping out of thirteenth-floor windows … same okes setting the bombs and crap like that. It'll be the same as on the Border, but we'll be fighting them here, in our country. I dunno … got a feeling that we going to get in."

I agreed with him. "I think they *will* take us. I wonder if we'll have to move, for the training … probably up to Pretoria. Tania won't be happy about it, we just moved down here to Cape Town."

"I dunno. We might also have to go through basic training again, or some bullshit like that."

We left the restaurant, glancing either way down the street for a suspicious looking blue Fiat with a broken light, but saw none.

The future looked bright.

Stan had always been a tough nut. I thought he would be an asset to BOSS. We had disclosed many differences between us during our time in Parachute Battalion; had once even shouted threats at each other in the midst of a battle, while we crawled on our bellies in the sand and advanced under fire, attacking an enemy base deep in Angola. We had yelled at one another, threatened to kick the other's ass, while bullets buzzed and cracked over our heads. Despite all this we had remained mates throughout our service. But now, even though we lived only a few miles apart in Cape Town, it seemed we had been trying to avoid seeing each other. We were both living with girlfriends, so the distance between us was probably quite natural, I thought. The army had been a different time; different rules; different values. Now it seemed we were disconnected, had cut each other adrift, while we struggled to find our new identities in civvy street.

Two weeks later I again collected Stan from the Wynberg station and we drove the same route to the offices of the South African Secret Police, overlooking the Atlantic. Both of us were dressed smartly once again; I was wearing plain slacks instead of my brown corduroys. But the same blond-haired BOSS agent didn't seem to notice my smart slacks. With a smile he told us that our applications had been declined by BOSS. Our services were not needed. Stan and I sat in silence for a moment and then I spoke up, seeing that I had nothing to lose.

"Why, what's the problem with us? We spent time fighting for our country in Angola."

"Look, don't take it personally. This is just the way your forms came back."

He seemed a nice enough guy, despite being a South African secret service employee. He saw our disappointment and gave us a smile, opening up, becoming friendly.

"I mean … you have a record long as your arm – what did you expect?" he laughed, as we stood up from our chairs. "Good luck, you guys."

Stan glared at him, delivering an extra high voltage version, as the blond spook handed us our rejection forms.

Finding another job wasn't as easy as I had anticipated; soon I began to feel frustrated at being jobless. I spent lots of time driving around to various interviews, but I was not offered anything other than door-to-door selling – encyclopaedias or home security systems. Reluctantly, I tried each of these options for a few weeks at a time, but I was unsuccessful at both, and I hated the work and was not good at it.

Then came a stroke of good luck: I discovered that an old school friend from my home town of Benoni was also in Cape Town, studying at the University of Cape Town (UCT). Marlon and I had been part of a gang of boys who hung together almost every weekend throughout high school. We had all drifted through high school in a cloud of smoke, hangovers, love bites and smiles. Music had been the bond between us, and Marlon and I had been in a rock and roll band together, playing at parties and small clubs on the weekends. We threw in our lot with a band called Warped; Marlon was the rhythm guitarist while I was the lead singer, belting out hard rock as best I could. For a variety of different, delinquent reasons I had laid waste to five separate high schools in my short school career. I had been a reluctant student but soon found that the marvellous, carefree ups and downs of high school were over in the blink of an eye – our entire gang and other friends parted ways to do our military service, lamenting, *a la* David Bowie, the disappearance of all our youthful, good times.

But now it was like old times again, having my mate, Marlon, in Cape Town. We had a lot of catching up to do as we had not seen much of each other in the last three years, having done our army service at different times. Marlon looked older, and a bit wiser, but still had the same offbeat sense of humour that had made us click in high school. He lived in residence on the university campus. On his days without classes I would blow off looking for work and hang out with him and a group of his student friends who rented a house in Observatory. It was a UCT student hang out; a quite large old house and there were always two or three UCT students lounging around on soft cushions on the couches in the living room. Invariably someone was rolling a joint. I liked the students but as much as I tried to fit in I quickly found that we lived in different realities; the only thing we had in common was our love for music.

"Hey! Listen to this new band ... R.E.M."

"Different sound," I said, nodding to the beat.

"Yeah, it's a new American band."

"It's got a different sound – it's not rock."

"Dude, it's the new sound, modern stuff, not so heavy."

I listened and while I enjoyed the high guitar I was not impressed. I shook my head, saying, "Too fast and light … what's the name again?"

"R.E.M."

"R.E.M?" I had never heard of them. The last two years in the army had been a black hole and I had missed a lot.

"*Ja.*"

"R.E.M., won't make it, but they're better than fucking Adam Ant!" I laughed.

I liked a heavier rock sound and thought R.E.M. too light, too much like pop music to make it big. My long-haired university friend argued against me, telling me that R.E.M. had what it takes to be huge. But I also didn't like the thin vocals.

"A Band needs to be heavy, man. Like Foreigner, Lou Gramm or Bad Company. These R.E.M. guys will never make it," I predicted.

I was a die-hard rock man and even though I tried to become friends with most of Marlon's UCT buddies, it seemed that I had little in common with them. I had just finished my action-packed military service on the Border between South West Africa and Angola, and I had a very different outlook and frame of mind from the long-haired students. I was clearly out of line with their way of thinking. My outlook was hard and rigid with little room for flexibility or forgiveness. These students were relaxed, easy going, well informed and, mostly, quite co-operative, although I was surprised at some of their leftist and radical political views. Frequently they spoke against the South African government, in a way that I had not heard before.

Usually I just sat quietly while they threw informed dialogue back and forth, discussing current affairs I knew nothing about. I was envious. Why wasn't I up to speed on the current topics they were talking about? As hard as I was trying to fit in with them, at the same time I felt a silent rage and disdain for their easy-going outlook and sophisticated conversation. Why were they so laid back? Didn't they know what was going on, north of our country, where my comrades and I had been fighting a bush war, just some months ago? The silent rage grew. Didn't they know how it felt to be woken up and kitted out with full frontline ammo in the middle of the night, and flown out at full speed in a fire force Puma helicopter, over the Border into Angola? Didn't they know how it felt to raise your rifle, bend your head into the sights and shoot as fast as possible at a figure in the bush, firing an AK-47 at you, or your comrades? To make eye contact with a man and pull the trigger before he could and watch him fall? Didn't they know what it felt like to accept that you might be dead in an hour – but please God let me do my job well, not let my comrades down, and kill the enemy before that happens.

I also had stories to tell, to add to the discussions in the old house where the students hung out, smoking their spliffs and chatting. But my stories always had terrible endings, people were killed, shot to pieces, so I sat quietly through most of the conversations. I was young at the time, when it was important to fit in and make new friends, so I pushed these feelings down and let them do all the talking. Maybe their view of our government was right? They were against national service, saying the military was a tool to enforce apartheid. Maybe they were right? Suddenly the things I had learned seemed irrelevant. It didn't seem that important to know how to look *through* the bush and not *at* the bush when searching for a hidden terrorist. Or to know how important it is to run no more than just three steps before you dive down, when doing fire and movement, advancing towards an enemy trench while under fire. The knowledge I had gained in the last two years now seemed irrelevant – and distasteful. Like a black hole in space my national service in Parachute Battalion had swallowed two years of my growth and knowledge of events, music, social changes, outlooks, world events, even sporting events. I had missed out. It seemed I had attended a very different school from my university friends, and I felt like the proverbial square peg trying to fit into a round hole.

Chapter Three

HANGIN' HARD, STAYIN' TOUGH

'Eye of the Tiger' ~ Survivor

I had to find something I could sink my teeth into ... so I decided to pursue something I knew I could do pretty well and which I had always wanted to give a proper shot. Something that I felt passionate about ... kicking ass!

I met up with my old Airborne mate, Kevin MacKay, a resident of Cape Town and a well-known Woodstock badass. Kevin had been a professional boxer even before he had joined the army to do his national service. He had been in my platoon and had become quite a legend in Parachute Battalion for various reasons; being able to throw some leather was one of them.

"Keep your hands up man ... and don't jump around like that. Just stand nice and solid and shoot fast from the shoulder ... *ja*, like that."

Kevin Mackay held his head low, his chin on his chest as he watched. The thick scar he had earned at Parachute Battalion ran from his forehead over his flattened, broken nose and into his top lip. It made his rough features look even more forbidding. He watched intently as I moved around the creaking ring, throwing punches. We were in Kevin's old gym, where he had boxed as a professional boxer, a 'pro'. It was situated, as many good gyms are, in a rundown building on the bad side of downtown Cape Town. There was a dark stairway with broken lights and red worn concrete steps leading up to the second floor and the gym. Many windows were filled with cardboard and the wooden floor creaked as boxers-in-training jumped rope or shadow boxed.

Kevin's old trainer, Mike, nodded his head as he watched, "*Ja*, you not bad, you hit hard and move fast ... just got to keep your hands up more."

"Sure, I'll train you. Come around as much as you can, we'll work on you ... get you some fights soon. As long as you don't mess around, like Kevin did, you might be good someday," he said, getting in a dig about Kevin's short and patchy professional boxing career.

I had boxed before, on and off, and had always kept in training at home, in the backyard, so I was no stranger to a good left, right left, hook combination. Punches had always come easy to me. I had trained in our backyard since high school, slamming the rain-soaked heavy bag until my fists were as hard as rocks. I had also developed a killer right hook that had saved me on frequent occasions, when it was called for. Even though a right hook is frowned on as a lead punch in boxing, my right hook shot out like a hydraulic piston, as fast as my straight left, and had saved my butt in many a good time turned bad situation, at a night club or on the street on the East Rand.

"You gotta keep your hands up ... these guys will get you. You not fighting some drunk palooka on the street. Keep 'em up high," Mike warned me, "try get here to the gym tomorrow and we can start training."

There was a good bunch of mostly Cape Coloured amateur boxers in the gym, plus a handful of professionals. I watched experienced, professional boxer, Bramley 'The Ghost' Whiteboy, the eldest of the five Whiteboy brothers, gliding around the ring, his tall frame and wide shoulders stooped, a serious look in his eye but relaxed and loose as he ducked and weaved in front of an imaginary foe. His brother, Chris Whiteboy, was just the opposite. Brash and cocky and quick to engage in a shouting match with anyone willing. I was impressed when I saw South African junior middleweight champion, Coenie Bekker, saunter into the gym, with attitude, just like a boxing champion is supposed to have. He looked around the gym, one eyebrow cocked as he made eye contact with everyone there, just to let them know the champ had arrived. Coenie glared at any small fry amateur boxer who came close to him. He pushed himself to the fore, in front of everyone, jumping rope and inspecting his broken teeth in the big cracked mirror, preparing for his upcoming fight against professional middleweight boxer, the KO artist and killer of giants, Charlie Weir, the 'Silver Assassin'.

I was sold. I wanted to be just like Coenie.

Soon I became friends with a tall German who visited the boxing gym a couple of times a week. Eric was not a boxer, but he was big and strong and came to the gym regularly, to work out and hit the bag. He told me that he worked security on the door for a Cape Town nightclub, close to the docks. Then he said he could do with some extra security help. Boom! Instantly I had a steady job. I was very chuffed and eagerly reported for duty at the night club door the next night. Eric gave me some instructions regarding security procedures on the door.

"Be friendly but firm ... no need to kick any one's ass unless they deserve it. It's not such a bad crowd here ... half of them are queer anyway."

So now I had regular work. Between a few days per week when I loaded fish off the trawlers at the docks, and working the door at night, at the club, I was making enough to get by. I worked six days a week and enjoyed it. I had come to like the Capetonians; they were a lot friendlier, quicker to crack a joke and a smile, than the folk back home in Johannesburg. Maybe the good humour for which Cape Coloureds are so well-known had rubbed off onto the average Capetonian; they were definitely more laid-back than people on the East Rand, where I came from. Even hard core *jollers* (party-goers)in the Cape seemed a more settled and reasonable bunch than their Johannesburg counterparts.

I had run into some Cape Town hippies earlier, during my job search. The girls wore long skirts and wild hair and had invited me to join them down at the beach, at one of their hangouts near the crashing waves, to drink some wine. They seemed a pleasant group, so I took them up on their invitation and arrived at their hangout late one afternoon. Among them was a man named Hennie, about thirty years old, tall and lean with a goatee and sun-bleached shaggy, sandy brown hair, but not as long as the others. He was tanned brown from the Cape Town sun, with muscular forearms and the hard, calloused hands of a worker. In fact, he seemed to be out of place here, among this commune of long-haired, bearded, softly spoken Cape Town hippies. Hennie was loud, with a heavy Afrikaans accent, blended with *rooker* (smoker) slang.

I had been drinking their cheap wine and smoking their weed and I was drunk and stoned. Fuck it. This weed was strong! The hippies had found the perfect place amongst the rocks to drink their wine and smoke their marijuana. I looked round at the Cape Town beach with its big round boulders and booming waves. Seagulls screamed as they flew in circles, squabbling amongst themselves. I sipped the cheap wine. It felt good to be out of the army. I looked at their dog. It was the first time I had seen what they told me was a border collie. This Cape Town beach dog had a scarf tied round his neck and he ran around chasing a ball, like an obsessed maniac. He looked like the happiest dog I had ever seen. I wasn't used to dogs like this; I was used to Transvaal plot dogs who didn't give a shit about any ball and chased cars or African farm workers, instead. This dog had one blue eye and one brown eye and stared at us like a lunatic, his tongue hanging out, until someone picked up the ball and threw it for him. But now everyone was too stoned and had stopped throwing the ball. The dog stared, waiting.

Hennie broke into the silence. "Hey! My bru, what were you saying before, about being with the parabats? You were talking about that ... that you and your *manne* (men) ambushed terrorists ... carry on telling us that story *broer* (brother)."

I was stoned and didn't want to talk but Hennie urged me on, with genuine interest.

I sat forward in my chair and tried to talk. My mouth was dry, my voice sounded distant.

"*Yes* ... up in Angola ..."

"Yeah, when that traitor terrorist was leading you guys to his buddies."

Hennie had not forgotten where I had stopped in the story I had been telling him, earlier.

I started talking slowly. "*Ja* well ... we were across the Border, patrolling in Angola, just a platoon of us. They had flown in this SWAPO deserter, in a Puma. He had been captured by South Africans somehow, I don't know, but he was a traitor who had turned on his own buddies. They had flown him to us, to lead our platoon to the position of his comrades. Our company was already in Angola when they brought him, we were split up in platoons 5 km apart on a four-week sweep, search and destroy operation ... we had been there for a week or so. "

"Looking for terrorists?"

"*Ja*, search and destroy, looking for terrorists ... so the chopper drops off this skinny SWAPO terrorist turncoat. He's dressed in a brand new browns (SADF Nutria Brown uniform). Just before we chow ... around five o'clock in the afternoon ... the lieutenant gets us together and tells us that sixteen of us are going to follow this SWAPO insurgent through the night and he is going to lead us to his buddies who have a base camp somewhere nearby. So the *terr* (terrorist) draws a map in the sand to show us the position of his mates, where they had planned to sleep, and who had what kind of weapon. This one had an RPG-7, this one had an RPD machine gun ... he said there were fifteen or so of them and they were roving SWAPO from Navy HQ. Afterwards the lieutenant lined us up and slowly walked down the rows. He handpicked sixteen of us from the platoon then he gave us our orders ... he said we would do a night attack on their position ... and he ended by telling us the orders are: 'To take no prisoners, to kill them all."

Hennie was quiet for once as he listened, all ears, as he slowly prepared another pipe. The rest of the stoned, long-haired group of Cape Town hippies had picked up on my slow, measured speech and had stopped their giggling and talking, they were following what I was saying. How could I tell these hippies what it's like to walk out to do a night attack on an enemy temporary base? Although I didn't feel like talking I couldn't stop myself telling them a story about one of the contacts ... on the Border ... just six months ago.

Soon I was back in the bush, oblivious to my audience sitting there quietly, listening while I remembered.

Lieutenant duPlessis silently urges us on, using hand signals and sixteen of us form up, unenthusiastically, into a rickety line. With our rifles pushed tight into our shoulders we walk purposefully, with faces of stone, across the moonlit clearing towards the black shadows of the thicket of trees, 40 metres away. I always walk too fast and I found myself in front of the V, the first one to step out of the moonlight of the small shona (clearing) and into the pitch-black shadows of the thicket of trees, expecting an AK-47 to open on me at close range. Right away in the dark shadows I see the embers of last night's small personal cooking fire, next to a shallow sleeping scrape. The embers of the little fire have been kicked back into life by the cold pre-dawn breeze. A small flame flickers. My eyes adjust quickly ... I see the shape of bedding and clothes, low shelves made from thin cut branches tied together, terrorist style; shallow scrapes for sleeping in the sand; the smell of food and dirty clothing; some cans, some cleared area.

They're here! We're right amongst them!

Consciously I brace myself for the inevitable burst of an AK-47. I glare like a demon into the dark, willing my eyes to see a human form before he sees me. Are we walking towards our deaths? The screaming silence of stalking through a terrorist sleeping area echoes in my ears. No hail of bullets! Like ghosts we step over their shallow sleeping scrapes, blankets and simple cooking utensils. Without stopping we pass through their well-concealed lair but see no human forms. No one here? Where are they? Yes, we've found the terrorist base, but no one is home!

"Go through. Go through, keep walking." I can feel Lieutenant Doep's intensity in the dark as he indicates urgently, silently, his hand waving. We pad silently through and away from the thicket, on towards a few shadowy trees, maybe 30 metres away. Lieutenant duPlessis indicates again, the familiar hand signal: 'Go down.'

It's a lemon, the SWAPO guerrillas have flown the coop. We have walked for seven hours, the whole night, out of the dark we walked right into their small base camp, but they have gone. Now what? Disappointed but thankful finally to have a break we go down onto the cold sand. No one says a word. No one makes a sound of disappointment. So close, I had seen the little cooking fire kicked back into life … I had smelled their food … I had smelled their dirty clothes.

The first glimpse of dawn begins to soften the black night. Now we take the opportunity for a brief rest, forty metres past the terrorist sleeping area, and wait for Lieutenant duPlessis to order the next move. What now? My mind flashes back to being human again. There's no one here, let's go back to the rest of our platoon. I feel exhausted. I carelessly drop my rifle onto the sand next to me and hug my knees for warmth. Fuck! It's cold. All we have on is our thin shirts and webbing. Why were we told we could not bring jackets? We are all disappointed, having walked the whole night for nothing. We sit in the cold, hugging our knees for maybe twenty minutes then, suddenly, we all hear a sound across the quiet dawn. It makes all sixteen of us hold our breath at the same time and look at each other. We all heard a laugh … then we heard a can being kicked not thirty or forty metres to the side of our position. All this time the terrorists we were hunting had been sitting no more than thirty odd metres from us!

My partner, John the Fox, and I turn our heads and glare at each other, confirming that we had both heard the noise, so close by. I pick up the rifle I had disappointedly thrown down in the sand. I shake off the sand. No orders are necessary, we have all heard the laughing close by, not a stone's throw away. No one says a word and we all rise as one man. The terrorists are right next to us! As quiet as killers the sixteen of us creep the short distance through the bush towards the sound. There, right in front of us in the early dawn, in a clearing about thirty metres away, we can just make out the dark figures of six or seven SWAPO guerrillas, making a small fire, talking very quietly, but with the occasional burst of muffled and suppressed laughter. How could they have been so quiet? On hands and knees we creep forward, undetected, onto a small natural rise in the sand, and wait. How had they been so quiet, so close to us? They must have just left their sleeping area that only minutes before we had walked through. If we had not become lost on the way we would have walked right in on them, asleep, and there would have been a point-blank shootout in the inky black shadows. What if one of us had made a noise? Or laughed, as they had done? They would have crept up on us just as we were now creeping up on them!

The lazy African dawn seemed to want to protect the SWAPO guerrillas. It was taking forever to give us enough light to pick our targets. Now a few more SWAPO guerrillas came down a path to join their friends, joking amongst themselves. We could smell their morning porridge on the small but blazing fire. A couple of them moved their arms up and down, some light exercise to keep warm in the pre-dawn chill. We wait ten ... maybe twenty minutes. It is now just light enough to see details on their clothing, to see their AK-47s propped against the trees.

In that time I traverse the sights of my rifle a dozen times; from between the shoulder blades of the men sitting at the fire with their backs to us, to the chests of a few on the other side of the fire, standing facing us, rubbing their hands together, looking down at the fire, talking to a group working on an upside-down bicycle. I settle on the terrorist rubbing his hands together when, without a signal, Horn lets fly with his RPG-7 rocket launcher. His rocket explodes with a huge BANG in a cloud of smoke and dust right in the midst of their cooking fire. All of us open fire as one, shooting as fast as a finger can pull the trigger. I get a double feed jam, clear it in seconds, shoot next to my boot to check, and keep shooting ... then I quickly change the taped-together magazines, pull back the bolt and keep on firing. Someone shouts ... we stand and charge forward through the dust and smoke. Everything in split seconds but also in slow motion.

Three or four of the guerrillas are dead around the fire. I see movement to my right, a terrorist lying on his stomach right next to me, desperately trying to push himself up, as if exercising. I wheel round in a second, glaring, and shoot him high between the shoulder blades. He collapses, dead, on his face, at my feet.

Another terrorist sits dazed and confused, flat on his backside next to the fire. John, as quick as a Fox, turns and shoots him through the head from three metres away. He falls forward onto his face, next to the fire. Within seconds, with no orders, we silently split up into pairs like hunting dogs and move into the dry bush, our rifles hard against our shoulders, eyes blazing, searching for any guerrillas who had run off, wounded. They can't have gone far.

Suddenly I lost all confidence about telling this story. I stopped talking, slowly lit a cigarette and looked out across the cold Atlantic Ocean. I was going to carry on with the second part of the story, but I realised that it was far too gruesome for these gentle hippies. We had caught all the stragglers who had escaped from the ambush, fallen and tried to hide and it had all been over in a few minutes. How could I tell them about the hungry pigs, crazed by the smell of blood, who entered the killing zone and immediately started eating the dead bodies?

My hands had begun to shake as I stared at the ocean. The group sitting around the cracked concrete table had not uttered a word while I was speaking. A couple of the girls were shaking their heads and peering at me through stoned and heavy eyelids, flicking the long ash from their Pall Mall cigarettes. Others were gazing at me with a faraway look, keeping quiet.

I felt remorse at having allowed Hennie to coax me into continuing with this story, which I had begun earlier, but then I had been telling it to Hennie, only. I felt very unsettled, very cold. There were goose bumps on my arms and I felt as though an electric charge was shooting through me. I could feel my heart pounding in my chest. Suddenly I felt like a killer who has just confessed to a premeditated mass murder. It didn't seem right to tell the story, at all, and having told it seemed to have killed the whole love and peace hippie vibe we had all been enjoying.

But Hennie, and only Hennie, seemed to appreciate my story of the ambush in Angola. He nodded enthusiastically and remarked, "Yes, the parabats were always in on the action, hey? I had a mate in the parabats and he said ..." Hennie rambled on, then tried to coax some more war stories out of me, but I shook my head.

I was completely sober and deeply regretted telling these friendly hippies about my army experience. I recognised the same strongly unsettled feeling I had experienced after telling some of my stories to the American Marine, a few weeks earlier. My mind was racing; my heart was thumping … I felt I could not sit another minute amongst this quiet and peaceful group, who were watching me so carefully. I had to get away.

When I confided in my Parabat comrade Stan I realised that he had his own demons and had not heard a word that I was saying.

Chapter Four

TAKING IT TO THE TOP

'Maniac on the Floor' ~ *Michael Sombello (from* **Flashdance***)*

Now Stan was a different kettle of fish altogether. Antony Stander, aka 'Stan', was a friend and Parachute Battalion comrade of mine who lived reasonably close by, in Cape Town, but 'Stan the Man' was very different from the university crowd with whom I had been trying to become friends.

I hadn't seen Stan for over a month or two, since our applications to join the South African secret police had been declined, to our disappointment. I wasn't sure what he was doing with himself and thought it might be good to catch up, so I gave him a call and arranged to get together for a beer. The last thing I remembered Stan telling me was that he had decided to stick with a manager's training course for Ster Kinekor, the South African movie company. This despite the grimace he assumed every time we spoke about it. I couldn't blame him, everything after our time on the Border seemed to be an anti-climax, a serious let-down. But, as I told him, at least he was holding down a job; I was still bouncing around between loading fish at the Cape Town docks and working security at the night club. Nevertheless, I struggled to visualise Stan as a movie house manager, in a shirt and tie, doing whatever cinema managers do – making sure that the popcorn machines worked, the tickets were printed, whatever. Stan was a serious guy and had proved himself a good soldier in action. Yet again I thought he had missed his calling and I could easily see Stan in a French legionnaire's uniform and white kepi, wagging his finger, warning a wayward tribal headman that he had better not step out of line.

The Simon's Town bar was quite full on this particular afternoon. Stan was nursing a Castle Lager, peeling the label off the bottle as he fidgeted. I had decided to confide in my Parachute Battalion comrade, to tell him about the hippies who had been so shocked when I told them what we had done on the Border, and I wanted to ask him, again, how he was coping as a civilian. Slowly and carefully I began to tell him I was having a bit of a hard time getting back into civvy life. I said it felt like an invisible wall had been built between myself and most others; and I didn't know if it was self-made, or not, and that I was feeling a bit detached from it all. I went on to tell him about the braai with Matt the Marine, at my flat, that I had experienced a mini freak out while telling him about some of our contacts on the Border, and that it had taken a day or so for me to see and feel the sunshine once again.

"It felt weird … like it was a sin. I mean, how do you tell someone about that ambush, when we crept up to those SWAPO insurgents, making breakfast and shot them all, or the Bushman clan, those kids and the woman? I felt like I was a bum, talking about it, like a killer." Again, I could see and feel those goose bumps as I spoke about this with Stan.

Stan was one of the few guys from Parachute Battalion that I had seen, since coming out. He looked around broodingly and didn't respond.

I sipped my beer and asked, "So what are we supposed to do – never talk about the fighting that went on? Just be quiet forever? "

No response. So I asked Stan how he was coping with getting back into the groove of Civvy Street. Was it all cool with him? Was he doing OK? No response.

Then I realised that Stan had hardly heard a word I had said. He sat there, peeling what was left of the label from his bottle of beer, his forehead knotted in a deep frown, his eyes black with anger, glaring over my shoulder at someone behind me. What the hell's going on? He had been distant ever since we had sat down to talk … and it dawned on me that I had been talking to myself.

Stan was famous for his 'I'll kill you for no good reason' stare, powerful enough (almost) to bend a silver spoon. He had used it to very good effect in the army. I turned to see who he was glaring at, in case some trouble was brewing behind us. There was nothing brewing. The guy that Stan was glaring at, apparently with murder on his mind, seemed a quite harmless, normal, sort of fellow, sitting in a booth against the window, trying to enjoy a quiet beer. But now he was squirming about, looking down at his beer, looking up, obviously disturbed by the two wild-eyed individuals, staring at him. Quickly I looked away and then back at Stan. For some reason Stan was trying to bore a hole through the poor guy's head with his icy stare.

I decided not to pursue the conversation about how he was coping with civilian life and switched to asking him why he thought we had been rejected as candidates for our recent application for the South African Secret Police. No response.

I didn't see much of Antony Stander after that. It was not long after this that my good friend 'Stan the Man', in the company of his own ghosts and demons, went on a rampage and robbed five banks in Cape Town, at gunpoint. After a short time on the run, leading the police on a wild goose chase, he was arrested, tried and sentenced, and began serving a 30-year prison term. Things looked very bleak for my Airborne friend. The gang infested Pollsmoor Prison was one of the roughest prisons in South Africa. Stan had spent a tough two years as a combat paratrooper, had been at the forefront of some of the biggest cross border operations into Angola, and was now facing a long, soul-crushing prison sentence. He had always been a hard man but, as year after year of his 30-year sentence slowly passed and he settled in for the long haul, he fell into the clutches of a Christian prison outreach group, of all things. The group had a profound effect on him – it changed his life forever. After seven years in prison, by the grace of a miraculous pardon, Antony Stander was released. He emerged from prison a changed and powerful man who, to this day, runs his own church in Cape Town, conducting bold Christian outreach programmes, walking into the dens and homes of drug dealers and ruthless gang leaders, to direct them to the way of the Lord. I learned about all this only 20 years later. *Salute* Stan! Airborne all the way!

On a humorous note, long after the event Stan told me this story: while serving his time in prison he was approached by a notorious prison gang leader, a Cape Coloured man. He persuaded Stan that the tattoo on his shoulder, depicting a swooping eagle (the emblem of the Parachute Battalion), created by me years before on the Angolan border, using a sewing needle and the ink from a broken ballpoint pen, had been so badly executed that the gang's tattooist, also in prison would have to cover it up with an image of a Roaring Lion. And Stan agreed.

So much for my bush tattoo skills.

§

I threw myself into training, driving to the boxing gym every day, where I felt as comfortable as I could. I had had a few amateur fights and was getting into shape. I went on long runs through the tall pine tree forests on the side of Table Mountain up to the Rhodes Memorial; spend half an hour shadow boxing under the pine trees, and then run back again. Each morning I turned our living room into a gym, shadow boxing around the furniture. I was determined to break into boxing for real, and even maybe fight as a professional boxer one day. One night at the gym I told Mike about this dream. He sucked air in through his teeth and nodded.

"It's a tough game, this boxing; in the pro's its kill or be killed. Swim with the sharks."

I waited, listening to him.

"Guys get hurt in this game …look how fucked up Arthur is. He's fucked."

I turned to glance at Big Arthur, shadow boxing in the corner.

"He's punchy, at twenty-eight years old … have you heard him talk?"

I watched Arthur move his feet, sluggishly, punching away at his reflection in the cracked mirror.

"And he won't stop fighting. He's fighting in a couple weeks at the Good Hope centre."

I could not have picked a worse time to tell Mike of my aspirations, about wanting to fight professionally. Arthur was the gym's heavy weight boxer, preparing himself for a bout, and Mike was concerned with him, not me and my uncertain future. Arthur was a big strong Xhosa man, six feet tall, with thick arms, a heavy chest and a seriously bad attitude. He looked about six years older than me, wore a permanent scowl on his forehead, his mouth was always turned down in a snarl and no, I had never heard him talk. I didn't think he *could* talk. He was an old seasoned professional on the downhill side of an unsensational boxing career. I had never heard him make a sound other than a few aggressive grunts at someone now and then, and he glowered at anyone who even looked at him. He didn't have a trainer and was flying solo, with Mike helping him out a bit, here and there.

Then Mike decided to test me, to see if I could walk the walk and not only talk the talk.

"Why don't you get in and do a few rounds with Arthur?" he suggested, casually.

He was asking me to sink or swim, so he could see what I had. Could I swim with the sharks?

Ugly Arthur the professional showed me no mercy from the first punch to the last. We sparred every other day for a few weeks or so. He cut me no slack and came out as if he was in a championship fight at the Good Hope fucking stadium. He tucked his head into his shoulders and skilfully hid behind his high guard. He held his hands high in front of his face like the old pro that he was. Even though I had a good punch and was able to land a few fast shots, they always seemed to hit his gloves. I was no match for this surly old professional. He bounced easily against the ropes, giving way to my attacks, then sucked me into his range and suddenly struck out with full force – lightning fast left and right hooks. I still had a lot to learn and, muzzy as he was, he caught me easily with my hands held at chin level. It was the first time I had been hit for real by a pro and instantly I felt the difference. These punches were very different from the punches in an amateur fight. In the days to come, after one or more of Arthur's punches, I would drive home in a daze, wiping the blood from my nose.

Invariably I was on the receiving end of the experienced punch drunk professional. But I improved quickly, thank God. One night I walked up the stairs into the gym and Arthur was nowhere to be seen. I hoped he had dropped down dead.

"Where's Arthur?" I asked, trying not to sound relieved.

'No, he's not here tonight. He's done with sparring, he fights next Friday. Are you going to come and watch … Good Hope Stadium?"

Instantly, I felt my constant headache ease up a bit from the good news. Arthur's absence was a very good thing for me … I don't think I could have handled any more. For close to a month now I had walked around with some low-grade concussion and a serious headache. In this game, you have to be humbled before being lionised, and I was not going to miss this boxing show with Arthur!

Tania and I sat high in the seats at Good Hope Stadium and watched the fights. Big mean Arthur came out in black shorts as one of the supporting bouts. Bright floodlights lit up the small ring and the full house crowd started chanting for another knock out. This time Arthur was facing a guy his own size, with arms and shoulders as big as his own. He moved around with his hands held high as usual and his back into the ropes. Arthur was trying to suck the other fighter in, as he had successfully sucked me in, as was his trick. He moved back into the ropes, playing possum, then quickly threw some very hard lightning left and right hooks almost lifting his feet off the canvas as he did. If any one of them had caught his opponent flush, it would have been good night for him.

But it didn't matter tonight … Arthur's punches seemed to have no effect on his opponent. The Other Big Fighter very quickly closed his range and was now throwing equally fast and heavy straight punches. Inevitably one of them ploughed right between Arthur's high guard. I felt a mean, secret satisfaction as we watched big Arthur collapse to the canvas in an untidy heap. Knocked Out.

Ah! So that's how you get through a high defence … you punch right through it! Lesson learned.

Big Arthur did not return to the gym.

I had a string of amateur fights in quick succession and won a few with cold knockouts (KOs). I found out, as did other boxers, that I had a very fast and hard KO right hook. Often, I would travel into Mitchell's Plain, a sprawling Coloured township about 20 km from Cape Town, to get my fights. I was becoming hooked on the pre-fight adrenalin and jittery nerves.

This was in the early 1980s and many of the gloves we used were stuffed with horsehair padding. They were already five years old, worn and flat with use; also, gloves then were smaller than the gloves in use today. We quickly learned to push aside the stuffing at the front of the glove, making it just a layer of leather covering our already wrapped knuckles. Taking a punch, like this, was like being hit with a rock; it was close to bare knuckle fighting. The new extra sponge padded and thumb-less gloves, only recently produced, had yet to make their way down to the boxing clubs.

My friend Marlon, living in Cape Town and studying at UCT, invited our group of university friends to watch one of my fights at the Mitchell's Plain disco venue. They all travelled together in a Volkswagen Kombi, excited at going to their first ever boxing tournament. We were the only 'whiteys' in the hall but that didn't change the outcome. My fight lasted no more than five seconds and consisted of just two very well-placed punches: one from my opponent; and a better one from me. The bell rang, my tall, long-armed opponent threw a very fast straight, catching me between the eyes and breaking my nose. A split second later I threw a vicious right hook; it came out like a piston rod, caught him flush on the temple and he was out cold, sleeping face down on the canvas.

Five seconds flat!

It took several minutes to wake him, and he had to be helped to his feet. When they finally held up my arm in victory, I glared at him, my nose still streaming blood and ruining the front of my Parachute Battalion vest. But the five-second stone cold knockout made me feel liberated and empowered. I would follow my own course! I had taken control of my life and my destination. I had the tools of the trade with me and I would smash my way up to the top. I would do it my way. I didn't care that my nose had been pushed aside at an ugly angle and was still running blood, which I could taste trickling down my throat.

A few days later Marlon and I met for breakfast and he told me that our UCT student friends had been quite shocked by the violence of the knockout. They had all agreed that boxing was vicious and distasteful. Marlon, my old school buddy, who had been the guitarist in our band in Benoni, thought the knockout had been spectacular and had argued in my favour. Our conversation had gone like this:

"What's Michelle and the gang say … did they enjoy it?"

Marlon grinned. "They didn't like it at all, they said it's not good to be so violent."

"What did they say about the five-second knock out?"

"They said I should try and get you to give up this boxing stuff."

I sat there, confused, for a second.

"Stop boxing? Why? I just got a five-second knockout!"

"Because it's too violent."

"Too violent?" I thought to myself, looking down at my breakfast plate. "Too fucking violent? What the fuck do they know about too much fucking violence! Most of them have been sitting in Cape Town University for two years, ever since high school, going to parties, smoking bongs … and they think this is violent! They have no fucking idea what level of violence I've just come from, up north, where stone faced youngsters their age had flown across the Border in helicopters at dawn, low and fast, to chase the hot spoor of a terrorist, in the hope of killing him. You think boxing is violent? Try attacking an enemy base camp dug in with trenches and bunkers, across the Border in Angola, while under fire from RPG-7s and 23 mm anti-aircraft cannons!"

I felt a few more mental concrete blocks being lifted, loaded and locked in place in The Wall; the mental wall that I was unwittingly building, between myself and a large part of the rest of society. I pondered the different realities to which the university students and I had been exposed Whose reality was right, theirs or mine? I decided that my reality was the real one – and smiled.

"Hey! You know what I've been thinking about?"

I had been hesitant to tell anyone, but Marlon was an old friend.

"What?"

So I told my old mate Marlon what I had been dreaming about. A vague dream that had first hatched while walking through the dry bush, patrolling in Angola and day dreaming of Civvy Street. I had thought it unrealistic and unattainable back then, but now the longer that I ran up the steep slopes of Table Mountain, the more times that I buried a hard, left hook into a heavy bag, the more I knew that it was possible. I imagined myself with the middle weight title belt around my waist and a long list of vanquished foes behind me. Why not? If they can do it, why not me? The dream had grown as I found peace in the solitude of hard training, becoming an obsession; and then the obsession started to grow when I found that I had a hard, knockout right hand that could end a fight in five seconds flat.

"Hey! I'm going to get my professional boxing license – I'm going to be the South African middleweight champion! Whaddya say?!"

Marlon smiled at me, sipping his steaming coffee; he didn't look surprised. He had been beside me in more than a few street fights in Benoni and he could see that I was serious.

"The South African middleweight title will be a long hard road, but I say go for it bro'. With a five second knock-out right hook like that, I think you can do it. Keep training brother!"

§

Tania knew she had crossed a line and bolted out of the bedroom, hair brush in hand, wearing only her panties. I was only a second behind her but was tangled up in the bed sheets and stumbled. She accelerated down the hall as fast as her shapely legs could carry her and I saw I had lost any advantage as her equally shapely backside disappeared out of sight. I grabbed the closest ammunition I could find and followed. She was a few feet from the safety of the living room nook as I hurled the big brass alarm clock, a gift from my mother "to make sure that you get up for work". It was a ridiculous thing with two bells on either side and little hammers that struck the bells and made a sound like the 'green light' buzzer that signalled GO! when you jumped from a C-130 aircraft. It was an infuriating means of waking up in the morning. I had aimed a safe good two feet above her head at the air vent above the front door when I let the fly with the clock. She had ducked into the living room a split second before the clock disintegrated. She popped her head out, her normally big eyes huge, to see if there was any threat of further hot pursuit. When she saw that I appeared satisfied with the detonation of the alarm clock she gave the shadow of a smile. But she was worried. Her next challenge was returning to the bedroom, to get dressed for work.

Tania and I still had deep feelings for one another, but our relationship was starting to take a serious dive. Looking back, I can see that the trouble started with one particular event. She and Janie, Marlon's good-looking but wayward hippie girlfriend, had gone to see the movie *Flashdance*, and Tania had returned to our flat with a determined, rebellious look in her eyes, reminding me of my horse I used to ride as a kid. The creature would stare at me, daring me, then try persistently to bite me and buck me off. Soon after Tania had watched the movie she had told me that I should learn to hold my mouth if I had nothing good to say. She had also informed me that the days of her keeping quiet were over. She had said all this in a matter of fact tone but with a certain authority that I had never seen in her before, yet it seemed to fit her well. Of course, I was in denial about any wrongdoing on my part and blamed the movie for this change. To this day I have not watched *Flashdance* but I assume it's about a woman who breaks loose from the chains, takes names and numbers and kicks ass, a power bitch inspirational movie. It must have been, because Marlon was getting the same treatment from Janie.

From that day on it seemed that whatever I said to Tania was challenged, and questioned, and her responses, invariably, were for me to button my lip. I wondered how many other previously good relationships had been ruined by this 'kick your man in the balls' movie that encouraged women to break free and take charge. I didn't know how to handle this new shift of power in our relationship, so I just let her have her way – which proved a mistake. Just like the guerrillas in the Angolan bush, if you showed any weakness, gave them an inch, they would take your arm and soon be running the show. Well, suddenly we had a new leader, and it wasn't me. Tania's unexpected coup was complete.

Apart from my boxing, which was going well, the Cape Town adventure was not working out. Tania and I were at odds over everything. My dead-end job working nights at the club was leading nowhere fast. I knew I had to find some real direction in the way of employment. Tania too had had it with her job and her bitch boss. While I found her new, independent persona attractive, we were butting heads at every turn. It seemed that our seven-year relationship was bang on time with the popular forecast of a 'seven-year itch'. We were fast coming apart.

Tania and I had been together for a beautiful fun-filled time ever since high school. We had met when she was fourteen and I was sixteen, and our relationship had continued all through my two years in the army. And when I walked out the gates of 1 Parachute Battalion in 1981, having recently returned from Operation Protea, a cross border incursion into the Cunene province in Angola, Tania was waiting for me. But before I could say ten words to her she had looked me in the eyes and told me I had changed. Maybe she had been right.

Sadly, we decided to pack it in and head back to Johannesburg, probably to break up when we got there. We sold all our stuff, all the furniture, all our pictures on the walls, our pinewood bed, the TV and pots and pans that we had bought with such excitement a year before. And so Tania and I left "the fairest Cape in all the world" and headed north over the high Hex River mountains, on the long drive back to Johannesburg. This time there was no stopping to skinny dip in the small, ice cold reservoirs beside the road in the hot Karoo semi-desert.

The adventure was over.

Chapter Five
BACK IN JOHANESBURG

'Heartache Tonight' ~ *The Eagles*

Leon was a tough fighter from Boksburg, the next town to the west of Benoni. I had watched him a few times when I visited the boxing gym, just across the road from the old Van Riebeeck Hotel. He was a slick boxer; tall and lean and moved easily around the ring with a side to side movement, his hands held high. One of the signs of a good fighter. One day, standing at the back of the gym, I watched him sparring with a black fighter. Leon destroyed his sparring opponent, employing a sharp left hand that shot out like a rod, followed by a crisp right that seemed on target for the whole sparring session, which had quickly become a full-on fight. The gym was run by *Oom* (uncle) Tom, who had not intervened to slow down the action. Leon was a good fighter.

He would not have been my first-choice opponent for my first fight as a pro, but that was the luck of the draw. My first professional fight would be the undercard or curtain-raiser to an international rumble between the South African hard-hitting knockout artist, Freddie Rafferty, and a strong, light heavyweight, Jonjo Greene, a Welshman. I was in great shape. I was lean and fast. My older brother, Murray, had been training me, pushing me hard. He had me running up and down the long field behind the family farmhouse, dragging a heavy tyre tied to my waist; he was also putting me through an unfamiliar workout, telling me that this is how the old-time boxers like Gene Tunney and Jack Dempsey had trained in the old days, "When men were men" he said. We had both read one of the books written by Dempsey, *Championship Fighting: Explosive Punching and Aggressive Defence*, which described how he had become the most famous heavyweight 'man killer' of all time. The book provided boxing tips and instructions and explained the philosophy behind Dempsey's 81 bouts, against some of the toughest fighters from the days of The Great Depression, in the 1930s.

Murray as Boxing Trainer: "This is the way to train, run up to that fence dragging this car tyre behind you, then turn and come back here, then shadow box for one round and then do it all again."

"All the way up there and back?"

"Yep."

"You sure?"

"Hey! No talking back to your trainer!"

Also, Murray had me doing some really strange exercises to get into shape for my first pro fight. He was working on my speed and had me snatching imaginary flies out of the air, doing explosive fast moves, cutting off the ring, and following through with six punch combinations. By the time the fight came I was lean and mean and *fast*.

I loved the fight atmosphere of the weigh-in at a Johannesburg hotel. Everyone was walking around wearing Old Buck Gin T-shirts, cameras flashed, reporters wrote in small notebooks. This was what it was all about! This was what I had been dreaming of, watching fighters like Arnold Taylor, Pierre Fourie, Charlie Weir, Roberto Durán, and Gene 'Mad Dog' Hatcher. These fighters looked like gods to me as they climbed through the ropes, gaunt and lean from running 500 kilometres and years of hard training, all of them poker-faced with dark eyes that showed no emotion, fighters with small red gloves as hard as apples, each one confident of his ability. These guys with their broken noses, the beginning of cauliflower ears, their slurred speech, fascinated me. I would soon find out if I could run with the pack.

But perhaps it had all been just a daydream, which would end with me being knocked out; embarrassing proof of being too slow, unable to punch … not good enough …can't fight, go home and try something else, try golf.

Leon came out of his corner moving like he had butter under his boots. I tried to match his slick moves but was a second behind him. He jolted his left hand at my face as he glided in and out. I tried moving from side to side and countered with a vicious left hook, trying to take his head off. I got a stiff left over the top for my trouble.

Fuck it! Can't catch him.

He was quicker than expected and I couldn't find my range. The crowd had quickly chosen their allegiances. Shouts of "Boksburg!" (for Leon) and

"Benoni!" (for me) filled the local Benoni Ice Rink turned boxing stadium. Leon seemed to smile as my punches crashed through the air where he had been a split second before. He made it look easy, as if he was slipping them without having to think. I could see why he was well known for his fast, left hand; he disguised his move and suddenly his glove was in my face. I walked back to my stool sucking deep breaths, thankful that the first round was over. But I had discovered one good thing in this round – I could hit harder than he could.

In the second round my nerves had settled down and I loosened up. I threw my combos, but my punches were still too long to really hurt him.

"Falling step, get closer!" I heard Murray's voice above the crowd.

I settled down, shortened my attack and started using Jack Dempsey's falling step. It seemed to work. The technique brought me closer to Leon. I was just beginning to find my range and open up with some hard shots in the middle of the round when Leon caught me with a short, powerful counter right hand. It landed square in my eye like a thunderbolt. In slow motion I had seen him time my attack, watched him drop his head and put his shoulder into his punch, but I had been in no position to move out of the way. It was the hardest punch I had ever felt. My brain exploded into a million stars fading to a black cloud ... instantly my nose and the back of my throat filled with that strange smell of iron that comes with a hard headshot. I felt the shock shoot right through the centre of my brain and all the way down my spine. Immediately I felt my right eye begin to swell.

Okaay ... so this is how it feels, catching a solid punch from a pro.

Even though my head was fuzzy and I was seeing stars I gave nothing away; I kept calm, my face deadpan and emotionless. Leon knew that he had hurt me and now he smiled broadly, whirling his right hand in circles above his head like Sugar Ray Leonard coming in for the kill. Then his mocking smile turned into an angry scowl and he came forward, determined and unblinking. I moved from side to side. I couldn't see properly out of my right eye had swelled up within in a few seconds and was almost closed. Then Leon tagged me with another hard hook that had my ear ringing.

Damn it!

The Boksburg supporters shouted wildly, seeing their man on the attack. The shouts came in waves ... my ear seemed not to be working properly.

He started throwing 'bombs', trying to finish me off, but his gloves passed millimetres from my head. I survived his relentless attack and walked back to the corner, breathing hard, and flopped onto the stool. My right eye was now swollen shut; I could not see out of it, at all.

My corner man, Bob Lang, pressed the cold enswell[1] hard onto my blossoming black eye as Murray hissed into my face.

"You got to knock him out bro'! Don't try to box. Go full out like you do in the gym."

I glared across the ring through my one good eye at Leon's corner. His support team seemed excited; his trainer's finger was flying through the air then pointing at me, indicating that he knew I was hurt; he was telling Leon to deliver the knockout blow. I felt a steely cold settle inside me. I was no fucking chump who had just fallen out of the olive tree. A stream of memories, contorted faces, sounds of battle flashed through my mind in a second.

I came out of the corner filled with a cold fury, strode across the ring and drove straight through Leon's guard, just the way that I had trained in the gym, with a lighting fast six punch combination. He seemed surprised but managed to cover up … but my hard punches drove his gloves back into his face. Immediately I attacked again, with a fast four punch combo, just the way I had practiced countless times in the garage. This time I caught him hard in the throat and saw him stagger. He tried to hide behind his gloves but now I knew I had learned how to get through a high defence. My arms felt like missiles and I sent them like RPG-7 rockets straight through his defences, which sent him sprawling onto the canvas. He looked up at me, wide-eyed with surprise that he was down, and took the count while sucking in precious air. He got up, confused, shaking his head, but signalled to his corner men that he was OK.

Well, tough shit buddy 'cause here I come again.

I knew it was over. I had found my range and my rhythm. His well-known ramrod left had lost its power and bounced harmlessly off my gloves. I had him on the run. He ducked and moved and I cut off his retreat, waiting for my time.

Now I've got you!

---

1 An enswell (sometimes called an 'end-swell' or eye iron) is a small piece of metal used by a second, corner or cutman, to apply pressure to a (boxing) injury to reduce swelling.

The game had changed. I was the hunter and he was the prey. He knew it and I knew it. There is an invisible energy in the ring when one man knows that the other man is about to beat him. I had been on the receiving end of this energy before, but not tonight. I cut off the ring and backed him onto the ropes. He faltered for a split second and dropped his hands to throw a last-ditch combination. It was just the opening I needed. In a flash I leapt forward like a loaded spring with a hard, furious, five punch combination. All the punches connected and sent Leon flying right through the ropes. He fell headfirst behind the judges' table and into the front row of chanting fans, his feet sticking out above their heads.

I raised my arm in victory and turned back to my corner while the crowd roared its approval of the knockout. Just what they had come to see, but perhaps they had been expecting it from Boksburg rather than Benoni.

It had been an exciting fight. The following morning Murray woke me by tossing the Sunday paper at me while I was still lying in bed. There was a deep, sharp headache right through the centre of my skull. I peered through puffed-up eyes at the black and white photo of the knockout in the sports section. My opponent's legs were sticking up from the front row of the audience; my arm was raised in victory. The main event, the Rafferty-Greene bout, featured a photo only a quarter of the size of mine. Freddy Rafferty had another win under his belt, but no knockout. While it felt good to have won my first professional fight with a knockout, my body hurt like hell. It felt as though someone had worked over every inch of my head, neck and shoulders with a ball-peen hammer. But I had won – and I was feeling good. In celebration I lit a Van Ryn cigarette I had nicked from my mother and walked into the backyard, to talk and joke with some of our farm workers who were eagerly waiting to hear if I had won or lost. I squinted through my right eye, still almost swollen shut, coughing as the smoke burned my lungs. I hadn't smoked for two weeks before the fight and had thought I would stop altogether.

Aw, fuck it. I'll quit before the next fight.

'Rebel Rebel' ~ *David Bowie*

Since returning to Johannesburg I had been lucky enough and successful too, to put together two very exciting changes in my life. The first was that I had applied for and been granted my professional boxing licence. I still didn't know if I had what it would take to hang with the pros, but I had been on fire to get into the professional ranks. I knew that most of the other pros had longer amateur experience, some of them with national colours. I was heading into uncharted water, with no aspirations or illusions about becoming a World Champion, but I knew I could hit hard. I had my eyes fixed on the South African middleweight boxing title. I loved the fierce competition and the bragging that went back and forth between local fighters with names like Kosie Van Vuuren, Bobby Chisale, Nat Moloi and Gerhard Botes. I was going to give it my best shot, win or lose. I would take no prisoners. I planned to stick to my rough, hard-hitting style and had no intention of becoming a student of the 'sweet science'. Knock 'em down, collect the cheque and go home – that was my plan.

Murray was my biggest fan and my very keen trainer. He was two years older than me, an out of the box thinker, and had been an inspiration to me, my entire life.

"Well, you're 23 years old, if you're going to do it, Gungie, you better go for it now," said Murray.

"Maybe I should keep boxing as an amateur for another year?"

"What for … more experience?"

"*Ja*, maybe?"

"I don't think another year is going to change anything. You're not going to become a Muhammad Ali in a year."

"You think I'll be able to hang in there, in the pros?"

"Yes, keep it simple and hit like hell. It's like Mike told you, sink or swim. We'll soon know."

On the Highveld, in the cold winter nights, the small amateur boxing gym in Benoni smelt like leather and sweat, the windows frosted over from the heat generated by the squad of young boxers, battling the heavy bags and sparring in the worn-out ring with sagging ropes. But the head trainer of our tough little boxing gym had a different view about my hopes and dreams.

"You can't turn professional, you haven't even got your Springbok colours yet," he said, looking at me with a condescending smirk. How dare I think of fighting as a professional?

He had stopped talking to me, turned his head and walked away whenever he saw me coming, making it clear that he wanted nothing to do with my plans of turning professional, even though I had recently collected a string of first round, stone cold knockout amateur wins on the East Rand. His scoffing didn't do me any harm, but his refusal to sign my application for a professional boxing license was an unexpected road block on my path to boxing success. I couldn't apply for a professional license if I couldn't get my amateur trainer to sign the papers. I hung around the gym for a week, trying to get a chance to argue my case. He avoided me, showing up late and leaving early, walking straight to his car without giving me a chance to talk to him.

It looked as though all hope was lost … until a couple of weeks later the gym's second-in-command coach, a great guy, who had been quietly watching this whole back and forth affair pulled me aside and told me to bring the application papers around to the gym, to him, the following Thursday. So I did just that. Without reading a word on the three-page application document he took his pen, confidently scrawled his signature across the bottom of the paperwork, then thrust the forms into my hand.

"Go for it. Give it your best my boy … remember, the pros is a dangerous game, you have to hit as hard as you can and keep your hands up high – you hold them too low."

"OK, I will, Gene. You watch."

I thought I recognised the grim expression on Gene's face. Perhaps he, too, had once had the same dream – to box as a professional – and for some reason his dream had been denied. Now he had scribbled his untidy signature on the ticket to my future professional boxing life. I thanked him from the bottom of my heart and walked out of the gym into the Highveld winter night, an equally cold smile on my face.

In South Africa at that time, the 1980s, it was not an automatic process from the application for, to the receipt of, a professional boxing license. No sir, not at all. Boxers who applied for their professional license in the Transvaal (now Gauteng) would have to assemble at a gym every six months to perform 'try outs' – to spar and show off their boxing skills in front of members of the South African National Boxing Control Commission (SANBCC), which, in 2002 was reinvented as Boxing South Africa (BSA). Stan Christodoulou himself, long-time chairman of the SANBCC, would be on hand to watch and decide whether or not a boxer had the right stuff for the pro ring.

We drove to the Johannesburg YMCA where the gym was run by well-known trainer 'Slagter' (Butcher) Van der Merwe. The old gym was crowded with at least thirty hopefuls, fighters from all over the Transvaal, who were eager to secure a future in professional boxing. I gloved up to face a strong, determined looking boxer whom I had never seen before. I was as cold as ice, on full automatic, allowing my training to envelop me.

The bell rang. I came out fast and aggressive, immediately on the attack, and produced the best thirty seconds of boxing that I had ever managed. My opponent stood no chance. My punches were as straight and fast and hard as a hydraulic punch machine. I was Charlie Weir! I was the slayer of all in front of me!

The big, determined, curly-haired hopeful was down on his butt within less than eight seconds. He got up to take the count and we continued. He seemed lost for ideas and rushed me. I shifted back on the balls of my feet, felt the ropes of the corner against my back, spun around, threw probably six stiff straight, left hand punches to his face as I turned in a semicircle and backed him into the same corner where he had held me.

Then I slammed a straight right with my shoulders raised, it caught him flush in the mouth and dropped him on the seat of his pants in the corner.

Thirty seconds!

"Stop! That's enough!" shouted Stan Christodoulou.

Finally, I was a pro. It was 1984.

Chapter Six

WAY DOWN INSIDE

'Africa' ~ *Toto*

It was more than a year since I had returned to Johannesburg, the City of Gold. Even though I had enjoyed my time living in beautiful Cape Town, it was good to be back on the East Rand. I understood how life worked here in Egoli. It seemed quicker, things moved at a faster pace, creating the illusion that everyone was on the move, unlike the relaxed, chilled vibe I had enjoyed in Cape Town, crammed between Table Mountain, the low clouds and the deep blue sea.

A second recent and exciting change in my life was that I had moved – up – from having been a plumbing apprentice to becoming a plumbing contractor, overnight. Now, it was lunchtime and I was eating my usual meal, a couple of burn-your-mouth hot Ma Baker meat pies, followed by a cool Nestle chocolate milk, and contemplating my run of good luck. My crew was busy working. I had overnight, literally, and without any prior planning, started my own plumbing company, working on new houses. I had gone, as usual, to work one morning as an apprentice with nine months experience and come home as a plumbing contractor – with a contract to plumb five new houses for a developer.

Life was not as exciting as for the Stander gang I was reading about in the newspaper, (no relation to my friend Stander who unbeknownst to me was pursuing the same pastime) . They were on a spree, robbing bank after bank and helping themselves to hundreds of thousands of rand; they were also on the run from the police. The money I was making was not as good as theirs, but it was good enough, and it had all happened really suddenly.

Soon after we returned from Cape Town, Tania and I had broken up. We were both very sad about it. At the same time, I had again started working as a plumbing apprentice with a few different companies. I had ended up with a small company that installed plumbing in the newly built homes popping up like mushrooms in a new neighbourhood outside Kempton Park. Bennie, my boss, was a boozer; a nice enough man but someone who thought he was a seriously tough guy after he had downed a couple of drinks. It was about noon on a sunny day and I was on the building site, balancing on a wooden roof truss, installing a copper pipe in the roof of a house when Bennie the Boss arrived on the scene, having enjoyed a couple lunch time beers. He started to bawl me out, from a distance, in front of the entire crew, for some or other reason to do with the copper pipe.

I leapt ten feet off the roof and landed with bent knees and feet together, like a good paratrooper should, and in a flash I had boozy Bennie up against the wall. I told him I would kick his ass all the way back to his little pickup truck if he ever shouted at me like that again, and, by the way – you can stick your job where the sun don't shine.

I threw my meagre set of tools into my small Renault, slammed the trunk closed and left the site. Then reality set in ... I knew I had screwed up, again. A few blocks away I pulled over and stopped at the side of the road to gather my composure.

What now?

Lost another job. It seemed I was unable to hold onto a job for longer than three months. I was deep in contemplation of my bleak future, trying to plan my next move when a light bulb flashed in my brain, delivering a really good idea, certainly one worth a try. I remembered that a few weeks earlier I had accompanied Bennie, my newest ex-boss, to visit a construction company looking for a plumbing contractor. The company was active in the area and I had watched as Bennie and the contractor scrutinised the blueprints of several new houses, waiting to be plumbed. Bennie had pushed his thick lenses up his nose and nodded, but the rest of his body language showed he was not too keen on the project. As we pulled out of the parking lot I asked him if he was going to take the contract. He shook his head.

"Naw, too much work. I'm not equipped to handle all those new houses," Bennie had told me.

At the time I had thought, "Well, OK, fine," and it had not crossed my mind again, until now.

Now my lightbulb idea was gaining traction. The problem was, I was not (yet) a plumbing contractor, I was barely even a plumber – I had logged only nine months of patchy plumbing experience, so far. I pondered this shortfall for a minute and then made up my mind. The hell with that! It doesn't matter … fortune favours the bold.

It was now only about half an hour since I had walked off the job. I started my Renault and headed straight across town to the construction company, just outside Kempton Park, which Bennie and I had visited a week previously. I walked into their reception area with the confidence of a man who doesn't know what he's in for and asked the manager a simple question.

"Are you guys still looking for a plumbing contractor?"

The blue-eyed manager hesitated for a second, peering up at me from behind his handlebar moustache. Slowly he inspected me.

Suddenly I was self-conscious about the black eye I was sporting, one of the results of my daily boxing training regime.

"Yes, we are, we need a plumber like yesterday," he answered, cautiously.

"Well, I'm a plumber and I can start working tomorrow, with the first house."

He sized me up, standing there in front of him.

"Oh? Really? Sure, sit down. Let me show you what we've got … what's your name?"

We shook hands. He was beaming now, as he stood up from his desk, pulled out a pile of rolled up blueprints and showed me a house for which I could start installing the plumbing, right away. He said he had a few more houses ready and waiting, right behind the first, and gave me a brief run down on the business of the construction company and how many houses they had ready for plumbing. Lots!

"Well, I can get started tomorrow with this one; probably do the second one the by end of next week. My guys work pretty fast," I lied.

I gave him a rough price which I had sucked out of my thumb en route to his office, for a basic bread and butter house. He smiled and said they had been paying a smaller amount per house, something like R9,000, if I remember correctly. Although it was less than my 'quote', it sounded a whole lot better than the R350 per week I had been earning as a plumber's apprentice. I told him his price was just fine by me.

"I'll be on site to start this house tomorrow; then I'll move on to this other house next week," pointing to the plans.

"No, no. Start this house second, and that'll be the third house."

"Oh, OK then. I'll do that one third."

"Well, thank you for having approached us. We were really in a pinch without a plumber. Come around tomorrow, if you want, and I'll have an advance payment of R3,000 ready for you."

"OK, good. I'll see you tomorrow, to pick up the cheque."

Great! Not more than three short hours after having told my drunk ex-boss to stick his job, and walking away as an unemployed apprentice, with a measly nine months of sporadic plumbing experience, I walked out of that office with a slap on the back from my new 'client' as a Plumbing Contractor. With the blueprints of the first three houses tucked under my arm. No one had asked me any ridiculous questions like: "Could we see your plumbing license?" or "Do you have liability insurance?" or "How long have you been in the plumbing business?" or "Do you even have a work truck?"

Little did they know how little I knew about the business of plumbing a house, from scratch. But we had shaken hands and patted each other on the shoulder – and the deal was done.

TIA brother! Who dares wins!

Straight off to downtown Kempton Park, to my father's office to ask if I could borrow a small amount of money for tools that I didn't have, grinders, step ladders, etc. My father smiled doubtfully as he wrote a cheque to me. From his office to the bank, from the bank to the hardware store, then straight to the city library to find a book about whole house plumbing systems. I studied it until midnight and woke up the next morning with a clear vision of how to plumb an entire house.

Within five or six days I had completed the rough plumbing on the first house and received another cheque for around R3,000 from the construction company. Apart from plumbing a hot water line to feed the toilet, which, when someone noticed steam coming from under the toilet lid, I had to redirect, my first house turned out just fine. Then the plaster and tile crew moved in to do their work and I moved on to the next house, to rough in the pipes – and get another deposit of R3,000. At breakfast I handed the cheques to my father, who chuckled delightedly. In the past couple of weeks I had made more money than I would have made in six months, as an apprentice plumber earning R350 per week.

To cap this incredible streak of good fortune our long-time housekeeper, Ida, rushed out of the kitchen early one morning, collared me and said that her boyfriend, Piet, was a first class, A number 1 plumber who, together with his team, just happened to be available and looking for work. Casually I suggested she ask him to come and meet me, as soon as possible.

Piet was waiting for me early the next morning, hat in hand, smiling from ear to ear, bearing a remarkable likeness to our South African middleweight champion at the time, Thulani 'Sugar Boy' Malinga. Piet had a really agreeable personality and smiled away while telling me that new construction was his specialty. I felt a burden the size of a newly bricked house lift from my shoulders. I had created an instant plumbing company, had new houses waiting for me, and now I had a skilled work crew. All this had been achieved virtually overnight and with *only nine months* of plumbing experience!

The Christmas summer that year, 1985, was sweltering; there seemed to be no end in sight to the drought, triggered by the recurring El Niño phenomenon, the cause of the worst drought to hit South Africa in 30 years. "The Vaal Dam is extremely low" was a phrase that made constant headlines in most newspapers at that time. Hot as it was, after two years in the army, followed by a year in Cape Town, it was great to be back on the family farm again, together with my sister Tracy, brother Murray and Mom and Dad – despite becoming aware that my parents' 30-year marriage was showing clear signs of coming apart at the seams.

My father Nicolaas was a well-known real estate agent and very active in the Witwatersrand Rifles, a reserve unit of the SA defence force. My mother Alice, as glamorous as ever, was still fully involved with her dance troupe, bringing smiles to old age homes and hospitals on the East Rand. She also played an active role as a sergeant in the Benoni Commando, a reserve army unit within the ten regional commands of the SADF (as it was then), a reserve army unit dedicated to serve the surrounding area of the East Rand.

But it would take more than a scorching summer and a major drought to suppress my mother's enthusiastic plans for celebrating the festive season in

1985. My mother must have had a premonition of events to come, because she had decided to 'go big' on Christmas day, with all her children at home for the first time in some years.

"Don't make any plans for Christmas; we are all having Christmas dinner together, at home," she had ordered.

While this was going to be a festivity with all the family, just as it had been in the past, unbeknown to us it would also be the last time we would ever celebrate as an entire family under one roof. In fact, it would be the last Christmas our family would spend together, in just one country, ever again.

So, on Christmas day we all gathered around our big dining room table under the large framed portrait on the wall – a grim Winston Churchill seated in an armchair, cigar in hand, scowling down at us as mom served our long-time family favourite, Chicken a la King over yellow rice peppered with plump, black raisins. All family quarrels were forgotten ... we all chatted and laughed, and my father and mother were all smiles ... just like the old days.

This time, there was an extra, grand reason for a family celebration. Tracy, my beautiful younger sister, sitting at the table with a tall paper hat perched on her platinum blonde hair, her cheeks stuffed with pumpkin and Chicken a la King, smiling, in between mouthfuls, a smile that could have melted the cold heart of the sternest minister in the *Nederduitse Gereformeerde Kerk* (Dutch Reformed Church) had just won a lucrative modelling contract with an international modelling agency called Elite Model Management.

At the ripe old age of 15 years, Tracy had appeared on the July 1985 front cover of *Cosmopolitan* magazine. My little sister! To be adorning the cover of the prestigious *Cosmopolitan* fashion magazine in itself was a marvellous feat. We were all so proud of Tracy, and what a thrill it had been to see her face on advertisements in news stands, in various shopping malls throughout the East Rand. Now, as a result of some quick thinking of Sherry, a family friend had ensured that Tracy was taken and introduced to Johnny Casablanca the head of the renowned Elite modelling agency. He had been in South Africa at that time to judge the Miss South Africa pageant. He had met Tracy and immediately offered her a two-year modelling contract in New York, Italy and Germany.

There was one small problem: my beautiful little sister, at 15 years of age, was still only halfway through high school; but Elite wanted to whisk her off to model in Europe and the 'Big Apple'. So, what was Tracy to do? Should she drop out of high school and take advantage of this once in a lifetime opportunity, to be a fashion model overseas/ Or stay at school and complete her matric year with all her friends? This had led to heated discussion within the family and another face-off between my father and mother.

My father had maintained that Tracy should *not* go overseas on this modelling contract but should stay in South Africa and finish high school. A wise and sensible suggestion. My mother, a theatrical actress who, once upon a time had been offered the chance to join a prominent theatre group in England but had declined this once-in-a-lifetime acting opportunity because of her obligations as a newly married wife, argued bitterly that Tracy should *accept* the contract, go abroad and think about finishing her matric later. Mom was desperate for Tracy not to have to experience the same regret. What a dilemma. This exhilarating prospect had been the cause of much excitement, and many pros-and-cons type discussions, which had gone on for weeks. What were we to do with our Tracy?

Each of my mother's extensive group of friends had driven out on a pilgrimage to the farm, ostensibly for tea and scones but really for serious discussion about this dilemma, as the deadline for signing the modelling contract loomed closer. Countless pots of steaming hot tea were brewed and served in the shade of the verandah of our big old farmhouse, while legions of old friends offered their opinions between dipping rusks or nibbling at scones. Even Tania, my old flame, looking as lovely as ever, had visited the farm to give her view and input. My mother, Alice, stood her ground, unwavering, insisting that Tracy drop high school and seize this once-in-a-lifetime opportunity to model in the US and Europe.; she could finish her schooling later. Her stance was supported by most of her friends. Murray and I also thought that she should go. Worn down by all this opposition my father finally had no choice but to capitulate, with a shrug of his shoulders and a wry grin. (I believe he was secretly glad she was going, but someone in the family had to play the role of the voice of reason.) My mother had won, and Tracy was soon to be whisked away overseas on a 747 jet, complete with a chaperone and a tutor, to begin her career as an international model. Bravo!

What we didn't know then, as we waved goodbye to my beautiful young sister, was that we would never again meet as a family of five, anywhere, ever. Our family would be separated, always, by a distance of 10,000 miles.

But for now, life was good. I had even been able to join a good band and was singing rock and roll again. Lance Dickinson, a good friend of mine from the old school gang days, and I had arranged to be interviewed by a talent agency in Hillbrow. My particular thing was belting out good hard rock and roll. The small, well-dressed Lebanese manager who ran the show gave me an audition and I got the job as doing a set as singer with the house band, but he was soon asking me to turn down the volume and sing softer dance songs, so everyone could relate; he wanted me to do current, softer hits. His several gold rings flashed as he waved his hands in the air, enthusing about Billy Joel, Bryan Adams and others, even Boney M.

I have nothing against Billy Joel or Bryan Adams, or even Phil Collins, but their stuff wasn't my style and I sure as hell wasn't going to do Boney M! I preferred harder rock – the Rolling Stones, Jethro Tull, Bad Company, Jimi Hendrix, Grand Funk Railroad – I needed some good hard rock to bite into. I told the manager that romantic ballads were not my thing, but he insisted, so the band and I spent miserable hours trying to work on a few current hits for an upcoming show at a Hillbrow hotel. The rest of the group looked and felt as gloomy as I did. We had a practice session and I tried a Bryan Adams and some other stuff, but I wasn't feeling the passion – and neither was the band. I could see the worry on the manager's face. At the end of the session I told him if I couldn't do at least some of the songs I had chosen I would quit. The show was scheduled for just a few days away, so he had his back to the wall. Again, he waved his hands and the gold rings flashed, but this time it was an irritated 'do what you want' sort of gesture. We began working on a few old Bad Company numbers and Grand Funk's 'Some kind of wonderful', which is a difficult, explosive song to sing but I managed. The band started pulling together again and we had a few good songs down, like 'Urgent' by Foreigner.

On the night of the show I was nervously drinking a rum and coke at the bar, watching the other performers while I waited for my turn on stage. Close to the bar I recognised a figure that looked familiar. He was doing an on-the-spot jig, pulling John Travolta dance moves, a big grin on his face; a grin I had seen many times before. It was my mate, John Delaney, from Parachute Battalion. In the two years since my exit from the army I had not seen anyone from the Battalion, except for Stan, in Cape Town, and that had been a while ago.

I attacked Delaney from his blind side and he was quick on the response. We laughed and ordered another double rum and coke and he told me what he had been up to. He looked pretty fucked up – aggressive, glaring at anyone who came close to us. We hardly spoke about the old times in Angola, but he did tell me that tough James Alders, who had been with our platoon in 1 Parachute Battalion, had recently killed himself playing Russian roulette in a Johannesburg bar. Apparently James had come across some punks with a revolver, talking about playing the lethal game of chance, and had challenged them. He told them if they had any balls they would put two bullets in the chamber. They did. James spun the cylinder, told them he would take the first shot, and did. Game over.

"How's your brother?" I asked. John's brother Neil had been a sought-after door gunner in an Alouette gunship during the Bush War. I had met him a couple of times when we were in the army. He was a good guy.

"He's not doing so good ... fucked up ...he's a quiet guy and keeps everything inside ... but fights all the time. You know, after he qualified as a door gunner, he shot twelve in his first contact, six of them were PBs (*plaaslike bevolking*, i.e. local population or civilians). With that 20 mm explosive filling and detonating fuse they ..."

I sipped my rum and listened.

Being a 20 mm door gunner in an Alouette gunship in the Border War was a prestigious position, brave crews coming in, flying low and exposed, in the face of imminent danger in a hot contact, providing much appreciated support for South African troops on the ground, like the cavalry of old. We would quickly punch our bush hats inside out, revealing the bright orange day-glo sticker on the inside of our hats, so as not to be shot by mistake by the fast shooting door gunner. The 20 mm explosive head cannon churned up the ground like the grim reaper himself. Decimating twelve people including six locals on your first contact could not have been a happy start as a helicopter door gunner, but I suppose it was part of the job. I thought of John's brother Neil. I remembered him as a quiet guy with a big grin on his face. In the last week of Operation Daisy – a major South African search and destroy operation in Angola, aimed at moveable, small SWAPO training base camps deep in Angola – I had witnessed first-hand what a 20 mm explosive head cannon did to the human body – men, women and children. It cut their bodies in half and sprayed their guts on the sand.

I walked slowly amongst the terrible aftermath, my rifle held tight in my shoulder, the barrel still burning hot from having shot three 35-round magazines as fast as I could.

BOOM BOOM BOOM! ... BOOM BOOOM BOOM!

Gunships always fired three burst salvoes.
At the top of the ridge we had come upon a scene of dreadful carnage and desperate fighting amid a haze of dust, smoke, the crack of gunfire and the sounds of wounded and dying men. The gas turbine of the two Alouette gunships making an ear-splitting scream, as the two helicopters flew in low tight orbits just above the tree tops and terrible scene below; Their rotor blades hammered loudly the tighter that they turned, with skill the pilot kept the craft tilted giving the flight engineer with his big helmet clear view of the ground below, firing his 20 mm explosive head cannon into the thick fog of battle below; secondary small explosion as the shell found it target. We were here to finish them off on the ground.

BOOM BOOM BOOM ... BOOM BOOM BOOM

The hellish scene and the perfect text book pincer movement had not taken very long to end.

"Cease fire cease fire cease fire!" someone shouted. "Forwaaaard!"
In jerks we stopped firing and charged forward, tripping and falling, across the rocky ground of the ridge, enveloped in thick dust and smoke our barrels still smoking. Some of the trees had been stripped of their leaves from the barrage of fire. Dead and broken bodies, in filthy tiger stripe camouflage uniforms, clutching AK-47s, were scattered all around; the fatally wounded were dying among the scrubby bushes; the sand, now burned black and white, had been churned up like a ploughed field by the 20 mm cannons ...a field ploughed by the Grim Reaper. What an awful mistake of war.

> *Who could see … through the dust and smoke in the heat of battle? It was a scene from Hades, never to be forgotten. Later that day we gathered up the enemy weapons, 29 AK-47 carrying them down to the helicopters. Before throwing them in a pile I struggled and twisted off a shiny silver bayonet from a shattered, blood spattered SKS soviet rifle to keep as a reminder.*

(I look at this bayonet, always on my desk, this very minute as I write these words, so many years later.)

I was lost in thought, thinking back to That Day, when John spoke loudly over the noise of the crowded Johannesburg night club. I shouted back to him, saying I was sorry that his brother seemed so fucked up.

"*Ja*, well, it's OK, it's OK. He'll be all right," John replied, looking a little disconnected.

I had become lost in my own thoughts, remembering that awful event on the ridge in Angola, so I was taken by surprise when the band began the opening bars of 'Urgent' –

"Hey! They're calling you!" shouted Delaney, thumping me on the shoulder.

I snapped back from the almost unthinkable memory of the Bushmen SWAPO, with their families, whom we had killed in the terrible chaos of war on the rocky ridge in Angola; I was back in the loud Hillbrow nightclub with the crowd cheering at the opening bars of the song. Quickly I downed the last of the double rum, punched my old army friend hard on his shoulder and leaped onto the stage. The red and yellow spotlights and disco lights went wild.

I knew this song off pat! I had sung it many times before, just the way Lou Gramm from Foreigner had shouted it. I felt like the man himself as I ripped through the song. 'Urgent' was a difficult song to sing but I nailed the impossible high notes one after the other, with not one falter … just like the record! I jumped around with Mick Jagger-like moves during the long, amazing saxophone solo. Anton the guitarist was smiling at me, showing that he was pleased with the vocals. I saw John's huge grin as he bopped up and down in the crowd.

It had been great to see one of the guys from Parachute Battalion again and at the end of the set I went looking for John Delaney, but he was lost somewhere in the bustling nightclub crowd. I was disappointed; I still wanted to talk with him about many things, but by the end of the night I was hammered. I searched my pockets for the bit of paper on which John had scribbled his phone number, but it had disappeared somewhere on the dance floor. Eighteen years would pass before I saw my mate, John Delaney, once more.

John and I had experienced a lot of life changing action together, while in Parachute Battalion, including the unforgettable, horrific scene on that rocky ridge deep in Angola.

When I saw John again, much later, he was still sporting the same infectious grin, but he had changed – he had become a minister. He had studied at and graduated from a seminary and, for ten years, had travelled to most of the countries in Africa, preaching God's word. He had even gone back into Angola, to the towns where we had waged war; he had also travelled to offer help to war torn Sri Lanka, and to Haiti, among other destitute locations in the world.

And then John and his wife had started a mission in Johannesburg, helping the poor.

It seemed that the guys from our platoon in Delta Company were making up for our time in the bush, at the tip of the spear.

Chapter Seven
MOVIN' ON

'Sweet Dreams (Are Made of This)' ~ *The Eurythmics*

My fellow up-and-coming local pro boxers did not quite know what to make of me. I had come out of nowhere and had not climbed up through the boxing ranks like most of them. Most of the younger professionals and amateurs on the East Rand had known each other for many years as they had come up through provincial, national and international tournaments together. I was a new face on the scene. I had turned professional as soon as I could, after a string of amateur fights that I had won mostly with stone cold first and second round knockouts and I didn't have much respect for my peers, I just wanted to get that Old Buck South African championship belt around my waist.

I saw this question written on the face of a well-known Springbok amateur boxer who had just turned professional, Bokkie Buys, as he and I squared up to spar on the concrete driveway of the big Boksburg house owned by World Boxing Association heavyweight champion, Gerrie Coetzee. The World Champ was not home as scheduled so, unable to get into the gym he had built in his backyard, our trainers decided to have us spar with one another under the floodlights of the WBA champion's four-car concrete driveway.

As a Springbok Bokkie Buys had many more years of boxing experience and skills than I did. As a spectator I had silently watched him fight at a number of high-level amateur tournaments, increasingly jealous of his slick boxing skills. Now here I stood, glaring at Bokkie as my trainer, Johnny, smeared Vaseline on my face and gloves. This was to be my test, right here tonight, under these lights. I suspected that Johnny had set it up because he was eager to see if I would sink or swim against a top boxer. Watching Bokkie watching me, I saw the puzzled look on his face, as we got ready to spar for the first time.

"Who the hell is this guy and where did he come from?" was written all over Bokkie's face.

Bokkie's trainer pushed his stopwatch and shouted, "Box!"

I came out fast, the only way that I knew how and let him know who I was right away, with a thud, as I threw a lightning power right cross that caught him hard on the side of the head. He wobbled and couldn't hide the surprise on his face. I had hurt him with one of my very first punches. I stuck to him like glue, giving him no chance to recover, and landed a few more clean, solid blows in my aggressive style. Bokkie tried to regain his composure and to apply his well-known straight combinations, but it was too late to change the momentum I had set. The night was mine. I was landing my punches almost at will. He held his gloves high, but I stepped in and punched right through his defence as I had learned from having watched big Arthur being knocked out, in Cape Town. I was coming out on top of the Springbok in our first sparring session! After two rounds of sparring it became obvious that Bokkie could not recover from the first round. His coach took off his headgear and said he was not going to spar anymore.

Welcome to the pro ranks buddy! I silently shouted to myself.

I kept my gloves laced and went another two rounds with a young, future South African champion, Fransie Badenhorst. I knew him well. Fransie was ranked number five or six in South Africa, then. He was a lot smaller but was always just too quick for me; he peppered me with some lightning fast shots as per usual. All the same, my trainer, Johnny Hogg, was well pleased.

"You did great tonight son, that's the way to do it, just like that."

"Was it OK?"

"Yes. Do you know who that was you were sparring with, first time tonight?"

"Bokkie Buys."

"Yes, Bokkie Buys. He's a Springbok and the up-and-comer on his way to the championship; and you beat him well tonight, son. You did great."

My new, diminutive, 4-foot, 11-inch trainer was pleased as punch and waved at me as he pulled away in his car, wearing a big smile.

That was the beginning of many a hot sparring session between me and the soon to be very well-known boxer, Bokkie Buys. We followed each other from gym to gym and always ended up having a good go at each other and I learned some valuable boxing tricks from him in the process. Sometimes Bokkie's Springbok boxing experience and combinations were effective, and I went home with a blue eye, my ears ringing; other times my unrelenting style and fast straight punches had his knees wobbling as I drove through his defences and rocked him back into the ropes. I had become an expert at driving through someone's defence.

I had progressed quickly from sparring with young club professionals to sparring against some of South Africa's top fighters, like SA light heavyweight champ Sakkie Horn; future SA super middleweight champ, Charles Oosthuizen; SA super bantamweight champ, Fransie Badenhorst; SA super welterweight champ, Coenie Bekker; SA welterweight champ Harold 'The Hammer' Volbrecht; even a session with heavyweight Pierre Coetzer; huge heavyweight champ Jimmy Abbott; and even WBA Lineal junior lightweight champ, Brian Mitchell. While sparring with the young up-and-coming boxing pros was all fun and games, although one could go home with a fat lip or a blue eye; stepping up to a seasoned professional boxer and South African champion, like Harold Volbrecht, Brian Mitchell or Sakkie Horn, was a different story altogether. A different league. These guys could send you to hospital pissing blood from solid body blows to the liver. Or drop you with a punch you hadn't even seen coming. These were the guys with whom I was rubbing gloves and shoulders; this was the boxing school of hard knocks; and all of a sudden, I was right in the middle of it.

Now, let me tell you what it's like to spar with Harold 'The Hammer' Volbrecht, ranked the Number 1 welterweight in the world.

The Hammer could suck the life out of a man before the fight had even started, simply by glaring at you from across the ring with enraged, solid black eyes. Harold had been the South African welterweight champion for fourteen years; he had successfully battered down *all* challengers to his 146-pound title with his steady, crafty style and hard-hitting overhand hammer. He was a born fighter, short with a slim waist and broad thick shoulders; a strong square jaw, and cunning, intelligent eyes that seemed to be constantly dilated with rage and blocked the colour from his eyes, making them look black as pits, tucked deep under a strong brow and forehead that looked like armour plating, covered with the scars from many previous battles. Altogether this spelled one clear thing – "I am going to fuck you up, *laaitie*! (youngster!)" – while he glowered at you from the other side of the ring.

Harold, reigning South African welterweight champion, would come out of his corner as calm and relaxed as if he was standing in front of his braai in his backyard. He held his hands up high which immediately deleted any chance of you landing a lucky blow. Although his black eyes were filled with an inner rage, he watched you calmly from behind the safety of his gloves, let you fire off your first punches which he caught easily in his glove, or simply avoided by moving his head an inch to either side. Sparring would pick up pace with Harold glaring at you, his eyes even blacker than before, seeming more pissed off than before.

Now you started to worry ... maybe I made him mad with that last punch ... was it too hard? Maybe I shouldn't hit so hard ... maybe I shouldn't hit at all? Should I open up and give my best, or will he make me pay the price by breaking my nose – again, like last time?

After giving you half a round or so, to let you think you were the one pushing the action, Harold would cut loose with a lightning quick, semi-overhand right, that landed as solid as a 4-pound hammer. It shook you to your boots and you knew, instantly, that you would have a headache for a week. It was almost impossible to read his punches, he let them fly with no warning telegraph movement. His signature kidney punches, when he had an opponent against the ropes, were short and very hard with a full shoulder and hip behind them. A few of his sparring partners, I had heard, had gone to hospital pissing blood from damaged kidneys. I believed it ... I had felt those hammers first-hand.

Now, I too could throw a pretty heavy shot during sparring, to make up for my lack of finer boxing skills. Harold, whom I knew from Benoni, and who I assumed did not really want to fuck me up more than he already had, by breaking my nose, developed a special way of showing me that I was cruising for a real fucking bruising, because I was sparring too hard. He and I finished a few particularly hard rounds of sparring and I could tell that he was really pissed off.

The next boxer to climb into the ring with him was an unfamiliar black middleweight. Harold traded punches with him for half a round and then unleashed his full fury – within seconds the black fighter was on his knees.

"Do you wanna spar or do you wanna fight!?" Harold shouted through his mouthpiece, standing over the fallen fighter, his black eyes enraged, like a pit bull.

"You doin' this because I'm black!" shouted the fighter, still on his knees.

"No! You going too hard! This is sparring, not fighting. But if you want to fight then let's fight!"

The boxer stumbled out of the ring moaning and complaining.

Instinctively I knew that Harold was sending *me* a message, loud and clear. He had used the unfamiliar boxer as a guinea pig to make his point. And I got the point.

From that day on I knew the boundaries to sparring with The Hammer and I kept it at just that … sparring.

I had met a well-known boxer, a champion at the gym who came in daily, his boxing kit stuffed into a deep maroon coloured 1 Parachute Battalion bag. I was curious. One day, at the beginning of working out, I asked him if he had been in Parachute Battalion, pointing at the duffel bag. He laughed and said, no he hadn't, a friend had given him the Parachute Battalion duffel bag as a gift and he thought it was a cool bag to use. He went on to tell me about his own army experience, how bored he had been walking patrol, standing guard, bullshitting around in the bush on the Border, how the time had dragged on and on for him. I said nothing as he talked, but I realised just how different our military experiences had been.

My time at Parachute Battalion had been action-packed and life-changing. Delta Company of 80/81 had comprised all sorts of troublemakers from different walks of life. As civilians they would never have given each other the time of day; now they were thrown together, galvanised through tough training, discipline and punishment into a well-oiled fighting machine of 100 men, who had cut down our nation's enemies, SWAPO and FAPLA, at almost every encounter. Together with our sister Hotel Company we had taken part in three major cross-border operations into Angola – high adventure which to us had seemed a normal part of being a paratrooper, but slowly the appeal had paled as the body count climbed into triple digits.

My personal crossroads had been the killing of almost an entire clan of Bushman SWAPO insurgents, who we had trapped on a rocky ridge, deep inside Angola, during Operation Daisy. It had all been over in about 45 minutes.

After the terrible killing on top of the rocky ridge I had walked alone as we slowly picked our way down from the rocky ridge, each at his own pace, in his own thoughts and each carrying a blood stained or shattered soviet weapon to throw on a pile down where the four Puma helicopters were waiting for us in a shona clearing five minutes' walk down from the ridge. I still held the silver bayonet that I had twisted off the blood stained and shattered stock of a SKS assault rifle that I threw in the pile of 29 enemy weapons at the Shona by the helicopters. We flew West in a V formation, low over the tree tops into a setting sun, the four Puma's with the two Alouette gunships and the spotter plane leading the way, just like a scene from the film Apocalypse Now, *departing as fast as we had arrived.*

We left only a handful of surviving women and children, rooted to the spot like stone statues, shocked, mute, staring dumbly at the horrifying carnage, all that was left of their clan of some 70 San people, decimated, shot to pieces, lying in the torn-up sand, scattered around the top of the small rocky ridge under bushes and in the open, the site of their last fight for survival. It would be their job to identify and bury.

Back at camp no one said anything about the women and children. Not one word. Just more of the unforeseen casualties of war.

As a youngster I had always been naturally optimistic, had always worn a smile, but I had also often been undermined by bouts of depression, dark patches where nothing made sense, which hung like cold winter days, were slow to pass. Now, lately, in the years just after the army these passing storms of dark clouds lasted longer and were more turbulent and violent. I knew from past experience that at all costs I had to protect my light, but it had become a lot tougher to do. I regretted nothing about the past, but now, after 1 Parachute Battalion, I definitely perceived the world differently. Bad things happen in any war.

Now at the age of 23, sometimes, while sitting alone, I questioned the moral value of what soldiers were expected to do, and did, while in uniform – kill a group of men without blinking an eye. Women and children caught in the middle. Unfortunate. What moral injury comes with this? What penance must be served, for this? We are not genetically programmed to kill. Back on Civvy Street all very different, as a civilian stringent rules and punishments govern acts that don't even come close to the acts committed in the war zone. Monster. Killer. Life in prison or the death sentence. "Thou shalt not kill" – the highest of the Ten Commandments. Is the sin of killing equal to breaking the other nine Commandments? What is so terribly sinful about killing? Is the sin in the killing, or in the breaking of society's laws? Of course, killing an enemy armed with an AK-47 trying to kill you is not even a question … nevertheless, the sudden and gruesome death of an armed, brave, 17-year-old SWAPO fighter was unsettling, seen up close.

The well-known boxer finally stopped talking about how bored he had been in the army and finished wrapping his hands in bandages. He punched his fists into his hands, to test his hand wraps, then stood up and danced around, shadow boxing in the small, musty Boksburg gym.

Part of me wanted to shout at him as loud as I could – tell him he had no right to walk around with a paratrooper's bag for his boxing kit if he had not been a paratrooper! I wanted to shout that there was a price to pay for being able carry a parabat bag, a price he hadn't paid! A price that he didn't know about or understand. Had he flown in low over the tree tops, clambered up the rocky ridge deep inside Angola, opened fire on the trapped Bushman clan, seen the children sucking their thumbs as we left them, standing among the shattered bodies of their parents, grandmothers, uncles and siblings? No.

Casually he asked me where I had done my time in the army. Instead of shouting at him like part of me wanted to, I started working out, sinking my left hook into the heavy bag. At the end of the round I walked up to him and told him I had spent my two years at 1 Parachute Battalion as a parabat and that I also had a duffel bag just like the one he was carrying. I was no longer in the mood to shout. He wouldn't have understood.

The big crowd moved slowly into their seats. We had all come to watch the showdown between the two South African heavyweights, Pierre Coetzer and Benny Knoetze, younger brother of the contender for the world heavyweight title, 'Die Bek van Boom Straat', (The Mouth of Tree Street), Kallie Knoetze. Tonight's fight for the South African heavyweight title had been on-and-off, again and again, and had been brewing for a long time.

The two big boxers entered the ring. I was rooting for Pierre Coetzer. I had always liked him with his big walrus moustache and snappy punches that shot straight from his shoulder. I had sparred against him once in a gym in Vereeniging – if you can call it sparring. He was twice my size and could have taken my head off, but he let me throw jabs at his mid-section. Not like the notorious 136 kg, 195.6 cm, Jimmy Abbott, with whom I had sparred at the Brixton gym – he had come full out and floored me with a body blow. Lesson learned. Never assume a much bigger boxer will cut you any slack.

I had long been aware that most white South African boxers (including me) loved to throw the big and hard *'Ek slaan jou dood'* punches – 'I'll punch you to death' blows. They were great when they worked, but after a few rounds they had sapped all your energy. The Americans seemed to throw an easier type of punch, shorter, with more thought behind it.

The fight began, generating currents of electricity among the crowd. It had been a back and forth fight, but now things were not looking good for Pierre. I was watching Coetzer's corner; Andries Steyn (his trainer) was working feverishly on his fighter, giving him advice that might save him, when my eye was caught by the ring girl who had just stepped into the ring. She was tall and slender, sexy, with ash blonde hair, a saucy smile and legs that wouldn't quit. The crowd went wild, whistling and cat calling. She sauntered around the ring like a cat, smiling from ear to ear, holding a sign high above her head, signalling the start of the third round.

And in the third round Bennie Knoetze went down in a heap; Pierre had caught him high on the forehead with a right hand. Bennie tried to get up off the canvas, looking a lot like his older brother, Kallie, at the end of the 8th round in the world heavyweight bout when Kallie had been knocked out by Big John Tate. Bennie was staggering around in the same drunken fashion, his mouth hanging open, his arms dangling at his sides. It was declared a knockout.

Both factions of fans – the jubilant and the disappointed – left the Ellis Park stadium making a lot of noise. I couldn't stop grinning, having witnessed this amazing comeback victory. The violent pantomime of overcoming life's hard knocks gave me hope. It seemed to symbolise the struggle we all called life – and offered a beautiful blueprint for snatching victory out of the jaws of certain death. To come back and win after having sustained such a heavy beating surely was a lesson to remember forever.

What is it that makes a man's spirit turn, in the last second of combat, away from defeat, towards victory? I have always loved this quote from Adlai Stevenson:

On the plains of hesitation lay the countless blackened bones of those who at the dawn of victory lay down to rest, and in resting died.

Surely victory is just around the corner for those who refuse to stop fighting ... who never give up?

Johnny Hogg and I went upstairs to attend the after party being held on the terrace. It was packed with boxing sponsors, media and officials alike. I felt lucky to be there, standing on the side, absorbing the atmosphere. I was munching a sandwich when I recognised the sexy, long-legged ring girl I had seen earlier. She was standing close to me, still smiling from ear to ear, one eye on the crowd and the other on the refreshments. I pushed through the throng of people and told her she had looked pretty darn good up in the ring, holding the round sign, but did she know she had been holding her sign upside down? She paused in mid bite, slowly lifted her eyebrows and looked at me, flustered, then she broke into a big lopsided grin, her brown eyes sparkling. I introduced myself and we began chatting.

"What kind of name is 'Danger' anyway?" she asked, chuckling sarcastically.

"It's not Danger – it's Granger ... with a G."

"So, Granger with a G, what happened to your eye with an E?"

"Cut it, boxing."

"Oh, another boxer?"

"Yeah ... maybe I can organise you to do one of my fights ... hit the big time!"

She gave a sexy, crooked smile and took another small bite of her cracker-with-cheese.

Her name was Lisa and she was very pretty; tall with exceptionally long, slender legs and long, straight, ash blonde hair. Her brown eyes lit up with excitement at the simplest of things, followed by a sexy, lopsided smile and a cocking of the head that pulled at her big dimples.

It turned out that she lived not far from me, in Benoni, and after an extended kissing session on our first date we started going out regularly. I would pick her up in my plumbing Ford Cortina *bakkie* with the black roof rack. This worked for the first few dates and then she informed me that it wouldn't do for her to be seen in the passenger seat of the blue work truck so we started using her car. Can't say I blamed her.

'Billie-Jean' ~ Michael Jackson

They say that fortune favours the bold, and when opportunity knocks you should open the door wide and pull it in with both hands. It was already 1986 and things were cracking; I was pulling rabbits out of my hat at every turn, like Chunky Charlie. I had met Tommy Panner, a successful building contractor and business man who lived in, and built luxury houses in, Bedfordview, a suburb in the shadow of Gillooly's Farm. I arranged to meet with him at his offices and together we went to look at some houses that needed plumbing. Tommy drove me around in his new hunter green, Jaguar XJ-SC convertible. I sank low in the passenger seat while he explained that the forerunner to the XJS had been the legendary E-type Jaguar. I looked at the dash, pale maple wood dotted with rows of small lights and switches that all meant something. The engine growled as we pulled out of his brick driveway. This was a lot different from my sky-blue Cortina *bakkie*.

Apprehension began to set in as I looked at the kind of houses that needed plumbing. A strange and unfortunate thing had happened in the last ten or so months. My plumbing learning curve had flattened out, due to me suddenly being a boss and having no one to teach me about plumbing. These double storey, five-bathroom luxury houses, with upscale plumbing fixtures the likes of which I had never seen before, were beyond my newly acquired plumbing skills. I was used to the bread and butter houses in Extension 4 in Kempton Park. I decided to try and steer the conversation away from these fancy houses towards a more general discussion.

"Do you have any other business interests, besides construction?"

"Yes, actually, I've just opened a few video stores."

"Good money in video stores?"

"Yes, not too bad, thing is to make sure you stock the right movies."

"Or a movie of your own," I replied, unwittingly.

It seemed I had said the right thing. Tommy lit up and turned to look at me.

"Right! These new self-help health and fitness videos are where the money is," Tommy answered with enthusiasm.

I had hit the nail on the head. We chatted briefly, and he told me that as good as the video business was, you could really make money if you made your *own* film, or self-help video, and held the rights to it.

As quick as a mongoose on a garden snake I grasped Tommy's wish to make a self-help video. I laughed casually and then remarked, confidently, that it was really funny that he should mention making a film, because, as it just so happened, besides plumbing, and together with my brother and my good friend Marlon, I already had a foot in the movie-making door; that I was actually in the process of changing direction, aiming for a full time career in the film industry.

Tommy raised an eyebrow, looked interested, and from then on all talk of plumbing his new luxury Bedfordview houses was forgotten. We talked only about film-making.

"Really, eh? What do you guys do?"

"Actually, we've just had a meeting recently, to try to decide what our next step in the film business is going to be; we also discussed some good film ideas."

"What direction are you taking?"

"It seems to us that self-help videos or documentaries are the way to go, just like you said."

Tommy nodded, scratched his unkempt beard and mulled over the prospect.

"If you could get a self-help video to sell worldwide, you could make some serious money," he mused.

"This video business is going crazy. You can make money even if you get into just a few European countries, never mind into America."

"You guys can do this; you can make a good self-help video?" Tommy asked cautiously.

"Sure, we can do it; we can make a damn good self-help video," I answered confidently.

"Hmm," Tommy scratched his scruffy beard again, thinking about it.

He drove slowly through the tree lined avenues of the upscale neighbourhood as we chatted. I told him he had found the right bunch of guys if he wanted to get a video made and I assured him that I would soon bring him some great ideas to explore. Plumbing forgotten, Tommy turned onto the main road and enthusiastically gunned his Jaguar XJ-SC with the six-cylinder engine, heading back to his construction headquarters.

I believe that Tommy later regretted the enthusiasm he had shown on that particular day, and our conversation about the possibility of making a self-help video. But I raced home to Murray and Marlon (now back in Jo'burg, having returned from four years at UCT), and told them to get some ideas ready … I had met someone interested in making movies who wanted some good ideas pronto. We held an urgent meeting and immediately started throwing ideas around for movies or self-help documentaries that might be successful. What could we do? None of us had so much as read a book on film-making, never mind attended a class on the topic.

We threw around a bunch of ideas and settled on a 'self-help' theme. Sex – yes but no. Street fighting – no. Self-defence – maybe. Self-defence for women … housewives … Yes! That's It! *Self-defence for the Housewife*! The crime rate in South Africa was soaring, but we had all become immune to the horrendous statistics and the crime rate did not bother us. But it was a hot topic. An issue to be addressed. We decided we would script, produce and direct an entire self-help video. This would be our big break into the film business.

Then, in the weeks to come, it proved impossible to get an audience with Tommy, to pursue our last conversation about making a video. Tommy was 'my' contact, I saw myself as our 'communications man', and I guarded my position jealously. Murray and Marlon would look at me sternly when I hung up the phone, no meeting scheduled, for the eighth, ninth, tenth time. Tommy had a chorus line of different secretaries who played the same game, every time: Tommy was out of town, for a week; Tommy was in a meeting; Tommy was overseas on vacation. A few times we even tried to drop in at his office, unannounced, to see if we could trick him into an impromptu meeting, tell him we were ready to roll … show him the story board we had put together … we were all set to make the movie he wanted to own … let's go, damn it!

A gorgeous, tall blonde in a short blue mini skirt, with legs that went up forever, looked deeply and sincerely into our eyes as she ushered us away from the front door.

"I am *so* sorry, but Tommy is *really* busy, and it's impossible to see him right now."

But surprisingly, today, *this* time, after three months of stonewalling, it was different. The beautiful blonde ushered the three of us into the upstairs office, smiling, seeming genuinely happy for us, as she bade us enter a cluttered office for our meeting with Tommy. We walked in talking in hushed tones, large boards tucked under our arms, picked our way between drafting boards and desks, top heavy with piles of construction blueprints. Tommy was seated at his desk, in front of the window. I had almost forgotten what the man looked like, I had not seen him for so long. He was a short, strong man, good-looking despite the indubitable beginnings of a paunch. He had concerned, intelligent green eyes, medium-length shaggy brown hair and an equally shaggy, nicotine-stained, full beard. His desk held an ashtray full of smoked cigarette butts. He introduced us to his wife – Lorraine – the same beautiful blonde woman who, I had always thought, was his secretary. She stood a full head taller than Tommy. We shook hands and I introduced him to my brother, Murray, and my friend, Marlon.

For a few minutes Tommy and I chatted about the plumbing and construction business being slow for this time of the year. We shook our heads and grumbled about it being a tough time in the construction industry. After a second or two of awkward silence, a small frown wrinkling his brow, Tommy finally asked what we had to show him. Murray and Marlon took over and described, eloquently, our vision for the self-help video. I unwrapped the bundles of storyboards as they spoke and started handing them around.

Tommy said nothing as we passed several big boards to him, retrieved them from him, and waited for his approval. Then he smiled, slowly, won over by the quality of the pencil illustrations Murray had used on a particular storyboard. He sank down further in his chair, his chin on his chest. His intelligent speckled green eyes darted from board to board. He gave a couple of grunts of understanding every now and then, as Murray and Marlon stood over him, fingers flying, pointing this way and that, working him over with their words, describing their vision, statistics and strategies for developing the market-ability of this 'necessary' self-defence video in South Africa, at this time. Hell, internationally, at this time.

We could see that the beautiful Lorraine was impressed.

"*Self-defence for the Housewife?*" she asked, thoughtfully, "it's a great subject for our crime ridden country." She added that she liked the story's twist and turns and its quirky humour. Tommy's severe expression grew less so, watching his wife getting excited about our ideas. Then he leaned back, slapped his desk loudly to get everybody's attention, and started to talk, enthusiastically.

Murray, Marlon and I sat forward on the edge of our chairs and listened intently.

Tommy went on at length about quantities, prices, markets, reprints and more. We agreed with everything he said, especially the bit about if we take it overseas the sky's the limit. We discussed ideas for an hour or more. Not once did anyone ask: Had we made a movie before? Written a script before? Worked in the movie industry? Had we (even) read a book on film making?

Tommy was standing up, squinting through his cigarette smoke, going through the storyboards again.

"Start setting it up ... get some quotes ... let's do this thing ... call me as soon as you have some estimates ... how long will it take?"

Both Tommy and Loraine walked us out, all the way to Murray's green Toyota Celica parked on the street, all of us chatting away like new best friends.

We drove home to Benoni feeling really excited. We were going to make a movie. We were in the driver's seat as directors, producers and the whole bloody bucket. Work of any sort ended for the three of us. My plumbing contracts suffered, and I quit looking for new work. The three of us drove around Johannesburg, dressed to kill, storyboards under our arms. We had agreed to attend all meetings and appointments together. Not one of us wanted to miss out on the fun of walking through the doors of the film production companies and set designers, to be courted as film-makers ... sipping coffee, munching croissants, listening to whatever they had to offer us.

Tommy had said that he had a good friend who worked at the SABC and who was friends with David Hall-Green, a top news announcer and the presenter of a very popular television series called *Police File*. Yes, we had said ... we'll meet with Hall-Green and show him the storyboard and treatment ... how much should we offer to pay him for his services?

We sat with David Hall-Green in the SABC cafeteria as the famous presenter of *Police File* worked his way through a plate of eggs and toast. His familiar face lit up as he skimmed through our storyboard. He chuckled, his mouth full of food; he sipped his coffee.

"Who are you guys working for again?"

"Passive Hound is the name of our production company."

"Oh … never heard of you chaps. Where are you based?"

"We're in Benoni."

"Oh … Benoni … how long did you say the shoot will be?"

"We'll need you for, let's say, a maximum of 3 days."

He put down his knife and fork as we handed him more of our storyboards. He laughed again at some of Murray's drawings.

"You know, this is a very current subject … self-defence for the housewife. I think it's a great idea … and very marketable."

David Hall-Green went on about the crime scene in SA and how it seemed to be getting worse. He said that our storyboard was creative and funny and well put together. One of us found his mojo and mentioned the small figure in our budget, allocated to his two days' shooting. He didn't flinch, just kept on eating his breakfast.

"Sure, I'll do it, count me in. Here's my number … call me with the details."

Silently we watched him swallow his last mouthful of eggs. David Hall-Green of *Police File* had just approved our film, said it seemed well put together and creative, and yes, he would present the movie for us.

Things were happening fast. Film makers on the move.

Chapter Eight
JOHNNY 'DUNDEE' HOGG

'Rock the Casbah' ~ *The Clash*

"This is my junior middleweight fighter … he's just starting out."

I leaned forward and extended my hand. Charlie Weir, king of the South African junior middleweight division, the slayer of giants and destroyer of all who entered the ring to oppose him, nodded, and gave me a gentle handshake.

I had learnt that most fighters had a soft handshake, they had nothing to prove by trying to crush your hand. Charlie was lean as an alley cat and mean as a badger. He stood off to the side of the crowd, casually dressed in jeans and sneakers. Johnny Hogg, my new trainer, a diminutive Scotsman, knew him well and chatted comfortably with him about the boxing scene. I inspected his slender face, surrounded by a mop of black hair with his famous silver streak front and centre, as he nodded agreement with Johnny's conversation. Despite his mild smile I could see that Charlie's eyes were as black and flat as those of a mamba.

Charlie aka 'The Silver Assassin' was a well-known smasher of heads and buckler of frames. Hordes of South African boxing fans had watched him in his blue pinstripe shorts as he carved his way through the junior middleweight division, destroying the likes of Sydney Bensch, Manning Galloway and all the others placed in front of him. He was a thrilling fighter who put it all on the line, attacking his opponent as if he owed Charlie money or had robbed his mother. His small red 12 oz gloves were like hatchets at the end of his skinny arms, cutting skin, smashing noses, breaking jaws as he furiously battered his opponents into submission, sending them through the ropes or rolling head over heels into the corner, usually within the first or second round of a fight. At that time, he had a reputation for having won approximately 21 fights, almost all knockouts. Yes, he had come unstuck a few times, but had been forgiven quickly by his fans. When a fighter provides the thrills, and gives his all, like

Charlie, he is bound to come unstuck sooner or later. We all knew this. Charlie Weir was my boxing idol and I wanted to smash heads and buckle frames just like he did. When we said our goodbyes, that day, to 'The Silver Assassin' I felt his gentle handshake again.

"Good luck with your boxing," he said to me, frowning slightly, an earnest look in his flat eyes.

I had recently entered the South African rankings as the Number 9 middleweight and felt proud to be included as a nationally ranked boxer.

§

Lisa, despite a naughty streak, was a classy girl who ran with an upscale crowd. There seemed to be an endless supply of parties and braais to attend, with Chris de Burgh being the music of choice, and thick lamb chops the popular cut. I smiled and slugged down Hansa while her beautiful friends laughed and nattered and sipped their Italian Cinzano. I had recently switched to drinking beer, it was less damaging, and I didn't feel like hell in the mornings when I had to run. All the same, I preferred a good stiff Oude Meester or Captain Morgan, but I had found that I always overdid it when drinking spirits. It would take me another twenty years to realise how heavy-handed I was and that I had been pouring triple shots my whole life. No shot glass measures in those days ... and I thought a triple was quite normal.

Lisa's group of friends were mostly model types, good looking, well dressed, who laughed loudly and openly winked at and flirted with each other's boyfriends. I got on well with them. They were constantly intrigued by my frequent facial nicks and bruises, and the occasional blue eye, from daily hard sparring, often with top South African boxers – Harold Volbrecht, Charles Oosthuizen, Fransie Badenhorst and Bokkie Buys and the like.

I was finding Lisa irresistible and began putting my training aside. She liked to wear fashionable wide-brimmed hats, as though for a day at the races. She was tall and elegant, so they suited her, and she looked sexy, so I didn't complain. Although she had a standoffish air about her she also had a naughty, impulsive side which I found quite addictive.

A hot afternoon get-together next to the pool was just beginning to get lively; a few of her friends had changed into bikinis and were relaxing on poolside loungers, sipping wine. Lisa was still wearing white slacks and high platform shoes, fussing around, mingling and introducing me to her friends. I was chatting about boxing to a photographer when she interrupted us, taking me by the arm.

"Oh Granger, I need you for a minute."

She led me away and into the house, as if wanting my help to fetch or carry something. Once inside she led me to a small back room where, with a slight smile she shut and locked the door, turned and gave me a long kiss. The party was noisy outside the window. She unbuckled her belt and let me slip my hand deep inside the front of her slacks, while we continued our passionate kiss. Then she unbuttoned her shirt but left her wide hat on ... and one thing led to another, as they do.

"I was getting bored out there," she offered, by way of explanation for her impulsive behaviour while we prepared to re-join the party.

"I can understand that," I muttered, under my breath.

Now, I had quickly learned that for this big-haired, Cinzano-sipping, modelling crowd, that Sundays were not a day of rest. While Saturdays were the curtain raiser, Sundays were treated as the main event, filled with braais and gatherings at Water World, where the bevy of beauties could strip down to their bikinis, lie on the green grass and suntan. I was all for it ... I was having a whale of a time. It was fun to be sipping a beer and flipping a metre of *boerewors* in the middle of the day; it certainly beat running 10 kilometres, which is what I normally did on Sundays.

My boxing training was starting to suffer, seriously, from this new routine of fun and games. All the late nights, Sunday afternoon braais and pretty girls were great fun – until I started catching more leather in the boxing gym than usual. I was sluggish; I had no extra zip; lesser sparring partners began catching me in the ring and beating me to the punch. I realised that running with the in-crowd was screwing up my training and derailing my mission to climb up the national ranks. Sunday had been my Holy Day for working out; the regular, extra-long Sunday morning run was the foundation that had set me up for the week ahead and a tough regimen of training at the boxing gym. The long

Sunday runs had been the foundation of my week's training schedule. Now I found myself running a quarter of the distance or, sometimes, not running at all on a Sunday morning. I thought I could catch up by jumping more rope at the gym on Monday or Tuesday. It didn't work; I never could catch up the hours I had lost. I was caught in the middle of wanting to go the full distance with this long-legged filly and getting enough early nights to be able to stick to my training regimen. My training began to falter as sexy Lisa's insatiable taste for restaurant steak with pepper sauce followed by late night dancing grew.

Not that I didn't enjoy partying on down with the best of them. I was going out, a lot, but not to the places that I used to frequent. I was intentionally staying away from the rougher places, trying to stay out of trouble. I still had friends who hung out at notorious local places like the New Hotel and Chimes Tavern, the oldest pub in Benoni, hidden amongst the old gold mine dumps. They were tough places; you could find yourself in a scrap in a second, just by standing in the wrong spot or having the wrong look on your face. Local head stompers and shit kickers, like wild-haired, big Jimmy Morris, would think nothing of slamming you into the bar rail just for looking at him *skeef* (skew), or for standing too close to him at the bar.

"*Wat kyk jy?*" (What are you looking at?) You would be lucky to get a warning like that.

Ass-kicking was practically a national sport in South Africa. In fact, only recently I had run into one of these renowned head stompers a minute after walking into a bar to look for my friend Paul on my way home from the gym. He was drunk and I was stone-cold sober, still sweating after sparring with Harold Volbrecht the number 1 welter weight in the world, less than an hour before. To me he moved like an ox in mud. Before the big head stomper's massive fist could find me I had slammed a solid four-punch combination into him that sent him to the floor, for a while. The entire bar cheered; apparently I had felled the pub bully. The East Rand was a tough place.

But, while my fast combination was good enough to floor the bar bully, these days it wasn't good enough to outsmart crafty junior middleweight up-and-comer Wayne Martin. He moved across the ring, side to side in his slick, peekaboo style, hiding behind his gloves, feinting with a left, then throwing a fast, right power shot that landed flush between my eyes. I threw a big right hand but caught fresh air as he darted to the side. Then he banged me with a combination that set me back on my heels. I tried to keep my hands up, but it was too late; Wayne had done his damage. My nose dripped beads of blood onto the already blood-spotted canvas. I wobbled as I climbed out of the ring, trying to gather my senses. It had been a hard shot.

"You OK?" laughed Wayne as he took off his gloves.

But Johnny Hogg didn't find it funny.

"For fuck's sake, son, keep your hands up!" Johnny was well aware that I had been slacking in the last couple months.

"We've got that fight coming up, son, what's wrong with you, damn it?"

"I haven't been feeling well."

"What? For two months … not feeling well? Wayne Martin's been catching you with his right all night long. Last week too."

I looked around me, nothing to say.

"You going to have to pick it up, pull yourself together, son. Start moving side to side with more snap. This guy Sereme that you fighting is a good boxer; he'll give you a good boxing lesson if you don't pick it up."

I was embarrassed, getting this dressing down from Johnny in front of the other boxers.

My ginger-haired, diminutive trainer had a heart of gold, but was also well-known for his fiery temper. This was the first time he had turned his temper on me. He stood there, hands on hips, glaring up at me with his beady, brown eyes. Johnny had been a fighter in the boxing booths in Scotland, back in the day, and he loved a good scrap. He had also trained the young Arnold Taylor, well-known in South Africa for having won the WBA bantamweight title in 1973 with a stone cold 14th round knockout of then world champion, Romeo Anaya.

"It takes a special mindset to get to the top in boxing, or any sport, a special drive, to make it to the top. You can't be normal. Normal isn't good enough, you have to be way better than normal."

I could see that Johnny was seriously upset so I backed off and held my mouth.

"You can't have a normal life … you have to sacrifice normal. You have to be as fast as lightning, hit harder, think quicker, be fitter than a racehorse. You understand this is what it takes to be a champion?"

I nodded.

"Do you?" he challenged me.

I said nothing.

"Nothing less than what I just said will do. Do you understand? If you can't give me this tell me now and we can part ways."

I nodded. It was dawning on me for the first time that this is, really, what it was going to take.

"Yes, I understand it, John."

He stared at me, looking grim, then cracked a small smile.

"Looks like you're going to have another shiner tomorrow, son."

"On top of the old one," I muttered.

Johnny Hogg chuckled.

'I'm Still Standing' ~ Elton John

South Africa is not for sissies … even the sissies are tough in this part of the world. With one of the highest crime rates in the world, citizens cannot afford to ignore a noise in the backyard at midnight, a barking dog, a suspicious-looking character on the corner. It was becoming a growing trend to live barricaded behind increasing layers of security, bright lights, high perimeter walls, electric fences and razor wire. It was a place where one had to be on the alert and ready to react if necessary. Even Lisa owned a small handgun which she often carried in her handbag and had brought with her to the local shooting range.

"Bend your knees and shoot with both hands."

Lisa pulled off a few shots from her small handgun; puffs of dust next to the empty 2 litre Coke bottles marked them as misses.

Jannie smiled. "It's difficult to do any really good shooting with a three-inch barrel. It takes time, many hours of practicing, but it's a handy weapon you can easily carry with you," he said.

Jannie spoke always in a slow deliberate tone, measuring every word he said. Moving equally slowly he opened up his small .38 revolver and loaded some hollow-point shells, explaining that they were twice as potent as the standard shells we had been using. Then he assumed his shooting stance, bent his knees slightly, and cracked off six rapid shots. The cracks were twice as loud as the shots we had fired, and the targets shattered, the dust spraying higher than before.

Lisa was dead impressed.

"That's the way to do it, Jannie!" I laughed, as he lowered the small handgun.

Jannie Nel was well built with developed arms and troubled blue eyes. He was a quiet guy whom my brother had met at the karate dojo while he was preparing for his black belt. Jannie was from Rhodesia (now Zimbabwe) and had been in the battle-hardened parachute Rhodesian Light Infantry (RLI), which had fought outstandingly during the Rhodesian bush war.

"Get your firearm license and we'll practice," he told me.

With Jannie's encouragement I had decided to get a handgun, for self-defence. I had driven through to a gun shop in Johannesburg a few times and after handling almost every small handgun in the glass case I had settled on a Ruger 357, nickel plated, with a three-inch barrel, a chunky revolver with rounded smooth edges and a big front sight, all of which fitted snugly in my hand. Although I had been raised with guns I was not a gun lover anymore. I had seen what guns can do, many times, first-hand, during my time in the army. I had also seen a .357 Magnum handgun in action in Civvy Street. I had been 30 yards from a group of ruffians in Sea Point who shot and killed a man in the street, claiming he was coming for them with a *nunchaku* – two sticks joined at one end with a short chain or thong. Although I had seen a pair of *nunchaku* lying on the sidewalk, close to the dead man who had fallen half under a parked car, he had been dressed in a three-piece suit and his screaming wife was beside him, wearing a long white evening dress. They had obviously been going out for the evening when the altercation had taken place.

No, I definitely was not in love with guns anymore, but I had thought I should get one for self-defence. So I applied for a firearm license and made an appointment for the interview at the police station. Should be easy ... just a quick interview before they sign off on my application and then I'll be off to pick up my new Ruger 357.

But the wiry blond policeman, wearing a cheap grey suit and thin tie, standing behind a bare wooden desk in an empty room inside the police station, seemed to have other ideas.

"So, let me see if I understand this ... you want to get a license for a firearm?"

"Yes, I've already paid a cash deposit for a revolver. Here's the receipt."

"What type is it?"

"A 357 revolver."

The blond policeman was silent. Then he turned, sat down, leaned back in his chair and removed a couple of pieces of paper from a brown folder. He examined them diligently and an odd smirk appeared on his face.

"Let me get this straight, you want a firearm license, but you have three arrests on your record?"

I was a little taken aback. I had not thought about those small blots on my copybook, but now I did ... and seeing that I had just finished two years in the army, fighting on the Border, I thought they wouldn't be a problem.

"Well, yes sir, but that was quite a few years ago, when I was in high school."

"Why do you want to get a firearm?"

"For self-defence."

"For self-defence?"

"Yes, that's what I said, for self-defence. I'm very responsible with a firearm. I recently finished two years of army national service and spent some time on the Border."

I was beginning to see that, for some reason, this police officer was going to give me trouble, which I had not anticipated at all.

"I am a very responsible person with a firearm and I just finished my two years' army service, as a paratrooper. I was on the Border and in Angola," I repeated, louder, in case perhaps he hadn't heard me the first time.

"It doesn't matter that you were in the army *or* on the Border. Your record says that you are a *dagga* (marijuana) smoker – and you think you can apply for a firearm license? You could be a danger to society with a weapon."

He tilted back on the legs of his wooden chair. His thin tie was black against his white shirt, his eyes were gleaming, and he was smirking while watching me intently.

"A danger to society?" I asked, confused.

'Yes, a danger to society."

I was surprised at his judgemental attitude. Why was he so accusatory? Why had I not anticipated this roadblock? I thought maybe he was confusing me with someone else, or that he hadn't understood what I was saying. I explained to him again … I was not the wayward high school kid I once had been.

"I was at 1 Parachute Battalion, and I am very well trained with weapons. I carried a weapon on me everywhere I went for two years. I was trained to handle a belt-fed LMG machine gun fed with a 50-round belt and jump from an airplane at 1,000 ft with the LMG strapped to my side. I slept and ate with a weapon next to me. I was in three major cross-border operations into Angola, fighting for my country and society."

"That doesn't change the fact that you have three previous arrests, and you are a *dagga* smoker, and a possible danger to society with a firearm."

"A what?"

"A *dagga* smoker."

I couldn't believe what I was hearing and felt a rush of anger. I knew it was all over and this fuckwit of a policeman in front of me was denying my firearm license and enjoying it. I stood up fast, shoving my wooden chair with the back of my legs, sending it sliding back a few feet. It was over and there was no point in showing this malicious prick any respect.

"*Dagga* smoker! Fuck you … what the fuck are you talking about? I've been in more fire fights than you've got fingers on your fucking hands."

"You see! Look at you! Look at how you're acting now," he pointed at me.

"Well then, screw you and fuck your license."

"Look, you see … you're losing your temper. I told you," he said, his eyes showing satisfaction at having trapped me.

I glared at him, still leaning back in his chair, wearing his arrogant smile. Now, with genuine anger, in one move I slammed my chair into the front of his desk. He quickly lost his smirk while struggling to balance his chair, grabbing the desk for support. I swung round and stomped out of the small bare room. The detective shouted something behind me as I walked out. I couldn't hear what he was saying but didn't miss the opportunity to walk back into the room and tell him to fuck off one more time. Then I left the police station and stormed off to my blue Ford Cortina. I had just failed, miserably, the interview for a firearm license.

The wheels of my Cortina blew up clouds of red dust as I drove fast up the long, dirt driveway to our farmhouse. I slammed the car door and the dogs came running up with their usual warm greeting. What the hell! The South African government claims that I'm not fit to carry a firearm? But I was OK for my two years of sweat and blood, fighting for my country during my national military service? Why not tell me I was unfit to carry a weapon before my company of 100 young men, fresh out of high school, flew across the Border into Angola, time after time, to attack terrorist bases, track down the enemies of our country ... and *kill* them. I had been considered A–OK, sharp number one ... good enough to be in the forefront, jumping trench to trench in cross border operations into Angola. Holy Shite! I even had a Pro Patria Medal signed by the Minister of Defence, saying that I was a good boy for "defending the country against terrorism".

I threw off my slacks and smart shirt, leaving them on the floor of my room. Something was seriously wrong with this picture!

Lisa agreed with me when I told her what had happened.

"Did you tell him you were in the army, in the parabats?"

"Yes, I told him."

"And?"

"And I'm not fit to carry a firearm ... I could be a danger to society."

Lisa held my gaze, her eyes wide.

"What about when you're called up to serve your next army camp? Will you be 'fit' to carry a firearm then?" she asked.

I didn't have an answer for her – but it was a damn good question.

§

I had often wondered about brave men. What's the opposite of a brave man ... a coward? Could familiarity with danger make a man braver? What if you made a conscious decision not to perform a dangerous act, because you had calculated it to be not worth the risk? Like sending six men into enemy-held territory to rescue one man ... when you know there is a great risk that the six men may be killed in the process. Why do it? Surely the cost outweighs the objective? Surely being around to look after your children and family is more important than jumping into a burning wreck to save a stranger? What makes a hero a hero?

I had once stood close by and witnessed a hero in action. Any one of us standing and watching could have performed that heroic deed, but it wasn't us, it was him. We stood and watched while he performed the heroic deed – for which he received the Honoris Crux, a medal awarded to members of the South African Defence Force for bravery in dangerous circumstances.

We were in Angola with Operation Daisy. The three-week cross-border operation, which intended to attack and destroy SWAPO bases deep in Angola, was turning out to be a fuck-up from start to finish. Our sister Hotel Company had attacked a SWAPO base camp deep inside Angola. The base camp had been well camouflaged, but they found it deserted, with food still on the cooking fires. (We, Delta Company, by chance caught all theses SWAPO escaping in a terrible and deadly trap not one hour later, just a few miles away, while they were making their escape.) Delta Company had been flown in quickly, in reserve for the attack, but now there was no need and we stood around, idly smoking and watching the Hotel Company guys load mountains of captured Soviet land mines and ammunition onto South African armoured vehicles. Suddenly there was a deafening explosion fifty yards from us, to our left. I turned just in time to see my friend, Derek Wood, flying through the air with the greatest of ease, like a Mexican rock diver, from the back of a Buffel. He landed flat on his back twenty metres away. A couple of us started forward to help Derek, writhing on the sand, but we turned back and got out of the way as platoon medics came running to assist him. He was alive, but blackened, and clearly in great pain.

In the meanwhile, the Buffel, a troop carrier, had instantly caught alight. We watched with interest. Very quickly the flames had taken the kit and were now licking high past the roll bar, flickering around the green wooden boxes of loaded, assorted Soviet ammunition, piled up amongst the burning kit.

Our platoon was backing away when, out of the corner of my eye, I saw a tall major running almost casually through the black smoke. He heaved open the heavy steel door of the burning Buffel and pulled himself up into the driver's seat. Black smoke enveloped the armoured vehicle while he struggled to start the engine, trying again and again until the big engine kicked into life. He turned the big wheels, the engine roared and the Buffel accelerated away from us. Flames had already engulfed the boxes of captured Soviet ammunition and the kit packed in the back. He drove the flaming Buffel, looking like a mobile funeral bier, two hundred metres away into a wide clearing, where it stopped. The vehicle was all but engulfed in flame and we held our collective breath when he did not appear. Suddenly we saw him break out of the black *cloud surrounding the Buffel like a smoke screen. Calmly he trotted back to us across the clearing looking as though he had just parked his car at the mall.*

I have always wondered what made the tall major jump into a burning vehicle loaded with enemy explosive and drive it away, from us. I have always remembered the casual, easy way he did it. What makes a hero do what he does? (The burnt-out hull of the Buffel was later loaded up on the back of a recovery truck and taken back to SA.)

I have come to the conclusion that there is no single, logical reason or explanation for heroic actions. That's why they're heroic. Men and women who perform acts of heroism do not even think about who will look after their family if they die while saving a life, or lives. And that's what makes them heroes. Wolraad Woltemade, Dick King and others. How many unsung heroic deeds have been performed in times of war, in civilian life, over the centuries, that have gone unrecorded?

It took me thirty years to discover over the internet that the man we had watched driving the burning troop carrier away from us was a Major Anderson, and that he had received the Honoris Crux medal for his bravery on that day. I also found out that soon after his heroic act – driving a burning vehicle loaded with Soviet ammunition to a safe distance from the rest of the troop – Major Anderson tragically had become a quadriplegic, the result of paralysis suffered during a car accident.

Chapter Nine

LEARNING FAST

'Crocodile Rock' ~ Elton John

It was around this time that Lisa left me for some foreign guy. She had pulled me aside one afternoon, making a point of not touching me, and told me in a soft and lovely tone that it didn't look as if it was going to work between us ... I was a nice guy but a little too rough around the edges. She said my name should have been Danger and not Granger.

In a way I was glad that it had ended, but I was also disappointed and moped around for a week thinking about why she had said I was too wild for her. Was it the boxing and the black and blue eyes? I didn't really go out that much anymore, anyway, so I didn't really know what she was getting at. When Johnny Hogg waved a signed fight contract under my face it was just what I needed to wash my hands of our whole affair.

"Pull yourself together son! Forget about this girl, it's time to focus on boxing."

I didn't say much, watching Johnny unload his huge trainer's bag ... gloves, head gear, groin guards, bandages and water bottles.

"You think she's the only girl in the world. Aye, she's a looker all right but there are many others ... hold still and push your hands in, all the way."

I pushed my wrapped hand deep into the red boxing glove until my fingers pushed hard against the inside. The gloves smelt like my new leather jacket.

"Maybe, but not all of them have legs as long as this one, Johnny."

"Aye, maybe son, doesn't matter ... those long legs won't get you to the middleweight title belt. This is what will get you to the title belt...in the gym every night, training even on a Friday night, and tomorrow on Saturday morning, and then an extra-long run on Sunday morning, like we used to do. That's what will get you to the top, son."

Johnny Hogg smiled, bent his head and expertly tied the long laces of my gloves.

"When you win the South African middleweight title there will be a girl with longer legs than this one that I will promise you." He winked at me.

"So John, are the girls better at the top?" I joked.

"Aye, son. Wait until you get there, the champion has his pick, you'll see."

I laughed at his Scottish humour.

"We'll just get past this guy, Willie Nolson, then we go for Michael Motsoene."

"Who is this Willie Nolson anyway?"

"He's an amateur star, undefeated in 72 amateur fights. The boxing board wants you to fight him in his pro debut."

"Is he any good? He must be, with 72 wins, even as an amateur boxer."

"He's a big hitter with a killer left hook. I've seen him fight. Knockout artist so you have to be on your toes, son. And keep your hands up!" Johnny said, trying not to look concerned.

I fumbled with my mouth guard. I was beginning to feel worried.

"Don't worry son, we'll work hard and give him a welcome to the pro's … we got to work on keeping your chin tucked in, someone's going to catch you sooner or later."

I had become closer to my trainer John Hogg after we had bumped heads and he had read me the riot act. A few days earlier we had stood on the sidewalk outside the Yeoville gym, on the way to our cars and he had looked up at me from his 4ft 11 in, his eyes fiery, and told me he was not taking the time to drive through Johannesburg rush hour traffic to the gym, just for the fun of it. He was doing it because he wanted a winner and a South African champion. He had said if I didn't change my recent shitty attitude we could part ways.

I smiled as I listened. Johnny Hogg was going to be my trainer for better or worse. Johnny and I did not have a written trainer/boxer contract between the two of us; everything, from day one when he had tracked me down, had come knocking on the front door offering to be my trainer and manager, had been agreed on the strength of a hand shake. I planned to keep it that way.

'China Girl' ~ *David Bowie*

The big American sparring partners for our South African World Heavyweight Boxing Champion, Gerrie Coetzee, sauntered into the Yeoville boxing gym, an easy lilt to their steps, carrying huge kit bags and a gigantic boom box. These particular heavyweights had been imported from the US to work with Gerrie every day, to prepare him for the upcoming first defence of his world title, against big Greg Page, another American. There were three of them and each one seemed bigger than the next. The biggest of the lot seemed to be about 6 ft 5 in, sported a half afro and carried a huge boom box on his shoulder.

After a few weeks of hard training I was just starting to get my old form back again, I was moving with snap, throwing four and six punch combinations. I had recently almost mastered the art of popping off my punches with next to no telegraph. It's all in the focus and relaxation. Focus and the concentration to let go with a punch straight from the shoulder, without pulling your arm or hand back even one half-inch. To shoot your arm from the stationary position straight into a 90-miles-an-hour punch, hit your target and pull the punch back at the same speed. Also, it's impossible to do if you're not in great shape or have not built up significant muscle behind the shoulder and shoulder blade to support the punch. The trick is to take it right from your shoulder, using your shoulder and lat (*latissimus dorsi*) muscles, as the trigger for the fast punch. No arm punching.

The take-off of a punch from the stationary position is the most important aspect. The first six inches of the punch must be the fastest part of the punch and must be executed with no tell-tale movement from the body. The punch has to come 'out the gate' at 90 miles an hour ... don't start the punch at 60 miles per hour then land it at 90 miles per hour. The shoulder, arm and even back shoulder blades must move *as one* for this to happen. Like a horse giving swift a kick with its hind legs. Everything moves at the same time. Having thrown 50,000 of these over the years I had recently, finally, been able to put the concept into reality. I was quite chuffed. It didn't always work but I was getting the hang of it and was often able to shoot my left hand right between the gloves of my sparring partner, nail him in the kisser and pull back before he could blink.

"Looks like a good left arm you got there, I'll look out for you in *The Ring* magazine," said Jackie McCoy, the American trainer who had come over to work with our Gerrie Coetzee. I smiled at his joke.

"Still got a long way to go before that," I joked.

"Oh, just keep training hard, you'll see."

"How's life in America?" I asked the famous boxing trainer.

"Life's good in the US, but it looks like you guys live pretty good over here in Africa as well."

The big black heavyweight with the afro raised an eyebrow as he looked my way.

"You fighting next Friday, in this tournament?" Jackie McCoy asked.

"Yes, I am."

"OK then, we'll all be there, and we'll watch your fight. Good luck," he smiled.

America … to me the place seemed so dynamic and huge. How had the country grown at such a rate? Wasn't America discovered around the same time as South Africa? I tried to remember the details from my school history books. What progress it had made in such a short time, the New World. Europe and its countries had been around for millennia. Deep down I yearned to see more of the world. All I had ever known was life in South Africa.

Johnny Hogg and I had worked hard. I was having early nights, taking long winter morning runs, doing wind sprints. I had spent long hours in the gym, slipping under left hooks and countering with a sharp, straight right cross and short left hook. I was learning to come in at an angle, using the bob-and-weave technique. Future world champion and Hall of Fame boxer, Brian Mitchell, was working in the gym daily. He peppered me as we sparred and I watched how he moved from the hips, using a side to side movement. He displayed his expertise, keeping this up, round after round, like a wind-up toy. I tried copying him and it seemed to work.

On fight night we drove to the black township of Vosloorus. My father had his 9 mm tucked into his belt. I was lean and mean. My cheeks were hollow and my eyes as black as Harold Volbrecht's, with whom I shared a dressing room.

"Go on son! Give it to him!" Johnny hissed in my ear as he put my mouthguard in place and then slapped me on the chin. He climbed out the ring, leaving me to face the stocky, muscle-bound Willie Nolson, who scowled at me without letting up, while five hundred black supporters sang for my blood and chanted for Willie to be the hatchet.

Willie charged me like a lion and immediately threw some powerful combinations. He held his head tucked in low and kept glaring at me with his little eyes, swinging his knockout hooks at my head. He let them loose like lightning, grunting as he put his whole body weight behind them. The black crowd cheered as his punches slammed into my arms and gloves like hammers. I could feel his power and backed up for a second, intimidated by his vicious attack. Now I could understand how he had beaten 72 opponents. I backed away and tried to work my left, but his attack was relentless. He caught the side of my head with a heavy blow that stunned me, blacking out my lights for a micro second. The crowd went wild as Willie turned up his brutal assault, now snarling and grunting as he swung his hard punches.

From the centre of a black fog of defeat I found a split second of intense clarity, stood my ground, and then stepped forward with some of the hardest punches I have ever thrown and extending my punches with my shoulder. Willie Nelson may have been undefeated in 72 amateur fights, he may have been named 'The Lion', but tonight he had run into a lion killer. I turned on him and drove forward with an attack more furious than his own, ploughing my counter attack through his onslaught. I saw his eyes roll back in his head as my fast, straight punches blasted, landing faster than his wide hooks, catching him on the forehead. He was clearly bewildered at finding himself wild-eyed and sprawled on the canvas within a minute of the opening bell. It had all changed and quickly.

I had learned my lesson from Harold Volbrecht, *When you're hurt, attack*!

I had rapidly turned the fight around and before the end of the first round I had him on the canvas, three times. It was over. On his last trip to the canvas he looked up at me, defeated, and stayed there, on his knees. As often happens in boxing, even in Africa, the predominantly black crowd quickly changed their alliance to the winner; now they clapped and whistled and cheered me as I walked to my corner. Conversely, Willie was booed by the spectators as he was slowly helped from the ring, still bleeding from the nose.

I noticed Jackie McCoy and the big American heavyweights sitting ringside, all of them wearing big, pleased smiles, happy with the outcome of the all action, first round knockout.

§

I had received a postcard from my old school friend, Darryl, who had been in the US for the past two years. In South Africa he had worked for the SABC as a sound engineer and had been over the moon about an opportunity to fly overseas and attend a three-month course on advanced sound engineering, in Texas. While there he had bought an old panel van and made his way to Hollywood, Los Angeles, where, by the looks of it, he was working as a sound engineer in a well-known music studio. Darryl was a man of few words and this card was only the second communication from him since he had left South Africa. I looked at the postcard and the glossy, colourful picture of the famous white 'Hollywood' sign which the world has come to know so well. Behind the sign the mountain looked a surreal green, the sky extra blue. The bottom corner showed an insert of Grauman's Chinese Theatre on the Hollywood Walk of Fame, where movie stars have their hand and footprints set in cement. I flipped it over and read:

> How's it bro, It's great here in Hollywood, California, living the life. Hope everything good on your side. I heard about the boxing. Pull in here to the USA for a visit, my china, Yankee girls are great,
> Your mate, Darryl

It was good to hear from Darryl and I kept the postcard on my desk for a couple weeks. Something about that postcard, with its picture of the famous 'Hollywood' sign, that had travelled around the world to land on my desk, fascinated me. I picked it up every coupla days and looked at the vivid photo and Darryl's untidy scrawl: "Pull in here to the USA for a visit, my china, Yankee girls are great."

Darryl was an old school friend, I had known him since we were thirteen. We always seemed to be at the same place at the same time, almost as if an ill-tempered fate was matching us together. He and I had burned through a few different high schools together, suffering the consequences of our spontaneous and misguided senses of adventure and humour. Marlon and Darryl were brothers, but Darryl and Leighton were the only members of the old gang to have pushed on with the music dream we had all indulged in, since forming our rock 'n' roll band in high school. We all had a blast as youngsters, our band played at parties, small night clubs and weekend resorts. I had been the singer and had some good moments, belting out hard rock from The Rolling Stones, The Who, Deep Purple, Free, Bad Company, Van Halen and more. At house parties we played hard, until my voice was hoarse, and our guitarist's fingers bled onto the strings. On Sundays we played, sometimes, at weekend resorts like Bapsfontein, or in the Battle of the Band competitions, where we strutted and jived, hoping to win the competition. It had always been about having a good time, attracting girls, having fun. For a few high school years our lives had revolved around The Band, girls and getting hammered.

I had seen little of Darryl in the last few years; our army service had been at different times. He had been a medic during his period of national service; afterwards he had trained and worked as a sound engineer at the SABC, before going overseas for a few months which had become a few years. This was only the second postcard I had received from my old friend – in 1985 there was no internet.

At the wise old age of 24 years I knew little about the west coast of America and even less about Los Angeles. My knowledge of New York was pretty much the same as anyone else I knew, tall buildings, throngs of people. But Los Angeles drew a blank in my head. Except, of course, the 'Dennis the Menace goes to Hollywood' comic. Strangely, it kept springing to mind as my only reference to Los Angeles.

I looked up to Johnny Hogg, my Scottish boxing trainer, as a man of the world. Well, he had come to South Africa from Scotland, so he knew more than I did.

"Los Angeles is not a good place son. That's where they make all the movies, the studios are there; Hollywood, it's a huge city and spread out and ugly. I don't think you'd like it there."

"Is it the same as New York with sky scrapers?"

"I'm not sure, son, but I know that it's very big, probably more than twelve million people or so."

"Twelve million people, in one city?"

"Aye, said it's quite big."

"Bigger than London?"

"London is a wee city compared to Los Angeles."

A wee city? How can London be a wee city? It's 2,000 years old. America was still a new country, probably only a few hundred years old. How can a city like LA grow so absolutely massive in such a short time?

"America is all about money, son. California by itself has one of the largest economies in the world. The state of California is richer than most nations, except for seven. It's capitalism at its finest."

"But we're also capitalist … what's the difference?"

"America has a very aggressive brand of capitalism. They step over the bodies of their countrymen to get a dollar. England is a little more socialist, can't climb up that easy."

"What do you mean? You can't climb up that easy?"

"The people and the system keep you in your place, they don't encourage you to rise up. In America you can rise, the people don't push you down."

"Sounds like a good thing, Johnny?"

"Can't say which is good or bad son. Just that the one is more of a rat race than the other."

"How many people in London?"

"About 8 million, son."

At 24 years old I struggled to imagine how a city could have eight million, never mind twelve million, residents. But by all accounts, it sounded as though my old school friend was having a gas in Los Angeles. I wondered what it was like in America. What was he doing … probably staying out all night chasing Yankee girls. He had said the girls were great.

Chapter Ten

PASSIVE HOUND

'Let's Dance' ~ David Bowie

"When do you guys start filming?"

"On Tuesday, Tommy, everything is set up."

"Where are your locations?"

"We're opening at sunrise with a shot over Johannesburg, then onto the Rosebank Mall then back here, to the Benoni area."

Initially, Tommy had been slow to feel excited about our film; but now that everything was set up he was calling us almost every day, to ask about the latest developments. He had even showed up at one of our meetings at the Stan Schmidt School of Karate, when we were looking for a karate expert to include in the video. I was still the main phone contact with Tommy, a position which I continued to guard jealously from my brother and Marlon.

"OK, please give me the address of the shooting locations ... I want to drop in and watch."

"Will do, Tommy, I'll let you know tomorrow."

This was going to be Tommy's big break into film business, as well as ours. Murray, Marlon and I were directing and producing – the whole banana. No one suspected that we all had zero film making experience. No one had asked us for our show reel. We had settled on a name and a logo for our film production company – Passive Hound Studio.

Finally, the big day arrived. Up at 05h00 we packed our three cars with storyboards, piles of prompt cards or idiot boards, make up, props, fake blood, wardrobe, tape, tools, pens, notebooks, duffel bags, cameras, jackets, folding chairs, buckets, dollies, a folding table and a pile of other things we may or may not have needed on the first day of the video shoot. We were to meet up with the professional film crew from Pro Video at a location in Bedfordview close to Gillooly's Farm where we were going to shoot the first scene, an early morning sunrise, an establishing shot over the city of Johannesburg. From there it was off to the busy Rosebank Mall where we filmed the gorgeous Kay, shopping, then being followed home from the mall to her kitchen, by a murderous bum. In the late afternoon we broke down the set, packed everything up and took off to the lake, to meet Keith Geyer who, at the time, was a 'black belt', a fifth dan in Shotokan karate and who was going to perform a *kata* against the African setting sun behind the lake, accompanied with a flowery monologue on the fighting spirit which can be summoned in times of need.

The next day we again watched the sun rise over Johannesburg. We were with the well-known SABC presenter of 'Police File', David Hall-Green, the narrator of our film. The long day's shoot was going to be held in two different locations. This required the smooth loading up and transporting of all the kit, from the Lock Company back to Benoni, without any hitches or lost time – we had stretched our budget to accommodate David for only two days. We dressed him in a variety of different guises, from a local gardener to a 50s rocker, in a leather jacket, driving a classic, purple Cadillac tailfin. We also had Tommy dressed as a bad guy, cruising the streets. The presenter of 'Police File' was a real pro. He glided through his narration with ease, relaxed, one hand in his pocket, smoothly reading the prompt boards I held in front of him, hardly moving his eyes while reading. We filmed him driving the purple Cadillac. I was having a blast.

No one in the shooting crew had picked up that we had no film experience. When the professional film crew questioned us about shot angles we answered, "Let's just stick to the storyboard." When they suggested a change to the storyboard to incorporate a more interesting sequence of shots, we shrugged our shoulders, looked at each other and said, "Sure. Why not? Sounds good ... let's do it."

Lights, camera, action! Let's go!

Sharon leapt at me with a high-pitched shriek, clawing at my eyes. She followed up with a punch to the throat and then a knee to the groin. I fell to the ground, as scripted, and she ended with a swift heel to my jaw, followed by another, triumphant, shriek – Aaaaiiieee!

Sharon was a thirty-five-year-old Rhodesian woman who conducted various anti-rape and self-defence classes for women. Having watched one of her classes in a community hall, we decided she was the ideal woman to feature in our video. She was all for it, very enthusiastic. We spent a few long days practicing with her, with me in the role of her 'attacker', and a few weeks later she was ready for her film debut.

Again, I was cast as the bad guy, the attacker. She punched me in the throat, nose and neck. She jabbed her fingers in my eyes and ears. She hit me with common household weapons – pots and pans, car keys and chairs – she twisted my arms, strangled me and kneed me in the balls for the whole day, from seven AM to seven PM. It was hard to resist the temptation to flatten her with a lightning bolt left hook, while she lunged at me again and again, using her ear-splitting screams and open hands, but I resisted the impulse. Sharon, too, was having a blast, throwing me around the room the whole day while the camera rolled.

After a few more days of shooting at a security gate and lock manufacturer, and at the police headquarters in downtown Johannesburg, we were done. Movie made. We had our video, *Self-defence for Housewives,* in the bag.

'Every Little Thing She Does is Magic' ~ Sting

Unexpectedly, I found myself back in the army, standing ready to jump out of a perfectly good aircraft. Let it not be said that the South African army did not work in wonderfully efficient ways. To be a civilian, busy plumbing one day, then two days later take off in a C-130 from the air force base in Pretoria, fly some 500 km, jump out of the aircraft and land in the thick Northern Transvaal bush, a few kilometres from the Zimbabwe border, along with my very own personal boxing trainer, who also had jumped out of the C-130, into the bush, with me.

I found myself marvelling at the competence of it all.

"Stand up! Hook up!"

I struggled to stand with the weight of the parachute on me. I steadied myself on the shoulder of the paratrooper in front of me, as I reached up and hooked the red parachute static line onto the cable that ran the length of the plane. An important aspect of jumping – not to be forgotten! I held on to the shoulder in front of me, for support, while the big Hercules C-130 pitched and lurched as the pilot slowly straightened the big plane out of the circle that had taken five minutes to complete. Now the engines changed their pitch as he began to line up with the Drop Zone ahead, slowing the C-130 to jumping speed. The big starboard and port doors opened with a loud hydraulic whine. Air was sucked into the aircraft with a noise that drowned out all forms of communication. Now it was all drills and hand signals. The jump dispatcher mouthed words that were lost in the wind and pumped his fist in the air. We all copied him and shouted in unison into the wind.

"Check equipment!"

We sounded off and checked helmet, emergency chute, hook up. The seventy troops all stood wide-legged, wide-eyed, chins tucked in ready to clear the aircraft in fifty seconds when the green light came on. Some things you never forget. It had been some years since I had jumped out of a perfectly good aircraft, but it all came back clearly. Steely-eyed instructors with big moustaches had hammered these exiting drills into us, day after day, until they had become second nature and we could do them without thinking. Our entire Company of paratroopers, each fitted with 60 kg of kit and weapons, could shuffle-run to clear the C-130 aircraft, last man out the door, in fifty seconds.

"One OK stick OK!"

Green light flicks on, the dispatcher's shout is lost in the wind, shuffle to the door. GoGoGo!

Look at the back of the jump helmet of the man in front of you, don't stumble now, shuffle-run- stamp to the door, getting faster now as the line thins out, daylight visible out the portside door, the line moving faster still, the dispatcher now standing back slapping and shouting as the troopers slip past him, as fast as beer cans on a production line, here I go … sucked out the door, keep your knees together, feel the shock of cold air, smell the exhaust for the big C-130 engines, tossed upside down, spun around as the slip stream catches me, falling … whaa! Lose my breath as my parachute catches air, opens with a hard jerk, look up … see my lines are twisted. Oh shit! OK. Kick with both legs and pull the toggle lines apart while kicking, go go, keep kicking buddy, the line twists not completely straight … OK! Fuck it! Good enough, quickly, must jettison. You're PWC (Personal Weapons Container), the heavy 60 kg hooked on my side … don't want to land with that on my side, break both knees! Hit the quick release clips, feel the heavy kit dropping, hanging on a 16 ft rope under me. OK, adjust your harness, look down. Relax now.

All quiet after the noise of the plane, just your own breath, look around and see seventy parachutes falling silently to the ground. And, of course, as a South African paratrooper no clear DZ underneath to land on like other armies ... just green African bush and a tree landing below. Nothing unusual ... pull down on the toggles to try to avoid landing in the extra high trees, ... feel the heat rising from the ground. OK, here we go, ground rush then a hard, sideways right landing, just miss the burnt tree stump and crash through a bush. Hit the ground hard and roll. Lie there for a couple seconds to catch my breath and do mental check. Unhurt, nothing broken. A good landing.

I could already feel the intense heat and hear the high-pitched singing of the sun beetles and the caw and cackle of African bush birds, startled by a Company of big-booted South African paratroopers dropping in 'out of the blue' to disturb their wild paradise.

§

It had been four years since I had jumped out of a C-130 but it felt like yesterday; all the drills had come back automatically.

I was on my first army camp since completing my two years' national service. This camp had come about very quickly and efficiently, which was the way the army *sometimes* worked. I had received a letter saying that I must report for duty, for a three-month army camp. Well, I had understood that being self-employed was a good enough reason for exclusion from these military camps – there would be no employer to pay anybody who was away for three months at a time. Also, the letter had arrived with just one week's notice to report.

Only two days before I had dropped my plumbing crew at the jobsite. I told them I would be back at 17h00 to pick them up, because I had to drive to Pretoria to Paratrooper Headquarters at Murray Hill, to explain to the commandant that unfortunately I was unable to attend my obligatory annual military camp, because I was self-employed, with my own plumbing business, with employees, and contracts with builders for jobs in progress, *and, on top of this*, I had signed a contract for a boxing match, to which I was committed, for which I was in training, which was coming up in just four weeks' time.

The blond commandant in charge of the three-month call-up scowled, his eyes gleaming, and deliberately shanghaied me. He told me I was going nowhere *but* on a three-month camp with 44 Parachute Brigade.

I called my brother from a payphone in the camp and asked him please to collect my work crew from the jobsite, explain to them that there would be no more work until I returned, probably only in three months' time. Then I called my boxing trainer, Johnny Hogg, and asked him please to get me a copy of the boxing contract for the fight with Shackleton Promotions.

The following day my father drove to Pretoria to bring me my army kit, from home, and the copy of the boxing contract as proof of my commitment to Shackleton, which I presented to the camp commandant. A little later I had a second audience with the camp commandant, to learn his decision about my circumstances. He told me that I would not be allowed to go home, I would have to do at least a three-week camp, instead of the three-month camp, but, yes – waving my boxing contract at me – I would be released in time for the boxing match ... which was four weeks away.

Hmm. How is this going to work, I wondered.

"This lieutenant, here," he pointed with his thumb over his shoulder "is going to be your boxing trainer while you are on military camp. He will make sure you get the training and exercise that you need, and extra food. You will be given time to run and train for your upcoming boxing match."

I turned and looked at the tall, two-pip lieutenant standing next to the desk, his hands behind his back, looking at me sheepishly. He was stooped, had the beginnings of a paunch and looked pretty un-athletic. So now, this lieutenant has been assigned to be my trainer and ensure that I am in tip-top shape when I face the hard-hitting Jacob 'Dancing Shoes' Morake? I wondered what the hell this lieutenant knew about professional boxing.

What the fuck?

I began to protest the importance, no, the necessity, of having my own professional trainer for this important boxing match, but I was shut down before I could say five words and quickly turned around to march out of the commandant's office. I left the building, resigned to the fact that I was in the army again. Oh well. I decided to give the army the benefit of the doubt. Maybe there was a good place to train … a boxing gym with a ring, a modern facility nearby, in Pretoria, where I could train.

Little did I know that we would be jumping into the bush the next day and all my training would take place under the mopane trees.

After our two companies had all landed in the thick bush, with full kit and few injuries, and trucked over dirt roads to tents pitched amongst the bush, about 200 of us, paratroopers, were assigned to our tents and sleeping arrangements. We resigned ourselves, settled down and began to make the most of a bad thing. We all milled around slowly in the oppressive heat of the Northern Transvaal bushveld, picking up kit, putting it down, trying to adjust to being back in the army again. But, once we had established ourselves in the bush, things began to take on quite a festive atmosphere, a reunion of sorts, as we stood in long lines for lunch, glancing around, looking for a familiar face, someone you knew from before, from our time at 1 Parachute Battalion. Even the corporals were relaxed. We were a mixed bag, some troops looked younger, had probably done their national service a few years after me. Finally, I was happy to recognise a couple guys from Delta and Hotel Companies, with whom I had done my two years. We arranged that we could all stay in one tent together.

We were young so we looked at each other suspiciously, trying to see who had changed in the last three years on Civvy Street. Who had gone either way, for better or for worse? We had shared some tough times in 1981. By midday the heat in the tent had already built up to almost unbearable, all the flaps hung open hoping to encourage any small hint of a breeze to come inside. A lean blond trooper who had been in D Company threw his kit on the bed and remarked: "Hey, remember that Russian tank that came at us in Operation Protea?" he said, out of the blue.

There was a short silence. But I had picked up what he'd said, and I was not the only one.

"Yep, and the Noddy car[2] took it out with one shot, blew the turret off, and it burnt in front of us," another trooper from Delta Company answered.

"Yes, that's right," I agreed, nodding quietly.

We all looked at each other silently, nodding. I was relieved that the blond

---

2   A small South African Eland armoured car with a 90 mm cannon.

trooper had mentioned the Soviet tank that had rushed out at us, because it confirmed a couple of things: one, that all those things really had happened, I wasn't dreaming; and two, the memory had been at the forefront of his mind, so I knew I was not the only one brooding about it.

"I thought maybe I had been imagining it, these past couple of years."

"No, it happened bro' … remember the contact at the waterhole, when Swanepoel and that lieutenant were shot?"

"No, I wasn't there but I heard about it," I said.

I unpacked my kit and started to fill my *kas* (cupboard) with browns – pants, shirts, short pants, a jacket – stuff that I that I had not unpacked for three years. I found some petrified boot polish and toothpaste at the bottom of my big army bag and even came across the small blue Bible that my parents had given me when I originally went into the army. In the front of the Bible there was an inscription from my father in shaky handwriting, saying that he loved me. It was a special find for me as I did not remember seeing it before; if I had read it during my time on the Border, I had forgotten about it. My father and I did not often express that kind of sentiment in those days.

"Hey! Remember those Mirage jets dropping those 1,000 lb bombs on those FAPLA, when we attacked Xangongo … fucking loooud!"

"Yeah, and how were the anti-aircraft guns, shooting back at them as they dived down, there was a Mirage or two that was hit by flak wasn't there?"

"They were 23 mm."

"*Ja*, it was like watching a movie."

"Were you guys in Operation Protea?" asked a younger paratrooper, wide-eyed, someone we had never seen before.

Suddenly it felt refreshing, even worthwhile, to be with guys who had been together with me in the army and on cross-border operations into Angola. These few guys held the same memories that I did. These few guys had probably told the same stories as I had, to their friends and family. They had heard the same orders, they had heard the same squeak and rattle of the Soviet tank tracks, the 1,000 lb bombs, the 23 mm anti-aircraft firing a few feet over our heads as we advanced towards the trenches. These men had been brothers in arms. All of us, fresh out of high school, doing our duty, ready or not so ready to die for our country. Pretty soon we were babbling like long lost family as we sorted out our tent and who would sleep where. We caught up on news.

A trooper told us, sadly, that he had heard that big Helmut Kruger from Ficksburg had been killed in a car accident, soon after finishing up with the army. Helmut had been one of the well-known and vibrant 'bungalow bulls', the main man of the bungalow, (usually the biggest, with the loudest mouth and a flash in his eye). It was a title that came and went quickly, the pecking order was forever changing within a platoon, but Kruger had been able to hold it longer than others.

I broke the sad news of how I had found out that another of our company comrades, 'Lange' van Rensburg, had also been killed, soon after leaving the army. Some months after I had finished my army service my mother and I had arrived, unannounced, (a practice quite acceptable in SA at the time) at Lange's home in the Karoo *dorp* (small town) of Beaufort West, looking for a place to stay the night, as we made the long road trip from Johannesburg to Cape Town. Lange's mother, whom I had never met before, had quietly opened the door to my knock. With a smile I told her that I had been in 1 Parachute Battalion with her son, Lange; was he home; and could we perhaps stay the night on our way to Cape Town? She was quiet for a moment, saying nothing, just looking at my mother and me standing on the door step. Then, still holding the door open in front of us, she quietly told us that just a few months previously, her son 'Lange' van Rensburg had been killed in a motorbike accident – but please, we were welcome to come in, and spend the night on our journey to Cape Town.

She was a dark-haired, good-looking woman, dressed in blue, her face etched with sadness. She led us through the old Karoo house with its long, narrow passage and high ceilings to the small kitchen, where she made us fresh coffee which was served with rusks at the small kitchen table. I felt quite moved, listening to the two mothers chatting softly while drinking coffee. Then she quietly led us to our room for the night and wished us a good night's sleep. I thought that the room we had slept in may well have been the bedroom that belonged to my Para D Company comrade, Lange.

The South African bushveld has a harsh beauty, tall grass scattered with dense clusters of roughly barked thorn trees and shrubs. It was summer, and the thick bush was green and hot. Sun beetles whined, exotic birds with long tails lazily flapped their wings in the shade. The bushveld is the jewel of South African bush, 50,000 square kilometres of a beautiful, sub-tropical, woodland eco region, bordered on the east by the Drakensberg escarpment; to the south by the Magaliesberg mountain range; and to the north by the Soutpansberg mountains, north of Louis Trichardt. The town was named after one of the two men who led their parties of *boer* (farmer) *Voortrekkers* into the area in the mid-1830s. The other man was Johannes (Hans) van Rensburg who led his *Voortrekker* party farther north, where all of them – men, women and children – were killed by the Manukosi people who inhabited the area at that time.

One Parachute Battalion had chosen a good place to simulate the heat of Angola for our annual training camp. Finally, we were sorted into platoons and sections and then I was called aside by a corporal. He told me that I would be promoted to lance corporal, for no good reason other than, it seemed, they were short a section leader. One thing that cannot be denied is the army's ability to provide an instant adventure; it felt good to walk through the thick green bush with a rifle, something which, probably, you would otherwise never have done while tangled up in the hum drum life on Civvy Street.

The word was that after a few weeks of orientation and refresh training, 250 or so paratroopers would be shipped back to the Johannesburg area as a show of strength, to control the violence that had erupted in five black townships near Vereeniging, in the Vaal Triangle. Some of the troops who had already done 'township duty' told us that it had been a miserable time. I was not looking forward to having to do township duty, but my mind was taken off this potential misery when, on the third or fourth morning, the tall, stooped, shifty-eyed lieutenant who had been assigned to duty as my boxing trainer, appeared among the tents as we were preparing to head into the bush on patrol for the day. He called my name.

"Take off your kit and get into your PT clothes, running shoes and shorts. It's time to start your training for your boxing match."

The other troops, laden with full kit, a rifle, wearing their browns, cast green-eyed, jealous looks my way as I went back to the tent and came out dressed in my shorts, a T-shirt and sneakers. The lieutenant, who was also just doing his annual training camp, looked as if he would be far more comfortable in Civvy Street, sitting in an armchair, watching a good TV show, rather than out here in the bushveld. We started talking about boxing and he confessed that he knew nothing at all about the noble art; his job was merely to ensure that I got enough exercise and extra food.

"What exercises do you usually do to get in shape?"

"Well, I run in the morning, with exercise and some sprints. Then at night I'll go to the gym, jump rope, work the bag and/or spar, but I suppose all I can do out here in the bush is shadow box."

"OK, that's fine. We'll start now, we'll get you in good shape for this fight. Also, orders are that you are to have extra food, so you'll go and eat after the other troops have eaten, and you have whatever you want, and more, during the day."

"Extra food?"

"Yes, in the morning we'll run. Then you'll eat, after the other troops, and have whatever you want and whenever you're hungry."

"Oh! OK."

"Are you hungry now?"

"No, I just had breakfast, not long ago."

I looked at him, feeling a little odd. He certainly seemed to be taking the 'keep him well-fed' aspect of his job seriously, all right.

Well! I had definitely lucked out on my first army camp! My own personal trainer, who gets told, by me, what I need to do and when, and who apparently arranges free access to the kitchen for 'extra food' whenever I feel hungry! Hmm, this isn't the army I remember! The quiet lieutenant ended up being a pleasant guy who also took advantage to get away from the daily routine of the military camp. He would drive slowly, far behind me, in a jeep while I ran. How lucky was I? To be heading out on long runs in this area, with only the sound of my sneakers crunching the red sand of the gravel road. In the mornings, while running, I enjoyed searching the dirt road, damp with morning dew, for animal spoor which told a wonderful tale of the activities of the night before. Big and small antelope spoor was plentiful, probably impala, the smooth smear of a snake spoor waving across the dirt road, maybe a black mamba, the footprints of large birds, and even the marks left by *shongololos* (millipedes).

Looking for spoor always took me back, instantly, to being in the operational area on the border of Angola. It became second nature to do a constant visual search of the soft sand of Ovamboland and Angola, looking for SWAPO spoor. It took a while to learn the skill, like learning to shoot in close combat with both eyes open, as the Airborne teaches.

"You have to learn to look *through* the bush not *at* it."

It had taken us a few months to master the art of looking through the bush and not at it, but finally a whole new world jumped out at us when we acquired the ability see into the bush, past the trunks, through the leaves and grass and through the bush behind them. This ability, looking through the bush, had served me well through many later instances. Once, as our company advanced cautiously towards a terrorist position far inside Angola, I walked, holding my rifle high, loosely in my shoulder, peering intensely through the thick bush and suddenly not forty yards in front of me I saw a SWAPO terrorist, behind trees calmly making his escape, moving through the shadows of the bush, then into an open *shona*. My eyes had picked him up a second before he slowly broke from the bush into the patch of sunlight. I was as surprised as he and for a second thought he might be one of ours. Quickly I shouldered my rifle again and half-heartedly shouted a command at him. For a split second, in slow motion, our eyes locked on each other as he turned to look at me. His eyes were wide as saucers – rooted to the spot he realised he was already dead. My own eyes were also both wide open glaring down my barrel – just as the Airborne had taught us. Then I pulled the trigger. I did not miss.

I stopped under the shade of a large green bushveld acacia tree and began shadow boxing, aiming at the hanging leaves, snapping out punches as fast as I could, blowing short breaths at the same time. Without a punch bag, working fast combinations aimed at hanging leaves was as good as it was going to get. I worked a few rounds, pulling my punches back as fast as they went out. The lieutenant watched from his jeep parked in the shade as I punched at the leaves. He looked at his watch.

"OK, that's three minutes. Take a rest."

"Just shout 'time' when the round is over," I said.

I worked the next couple of rounds, building up speed as I moved around in the shade of the acacia tree, shooting my jab at the leaves. I found some lower hanging leaves and bobbed and weaved from side to side under them. I was pouring with sweat in the bushveld heat.

"Time!" shouted the lieutenant from the jeep.

I sat down on a tree stump, dripping with sweat. This wasn't working so well.

"If you punch those thorns they'll hurt you," the lieutenant remarked, making a surprisingly keen observation.

"Yep, Lieutenant. I'll try not to hit the thorns."

I couldn't stay focused as I trained under the acacia. My mind was wandering.

What was my friend, Darryl, doing in Los Angeles, California? Was he living a life of luxury, partying on down, drinking rum with a Californian girl on each arm? Was he hanging out with music stars, with mirrors on the ceiling, drinking pink champagne on ice? Why had he not come back to South Africa, was Darryl a prisoner who could never leave I mused? His postcard had sounded like a free-spirited message sent from the 'other side', from some Garden of Eden.

"Pull in china, the Yankee girls are great. Your mate, Darryl."

I had heard songs of California, the Hollywood hills and Sunset Strip. At 25 years all I had ever known was South Africa. I wanted to see the world. I wanted to see other countries. Europe, America, the East. How did people in other countries live their lives? There must be more out there than this, punching at the mopane tree leaves.

"Time!"

Hordes of *muggies* (midges) crazed by my sweat circled my head as I bobbed and weaved under the leaves. I spent another half hour shuffling around in the soft, thick bushveld sand, practicing my footwork, but it wasn't going well. The sun had reached its mid-morning intensity and the heat hung in the bush like a fog. My clumsy footwork was kicking up dust which was washed into my eyes by my sweat. This bushveld training was not working out; my opponent Morake was probably going to kick the crap out of me. And rightly so. My brown army T-shirt was drenched.

"I'm done Lieutenant. Let's head back, I'll ride with you in the jeep."

"You not going to run back?" the lieutenant asked, with concern.

"No, I'm not."

The lieutenant, who had started to look bored, had dozed off in the shade of the mopane tree, happily turned the ignition of the old jeep.

"Sure, hop in. Report to the kitchen when we get back and you can have some extra food," he offered, generously.

What was this thing about extra food they were trying to stuff down me? As if food alone can win a fight! But the lieutenant had been given an order to keep me well fed and he was sticking to it. I needed to lose weight, not gain weight! After a week and a half of training in the hot bush, punching acacia/mopane leaves, a major called me in and released me from the training camp.

"Good luck with your boxing match. I hope the training we have provided here has been sufficient for you," he said, smiling, as he handed me a train ticket back to Benoni.

All I had done during my bush training was sweat a lot and eat a lot. I hadn't sparred, hadn't hit mitts, hadn't used a heavy bag, or a speed bag … just punched at acacia/mopane leaves and kicked up dirt.

"Yeah right, thanks, it's been great," I mumbled, and saluted.

'Hotel California' ~ The Eagles

The boxing match was held in a black township not far from the city of Johannesburg. It was troubled times in South Africa; apartheid was like a 40-year-old Cadillac, slowly falling apart, with the last wheel stuck in a ditch as Neil Young might sing. Now the wheels of apartheid were finally coming off. As usual, the mostly black boxing crowd chanted for my head on a spear as an official introduced the fighters. Morake and I glared at each other across the ring. This might very well be the same township that my mates at 1 Parachute Battalion, whom I had last seen a week ago, were patrolling, doing township security duty this very minute, while I paced in my corner. I felt in surprisingly good shape after doing most of my training for the fight by myself in the bush, shadow boxing against the hot drooping leaves of acacia/mopane trees. I felt lean and fast but mostly just pissed off. As usual the fight exploded with a bang. I started really fast with a hard attack that had Morake reeling back but hiding behind a high guard. He was defending only, but then it seemed I had woken a hidden tiger inside him; I heard him grunting as he stood his ground, matching me punch for punch in an action-packed first round. He had caught me with a few hard blows, but I was faster, and for every punch he threw, I threw two or three.

In the second round Morake made some mistakes; he started dropping his hands and staying in one position a second too long. I could see that it was just a matter of time before I could land a telling shot. He kept up his somewhat awkward style of bobbing and weaving, but pretty soon I caught him with a short left right combination and he went sprawling across the canvas, only to jump up as soon as he could and signal to his corner that he was unhurt.

The mainly black African crowd bayed in support of their plucky fighter as he managed to slip out of a few tight spots, but I kept up my relentlessly aggressive attack, moving forward, missing by millimetres, until finally he faulted against the ropes for a second too long and I was able to smash a solid straight right from my shoulder to his chin. It dropped him to his knees. He got up on wobbly legs to beat the count, but staggered forward with glazed eyes, almost into the ref's arms and was counted out. I respected Morake and patted him on the back as he climbed out the ring, but he didn't look too appreciative. The black spectators were not happy either; the whistles and chants didn't stop as we walked through the small hallway to the old, dirty dressing room.

"Rough crowd … what's the problem?" I asked.

Johnny quickly pulled my gloves off and cut the hand wrap bandages away from my hands, using scissors He looked nervous and kept glancing at the door into the dressing room.

"What's the problem?"

"I think they don't like the decision, son. He got up before the bell but was counted out."

"He was finished, Johnny, I could see it in his eyes, he fell into the ref as he got up."

"Aye, you beat the blazes out of him, son, no doubt about that. Let's get out of here, you going to need stitches for that eye again."

Early in my boxing life I had chalked up a deep cut above my eye, which had never healed properly. It seemed that every fight, sometimes even a sparring session, would open it up again, and I was getting used to fighting with blood running into my eye. It was going to be another late-night trip to the local emergency room in a small town, with a nurse giving me more late-night Frankenstein stitches in a quiet, cold, side room. My dad looked around uneasily at the seemingly angry black boxing crowd, milling around us as we walked to our car, anxious to find our way out of the township. I felt a small sense of security, knowing that my father always carried his Star 9 mm pistol with a 15-round clip under his big sheepskin jacket on outings like this. I was never permitted to carry a firearm.

The evening made me wonder about the future of South Africa. There seemed to be no end to the township riots; it had begun to feel as though a major civil upheaval was in sight.

§

Although I had been excited about winning the last fight with a KO, and I wanted to fight again as soon as possible, there was something I had been keeping from Johnny. I wanted to tell him … but I knew he was not going to like it.

"What do you mean? You going to America, son? What for? We just getting started here … you're doing so good. Look what the papers are saying about you … they say you the most exciting fighter in the country. Read it here."

I had met Johnny Hogg at the Yeoville boxing gym a few days after the fight, for a light workout. He had said he wanted to discuss the next fight, coming up soon, against Johan Horn, who was a hard hitter. Johnny had come in late, bringing with him a newspaper with a small article about the Morake fight, to show me. But I had forestalled him, telling him about my latest Big Decision. And he didn't like it. As expected.

Johnny threw down the newspaper and I read the bold headline of a small, three-column article on the upcoming fight.

"Korff can be next boxing drawcard."

Johnny was watching me, carefully.

"You can be South African champion if you keep knocking them down like this. If you leave now this was all for naught, all this hard work, for nothing."

"I'll train while I'm in Los Angeles, Johnny, and maybe even get a couple fights. I'll be back in three, maybe four, months' time and we can carry on, you'll see."

"You can't just go fight overseas son, it's just not that simple."

"What about that American trainer that you know, Jackie McCoy, maybe I can go to his gym?"

"Things are working for you *here* ... you're winning fights, you're knocking them out! You are ranked number nine now and Leonard Neill (a boxing journalist) says he heard from the board that you soon going to be ranked number five in South Africa. You can't get sidetracked now! Stay on course. Go to America later, in a year or two. America will still be there."

I knew that the workout was over, started packing my gym bag, hooded my head with a towel as we walked out of the Yeoville gym. I had made up my mind; I was going to America – I was going to see the world. And that was that.

But Johnny Hogg my trainer was adamant that I should not go to America, *not now*. It was dark when we left the gym and walked to our vehicles. I had picked up another shiner which had almost shut my eye and I drove home carefully, deep in thought.

Was it the right thing to go to America now? Maybe Johnny was right. Maybe I should stay, train hard, fight Johan Horn and the others. Keep the ball rolling and go travelling later.

A week later Johnny and I met again and I told him that I was determined to go, *now*. But I would continue training in America and come back with valuable experience. This seemed to go some way towards placating my feisty Scottish trainer. At least he was thinking about it.

"Johnny, I'll work out in the American gyms, get some experience, come back to South Africa and then we can really go to it. American boxing experience can't do me any harm."

I convinced Johnny that a few months in America would be a great thing for my boxing. He nodded his agreement now, seeing a different picture.

"OK. I'll call Jackie McCoy in Los Angeles and you can spend some time training with him. Then also with Jim Jacobs in New York ... this might work out well, son."

"Johnny, I'll be back in about three months or so. I'll train hard over there, when I come back we can carry on and get ourselves that middleweight title."

Johnny was smiling as I shook his hand. I was relieved ...and excited.

"You'll see ... it'll all work out Johnny!"

But I would never see my fiery boxing trainer and friend, Johnny 'Dundee' Hogg, again. Ever.

§

A week later we held the 'home premiere' of our self-help video, in Tommy's plush living room. Producing and directing the video had been three months of fun, and a lot of hard work, but it was done and dusted and we were ready for the red carpet premiere of *Self Defence for Housewives* by Passive Hound Studios.

I felt awkward sitting in Tommy's lounge on the edge of an oxblood leather chair, the remnants of my black eye still visible, in the company of his beautiful wife, Lorraine, and a few of his friends. I sipped at a cold Castle lager and munched snacks while we waited for Murray and Marlon. I was the forward party, sent to prepare the ground for the red carpet premiere of our self-defence video.

Tommy was finally going to see, from start to finish, the movie he had financed. We all hoped the video was going to make some money for Tommy and Passive Hound Studios, that it would be our big break into the movie making business. Murray and Marlon had spent two days in the post production studio, watching professionals busy with the editing and post production process. They were still there, putting the finishing touches to the movie. We had told Tommy that he would get to view the finished product at his house, at five PM. It was now getting on for nine PM. I had been sent ahead to calm the waters, to assure Tommy and friends that the video would be viewed tonight. I had been sitting there for well over an hour, making small talk.

"I heard you are going to America?"

"I'm going over to visit a friend and have a couple fights, if I can. I'll be back, probably in three to four months' time."

"Fantastic country. I was in Atlanta not long ago, an amazing place, America."

"Do you like boxing? Doesn't it hurt when you get hit?" Tommy's gorgeous wife enquired, peering at my black eye which had begun to turn yellow.

"Aw ... not really ... sometimes, maybe."

I was always lost for words when she turned her attention to me, and Tommy always laughed at my awkwardness.

Outside a car door slammed and the German Shepherd started barking.

"I think they've arrived," I said, with relief.

Murray and Marlon strode into the trendy living room to applause. They were grinning from ear to ear and flourished the *Self Defence for the Housewife* cassette, hot from the editing room. Tommy poured a round of celebratory drinks and the video was ceremoniously slipped into the VHS player. The show started.

Tommy slapped his thighs with both hands and sat forward, looking around the room, laughing, showing his brown smoke-stained teeth, his green eyes shining. Lorraine was smiling expectantly.

"This is great ... bloody fantastic, well done!"

The video was good. Even I was surprised, not having seen the complete, edited and finished product. Not bad for a bunch of guys who had taken a chance, not knowing the first thing about film making. The professional editing and soundtrack pulled it all together. David Hall-Green's performance was flawless; his posh, hot potato voice gave the production authority and he highlighted some similarities between our video and the current, popular TV show *Police File*, for which he was so well known. The murder scene was gory ... Captain Peach was impressive. The funny scenes flowed smoothly into each other, thanks to the professional editing and sound. There were several comic moments, with the famous David Hall-Green dressed in an array of costumes from thug to delivery boy. Tommy roared with laughter when he appeared on-screen, dressed in a leather jacket emulating a 50s rocker, doing a drive-by in a purple '56 Cadillac with tailfins as high as your chest. The self-defence instruction section was insightful and interesting – with me being tossed around by the prepared, trained for action 'housewife' Sharon.

The End

DIRECTED AND PRODUCED BY MARLON HEILBRUNN
AND MURRAY AND GRANGER KORFF

"This is great! This video is going to go straight to Atlanta in America," Tommy announced when the movie was over. He was ecstatic. He now had a self-help video, which he owned, which he could market through his own video stores in South Africa, and intended marketing overseas. He kept asking questions and seemed genuinely surprised that the end product had turned out so well; he also seemed well pleased with his investment.

I was doubly excited. My name was on the video as director and producer, and I was leaving for California in a few weeks, to visit my old friend Darryl, and possibly have a few fights to get some experience. I had managed to buy an inexpensive airline ticket on an 'under 25 years old' special being advertised by South African Airways. I had only just qualified for the age limited special and would have to fly to California the night I turned 25 years old – which was coming up in just a few weeks. California here I come!

The few weeks left before my birthday flashed by. I had finished my plumbing jobs and, despite the fact that it was going to be a short trip, I had told Piet and the work crew that I was shutting down and going away for three months and would call for them when I returned. Leaving everything to the last minute, as usual, I packed hurriedly for the trip, throwing some clothes into my green hiking backpack, together with some boxing gloves, a headguard and a copy of *Self Defence for the Housewife*. At the last minute I threw in my army photograph album with photos from my time in 1 Parachute Battalion, to show my mate Darryl in Los Angeles. I knew he would be interested. I didn't bother taking any photos of my family and friends – there was no need, I would be back in South Africa shortly. The departure day came up so quickly that I did not even have time to say good bye to most of my friends and I had to say a quick goodbye to my Dad over the phone, because he was working late.

"See you in about three months, Pa."

"Travel safely, son, and take care, love you."

My mother and Leighton, one of my childhood friends, saw me off at Jan Smuts International airport.

"See you when you get back – soon," my mother said, and gave me a hug.

"Just a few months, Mom," as I hugged her good bye.

Chapter Eleven
CITY OF ANGELS

'Careless Whisper' ~ *Wham!*

I arrived on the West Coast of America on August 28th 1985, on my 26th birthday. August was midsummer in California and sweat dripped off my forehead as I stepped off the Greyhound bus that had finally stopped, after a five-day trip from hell, non-stop, across America from New York to Los Angeles. The bus had finally stopped outside the dramatically designed Union Station, a combination of what looked like Art Deco and Spanish architectural styles, in Downtown Los Angeles. I unloaded my kit, scratching at my seven-day-old beard, not having shaved since leaving South Africa a week before, and looked around me at the tall buildings of Downtown Los Angeles. I was disappointed – I had thought that the city would be bigger, like I had seen in photographs. Like New York. I kept an eye on my green backpack, small suitcase and South African made 'Noble' boxing gloves. My muscles and bones were as stiff as a man who'd been in solitary for a week and as a lean middleweight my butt ached from the five days and nights on the hard Greyhound bus seats, advertised as a 'Luxury Bus' on the Greyhound adverts. My closest memory of being this uncomfortable was sitting in an army Buffel troop carrier, for days at a time, shoulder to shoulder and knee to knee with troops, all of us loaded with kit. The five days on the old Greyhound bus had made me feel even worse!

I knew very little about Los Angeles except that it was an endless urban sprawl, and an ugly city, according to my boxing trainer, Johnny Hogg. It looked OK to me. Tall palm trees lined Alameda Street. Big American gas guzzler cars from the 70s were still plentiful on the roads, along with many other makes and models that I did not recognise. The sounds of the city and the scorching heat radiated off the glass high rise buildings. I was surrounded by concrete freeway overpasses, tarred roads and the smell of vehicle emissions mixed with unfamiliar spicy food. I smoked another cigarette … I was smoking more than usual and combined with travelling for a week it made me feel sluggish. I wandered around, slowly exploring the front of Union Station.

So this is downtown Los Angeles …

Folk standing nearby leapt back from the kerb with me, when Darryl arrived to pick me up, making an expected dramatic entrance into the parking lot of the Union Station. He literally pulled his van onto the walkway, tyres screeching as he came to halt. Not in the least embarrassed, wearing a huge grin, he flung the door open right there. It was really good to see my mischievous South African schoolmate and old friend, once again, I had not seen him for some four years. He looked a bit older and a bit wilder. We slapped each other's backs and he carelessly tossed my gear through the side door of his old square '69 Dodge panel van, sporting an old railway sleeper for a front bumper. Darryl was in good spirits; it seemed that his stay in America had suited him well. He looked confident and outgoing.

"Welcome to America, the land of the free. You look like shit bru, what cuts with the beard?"

I felt and looked ragged. I had landed in New York after a long 17-hour flight, with only three hundred dollars to my name. I called Darryl and he suggested that I take a $99 Greyhound bus ride from New York to Los Angeles. Neither of us realised the huge distance involved, driving from the east coast to the west coast of America. I had spent five days and nights on the bloody bus and I had a large bone to pick with Daryl.

"Why the hell did you tell me to take the bus from New York? It took five days to get here, sitting and sleeping in the same seat!"

"Why so long?"

"I dunno – you tell me. You're the one living here, who advised me to take bus – I should have flown!"

"Naw, would have cost much more bru. At least you here now and it cost you only $99."

"$99 is not worth five days on a bus. The bus went down all the way south through Saint Louis, in Missouri, before it came crossed to the west. I even saw the Saint Louis Gateway Arch!"

"Jeez! You went that far?" Darryl exclaimed.

Who knew America was so damn big! Many passengers had climbed off the bus, many others had climbed on, during the journey. Only one other passenger had stayed the course, travelled the entire distance from New York to Los Angeles on the Greyhound – a young anaemic-looking Chinese fellow, wearing thick spectacles. From sheer boredom he took it upon himself to give me 'American lessons' which he took very seriously, while we watched the American mid-west farms, fields and graffiti-filled neighbourhoods flash past, city after city, town after town.

Yet again my Chinese tutor raised his finger to push his glasses up his nose, they kept sliding down his small, flat nose, while explaining in a heavy Chinese accent, "In Amelica Budweiser number one beer. Evelyone dlink Budweiser. Amelican people want the job done light away … no wait for tommolow, tommolow too late," and "If you work vely hard, can make some success in Amelica." These are some of his lessons that I remember.

Darryl, originally from our hometown, Benoni, had settled into a small single-roomed apartment at the foot of the Hollywood Hills, a block up from Hollywood Boulevard. The apartment block was an interesting looking seven or eight storey art deco building which, according to the brass plaque in the old black cage door elevator, had been declared a historical monument.

"It's a cool building, I'll introduce you to some of the *mal* (mad) people living here," Darryl chuckled.

"Errol Flynn used to live here," he said, pointing to another brass plaque that confirmed confirming this fact, while I squeezed my bags into the small old-fashioned cage elevator.

We walked into the small, bachelor pad apartment which he shared with three other South Africans who all kipped on the floor. It was Darryl's place, so he had the only bed. He explained the house rules: "They're hardly ever here, if they're not at their girlfriends then they come crash here, late at night. Got to keep the apartment clean and tidy, like in the army, *mooi netjies* (nice and neat), no *varkshok* (pig sty) stuff. Everyone has to work; no-one gets to just hang around the apartment. We'll give you a break, seeing as you've just arrived, but you have to find a job as soon as possible."

We had not seen each other in a few years and couldn't stop talking. I took up a position at the window, gazing out at the Hollywood Hills and coming with the heat the sweet smell of jasmine, or maybe callidas, wafting down from the hills to mix with smell of city smog. Darryl was longing for news from back home. I told him about the exciting stuff that had been going on in South Africa for the last three years: about returning to Johannesburg from Cape Town, my plumbing business, the self-defence video, and I told him also that my boxing had been going well. He asked about old friends, some of the good times he had missed, and told me about life in the US. I told him about my sister, Tracy, winning the 'face of the eighties' competition in South Africa, being featured on the front cover of *Cosmopolitan* magazine and going overseas to model, all at only 15 years old.

Our catch-up session finally started winding down and Darryl suggested we go for a walk down Hollywood Boulevard, so he could show me the neighbourhood.

Hollywood Blvd was one block away. We dodged thick traffic crossing the wide streets, there were throngs of tourists in California for the summer. Boy, this was not like small town Benoni, where I had just come from! The sidewalks were filled with a mixture of long-haired Hollywood locals and groups of tourists festooned with cameras; there were endless stores next to each other selling the same Hollywood tourist paraphernalia – T-shirts, fake Emmy award statures, framed posters in all the shop windows, Marilyn Monroe, Elvis and John Wayne seemed to be the most popular; James Dean also scowled down from every other store front wall.

We weaved in and out of a thick morass of weirdos, bums and crazy people, their faces black with layers of dirt, babbling to the wall and anyone who made eye contact with them. Long-haired kids on skateboards raced in and out of the crowd, brushing past pedestrians at dodgy speeds. I paused to look down at David Bowie's star on the Hollywood Walk of Fame, while Darryl chattered on about the last three years in America. He had taken a course in Texas for sound engineers then bought a van and travelled up to Los Angeles, with quite a few adventures along the way. He was telling me about a nutcase in a motel putting a revolver against his head and making off with a lot of his stuff.

"Some of these Yanks are crazy bru," Darryl said, grinning hugely. I noticed that one of the new Los Angeles habits my old friend had acquired was to wear sunglasses 24/7, even in the middle of the night or when at the movies.

City of Angels

"This is it buddy, Hollywood – this is where it all happens," he announced as we sat down at a small table in the Snow White restaurant. He introduced me to Doris, owner of the Snow White Diner, a cynical, had been good-looking once upon a time, Austrian woman. She had come to Hollywood many years ago, hoping to find something more than running a diner on Hollywood Boulevard. She took my breakfast order and replied to Darryl's comment with a scornful look.

"Look at all these tourists who've come to Hollywood. It's a dump and they walking up and down these side streets looking for something, but all they see is bums and weirdos."

"Is Hollywood a dump?" I asked naively.

She gave me the benefit of what might have been a smile. It said clearly that I was fresh meat to the Hollywood scene.

Directed by Darryl I ordered my first American breakfast – pancakes and maple syrup with sausage and eggs over-easy and hash browns.

§

After a few days of chatting our heads off till late at night, I came down to earth and decided I needed to get a job. So I thumbed through my little phone book and found the phone number given to me by the travel agent in Benoni, who had sold me my airline ticket.

"I know someone who lives in Hollywood," she had told me, "he's a plumber in Hollywood, his name is Mike."

"What a coincidence! I'm also a plumber, and I'm also going to stay in Hollywood. If you give me his number, I'll definitely look him up when I get there."

What a handy twist of fate: a fellow South African, a plumber, living in Los Angeles.

So I called Mike and told him I had just arrived in LA, from South Africa, a week ago, and I had been given his number by a travel agent in Benoni – and I was a plumber, looking for work.

"*Izit*, my china? *Ja*, OK. Meet me at the corner of Sunset and Le Brea Wednesday at 07h30. I'm busy with a main sewer line and need some diggers."

I was to learn that Mike and most of his South African connections now living in LA, used South African slang, most of the time, as in: "*Izit*, my china?" meaning "Really (is it), my friend?"

"Diggers? Where're your Bantus?"

"No Bantus here, my china, but if you want work, I've got some digging for you."

Beggars can't be choosers, so within a few days of arriving in the US I was working. I met Mike, a muscle-bound Lebanese weightlifter from the southern suburbs in Johannesburg who had been in Los Angeles for four or five years and had not forgotten any of his Jo'burg slang. Mike seemed a nice guy and eagerly asked for news about South Africa. He seemed to slip into trance, nodding as he listened to me nattering away about the old country. It looked as though he missed South Africa terribly; there was a distant, wounded expression in his eyes as I spoke about our country at the tip of Africa. He was a strong guy who worked out, lifting weights, every day. He wore a loud mostly red oversized American worker's plaid shirt, and a huge smile.

"I go to the gym, work out at midnight, my china, at the 24 hours' fitness club, there's no one in the gym, that's the way I like it."

There's a weightlifting gym that's open 24 hours a day? I was learning.

We rode through the thick morning traffic in a plumbing van that smelled just like mine, in South Africa, and entered the six lane 101 Freeway, heading over the Hollywood Hills. I was absolutely gobsmacked, looking at the freeway ahead of us, jammed with cars. I had never seen so many cars together on one road before. I had never seen such a traffic jam, as far as the eyes could see, two six lane freeways, both sides moving at five miles per hour.

"*Ag*, this is normal bru ... this traffic jam probably carries on for twenty miles, we'll get to the job at about nine or so, two hours' drive ... if there was no traffic we could be there in twenty minutes."

Finally, we arrived at the job and I got to meet Herold, the owner of the small plumbing company, who also used South African slang all the time. He had been in LA for about seven or eight years and had a small but busy plumbing business which served the Hollywood area and the Hills, mostly. Herold was a good South African guy with – it being 1985 – a mullet hairdo about five inches high, which made him seem taller than he really was.

"They were going to make me a lieutenant in the army, but it didn't happen," he told me, when I brought up the subject of national service. He ran his little plumbing outfit with a firm hand and could easily have been a competent lieutenant. He knew an endless number of customers in the film industry, half of whom seemed to be gay, weird or eccentric or all three.

"They all fucking *mal* here, you'll see, my china."

Working with Herold was quite an entertainment. Listening to Herold and Lebanese Mike talking about the day's work ahead was a continual series of grunts and the perennial phrase, "*Ja, izit,* my china?" Not that I was any better. At 26 years old my own vocabulary was littered thickly with South African slang.

Working for Herold in his plumbing company was a real lifesaver for me. I had arrived in Los Angeles with only $90 in my pocket after the long trip, coast to coast. I was happy to be digging trenches and I did not complain. I remembered how easy and enthusiastically my smiling Zulu labourer would dig trenches for me in South Africa. I was in good physical shape, I needed the money, so I jumped in, determined to show them how to dig a proper trench. I copied the style of my Zulu digger, holding the shovel low down the handle, the way King Shaka Zulu had taught his *impis* (regiments) to hold their stabbing spears.

I was now the Zulu. Welcome to America.

'A View to a Kill' ~ *Duran Duran*

After work I would spend long nights hanging out with Darryl in the recording studio where he worked behind the sound mixing desk. Darryl, wearing his perennial shades, even in the dimly lit studio in the middle of the night, seemed to know what he was doing. He tweaked the endless rows of knobs and gave confident instructions to the musicians. Generally, he booked his clients for the graveyard shift when he could squeeze them in at a better rate. His clients were mostly soul brothers, playing R&B music or hip hop. Darryl had always displayed a very keen sense of humour and had been able to get on with everyone – and nothing had changed. I had never known anyone with a better rapport with blacks in Africa than Darryl. Even the surliest *tsotsis* (street thugs) would light up from ear to ear when Darryl started jive talking with them, mimicking their accents, using *Fanagalo*, the *lingua franca* used on the mines and recognised by most white South Africans living on the Highveld. He did the same thing in LA, where he was known as Dr Africa, and got the same reaction from the black homeboys there. He had all the soul brothers among his late-night clientele eating out of his hands in the studio earning the name "Dr Africa" from them for his ability to mix the perfect sound.

§

Around this time I met John Wood, the manager and co-owner of Studio Masters, a well-known music studio at which Darryl worked – mostly late night sessions. John was a boxing enthusiast and when Darryl had told him that I was a pro boxer he wanted to get together. I met him in his studio on Beverly Boulevard and was fascinated by all his boxing magazines and the impressive collectables on the walls of his office.

"I know Bobby Chacon very well, old friend of mine. Jerry Quarry, Archie Moore as well. Also Mike Weaver."

John was a nice guy. Like most Americans I had met so far, John had the gift of the gab and he suggested that we should get a fight arranged, as soon as possible. We piled into his convertible Alfa Romeo and headed down to the Main Street gym. John knew one of the trainers there and introduced me as a pro boxer from South Africa.

"You're a fighter from South Africa?"

"Yes, I'm a boxer."

"We call them fighters over here," he informed me

"OK, I'm a fighter from South Africa."

The gym was a big old building standing in the shadows of LA's tall downtown buildings. It was the biggest gym I had ever seen, with two rings, and even though it was midday on a weekday, there were a dozen or so fighters jumping rope and hitting the heavy bags. The gym smelled like wet leather and wintergreen, just like the gyms back home. I geared up and did a few rounds of shadow boxing in front of the big mirrors, but I was more interested in looking at the other boxers than watching myself in the mirror. The trainer with whom John was chatting came over, gloved me up, and I stepped into the big ring with countless blood spots splattered all over the old canvas. I sparred two rounds with a short, stocky Mexican who came at me with some good hooks to the body and head. I was not in good shape, I had hardly been running in the last month or more, so I didn't press an attack, but I moved easily, avoided his hooks and slipped a few good straight hands down the pipe, between his wide-open defence.

"The Mexican fighters like to hook a lot, also to the body, so watch out," said the gym manager and promoter, Jimmy Gilio, speaking loudly as I took off my headguard and threw my South African made Nobel gloves which I had brought with me, all the way across the world, into my bag.

Jimmy's office featured a big blow-up of a black and white photo, 3ft by 2ft, showing him as a ex-pro boxer in the middle of the ring, on his hands and knees, his mouth hanging open, his eyes staring blankly into the crowd. In the picture he had been savagely knocked out and was trying to get up but obviously couldn't. Jimmy was proud of that photo.

"I got my ass kicked on that one ... but the main thing is that I was in there, trying and doing it. Not everyone can do this sort of thing. You not bad kid, you got a good right hand and you hit hard, that's what you have to have in this game. How's the boxing in South Africa? You got a heavyweight champion, Gerry Coetzee, he's got that bionic right hand filled with metal, he hits like hell."

"Yeah, I know Gerrie Coetzee, we're from the same town. I used to spar with his brothers, in his gym behind his house ... I watched Gerrie bend a heavy bag in the gym as if it was a soft bag."

"Well, if you learned a few tricks from him, you might be OK. I'll try getting something going for you here, in the meantime, start getting in shape. How much you weigh?"

"I can get down to 160 pounds – 75.2 kgs."

Jimmy was Italian American and the promoter at the Los Angeles Grand Olympic Auditorium. He spoke with an east coast accent and sounded just like an actor in a bad boxing movie.

"OK, kid. We'll get you in on a show at middleweight."

I started doing some serious running for the first time since I had arrived, and I dropped the cigarettes to just a couple a week. There was one problem: I soon realised that it was not going to be that simple to do roadwork – there was no place to run in the middle of Hollywood. No long dirt roads to run on, like 'back on the farm' in South Africa. I started exploring the neighbourhoods of Hollywood Hills, running up and down winding roads filled with overgrown bougainvillea and wrought iron gates. I soon found a flatter route and huffed and puffed my way past the eerie looking Magic Hotel, down to La Brea along a quiet section of Hollywood Boulevard, and up a side street that led into hiking trail area. I was quite out of shape, having hardly trained in the last two months, unusual for me.

It was a week or so before I established my training routine and could run at an easy pace on the concrete Hollywood sidewalks. It took me a few days, but I found that the strange puking thing that always seemed to happen in the same place, as I was going down busy Franklin Ave in rush hour, was thanks to the exhaust fumes from the traffic, hanging thickly in the long section of road, which I was sucking in deeply, while running. The gasoline here smelled different to the petrol fumes back home.

Jimmy Gilio had recommended a boxing gym closer to Darryl's pad than his own place in downtown LA. Problem: Darryl was the only one with a car who could give me a ride to the gym. So, over the next few weeks, in between digging ditches and running down Hollywood Boulevard, sucking in fumes, Darryl and I drove down to Frankie Goodman's gym in Van Nuys.

"Let me be your manager for this boxing stuff. I know how these Yankee minds work … I can do this."

"No way!" I said. Darryl was not going to be my boxing manager.

"C'mon man, what you talking? You need a Yiddishe boy as your manager. I've got the gift of the gab."

"No way, not going to happen."

"Let me do this."

"No, this is boxing, and you know zero, zilch, *nothing* about this business. No way, sorry bro."

I was determined that Darryl would not become my manager. Boxing is a serious business, you have to know what you're talking about in this game, you can't willy-nilly say something that doesn't make sense. You have to know your facts – weight classes, who the champions are, what the current topics are, gym etiquette … none of these were topics for a beginner.

Darryl moped for a few days, just wasn't himself, clearly disappointed that I had not granted him manager status. A position, he claimed, for which he was naturally suited, being in the music business where, he said, he promoted people every day in his music circles. I listened to him for hours as he pleaded his case. It was probably the third day when I gave in to Darryl and said yes, alright, he could be my boxing manager.

Darryl was downright chuffed and took to the task as easily as a good Jewish boy ordering pickles and gefilte fish in a deli. I cringed as he told all and sundry that I was in LA to take names and kick some ass. He described my boxing style as 'sting like a bee' when actually my technique was more like the 'stand and slug' variety. I had to take him aside and give him some lessons in boxing etiquette. It's not a good thing to bullshit in boxing circles – it'll come back to bite you.

Frankie Goodman was a well-known old timer in the LA boxing game. He had an upstairs boxing gym on Van Nuys Blvd filled with pictures and posters of famous Mexican fighters I had never heard of. Apparently Frankie had been a top fighter in his day. He wore his trousers high, above his waist and finger-combed his thinning hair while he inspected me. Interestingly I noticed that Frankie wore his belt buckle on the side, near his hip, not in front, as everyone else did.

"You look like you can bang … what are you? Middleweight?"

"Yes. I can make 160 pounds."

"Who's this guy?" he asked, nodding at Darryl next to me.

"This is my manager," I mumbled, unenthusiastically.

"And trainer," Darryl added, and I nodded to confirm this.

"You have a fight at the Olympic, eh? That place is a famous bit of history. OK, let's get you warmed up and see what we got."

For a few days I visited the gym to jump rope and shadow box. I couldn't have Darryl hold the hand mitts for me, it would have exposed him straight away as someone who knew very little about the boxing game, so I would go straight on to heavy bag work. On a few occasions I managed to stop Darryl from wandering off to talk to the other boxers and Frankie. There are many subtle dos and don'ts in boxing gyms; chit chatting with other boxers is just not on.

So, I'm set to spar early one afternoon with Frankie's young Mexican fighter; he has just turned professional and will soon have his second fight. He looks serious, moving around in his corner, gloved-up, headguard on, waiting for me to get ready. Darryl is gloving me up and it's taking much longer than it should.

He is having a hard time tying my gloves, while I am giving him quiet instructions from the corner of my mouth, under the watchful gaze of Frankie and the Mexican fighter. All the time Darryl is chatting, looking around, telling everyone that the time has come to separate the men from the boys. Finally, I'm standing in the ring, gloved up, while Darryl tries to put my leather headguard on me, still looking over his shoulder, still talking non-stop. My old school friend from Benoni has never before put a boxing headguard on anyone, in his life.

A small crowd has gathered, waiting to see the South African taking names and kicking ass. I feel leather covering my face, even my eyes. Something is wrong! Then I feel Darryl trying to fasten the leather chinstrap behind my head. The strap is supposed to be under my chin!

Finally, I hear Frankie Goodman saying, loud and clear, "You putting that headguard on back to front, son."

There is silence in the gym. We are *so* busted! I cringe inside but actually I'm relieved that the sham is over. I knew, from the start, that agreeing to Darryl being my manager/trainer had been a bad idea. Darryl laughs and takes the headguard off, joking about American headguards being so fucked up that they look back to front as he tries to put it on my head a second time.

I wave off his attempts, speaking loudly through my mouthguard, spilling the beans to Frankie Goodman. I tell him that my friend is not acquainted with boxing, he is just a good, old friend who is helping me out, because I have just arrived in LA from South Africa. But I do know about boxing, very well, so let's get on with the sparring.

Frankie nods his agreement.

I am determined to regain the respect I have lost in the back-to-front headguard incident and come out hard. I had gained experience sparring with top notch fighters like Harold Volbrecht, and I had learned not to give any new sparring partner a chance. Come out hard.

I do just that. I come out banging, not giving the Mexican fighter a chance to recover. After five rounds Frankie calls it. I have come out on top of the sparring.

"Yes, you not bad, you have a good punch. Try work the body more and move your head some." Frankie seems quite impressed.

On the drive back to Hollywood Darryl is promptly fired from his position as my manager-cum-trainer; instead he is bumped down to assistant and bucket boy. He is disappointed, of course, but accepts it cheerfully enough. Once a *tjommie* always a *tjommie*(pal).

Chapter Twelve
KNEE DEEP

'We Built this City' ~ *Jefferson Starship*

At least the work from Herold's plumbing business was constant and kept me with some money in my pocket. I also used the digging as exercise, making a full day's work-out of it; I tackled it with vigour and was drenched in sweat at the end of the afternoon.

Darryl and I had finished digging a sewer line and had just arrived home. As I cleaned up Darryl checked his answering machine. It was 1987 so his was the first phone answering machine I had ever seen.

He shouted from the other room: "Hey there's a message for you! From that promoter, Jimmy Gilio, he wants you to call him; he has a fight for you."

I listened to Jimmy's message. It was about five PM so I called him right away. I had learned to be cautious in my short boxing career and knew I had to be noncommittal. I asked him what was going on.

"I got someone for you at catch weight of 158 pounds, for a show at the Olympic Auditorium. It's on the 30th so that gives you about three weeks to get ready and in shape. Yeah, he's a palooka from Mexico, don't worry about it. What's that? Oh, yeah, five hundred dollars after the fight, call me tomorrow and let me know. This could be good for you, kid."

I told him I would let him know, but I knew I shouldn't accept this fight because I was not in fighting shape.

"Hey bro, you going to take the fight, right?"

"I don't think so, I don't think I'm going to take it, I'm not in shape."

"You are in shape! You've been running and you've been to the gym a few times."

Darryl had no idea what "in fighting shape" meant. It meant a good six weeks or more of hard training, building it up, bringing it to a peak, then backing off for three or four days before the fight, doing not much more than walking and stretching.

"You got to do it, this is your chance!"

"No, I am *not* in shape; I'm *not* going to do it."

Darryl continued hassling me about doing the fight as we cooked dinner on the gas stove. He dumped a can of brown bean mix in a pot.

"What's that?"

"This is called chilli, its good stuff."

American chilli. It tasted good. I had never seen it before, but I had read about it in cowboy books.

As a kid, during the seemingly never-ending Christmas school holidays, I had lain on my bed reading cowboy books ... about McAllister (by Matt Chisholm) and Dusty Fog (by J.T. Edson). McAllister and Dusty Fog were cowboys who rode the Wild West on their trusty Roan horses, escaping from the law or hunting bad hombres. What these two cowboys had in common was their love for a plate of chilli with beans, cooked over a small fire, hidden from view out on the cold prairie, or in a saloon after many long dusty days on the trail. I had long been mystified about what 'chilli' actually was ... the only chilli that I knew about was red or orange capsicum peppers. Were these cowboys eating a plateful of hot chilli peppers? They must have had strong stomachs in those days, to cook and eat an entire plate of hot chilli peppers!

I chewed small tasty chunks of minced meat in brown savoury sauce, mixed with beans. So this is what chilli is! Small discoveries. I was learning. This is what McAllister and Dusty Fog ate out on the prairie ... another life mystery solved. After having a good meal of chilli, just like my cowboy hero McAllister, with his long Navy Colt out on the prairie, my cautious good sense was overtaken by my love of a good fight.

"*Ja*, OK ... why not? Let's do this Olympic Auditorium fight thing."

I called Jimmy the next day and said I would take the fight.

"Good for you! Work out hard ... make sure that you make the weight. Call me next week and come down here to sign the contract."

I started working out twice a day, after running early in the morning. No place to run in centre of Hollywood and I had no car. No quiet, long dirt roads like at home in South Africa. Traffic roared past me on busy Franklin Ave. It was the same route I had used before, but I had learned that if I walked past the block or two where the heavy car exhaust fumes lingered, in a dip, I could avoid having to puke. Then I would turn and run uphill to get higher than the layer of exhaust fumes. At night, when Darryl got home from work we drove to Frankie Goodman's gym in Van Nuys and I was able to get in some sparring, with the same kid and another light heavyweight, bigger than me. I went in hard. I had learned that that was the only way. You can't spar halfway, especially with fighters you don't know. Invariably you'll come off second best if you went easy, either by sparring with someone better than you, or some 'green' guy could catch you with a lucky shot and make you look like a fool. No, going at it full on is the only way ... if you can't take the heat then get out the kitchen!

I had been training hard for just over a week when Darryl's Dodge '69 van broke down and had to be towed to a workshop from somewhere on La Brea Boulevard.

"The van's fucked. I think the clutch rod has gone, it's happened before."

Darryl and I walked home from the mechanic's place. He was a guy from New York and told us that it was indeed the clutch rod, but that the fuel pump was also involved. The repair would take a few days and also all the money in our possession. So now we had no transport and no money. The money part we could deal with, but not being able to drive to the boxing gym and missing the sparring that I needed, for a fight just two weeks away, was a bigger issue. I was thinking about calling Jimmy Gilio and pulling out of the fight. I knew it was just not right going in to a fight less than half-cocked.

"You need that money bro, you should do it. $500 is more than you make a week, digging for Herold. He's paying only $50 a day."

"Well, OK. Forget the gym then, I'll just have to do what I can and train in the park."

'Money for Nothing' ~ Dire Straits

I scribbled my signature on the fight contract in Jimmy Gilio's small office at the side of the Main Street gym in Los Angeles, only too aware of the huge dramatic black and white photo behind his desk of him years ago as a boxer getting up groggily from the canvas, his eyes blank, his mouth hanging open, the pic he was so proud of. It rang through my head what Jimmy had told me with a smile when I had asked him about the photo before, "We can't all be winners. Professional boxing is a very tough game!"

I was being billed as an overseas South African fighter on the undercard for a WBC eliminator between Rene Arredondo and another Mexican fighter, I think it was Rodolfo 'Gato' González. It was going to be a full house. I knew I was not in shape for the fight ... I could hear my former trainer, Johnny Hogg, advising me in his Scottish accent, "Don't do it, you have to be in shape, son." But I needed the $500.

The contract business over, Jimmy asked, "Have you seen the Grand Olympic Auditorium?"

"No, I haven't. Where is it?" I replied.

"Right there," Jimmy pointed out his office window at an old, square, four storey building, which took up most of a big city block.

"I want to take you across the street into the Olympic Auditorium, so that you don't get overwhelmed when you walk in there next week. This is going to be a sold-out championship show, there will be 10,000 people in the stands."

We walked across the road to the huge, old box like building that took up half a city block. Jimmy Gilio heaved open the main double door of the Grand Olympic Auditorium. We walked inside and paused in the dark entrance, so our eyes could get accustomed to the subdued light. All I could see was an old boxing ring in the middle of the massive, dimly lit auditorium, the walls and floors of which were constructed from chipped, crude concrete. The threadbare boxing ring looked small in the centre of the vast space, surrounded by three tiers of benched seating, old metal seats with scratched paint, packed closely together. In the dim light I couldn't see into the top bleachers, angled steeply into the high, dark corners of the historic building. There were big, flashing lights on each of the two opposing corners of the ring, something I had never seen before.

They probably start flashing when the round starts, I thought.

"Ten thousand people?" I asked.

"Yeah. This is where they filmed the movie, *Rocky*," he said, loudly.

I must have had 'small town' written all over my face. Even though I said nothing Jimmy knew I was impressed.

"It was built for the 1932 Olympics, designed just for boxing. When you fight here this auditorium will be packed, there'll be 10,000 people, all shouting and screaming. Walk around, get the feel of it, check it out. This is an old, historical place and lots of fighters get psyched out when they walk into this place for the first time, especially when it's packed with people. Go on, get into the ring and walk around."

I climbed stiffly into the ring. I hadn't even passed the 'stiff' stage of working out ... and I was fighting next week.

The movie Rocky *was filmed here*, I thought, bouncing up and down, testing the wooden boards under the old canvas. The canvas too, was not like anything I had ever seen before – this canvas was dotted with thousands of black beads of old, dried blood. I tried to imagine the auditorium filled with people. Shit! It sure wasn't like any of the small venues where I had fought in the townships in South Africa. The biggest crowd I had fought in front of, back home, must have been maybe a thousand people, in a black township.

Welcome to LA, buddy!

The promoter's voice echoed in the empty auditorium, his New York accent magnified as he shouted to me, "All the greats in the world have boxed here. You name 'em ... Joe Louis, Henry Armstrong, Rocky Marciano, Ray Robinson, Muhammad Ali, Jerry Quarry ... they all fought here. Quite a place, eh, what you think?"

I was awestruck, so I simply nodded. It looked like a twenty-one-foot ring. Every boxing ring has a feel of its own. The ropes are different in every ring. Some ropes have spring, others have sag. The padding in each ring feels different. Some rings are hard and fast, others are cushy and pull at your feet like sticky mud. This old ring felt cushy and soft. It was a ring made for punchers not movers, small, with a soft canvas. I made a mental note of how it felt under my feet as I twisted and threw a set of combinations. Certainly, the whole place was daunting. How many old fighters had walked up these aisles? Fought in this ring ... won or lost, gone home victorious or battered and broken, maybe never to be the same man again. I looked up into the high, dark seats. The iconic Grand Olympic Auditorium with its 10,000 empty seats looked quite scary in the shadowy light. My imagination evoked some strange creatures, the ghostly spirits of old, brain-damaged, broken fighters, lurking up there in the dark top bleachers! I was glad that Jimmy Gilio had introduced me to the auditorium; it was easy to see how one could be overwhelmed by the architecture and history of the Grand Olympic Auditorium, with a full house of screaming boxing fans.

§

"You fighting at the Olympic, eh? You gonna give me tickets?"

We were paying the rest of the money for the clutch job on the Dodge van and our car mechanic, constantly flexing his tattoo-covered biceps, was more excited than me about the fight.

"Hey! The Olympic is a big place to fight at … you know that's where they filmed the *Rocky* movie? We gotta hang out some time … go to a coupla bars I know, you know …sorta coupla guys hangin' out."

I laughed at the mechanic's enthusiasm and told him that after I had won the fight we would go for a beer. It seemed that everyone knew about the famous Grand Olympic Auditorium, except me. At least he had fixed the van and we now had our transport back, but it was already too late for the gym work I needed to have done. For over a week I had been working out in the hiking trails in the hills, doing some exercises I had learned in Parachute Battalion, shadow boxing and snapping fast punches at hanging leaves, getting more than a few strange looks from passing hikers. Now, with the van fixed, I could get a few nights sparring at the gym and then it would already be time to stop.

There was even going to be a pre-event briefing for the fight, at some local downtown hotel, and Jimmy had said that I must attend. It was fun …being billed as an overseas fighter I even got to talk in front of clicking cameras on Mexican TV. I was unprepared for having to talk, and I had to wing it, standing at the wooden high desk, facing the surprisingly big group of paparazzi. A reporter asked me if I supported the apartheid policy of my country and I fumbled through my response. I had no trainer or manager to support me and I felt isolated, surrounded by mainly Mexicans babbling away at each other in Spanish. Maybe this is how Harold Volbrecht had felt, before his fight with José 'Pipino' Cuevas González, the Mexican KO king.

Back at the plumbing company Herold had a new sewer line installation underway in the Hollywood Hills, and he had to get it finished before the weekend.

"Can you help me, my china? We need to get this main sewer line in. This bitch is really riding me hard. I was supposed to get this finished last week."

Herold had been good to me and I didn't want to let him down.

"I can dig for you on Thursday, Herold, but Friday I have to take off; I have a fight that night."

"*Ja*, but can't you just work maybe half the day, and get off early?"

"Herold, I need all the energy I can get for Friday night. I can't be digging a fucking trench in the morning and go into a fight all fucked up with dirt after digging!" I was getting upset.

"I'm also not digging on Friday; I'm going to be in his corner," said Darryl.

It took some time to get through to him, and even then Herold was none too pleased, but he finally understood the situation.

On Friday morning we went to the weigh-in at the Olympic Auditorium. The place was full of reporters. Apparently, it was going to be a big fight, even though I had never heard of any of the Mexican guys fighting on the headliners. I had seen my opponent – he had a broken nose, seriously pushed over to one side of his face, and he had an inch of height over me. We shook hands and had a few photos taken, the two of us standing next to each other in the ring, in boxing stance. He smiled a lot. I took another chance to have a quick look at the cheap seats, high at the top of the dark bleachers. I was fascinated with them. They were as dark as before, even though quite a few lights were shining in the Auditorium. I wondered what small rodents and rats lived up there.

"He seems like a nice guy," Darryl said, referring to my Mexican opponent as we tucked in to a big steak lunch with the extra, good luck money Herold had given us, just for this occasion. I had been starving myself to make the weight, living on canned tuna fish for the last two weeks.

"Maybe. But he didn't get a broken nose like that from being a nice guy."

"Well, the broken nose could be a good thing."

"How's that?"

"It shows he has been fucked up, badly, before."

"Naw, doesn't work like that in boxing, probably means the opposite."

"So, if you *don't* get your nose broken, it means that you not a good boxer?" Darryl queried, puzzled.

"No. You see, that's where your judgement is wrong in this boxing thing. A broken nose has nothing to do with it, even great boxers have broken noses … everyone gets hit in boxing, win or lose! A broken nose means he has learned many painful lessons and probably won't make those mistakes again in his next fight."

The big steak and the French fries were delicious. I even had a side plate of pasta, as Jimmy Gilio had instructed me, for the carbs. My body seemed to suck in and digest the food right away. Immediately I felt better and stronger than I had during the entire preceding fortnight, eating canned tuna only.

'The Heat is on' ~ Glenn Frey

We left early that night and drove to downtown LA in Darryl's old serial killer van. I went down into the bowels of the Auditorium, into its changing rooms with their rough concrete walls painted institutional light green. I was way too early and tried to sleep in the corner, but I didn't have much luck.

"Hey! Wakey wakey! C'mon let's get you bandaged up."

I had asked the trainer, Frankie Goodman, to be my corner man; I didn't know anyone else in Los Angeles.

He had agreed but had made it clear that he wanted his percent of my small purse in return for his services. I didn't care. I sat backwards on a chair while he wrapped my hands. He wrapped them tighter and firmer than Johnny Hogg had done, using a criss-cross style I had not seen before, but it felt good.

"Looks like a good crowd here tonight, kid. Don't worry about a thing, just go out there and focus on your opponent. Don't let your hands down … like you were doing in sparring. Don't know who this kid is that you fightin'. He has a record of only a couple fights, but that's here in the US. He probably had a lot more in Mexico that no one knows about. The guys at the gym said to tell you good luck."

I was the third fight on the bill, so I didn't have to wait that long. The only fighter sharing the changing room with me was billed before me, in a four rounder. Frankie went out to watch the fight while I paced the dressing room with my boxing gloves on. I threw combinations and tried to focus. My arms still felt stiff from the push-ups I had been doing in the park, but I had my speed and felt strong. I punched at the old broken lockers. Maybe Joe Louis had been in this very dressing room getting ready for a bout. Maybe Ray Robinson had paced up and down right here as I was doing now, punching at these lockers.

Suddenly I felt a familiar shortness of breath and my chest tightened up and I couldn't breathe. It got worse and I felt the need to retch. I spat globs of spit into a trash bucket filled with cut hand wraps and tape. I was bent over the bucket, struggling to get my breath, my eyes streaming.

Fuck! This is all I need now!

I was no stranger to this feeling. I had often before had this strange attack, sometimes during training or running, but never *before* a fight. It usually left me with blocked airways, dry heaves and eyes filled with water, but then it would pass, quickly, and after a few minutes of relaxing and slow deep breathing it vanished, leaving no lasting effects, as if it hadn't happened at all. (It was years later, when I heard Iron Mike Tyson say during an interview that he had suffered from exercise-induced asthma throughout his boxing career, that I realised these were *asthma* attacks. Snap! Thirty years later I finally understood that my bouts of compromised breathing had been the same thing.)

I sat down on the folding chair and breathed slowly and deeply through my nose. It was not the first time I had experienced this breathing spasm sort of thing … on one occasion it had almost got me killed. It had happened during a four-week search and destroy operation in Angola, when our platoon's afternoon hide-out had been compromised …

… by an old grey-haired Angolan local, who walked past us, close-by, assuming a look of disbelief as he spotted us, white men, resting under the trees in his country. We quickly shanghaied him, knowing that he would compromise our position if we let him go. The awkward situation of what to do with the old man fixed itself when, after questioning him on the whereabouts of SWAPO, our enemy, the old man casually announced that there was a SWAPO base not far from our position, and then offered to take us there, because they had been bothering his daughters.

After discussion we kitted up in the mid-afternoon and followed the old man in a V formation (even though the radio was down and we had no comms at the time) as he picked his way north along a small footpath. The footpath quickly grew wider as it joined up with other paths. Soon, with our small formation of Paratroopers now travelling close together, we came to a small town of maybe thirty well looked after and painted brick shanty buildings, and an old dilapidated Portuguese church, with broken orange roof tiles and a tall steeple. The Angolan locals came out of the buildings and gawked at us in disbelief from their shaded verandahs. What were South African troops doing in Angola, …walking through their town?

We were equally surprised, walking cautiously through the small town which, unbeknown to us, had been so close to our hideout. These were Angolan civilians, with whom we had no quarrel. But only ten minutes later, as we left the other side of the small town and crossed into an open chana, *we ran into the hornet's nest of armed soldiers that the old man had spoken about. They opened fire on us the moment they saw us. Immediately it became a running firefight. We were caught without cover in the open clearing and there was heavy fire coming at us from the tree line ahead. We dived down, as flat as possible, and began firing into the trees. Someone shouted, "Up!" and we ran forward in odd numbers then diving to the ground doing buddy buddy fire and movement, drenched in sweat, shouting encouragement to each other and shooting below the tell-tale white gunsmoke, hanging above their hidden positions, and at figures dashing between the trees, then diving down, flat, again. Doogy's LMG opened up and emboldened us, his long bursts kicked up dust and brought down showers of leaves from the trees ahead … dive for cover again, observe, look for a target, there … shoot, heave yourself up and run forward, down again.*

With precision timing two helicopter gunships flew in, like the cavalry in a western, orbiting in tight circles, blasting away with their 20 mm cannons. The insurgents who had been hidden in the tree line, firing, now panicked and bolted, fast as rabbits, in different directions, but quickly stumbled and fell as our bullets found them. Soon our platoon of 25 was among the trees, spread out, barrels burning hot, searching for stragglers still taking pot shots from hidden positions further in the trees. I was at the end of the line, rifle pushed against my shoulder, searching the bush with hard eyes, when I felt a choking sensation coming over me. Suddenly my chest tightened in a body wrenching spasm. Struggling to breathe I was driven to bend over, dry heaving, my rifle pointing to the ground.

"Gungie! Gungie!"

I heard Greef and Johnny Fox shouting my name in tones of unmistakable and imminent danger. In mid retch, my eyes blinded by tears, I tried to force myself upright. Half hunched-over I fired six or seven rapid shots in front of me. They were followed by the crack of bullets very close to my body. Seconds later, my vision blurred by tears and gunsmoke, I saw a SWAPO terrorist lying on his side, half under a bush where he had been trying to hide, not more than twenty feet in front of me, to my right. I had been bent over retching, right in front of him.

He lay on his side, dead, one arm stretched under his head and woolly Afro, the other still clutching his worn and shiny AK-47 to his chest, killed by the instant reactions of Paul Greef and John the Fox.

My comrades had saved me from being shot and killed while having an asthma attack 20 feet in front of a concealed terrorist. What a way to go, killed in mid retch. Not a great outcome!

After some slow, deep breathing in the Olympic locker room the choking sensation subsided, thankfully. I could breathe again. I felt I was ready to go again, right as rain.

What the hell was that about?

I threw another combination at the lockers, and felt none the worse for wear. I needed to hit something. Why wasn't Frankie here, with some hand pads, or something?

I heard the huge crowd shouting, fit to bring the roof down. Must be a hell of a fight going on out there. The full house of Mexicans produced a tidal wave of noise that reverberated down and flooded through the concrete hallways into the dressing room. I tried to detach myself from the excitement and achieved a dead, emotionless feeling inside, like I had in Angola, before a firefight or going into a contact. I hit the wall hard with a combination and gave a loud shout to release my energy.

The fighter before me returned from his fight, walking quickly into the dressing room with blood streaming down his chest. It looked like he had lost the fight but found a broken nose. His trainer made him lie down on the bench, pushed his head back and pinched his nose.

Frankie rushed in grinning. "Good fight, what a crowd. OK. Let's go, we're up next …let's go. You! Darryl! Bring that bucket, sponge, all that stuff right there. OK, let's go, it's a big crowd, kid, let's go."

I was ready. We walked under the round arches into the main walkway. Even though I had been mentally prepared, I could not help but be a little taken back by the mass of humanity – 10,000 people, packed shoulder to shoulder, to the roof, filled the Auditorium. Frankie led the way through the walkway and Mexicans glared and shouted at me as I moved towards the ring. Everyone seemed to be holding a plastic cup of beer and the noise was deafening. I looked straight ahead, focused on the ring, all lit up with bright old ring lights, hanging low. Now, suddenly, with the crowd and the noise, I recognised the boxing ring from the *Rocky* movie!

I rubbed my boots in the resin tray and was just about to get in the ring when Darryl got into a shoving match with a Mexican in the front row. It was becoming quite heavy. Darryl, who was not a fighter, shoved the guy back into his seat. I turned around to see what was going on but Frankie grabbed me and pushed me into the ring. I got up through the ropes and paced a couple of laps around the ring.

Now that I was actually inside the ring my nerves had left me – I was back to my old self, comfortably numb, just wanting to get it on. I tried not looking at the crowd while I paced. My opponent was taking his time. I paced back and forth like a caged lion and finally looked around me. The place was packed to the roof with what seemed to be mainly Mexicans. The bleachers seemed to hang almost over the ring and everyone seemed so close. Once again I looked up, into the top bleachers in the dark, high corners of the Auditorium, and was relieved to see them alive with people, not ghostly figures or the sort of animals appropriate to those high, dark and dusty corners.

Finally, my opponent began his entrance into the auditorium. I heard the familiar roar of approval from the crowd – and then an unfamiliar sound. What the hell was going on? I turned to see him making his way towards the ring, wearing a full Indian headdress of yellow feathers, with a tail that fell to the back of his knees. He was followed by an entourage of at least ten drummers, prancing and beating upright Mexican drums. Perhaps they were Aztec drums? The crowd went wild, cheering and whistling as he waved and headed towards us. Frankie laughed and shook his head. The fighter sure looked impressive, didn't look like the 'palooka' that Jimmy the promoter had told me he was. He got into the ring, performed a short war dance, then ran around in a circle. His entourage stood outside the ring, beating their drums for a few more minutes before disappearing. I watched him as he pumped up the crowd. His shoulders looked broader … he looked taller than he had at the weigh-in.

The ring was small; a 21 ft puncher's ring, with no place to run. I decided then and there that I was not going to fuck around – I was going to jump him early.

"I'm going to do it just like Charlie Weir … knock him out fast and we all go home," I thought to myself.

It's just the way it was going to have to be. I knew I was not in good shape for the fight. I had been training for only three weeks and even that had been in poor training conditions – running down Hollywood Boulevard gulping down gas fumes. A young, soon to be famous, Jimmy Lennon Junior introduced me as having arrived in LA by way of the Republic of South Africa. I raised and pumped my hand in the air – and was completely taken by surprise when the enormous crowd made known its anti-South African feeling, right away, booing and jeering in unison. It sounded like the roof was going to come down. I felt the sting of my country's sins and its well-known apartheid policy in no uncertain terms. The 10,000-strong crowd booed relentlessly for a minute straight.

Shit, I didn't do anything, why they booing me?!

Strangely it felt similar to the first time I had been shot at, when that bullet cracked past my ear and I realised I was in someone's rifle sights and they were actually trying to kill me. For only a microsecond, my ridiculous response had been: *Why are they trying to kill me? I'm a good guy?*

I had never been booed so badly before, even at my fights in black townships in South Africa. These American boxing fans, mostly Latinos really put their hearts into it; they let me know that they *really* did not like me or my home country, South Africa. But I forgave them because they didn't know the truth, they knew only what they saw on television.

I shook hands with my opponent, now without his headdress, in the middle of the ring and he smiled at me from behind the broken lump that once had been his nose.

I walked back to the corner and managed a stiff wink at Darryl. A loud buzzer went off, sounding like the buzzer for jumping out of a C-130, and big red lights flashed from the corner posts, signalling the beginning of the first round.

What the fuck! Flashing lights on the corner posts?

I came out of my corner, moved to my left and circled around, my hands held high, my left foot firmly on the canvas, pointing toward my target. He stood back and watched me. I feinted a few straight left hands and moved my head as he feinted a few back. I started to move my head from side to side as I tried to find my rhythm, waiting for an opening. He hid behind his gloves and wouldn't give me one.

The hell with you, let's do this thing!

I turned the switch and jumped forward with a fast double-handed attack that flew in through his defence. My signature attack. I tagged him flush and I could feel straight away that I had hurt him with my first few punches. He backed off, surprised by my quick, hard attack, but I stayed on him and backed him into the ropes. He tried to fight back but my attack was in full swing and all he could do was try and cover up. The ref broke us apart. As the ref dropped his hand, telling us to box, I immediately jumped in again with the same fast and hard combinations. The crowd went wild. I had him against the ropes again, got through with a few solid punches and one good right hand to his head. I could see his legs buckle and knew I had hurt him again; He held his hands up but didn't go down. He held me and caught me with a weak uppercut. I pushed back into the centre of the ring and drew him out from the ropes. As soon as I could I jumped into another hard attack that put him back into the ropes.

Anytime now ... one more solid right hand is all I need and you down. C'mon. Go down. Yes!! Got you again!

I shouted to myself as I felt my punches land: *Keep going ... breathe!*

He tagged me with a short right hand. No big deal. I covered up, not really hurt, as he tried to follow up, but I bobbed and weaved my way out against the ropes. I caught a flash of Darryl's face, ringside, as I spun around and pushed my attacker into the corner. Darryl had a fiery look in his eyes and was shouting at me. But I couldn't hear him above the 10,000 Mexicans roaring for me to drop where I stood, like a sack of beans.

After an all-action first round I walked to my corner sucking hard for breath. My legs felt like jelly. I sat down and listened to the crowd. They were obviously enjoying the all action, nonstop round; the crowd at the famous Grand Olympic Auditorium was roaring its approval.

"Try set him up with the right hand, take your time and try to set him up," Frankie advised me. But my ears were closed to Frankie's advice and my eyes were ablaze. I knew there was only one way to do this, and it would be over soon, one way or the other. Him or me. I drew in deep draughts of air as the ring girl ducked through the ropes. The huge Mexican crowd was deafening.

Why the fuck are they shouting so much?

I stood up on shaky legs, moved to my right, my left foot firmly on the canvas in front of me, my left knee and foot pointed toward my opponent, just like Bokkie Buys had taught me. I waited this time, watching him. He seemed wary and there was blood oozing from his nostril. We moved around the ring, watching each other, our hands up. I moved my head from side to side and found a broken rhythm.

Watch him, watch him ... now! No, no ... wait. Now! Boom Boom! Gotcha! OK one more, one more. Now ... too slow. OK, don't worry ... now! Now move, move, move your head, move your head, move your head.

His flurry of punches missed as I bobbed and weaved.

Get your legs working ... work legs. OK. Relax ...relax, breathe! Don't show him you're tired, don't show it! Hands up! Keep your hands up! Breathe and relax. Good shot! Got you!

Silently I shouted at myself as I traded hard blows with my tough opponent.

He flicked out a left that was a split second too slow. It was all I was waiting for. I sprung forward again with a furious attack and got through his gloves just like I had in the first round. Yet again I felt him buckle as my right hand found its mark and he sagged into the ropes. I backed off, trying to lure him out from his defensive shell. We watched each other through puffed eyes. I jumped in again but this time he was able to manoeuvre out of my attack, moving to the side. He was finding my rhythm and starting to time me.

He came forward with an attack and every one of those 10,000 Mexicans roared their encouragement. I covered up and now he was pushing me into the ropes. He wasn't hurting me, so I let him attack, keeping my hands high as I tried to suck in air. I was having to dig very deep for energy. My gas tank was running very low. But I had always been blessed with the ability to recover quickly and soon I was pressing my attack on him again. I knew I had hurt him with a few, good, hard punches – I needed just one more *koek* shot (take the cake punch) to close out.

One more ... I need to land just one more solid right hand, buddy, and you down ... just one more!

I was able to get an attack but couldn't get the solid right that I needed. In the third round I noticed a calmer look in his eyes, as he watched me from behind his gloves. He seemed to be holding something back. Something was up. Is he tired? Is he hurt?

I interpreted his look as having been hurt from my right hand and decided now was the time to use my small reserve of energy for an attack. With a grunt I stepped forward, punching him back into the ropes again ... with satisfaction I saw him wince as I tagged him again. As he backed off I came forward and saw him drop his left hand low to his chest.

OK mother fucker, I got you!

I saw an opening and jumped in with a left right attack, only to realise too late that his low left hand had tricked me into an ambush. It was a fake.

As I came in low he dropped his head and threw a solid right hand punch that caught me like a hammer under my eye. It was a 'blind man right hand', thrown straight, with all his strength, the kind you can even close your eyes and give it your all. The same kind of punch that would floor Mannie Pacquiao many years into the future. My head exploded into sudden blackness with flashes of white and gold bright explosions. Instantly I smelt the familiar tang of blood and iron that always comes from a hard head punch and found myself on the seat of my pants.

Milliseconds later I had scanned myself, done my damage control, found that I was good and could carry on. I turned, to try to get up, but stopped on all fours, blinking and looking around at the crowd. Everyone was double, everyone was blurred. They were jumping up and down, frantically, but no sound was coming out of their mouths. What the fuck! The frantic roar from the Mexican crowd sounded mute and far away. Perhaps they were in another building?

I stared across the ring which looked to be tilted at an angle; it had too many ropes. I had a blurry view of the other fighter, in the neutral corner, looking like a monster with three heads all moving at the same time. Behind him I saw the big red buzzer, and the flashing lights on the corner posts.

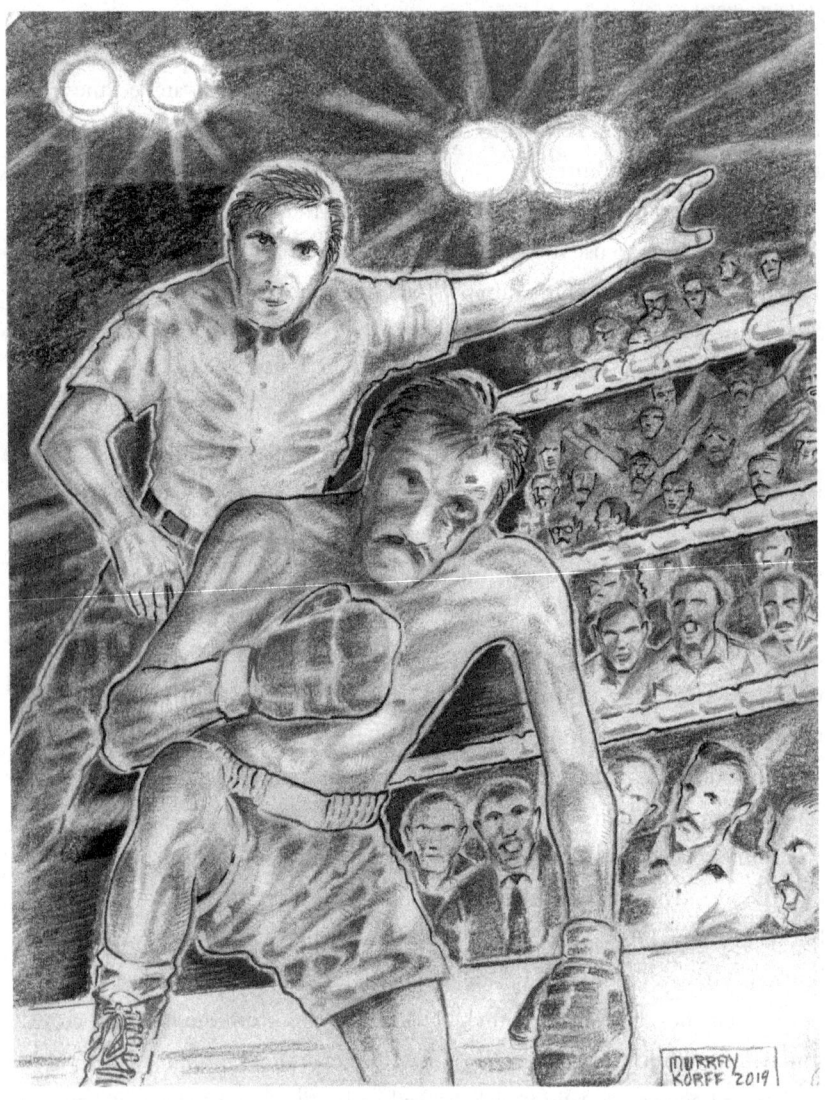

Fighting overseas in the height of the anti apartheid era the crowd bayed for my blood.

What are those fucking things anyway; flashing red lights with a buzzer on a fucking ring post? Who's ever heard of that?

The ref was counting. I got up, halfway, but was still on one knee. I looked down, took a deep breath and saw a big glob of blood and snot drop onto the canvas. Everything was happening in slow motion, far away, but then suddenly my ears popped and opened up to the roar of the huge crowd, delighted to see me down and bleeding.

"I'm OK. I'm OK," I thought ... and took a deep breath. As any fighter will know, there are very few times you can feel as alone as when you are in a boxing ring, hurt, tired, almost unable to continue – and the crowd is against you, baying for you to get fucked up, hurt and knocked out. A strange feeling. Maybe even worse than being shot at?

The shouting of those 10,000 people was deafening. I stood up, looking at the ref's fingers. This is what it must have been like for Kallie Knoetze standing up with Big John Tate. I was a second too late and the ref signalled with waving arms that it was all over. I turned and stumbled back to my corner.

"What the hell ... I'm OK ... I can carry on."

But it was over. With a final signal from the ref the Olympic Auditorium crowd surged to its feet, roaring its approval of the short, brutal fight. The tone had changed from menacing to satisfied – they'd had their money's worth.

Frankie Goodman smiled from ear to ear as he towelled my face. A first. I had never seen him smile before.

"Don't you worry, it was a great fight, kid. You fought great. Listen to that crowd."

I took a few big gulps of water and let Frankie clean me up some more. I was a little more of my usual self and walked on wobbly legs to the centre of the ring as the ref raised his arm. The crowd ate it up. I smiled and shook my opponent's hand in the middle of the ring. He smiled back, with puffed eyes and a bleeding nose. He was wearing his huge yellow-feathered full headdress at an angle on his head. His troupe of supporters had climbed up into the ring and were beating their drums.

My worthy opponent, Mauro 'Indio' Veronica from Mexico, looked at the announcer, grabbed the microphone, shook his head from side to side, and in broken English, through puffed-up lips and a big, crooked smile, he said: "You can hit *veerrry* hard my friend, *veerry* hard!"

I smiled, thanked him for the fight and wished him good luck. (His next fight would be a KO loss against the legendary 'Terrible' Terry Norris, in which he had Norris bent over in trouble just before the legend landed one of his lightning right hands.)

I climbed out through the ropes on unsteady legs and walked up the long aisle as the massive crowd continued whistling and cheering. Just before leaving the crowded, seated area a Mexican spectator jumped up from his seat, right in front of me, holding his hands in front of him as if holding a set of bull's balls.

"You have *beeeiiig* balls *amigo*! *Beeeiiig* balls!"

I smiled at him from behind my puffed-up eyelids. This Mexican boxing fan never ever knew it, but his enthusiastic gesture of approval about the good, all-action fight meant a lot to me. For a long time after that bout it was a small comfort that made me feel a whole lot better about having lost.

Mexican fans love a good fight.

1 Parachute Battalion's legendary RSM Sakkie Marais in full swing.

1981 Cross border 'Operation Protea' leadership group. Legendary Parachute Bn. RSM Sakkie Marais standing centre. Deadly Delta Company CO Capt. Leipoldt kneeling front.

Anthony Stander aka Stan as he is today preaching the gospel.

Boxing as an amateur in Cape Town.

'Deadly' Delta Company 1980 to '81 1 Parachute Battalion.

Honoured, years later, to march with my father Sgnt. Maj. Nic Korff, Witwatersrand Rifles.

My beautiful mother Alice showing off her new Sgt. stripes.

My Lovely sister at 15 years old on Cosmopolitan cover that launched her international modelling career at an early age.

Alpha Company on solemn parade honouring twelve of their own KIA when their helicopter was shot out of the sky while flying low level during operations in Angola. Salute A Company.

Small contingent of '81 Delta and Hotel Company troops meeting after 2 decades.

Weigh-in prior to boxing at the Grand Olympic Auditorium, Los Angeles.

My wonderful daughter Natalie, Los Angeles.

The authors book 19 with a Bullet *displayed in museum on the bush war at 44 Parachute Brigade.*

The author in later years at 44 Parachute Brigade museum on the bush war (formally 1 Parachute Bn.) His book 19 with a Bullet *of his time as a paratrooper displayed amongst captured Soviet equipment.*

Chapter Thirteen

PAIN, NOW NOT WASTED

'Shout' ~ *Tears for Fears*

I was devastated that I had lost the fight, despite having known there was a good chance I might lose. I had not been in top shape and had taken the fight too fast. But I had hoped, nevertheless, that I could count on catching him with a good right-hand punch and save the day. It had almost paid off because I had had him hurt but carelessly walked into his trick. I had always believed my right hand could get me out of a pinch when necessary. No such luck.

The next day I felt like hell. I got up late and moved around slowly as I made a cup of tea. I felt nauseous and I ached all over. I had a big blue eye and a severe headache that went all the way down my spine. The back of my neck was stiff as a board and every inch of my body hurt, as if someone had worked me over in microscopic detail, using a small hammer. My back was marked red and blue from the ropes and my thighs were so stiff that I had a hard time walking. Holy Moly! Even my lungs hurt! Amazing how fucked up you can get in just a few hard rounds of real fighting.

A couple of days later, after a few good meals, I was moving more easily and we drove out to the gym in Van Nuys. Frankie Goodman chuckled when I told him that I felt so bad about losing the fight.

"Boy! You don't like to box much do you? And you know how to turn a boxing match into a fight really fast, eh? Don't worry son, don't feel bad about it, its life in the big city! I don't know what it's like in your country, but boxing is a damn tough game here in America. You did great; you went in and gave 'em a hell of a fight. The crowd didn't shout like that even for the main event – and that was Rodolfo 'El Gato' González, the Mexican all-time hero! Your fight was the best of the night, no doubt. All action. Don't worry about a thing, you hold your head up. Go back home to your country and you tell 'em that you won the fight, and that's all there is to it."

I thanked Frankie Goodman for his help and encouragement, gave him his share of my small purse and we parted ways. We drove back to Hollywood with me deep in thought. Boxing is the only sport in the world that produces such utter desolation, such emptiness, in the fighter who loses the contest. It's not a tennis match in which you failed to hit the ball, or a cycle race in which you failed to ride your bicycle as fast as the other guy. Boxing is *mano a mano* ... and the loser fails to beat the other man in the fight – he beats *you* in the fight! You are knocked out, unconscious on the floor! I felt an uncomfortable squirming deep in the pit of my stomach. I wondered how 'champion' boxers felt after losing a big championship bout. Without a doubt these American fighters were better boxers than the fighters I had faced in South Africa; they were more relaxed *and* more skilled. But – I comforted myself – it was all a good learning experience that would help me when I went back to fight in South Africa and get that middleweight title.

Darryl was aware of my brooding but was cheerful, even philosophical, about the whole thing.

"Look bru, you did good. Who else from South Africa has fought at the Grand Olympic Auditorium hey? You probably the only one. So what you lost? You heard all those Mexicans. Fuck! I never knew they hated South Africans that much. But afterwards ... they loved the fight afterwards."

"You think they were booing because we were from South Africa?"

"Absolutely! They all went ape shit when they announced you being from South Africa."

'What the hell do they know about South Africa anyway?"

"See it on the news bru, even in Spanish. We're racists, the world hates us bru."

"I didn't realise it was *that* much."

"Yep. And all the TV news shows are negative. They don't show what a great country it is, they don't say anything about the bombs planted by the ANC, nothing about blowing up innocent people."

Darryl was on a rant; he was genuinely upset about the skewed view of our home country. He jammed his sunglasses hard onto his nose and speeded up, driving the old '69 Dodge aggressively through the traffic.

"Hey! Slow down bro!"

"The other thing is that none of these Yanks, not one, has heard about the 40,000 Cuban troops on our border. Or what's going on up on our border. They think that communism is a joke … Russia is on our doorstep and we must have free and fair elections? Fuck them is what I say."

"No one knows?"

"No one knows about South Africa's Border War, only thing anyone knows about here is about America."

I thought back to Matt the Marine, who had said he'd known nothing about South Africa, except about apartheid, before being stationed there as a guard at the US Embassy, in Cape Town. It was clear, now, that he had not been exaggerating.

"Americans don't even know where our country is bro, never mind the 40,000 Cuban troops on our border," I said quietly.

Darryl calmed down, concentrating as he changed lanes on the busy freeway and turned off into Hollywood. I still had a headache and didn't want to talk about South Africa anymore, or about boxing. But I was beginning to feel a little better after the pep talk from Frankie Goodman about life in the big city. Get over it, he had said, and move on … you got to be able to take an ass beating as good as you can give one, especially in this town. Frankie had been around the Los Angeles fight game for years and knew it was no easy business.

"I don't really understand all that communist shit they fed us," I mumbled, coming back to reality.

Having come from South Africa only recently, I was still taken aback by the negative response when people found out that Darryl and I came from South Africa. Americans loved our accent and conversation would be going well, big smiles all round … until they asked, "What part of Australia are you from?"

"I'm not from Australia, I'm from South Africa."

Then there was a pause while the penny dropped. Hmm … South Africa, apartheid, Steve Biko, free Mandela. Eyes widened and darted from side to side, facial expressions changed, smiles vanished. Recently, at the Auditorium, Darryl and I had felt the loathing directed at our country when 10,000 boxing fans had booed us, unmercifully, just for being South African. It had been a real eye opener for me ... and it wasn't helping to ease the depression that had set in after losing the fight.

§

"Oh! What happened to your eye?" asked Zan, the pretty blonde upstairs neighbour with the perpetual smile, bumping into us at the cage elevator in the hallway.

"Oh, you a boxer? Really? I didn't know that. You know, my roommate's father is a boxer. Jake LaMotta, have you ever heard of him?"

"You mean Jake LaMotta – The Raging Bull?"

"I don't know much about boxing, but I think he's quite famous," said Zan, doubtfully.

Jake LaMotta was a legend, definitely famous – mostly for having been the first boxer to defeat Sugar Ray Robinson, in 1943. So famous that they'd made a movie about him, with Robert de Niro in the starring role. I was impressed, and curious about his daughter, our upstairs neighbour.

The next day, a rainy, cold afternoon, Zan called and we met her in the hallway, together with her attractive roommate, Stephanie LaMotta, who gave my battered face a thorough, matter of fact inspection.

"Hmm. You lost the fight, eh? It sure looks like it."

She was from New York, Italian, and didn't pull her punches.

"You should see the other guy," I laughed.

"Yeah, right," she smiled.

It was great meeting and getting to know Stephanie LaMotta; her tough New York humour helped me forget about having lost the fight.

"Oh, don't worry about it, you'll win the next one. That's boxing. Can't win them all."

Stephanie and I soon became an item, grooving around Hollywood in her little VW bug. She was a pistol but also an old-fashioned girl who was not into any casual hanky-panky. But she knew her way into the back doors of several high society haunts in Hollywood and seemed to have an endless group of girlfriends, always dropping in to say "Hi!" with big American smiles and perfect teeth. The fact that she was living upstairs was pretty convenient. At the drop of a hat we would stuff ourselves into her VW and cruise the streets of Hollywood. She took us to a variety of restaurants, bars and hideaways where she was greeted enthusiastically by patrons and owners alike, hugs and kisses all round. Hollywood was like a giant Hillbrow and Stephanie seemed to know everyone there was to be known in the town.

On one occasion we dashed through a cloudburst and tumbled into Gio's Italian Restaurant on Sunset Boulevard, where we ran into Evel Knievel, the famous motorcycle daredevil, sitting at the bar tucking into a steaming plate of pasta. He looked up from his plate, nodded at Stephanie and asked how things were going with her. He had bright blue eyes and an unwavering stare.

"How's your father doing?" he asked.

"Dad's doing fine. Hey Evel, this is my friend Granger. He's a boxer, from South Africa."

Evel Knievel levelled his bright blue eyes at me and gave me a serious stare down. He looked a little older, but you could tell he was still a no-nonsense guy. I smiled and said I was pleased to meet him. Hell, now who hadn't heard of Evel Knievel? I remembered him saying, about jumping the Snake River Canyon, that he was going to "… spit at the canyon wall face-to-face if the parachutes don't open". Evel lived in a big RV bus which was parked in the parking lot. He spent his time touring around the country, making his living from public appearances and talks. He looked like a normal sort of guy, but for that insanely intense stare. Well, I guess the eyes are the windows of the soul.

It was a wet night out so we settled down at the bar at Gio's and, on Stefanie's recommendation, I had my first ever, but definitely not my last, Long Island Iced Tea. It was one hell of a drink – a mixture of vodka, tequila, light rum, triple sec, gin, with a dash of cola. The cola turned the concoction the colour of tea, hence its name. You went temporarily deaf if you sipped it fast, through a straw … it was like sipping liquid heroin, you could feel the fire run through your veins. Right away it became my drink of choice. While I was trying to digest the complex, sour taste of Long Island Iced Tea, Stephanie told me how Evel had once taken a baseball bat to the knees of a guy who had crossed him. She spoke loudly, smiling, and then in a loud stage whisper she told me that Evel Knievel wasn't a guy you wanted to fuck around with, ever.

Evel seemed absorbed in his pasta dinner and ignored her, but the regulars laughed. They all seemed to know each other.

Stephanie LaMotta was a real character. She was good looking and tough, spoke with a typical New York accent and her eyes narrowed to slits whenever she laughed. She had thick brunette hair which reached halfway down her back and framed her face with its big brown eyes and customary, quirky 'don't give me any bullshit' expression. She was able to bring a buzz to any room at any time; and had the knack of making everything she said sound very important and very urgent.

"I knocked out a mugger in New York."

"Why? What did he ever do to you?"

"What do you mean, "what did he do to me", he tried to rob me, you goon!" looking at me as though I had sprouted another head.

I was learning that my dry South Africa humour did not go down well in the US. She described, loudly enough for the entire bar to hear, how she had been followed by two muggers in New York. At a street corner one of them had shoved her and tried to snatch her bag. She had let fly with a left hook, just as you would have expected the daughter of the Raging Bull to do. It landed flush and the mugger had dropped, lights out, on the sidewalk. Some weeks later she showed me a newspaper clipping about this event. In the photo her fist was held high and the headlines read: "LaMotta knocks mugger cold". I was impressed.

We said good night to Evel Knievel and left Gio's, heading home through the rain with Stephanie driving – I was blitzed on the strong Long Island Iced Tea.

§

It was unusually cold and wet for this time of the year in Los Angeles and several of the busy city streets flooded in the busy intersections. I was starting to get into the vibe of Tinseltown. Hollywood was riddled with old buildings in the Art Deco style, which had been all the rage during the golden age of Hollywood. Its famous boulevards – Sunset, Hollywood and Santa Monica – travelled for 30 miles to the west, from downtown LA to the Pacific

Ocean. I still had no car and it seemed I was always wet, walking around town, exploring, catching a hamburger on the star engraved sidewalks of Hollywood Boulevard. Darryl pointed out the famous cylindrical Capitol Records Tower on Vine Street, and Mann's Chinese Theatre, with its concrete blocks bearing the signatures, footprints and handprints of many of Hollywood's most famous stars. Funnily enough, I had only ever seen photos of these buildings in the 'Dennis the Menace goes to Hollywood' comic, when I had been a young boy in Benoni.

Even though the feel of the city was intoxicating, and I was fired up with potential new prospects, I found a block and that my thoughts of South Africa and my action-packed time in Parachute Battalion were always nearby, just a heartbeat away.

At night, the Hollywood freaks came out.

I woke to the hammering of the blades of an LAPD helicopter close above our building, its bright searchlights penetrating into our small apartment like a 20 mm cannon, illuminating the space as bright as an explosion for a second. The chopper turned and hovered over the small bushy park next to our building, its blades making a familiar noise – *whap whap whap.*

If there had been terrorists in that park they would have been cut down by the helicopter by now.

That was my first thought on waking, wide-eyed.

My roommates seemed to be used to the disturbance and continued sleeping. I lay awake, memories of incursions deep inside Angola churning through my mind as I lay in my bed, listening to the sound of the chopper angrily circling, low, directly above our building again.

Whap whap whap.

The two SAAF helicopter gunships circle in a tight orbit just above us, not much higher than the tree tops. Our five Buffel troop carriers crash into the dusty thicket in Ovamboland, being targeted by the gunships. Boom Boom Boom. Always three bursts at a time.

We're all standing up now, braced inside the Buffel, our rifles pushed tight into our shoulders, our hard eyes searching the bush surrounding us. This is it! The gunships circle, come around over us, blasting their 20 mm explosive head cannons into the bush

not forty metres from us. The small thicket of bushes and trees is quickly enveloped in a foggy shroud of dust and smoke.
BOOM BOOM BOOM!!
"Where the fuck are they? I can't see them!"
"Drive in! Drive in!" Our lieutenant shouts to the driver and the big South African-made troop carrier creeps forward, deeper into the bush, pushing over and breaking thin trees as it moves. Dust, leaves and smoke. I stand, glaring into the bush, looking for targets. This is my first action.
"There! There!" shouts John Delaney, bending his head into his sights. He begins shooting into the bushes. I still can't see a damn thing. John shouts as he shoots into the bushes. Suddenly a small form in a dirty brown uniform comes struggling and pushing through the thorn bush, oblivious to our Buffel as he tries to escape the hellish destruction from the 20 mm gunship cannon behind him. He's the first live SWAPO terrorist I have ever seen. Finally, SWAPO!
My rifle kicks in my shoulder as we all open fire and the terrorist dies in a bush, in a hail of South African bullets. My shoulder aches as I look through the bush for more terrorists. Gunsmoke hangs over our open troop carrier. The noisy helicopter gunships are still spinning in a tight circle above us, their turbines screaming and blades hammering, but they have stopped firing their cannons. There is shooting from the Buffels on the other side of the thicket and we hear the buzz and crack of their rounds coming past us from the other side.
"Watch out! Watch out!"
The shooting escalates on the other side of the thicket then slowly dies down as the killing stops.
"Cease fire! Cease fire!"
Quickly everyone disembarks from the Buffel and lines up to scout the area, relieved that the contact is over. One of the helicopter gunships lands in a clearing and the crew joins us, to inspect their handiwork. We search the thicket and drag out four bodies, putting them together in a clearing. Then we light our cigarettes. These terrorists look no older than fifteen or sixteen … but they're wearing SWAPO uniforms/
The SADF rules of engagement say that we have to bring dead terrorists back to base, for finger printing and recording. We hoist the bodies up onto the bumpers and storage bins of the Buffels, using rope to tie them down. The brain falls out of the shattered skull of one of the sixteen-year-olds, as we drag him to the troop carrier. Their faces

are already covered in dust and blood-clotted sand. I wonder at their terror in their last moments when they knew that they were surrounded, at the end. They were only teenagers, yet they were dressed to kill in the enemy's communist uniform. A uniform that represented terror, landmines that killed civilians, rape, the abduction of children to be trained as soldiers ... as no doubt had happened to these dead teenagers themselves.

We drive off. I feel sad as I look back at the scene, watching the fierce African sun sink down behind the thorn trees. I wonder if their mothers will ever find out what has happened to their young sons. The only evidence of the killing that has taken place today, here in the dry African bush, is the mostly intact brain of one of the young freedom fighters, lying in the sand among the tyre tracks and boot prints. By morning the yipping jackals and hyenas will have taken care of that too. Then there will be nothing but tyre tracks, boot prints and some paw prints in the sand.

The noise made by the blades of the LAPD helicopter increased and then started to fade as the chopper broke away, heading east towards Downtown LA. Just like our South African gunships they couldn't stay in the air for long. Sirens wailed, coming up Hollywood Boulevard.

I lay on the small fold-out stretcher and listened to my roommates snoring, deeply asleep.

Here I was, trying to fit into a new culture while a battle still raged inside me. I felt as though I was carrying a dead man over my shoulder. I did not fall asleep again.

Chapter Fourteen

IF I STUMBLE AND FALL

'One More Night' ~ Phil Collins

My friend Thomson – he's a producer – says he wants to see your movie," Darryl announced.

So we walked the short distance to Thomson's pad and slipped the VHS tape of *Self Defence for Housewives*, produced and directed by Murray, Marlon and me in South Africa, into his cassette player for Thomson to watch.

Thomson sat there, fully engrossed, viewing the forty-three-minute self-defence video while eating his dinner and talking on the phone all at the same time. I was beginning to realise that these particular activities constituted a set of multi-tasking skills common to most of the Americans I had met so far.

It turned out that Thomson wasn't too impressed with our movie.

"Yeah, you dudes are kind of stiff in this movie, I mean we can market it as some sort of South African martial art form, you know, it could be like a special thing that you guys do over there, you know … Do you have any other stuff? I'm looking for any kind of weird and bizarre behaviour and strange stuff from other countries."

I told him that I didn't have any other "weird or bizarre" South African stuff on me, but that I could certainly send some drum messages and smoke signals back to the homeland, to see if I could get hold of some.

Thomson said he would show some people the self-defence video and see what he could do, but I would have to get signed authority from the copyright holder. That wouldn't be a problem; I could easily contact Tommy in Bedfordview. I was sure he would be glad to hear from me. In the meantime, it seemed that Thomson had taken a liking to me. He said he might have a part time job for me, as a driver for a small printing business in which he had an interest. The business designed and printed HBO advertising – door hangers and flyers – and they needed a reliable driver; the old guy they had using before had gone MIA while doing deliveries. I was quite excited about the new job. I didn't mind digging trenches for Herold but it would be great to get something easier.

It was getting close to Christmas, my first Christmas in a cold climate. The high Saint Gabriel Mountains behind Downtown Los Angeles were covered in snow and the wind that blew from them into the city was icy and wet. California has its rainy season in the winter, like Cape Town, so the cold, pouring rain had the makings of a very cold, wet Christmas.

"This is the way Christmas is meant to be," Darryl informed me, "it's supposed to be cold and snowy, just the way it looks on Christmas cards. Back in South Africa we have to produce fake snow, cotton wool usually, for the tree and the mantlepiece, because our Christmas is in the summer. And we think that's normal, how weird is that? Why not just have Christmas cards that show Santa in summer gear?"

He had a point, I'd never thought of that before.

Bright and cheerful coloured lights twinkled on the balconies in Hollywood and from the front of houses and stores in the suburbs. I had brought with me only a few light clothes from South Africa and with limited funds I had to beg, borrow and steal a few woollies and a jacket. I had originally planned to return to South Africa in early January, after three months in the US, but more and more it seemed I would not be keeping my appointment with the SAA Jumbo Jet. I was just starting to have a good time and didn't feel like going home just yet. My tourist visa was good for six months so I casually decided I would stay a bit longer, and probably head home round about March.

I had spoken to my family only a few times since I had arrived. Darryl, being the *ou man* (veteran) of living in America, was in charge of the phone bill. All I knew was that it was *"very* expensive" to call South Africa, so any call I made was late at night, brief and loud. In between I wrote a few hasty letters home. No internet, cell phones or computers in 1986.

My new job as a driver and deliveryman for Thomson's printing business was starting to keep me busy. I was using my own newly bought car for which I had paid $400 and was amazed that I could put in just $10 of gas for a whole day, plus I could actually read the numbers on the gas pump. In South Africa the numbers on the fuel pumps flew by in a blur. But it was definitely no joke driving on the inter-connected busy freeway system in Downtown Los Angeles, in a small underpowered vehicle, especially when you had no clue about how to find your way around the enormous city. I would begin the nerve-racking day by entering the freeway via an entrance ramp that dumped my little under-powered junker of a car straight into the fast lane on a mile-and-a-half of uphill, in morning rush hour traffic, with a solid white line, so I couldn't move out of the way of the pack of fast cars coming up behind me, wanting to accelerate, impatient to get to work. Middle fingers and honking horns were my usual start to the day.

"Fuck you too! Give me a break man, I'm a tourist!"

The Interstate 5 (the I-5, or the Santa Ana Freeway to people in LA) is a well-worn highway, busy 24/7, often congested. It serves as the main thoroughfare for 18 wheelers, concrete trucks, delivery trucks, you name it. It had been built in the mid-50s and its old, brown concrete overpasses and bridges, underpasses and walls, were bounded by the grubby no man's land on either side, covered with thick bush in which you could hide a body for weeks, if needed. The walls were covered in graffiti – the word *chaka* was sprayed, graffiti-style, on every other pillar in bold black paint all the way across Los Angeles. The fences were masked by papers and plastic bags blown by the wind, high tension wires ran zig zag over head above the wide, man-made concrete river that snaked through the city of LA. It felt like taking your life in your hands, weaving in and out among the semi-trailers and speeding cars in my old underpowered car, hoping to catch the right exit ramp.

I quickly learned a few lessons about how efficiently traffic enforcement was managed in big American cities. Traffic police in the US were definitely a far cry from the slow moving, dreaming-of-my-holiday-in-Durban traffic cops I was accustomed to in Benoni. This was a different scene all together. Life in the big city, baby. If you think you can pop in for three minutes to buy a Coke, without feeding the parking meter, or run in and drop off a quick pile of door hangers while in a no parking zone, or, worse, a blue handicapped zone – think again. Those big traffic control mamas, with asses the size of your chest, clad in tight khaki pants secured with a leather belt, would slap a $120 parking violation ticket on your windshield before you could sing 'Shosholoza'. It seemed they had defined routes which they circled, over and over. I had an officer on a motorbike almost shaking with rage when I casually left my car parked in a blue 'handicapped parking only' zone, to drop off some flyers. When I returned he was writing out a $350 ticket, almost pushing his pen through his ticket pad, he was writing with such conviction. I asked him what the problem was and explained that I had been dropping off a few items, for only a minute. No response. I mentioned that I had recently arrived from South Africa and had never before seen a handicapped parking zone. No response. I told we didn't have such things where I came from ... handicapped people in South Africa all had to find their parking spaces and make do, just like everyone else. This seemed to make him even more angry.

"OK, I'm sorry, I didn't know," I said, realising I would have to treat this embarrassing incident as yet another American learning experience.

I had been going to try to make light of it, crack a joke, but I had already realised that the casual South African joking vibe didn't hold much water in LA. I also didn't know that handicapped parking zones were such hallowed ground for traffic cops *and* other motorists – as they should be, I came to realise. Now I knew and it made sense. We didn't yet have handicapped parking where I came from, and actually I had no idea how handicapped South Africans coped. Hmmm, I would have to think about that one ... why didn't we have special parking for handicapped people in South Africa? (Parking bays reserved for handicapped people have since become standard practice in South Africa, although, I'm told, these special bays are not really treated as hallowed ground, by traffic cops or other motorists.)

I tossed his ticket into the glove compartment with all the others. At $350 it was the most expensive ticket I had been given, at that point. I was not too concerned about the growing pile of infringement notices in the glove box – after all, I was leaving to go back to South Africa in a few months.

Darryl shook his head and laughed at me when I told him about the cop's reaction to me parking in the handicap zone.

"You a *roofie* (rookie) here bro ... you still going to learn lots of things."

§

Darryl was buzzing with excitement, desperate to give me the news.

"I'm telling you bru, you are going to *love* skiing – it's the *most fun* thing you'll *ever* do."

"What's it like, is it difficult?"

"Naw, you just stand up, point your skis downhill, and go. I've done it once and I had a gas."

Darryl was over the moon. One of our roommates, Reg, had hooked up with an older girl who had a condo in Lake Tahoe, which was about or seven or eight hours north from LA. Tahoe was supposedly a beautiful area, high in the Sierra Nevada mountains, with a beautiful lake for summer fun, and a well-known ski resort for winter entertainment. In the Lake Tahoe area, the mountain peaks range from 5,000 feet to more than 9,000 feet. Darryl and I planned to drive up in my small underpowered car and meet them on the slopes. We had been warned about the freezing temperatures on the ski slopes but, as usual, money (or the lack of it) was an issue, so we bought some cheap gloves on Hollywood Boulevard, like the knitted ones we had worn at school, and some extra woollies. We packed our gear and hit the highway. This was going to be an exciting adventure *and* it was going to be great to get out of the city and see something of America, finally.

The only radio station that came in clearly all the way was a religious radio station which was killing the vibe, so we turned off the radio and told each other stories as we drove along the busy interstate freeway. It seemed to take forever before we eventually left the sprawl of LA, when it was easy to see that the huge city had been built in a desert – but we could still see the city graffiti on the overpasses and other seemingly impossible places in which to spray one's name.

"Jeez! Looks like that Chaka guy has sprayed his graffiti everywhere. Look! There it is on that bridge."

"How the hell does he get up there? And what's he trying to say … something about Shaka Zulu?"

"Only if he's a gangster who knows his southern African history!"

Didn't know if this Chaka guy was a gangster, but he was certainly committed to spraying his name on every wall in the whole of huge LA county and elsewhere. We were two hours out of LA town and still we could see his tag all over, in many different places. Gradually the scenery changed to raggedy mountain scrub and then tall pine trees, as we gained altitude. Even our committed graffiti artist, Chaka, had not ventured this far.

Years later, when Chaka 'the tagger' was arrested, he had become one of the most notorious graffiti taggers of the 20th century. It was estimated that he had tagged the name 'Chaka' in 50,000 different places on public and private property, all the way from LA to San Francisco – and had caused half a million dollars in damages. In court he testified that he would drive hundreds of miles, daily, and go through hundreds of cans of spray paint, daily, in pursuit of his goal – to tag his name throughout Los Angeles County and beyond. Finally, he was arrested and sentenced to probation plus 1,500 hours of cleaning up graffiti. News services reported that, as he left the court house, he managed to carve his name on the courthouse elevator, on his way out of the building, so he was arrested and charged again.

The scraggly, steep rocky mountains, covered in pine trees, looked just like the photos in the books and magazines my American uncle had brought with him, when visiting our family in South Africa. My mother's brother, our Uncle John, had lived in Colorado and was the source of my childhood pictorial knowledge of America.

The weather started to get colder as we climbed higher. Shortly before reaching Tahoe we started to see snow. We consulted the map and eventually found a long winding mountain road towards Tahoe. We were just starting to get excited when we came upon a roadblock and were told that we had to get 'tyre chains' before we could proceed further.

"Tyre chains? What do you mean, tyre chains?"

The patrolman thought we were fooling when we looked at him in confusion and explained that we had never heard of tyre chains before. What the heck is a tyre chain, anyway?

"You need to get tyre chains on your vehicle or you don't go up!"

He strode off, clearly sceptical about our professed ignorance.

Obviously, we did not *have* chains, we had never even *heard* of tyre chains before. Chains that you put on your tyres? I had a problem trying to picture chains on a tyre. We asked a couple of passing motorists and learned that we could purchase some chains at the store at the bottom of the mountain, the one we had passed half-an-hour before. So we drove back to the store and bought the chains.

Then we had to figure out how to put the network of chains on the tyres of the van. Darryl and I, like Dumb and Dumber, fussed and fiddled with the chains, right in front of the store, clueless about how to attach the spider's web of chains to the tyres on the van. An impossible task ... unless you lifted the car tyre off the ground? It was only when a friendly trucker came to help us out that we were able to see how they worked.

"Look here, guys. Just lay the chains out like this, yes, long ways, in front of the wheels ... then drive your van over them, but stop with your wheels on the chains, then wrap the chains up and around, over the tyres, and then connect them. Easy peasy. But you guys are from England, you should know about snow."

"No, we're from South Africa, very little snow in South Africa."

"Y'all from Africa? But you're white!"

"Yes, we're white ... actually, there are many white people in South Africa ... but no snow."

"South Africa? How about that? Now, you gotta drive slow, hear, or you can throw a chain."

"The chains don't harm the tyres?"

"No, just take it easy. Enjoy your trip and welcome to America." He chuckled at our witlessness, slapped us on our backs, and left.

We returned to the roadblock, stared down the patrolman, and continued up the mountain.

We arrived late in the afternoon to find that the condo was perfectly situated, not far from the ski slopes. Snow was piled thickly on the rooftops and long icicles hung from the eaves. It looked just like the winter wonderland depicted on Christmas cards on mantlepieces back in South Africa, where we sweated through our midsummer Christmases, year after year.

"Let's hit the slopes1 It's going to be night skiing!" Darryl announced.

Darryl and I smiled with anticipation as we tried on the rental ski boots, changing sizes a couple times before we could even start looking at the skis.

"Beginner or intermediate?"

"Intermediate," barked Darryl, super confident, still wearing his dark glasses.

The skinny young kid handed over the longer, faster, intermediate skis. It took another half-an-hour to put them on. Then we stumbled outside, falling over a dozen or so times, on the flat snow in front of the building.

"Let's go to the ski lifts and head to the top," said Darryl, our man of many previous skiing experiences.

"Sure thing," I agreed, enthusiastically.

No bunny slopes, no practice slopes… no half day ski lesson like any sensible first-time skier … no asking how it's done. Benoni style *ou maat* (old friend) … straight to the ski lift and all the way to the top.

"Wow, this is not easy." I was out of breath, just from crossing the short, flat distance to the ski lift. Another falling over ordeal.

Not more than fifteen minutes after we had stepped into our skis we were sitting in the ski lift, on our way – up – to the very top of the mountain.

"One-way ticket *boet*! All the way to the top!" Darryl laughed

I was *game*. I didn't know, then, that there were different levels or slopes. What for? Different experience levels? Never heard of them.

"The Black Diamond Triple X slope is the best. Let's hit it," Darryl chirped, determined to show me how it was done.

A Black Diamond Triple X slope? Never heard of it.

"Dude, you gotta take off your sunglasses, it's night, how are you going to see?" I asked.

Darryl ignored me.

It was most definitely night-time and while the floodlights shone on the ski slopes the rest of the mountain was black. I was getting a bit worried, watching most of the skiers getting off the ski lift at various levels, leaving just a few of us 'hardy and experienced' skiers to ride up into the clouds at the very top of the mountain. It began to get very, very cold as the lift headed up, up into the wet clouds. I zipped up my cheap jacket, as far as it would go, and glanced down below us.

We were at least eighty feet or more above the cold, lonely slopes. The giant rough-barked pine trees stood like frozen prehistoric statues, throwing grotesquely twisted shadows from gnarled branches onto the snow, backlit by the huge floodlights. These magnificent pines with their faded grey bark looked like part of the cold rock; they must have been standing in this freeze for hundreds of years. They were huge. Rapidly it became colder than I had ever felt before, in my entire life, then we saw lights ahead.

"Here comes the exit! Get ready, just jump off and land on your skis," advised my champeen skiing companion.

I tried to estimate my take off from the ski lift, misjudged it by miles and fell, clumsily, all tangled up in the lift. To my surprise, Darryl did the same.

The attendant looked annoyed and had to stop the lift so we could climb off and pick up our skis. Our cheap woollen gloves and jeans were seriously out of place among the brightly coloured, expensive, cosy ski outfits worn by the small group of experienced, smiling skiers who were preparing to set off down the very steep slope in front of us. Believe it or not, at this point I was still under the impression that skiing would be easy, a natural part of just sliding downhill, sort of. I was quite surprised to find, three seconds later, that this was not so. A very cold, rude awakening, if you will.

I suppose it's akin to someone with little or no boxing experience thinking they can stand firm against a good fighter. Looks so easy from the outside … just get in the ring, throw some hard punches that land on the other guy, easy stuff, then keep moving out of his reach. Maybe our beginner even trains in the gym for weeks or months and thinks he will do just fine. Then one day he gets in the ring with an experienced boxer. Just climbing through the ropes will have lost him some steam. But at this point he still believes he is going to do OK. Perhaps, for a few seconds, even after the bell rings, he still thinks he will be alright … but then the experienced boxer comes out with his hands held high, his body moving loosely, in a way our beginner cannot possibly comprehend … and the idiot realises he has been fooling himself for months. What a massive mistake he's made, even thinking he has what it takes to be in the ring! Then the experienced boxer easily lands his first lightning solid punch, out of nowhere. The punch lands hard, right on his nose, knocking the snot back down his throat. His eyes roll in his head. That's when he knows he is about to get fucked up – and there's not a thing he can do about it.

Well, that's exactly how I felt as I hit the hard, icy slope in a bone jarring fall within the first three yards of my long education down the Black Diamond Triple X slope. I went sprawling downhill, upside down, ice pouring into my jeans and under my jacket. Slowly I managed to position my body so that my head was uphill, only to find that both my skis had come off. I watched them sliding farther and farther away, coming to rest in different positions, many long metres downhill. To my surprise, yet again, Darryl was on the other side of the icy track, flat on his back in a similar position.

I looked down the dark mountain and understood just how high we were ... I couldn't even see the lights at the bottom. That's when I realised we were both about to get fucked up – and there was nothing we could do about it.

We were at roughly the same height as the clouds and the biting, cold wind, which was picking up speed. The last few very experienced Black Diamond Triple X skiers of the night whipped past us, like ghosts on steroids, gone in seconds. I had quit trying to get my skis back on – it was impossible. I realised that, as fun as it was all supposed to be, we were in a very bad situation. Up in the clouds at the top of the highest peak, at night, in the freezing sub-zero temperature, hardly anyone around us, a snowstorm rolling in ... and we couldn't ski. This time, my mate Darryl had really fucked up. What was that suggestion about going straight to the top of the mountain?

I had taken to sliding down on my ass, throwing my skis ahead of me. I found a level patch and decided to try skiing upright. It took an age to clip the long skis into my strange boots. My fingers were frozen. I stood up, travelled about three metres and fell so hard that I lost my breath.

"Darryl?"

"*Ja!*"

"Are you OK?"

"No!"

"Where are you?'

"I'm over the side ... help me up."

"I can't. I can't move."

"This is so fucked! I need help bru ... I can't get out this furrow."

It took me ten minutes to slide, on my ass, to the side of the ski trail. Darryl was in the slushy snow, skis off, and said he had hurt his leg. His sunglasses were lying in the snow, crushed and bent, about a metre away from him. It took us some time, but I was able to get his hand and pull him back up onto the ski track.

Silence, deep breathing, pauses, and trying to stay calm.

"What the fuck you bring us up here for man, it's almost vertical!"

"I didn't know! It's not the same as last time I skied! Fuck its cold," Darryl proclaimed, trying to put his bent sunglasses back on his nose.

"Throw those fucking things away! They're broken!" I shouted.

Darryl and I had been in some tough situations before, but this was now taking on a serious tone. Our cheap woollen gloves and jeans had quickly become soaked through. Pain had been burning the bones of my hands and legs, but I couldn't tell whether they were burning hot or ice cold. Now some serious agony began to take hold. No one stopped to help us or offer advice. There were very few skiers on the slopes now, and the last of them zipped past in a spray of snow, vanishing within seconds.

It had been dark for some time and although the flood lights lit up the ski slopes, the terrain on either side was in the pitch dark. Now, at last, we were encouraged by the sight of the twinkling lights of the ski lodge, very far below. We still had a long way to go, sliding downhill on our backsides. We were soaking wet and very cold. Anyone who has sat on his bum in sopping wet clothes, in the snow, at 9,000 ft, will recognise the feeling. My whole body was shaking, violently, and I was unable to control it or stop it. I was long past caring if I was ice cold or boiling hot.

"What time you think they close down? Maybe they'll leave us here!" Darryl sounded close to panicking.

"Don't know, if they shut everything down we could fucking die up here. We have to keep moving down, even if we have to slide … we have to keep moving downhill, let's go."

I had kicked back into army emergency mode, I was thinking survival.

I could hardly hold the skis and did not bother to try putting them on. I started sliding on my ass, trudging when I could. After an hour and half of this, trying to stay calm while fighting off the pain from our frozen wet gloves, we were halfway down the mountain. The slope had levelled out a bit and we both breathed sighs of relief. At least we could see the lights of the lodge below the low clouds and every metre we slid or trudged was closer to safety, warmth and comfort.

It took a long, long time to get down the mountain, and ice-cold hands in soaking wet gloves made it almost unbearable. We made it just as the ski lodge was closing for the evening. I left my skis in the snow and hobbled, dripping, to the locker room to hold my hands under hot, running water. The pain of the circulation returning to my hands was excruciating … equal to the pain of injecting tincture of benzoin into blisters. Darryl was at the other sink, also in great pain.

"What a fuck up man! I am never, ever going to listen to you again!"

I was mad at Darryl for having taken us so high, to the top of the mountain, when neither of us could ski. I decided that even though my best bud had been living in America for the past four years, and I had been happy for him to take the lead on decision-making, because he knew the ropes in the US better than I, he was now being demoted from corporal back to private troop, as a result of his bad leadership skills.

"What the fuck bru! You almost killed us. I am *never* going to listen to you again."

§

Back in the warm ski cabin, standing close to the roaring fire, a few rums later, we recovered enough to laugh at ourselves with Reg and his friends. The group of cheerful Americans roared with laughter while we told them about our ordeal on the Black Diamond Triple X slope. They said that despite being pretty good skiers they had never attempted the Triple X slope themselves, it was way too steep and *definitely* only for seriously experienced skiers. Hearing this I threw some grim looks at Darryl, but after a few stiff Captain Morgans he and I were able to see the humour in the situation and we laughed with them, laughing at us.

Reg was getting blitzed.

"I know a South African guy in the movie business. When we get back I'll arrange a meeting for you guys … maybe he can do something with that movie of yours."

"That sounds great, Reg. What does he do?"

"He's a stuntman, but he knows people in the movie industry, you know."

"Sure, sounds good. I need a lucky break."

The next morning I woke with the sunshine and marvelled at the snowy wonderland and the icicles, three feet long, hanging from the snow laden cabin roof. We decided to give skiing another try and this time we chose a few of the easier slopes for beginners. It was altogether more pleasant than the first shocking sink or swim experience of the night before. Soon Darryl and I were shooting straight down the medium slope for quite long stretches, before ploughing hard into the snow, skis flying, again, but at least this was happening in daylight and we were able to get up and do it again.

Round about midday Darryl fell hard and one of his skis hit him on the side of the head. I told him he should stop as the contusion on the side of his head had quickly swelled into a bump the size of an orange. Reluctantly he turned in his skis. I did the same, less reluctantly. I had had my fill with this fucking skiing business. I was a Transvaaler who enjoyed the open veldt and long dirt roads and I had learned that skiing was a really dangerous sport. This was confirmed a few years later when Sonny Bono, of Sonny and Cher fame, was killed on the very same ski slope, when he collided with a 100-year-old pine tree.

We drove home to Los Angeles the next night, using a different route someone had recommended, which was supposed to be shorter. The rear side-window of the car had fallen out so we stuffed a sleeping bag into it, to block the biting cold from outside. Luckily the small car had a killer heater, but unluckily the only radio station it could pick up was that same Christian radio station. We were both quite bruised and exhausted from our skiing trip. Darryl was seriously not feeling well; he had a massive contusion on his temple and cheek bone and slept on the backseat while I drove slowly through the dark night.

I was tired, day dreaming about South Africa. I looked around me and thought that how odd it was that a section of the road reminded me of the Old Pretoria road, travelling past Olifantsfontein, with the lights of the plots in the distance on the left. I wondered about my family.

Tracy, my sister, was now in Germany, still modelling for the well-known Ford modelling agency. Now sixteen years old. It was a bit young to be on her own in Europe and I was worried about her. My mother had recently sent me a few of her 'front covers' from Italian and German magazines. She looked as lovely as ever, with her high cheek bones and almond-shaped, slanted eyes. It was hard to believe she was my little sister.

I had recently been missing my family, life on the family plot, the bunch of five dogs, roughhousing with them, going for runs with them. I missed the people of South Africa but consoled myself as I struggled to stay awake, reminding myself I would probably be back in South Africa in the next three months.

Ahead of me the car lights illuminated a road sign and I thought I was in a time warp. The green road sign looked old and chipped, but I could undoubtedly read 'Johannesburg 40 miles' and under that, 'Randburg 50 miles'.

"What the hell? Johannesburg 40 miles!?"

The blackness of midnight wrapped around me, save for some lights in the distance that looked for all the world like the lights of Olifantsfontein.

"Johannesburg!?" I barked aloud.

I knew I was not a crazy man but what the fuck was going on here? Why had I just seen a road sign for Johannesburg and Randburg? For a few seconds I was seriously confused.

"What the fuck! I'm in California, in the United States of America … but I just passed a sign telling me that the turnoff to Johannesburg and Randburg is coming up ahead?"

I told myself that there had to be a simple explanation for this crazy road sign, somehow, so I turned my head and spoke to Darryl, fast asleep on the back seat.

"Hey! Darryl! I've just seen a road sign that says Johannesburg is coming up soon."

"*Ja*, right. Let's go to Hillbrow for a late-night shawarma. Leave me alone, my head hurts."

"I've just seen a sign for Johannesburg."

"Fuck off man. It's not funny, I'm trying to sleep."

I thought about this strange freeway sign for most of the long drive back to Hollywood.

We drove into Los Angeles just as the sun was rising and the wide five-lane freeway had never looked more beautiful. I could see every detail of the fine web of patchwork cracks on the hard, well-used black asphalt, in the reflection from the rising sun. Yes! Back in the city. Screw the freezing cold snow and slippery mountains slopes! Africans don't do snow! No wonder I hadn't seen one black person on the slopes.

Darryl was waking so I told him again about the mysterious Johannesburg road sign, but he just grunted, saying he didn't have time for nonsense. The next day I started asking a few random people about this mystery. No one seemed to know anything about a sign to Johannesburg in California. It was driving me crazy until, a few nights later, I found the answer to the conundrum. A knowledgeable bar-fly at Gio's Restaurant on Sunset Boulevard, told me that there were two small towns in California, which, in the days of the Californian Gold Rush, had been named after Johannesburg and Randburg in South Africa. In fact, this guy was so well informed he could tell me facts about my own country that I had never heard of before.

I found myself nodding and questioning him about my own country, as if he was the South African and I was the foreigner.

'One Night in Bangkok' ~ *Murray Head*

Eddie was a tough-looking little guy. The first time I met him he was sitting in the trendy West Beach Bar and Grill, smoking a cigar almost longer than his shoe. I had seen him at the club before but I hadn't known he was a South African. He seemed to think that he was a gangster or something, always lounging around, smoking a ridiculously huge cigar, talking to black rappers and wannabes. Despite being very short he looked strong and confident and gave the impression he could be dangerous. I introduced myself, told him that Reg was my roommate, and that I was the man with the movie from South Africa.

From behind a cloud of cigar smoke Eddie told me he had been in the states for a while and was a successful stuntman in the movie industry. He sipped a big tumbler of what looked like cognac on the rocks, slowly looking me up and down as he puffed on his cigar, with attitude to spare.

"Yeah, Reg told me about your video. Where you from in South Africa?"

"Benoni, near Johannesburg."

He blew a cloud of smoke at me and told me was from Rhodesia.

I responded jokingly, saying there was nothing wrong with being Rhodesian and it wasn't his fault. He didn't seem to like the joke and I felt a little tension building as he swirled the amber liquid in his glass. I didn't really care how he took the joke, but from genuine interest I asked him if he had been in the Rhodesian Bush War. His eyes lit up, he looked at me with new interest and replied yes, he had been part of the Rhodesian Bush War. My query had broken the chilly atmosphere; I reached out and shook his hand again. It was always good to meet someone who had been in the African bush, shooting 'gooks'. We sat and chatted about the bush for a while. West Beach was a lively upscale restaurant bar in Venice beach. The young, slick yuppie crowd that crammed the place shoulder to shoulder was well dressed and well connected. Frank Stallone was a regular and sat a few stools away from us, sipping a cocktail.

"Sure, I can have a look at your movie. What's it about again?"

"It's a self-defence self-help video for housewives."

"Hmm … any pussy in it?"

"Not really, other than a few amazons, but we can always add something to it," I joked.

Eddie seemed an OK kind of guy but I have never trusted anyone looking so short and strong. And Eddie looked dangerous. He was one of those short guys capable of kicking a big guy's ass quickly and effectively. He told me he had left Rhodesia some seven years before and that he was doing well, working as a stuntman in Hollywood. He casually mentioned a few movies I had never heard of and said he had been paid $18,000 for one stunt. He said he was well connected with many companies involved in the movie business in Hollywood and that he should be able to get something together with the self defence video. I smiled enthusiastically and suggested that we could market it as a self-defence video, created in a uniquely South African style. He said that was a good idea and was beginning to sound excited, puffing away at an oversized cigar. After a couple drinks we walked out to Eddie's car, parked in an alleyway in Venice beach, where he expertly laid out some long fluffy white lines on the centre console.

It was Los Angeles 1987 and cocaine was everywhere. Every other well-dressed yuppie at the West Beach club was rubbing his nose and talking incessantly. Girls with big hair carried it in their handbags. Guys had it folded and stashed in their socks. Years later I learned I had arrived in Los Angeles in the middle of what came to be known as the cocaine epidemic of the 80s. Ronald Reagan had declared a war on drugs but everyone had a connection. It seemed that, almost once a week, there were reports on the TV news of some sports star getting bust or dropping dead on the practice court from a cocaine-induced heart attack. On the street it was the recreational drug for lawyers, salesmen, sports stars, stock brokers, entertainers, sales girls and good-looking party MILFs. Cocaine was a high society drug considered both recreational and glamorous, with only one rule – don't do too much and become addicted.

At that time, the new television programme, *Miami Vice* was a huge hit. The hip music and new style of close-up-and-fast-moving camera shots, mostly of swarthy, unshaven cocaine dealers in banana speedboats, racing through the Florida Keys, was so cutting edge that re-runs played as recorded background entertainment in bars and cantinas throughout Los Angeles. The Don Johnson look was in and soon, like many other young men, I was routinely wearing a T-shirt, sports jacket and loafers without socks.

"This stuff comes direct from the Medellin Cartel through Miami and the Dominican Republic. I live in Florida, *broer*, and it's all over the place. You can buy a key (kilogram) for $16,000 still with the Medellin Cartel scorpion stamp on it. They fly it in on Lear Jets … one of them crashed a while back and it was packed, floor to ceiling, with powder. Hey! You wanna make yourself a quick 10k?"

I was sitting back in the passenger seat, feeling the pure cocaine coursing through my body. The back of my tongue and throat was numb and I had started sniffing straight away. It was not my first rodeo, but this was some quality stuff.

"How?"

"Easy money. Just drive a car from LA to Texas and hand over the keys when you get there."

"The keys?"

"The keys."

"How many keys?"

He laughed and lit up another huge cigar. It looked ridiculous in his small hand.

"Plenty keys. They all welded into the framework of the car. Chances of getting bust are next to nothing, especially if you white. They need white guys to do it; the black guys are always getting pulled over, especially through Texas."

I thought about it – 10k was a lot of money, $10,000. I was odd jobbing and driving for a few hundred a week.

"Seriously? Have you done this?"

"Naw, but I know someone who does, if you're interested. Make a few good runs and you can make 30k, maybe 40k, in a few months."

Quickly I did the math. Do the run at $10,000, perhaps four times, making a total of $40,000. Convert this to South African rand … in those days the exchange rate was about seven or eight rand to the dollar … so you get maybe R320,000. In 1987 this was big money! Strap it around you and fly back to South Africa, with R320,000! Money for jam!

We went back into the bar and drank some brandy and coke, South African style. Unheard of to mix brandy with coke in America. I wasn't sure if Eddie was everything he said he was, but I knew one thing for sure – he had excellent cocaine. Actually, two things, for sure – he could drive like the stuntman he said he was. He gave me a 20-mile hair-raising drive through the thick Friday night traffic, from Venice to Hollywood, without slowing the pace once. I don't scare easily but he had me gripping the panic handle on his small souped-up Audi as though my life depended on it. No one spoke. He drove as though in a car chase scene in a movie, swerving in and out of the traffic, working the gear stick and screeching to a stop mere inches from the car in front, at every red light. It was a flawless exhibition of precision, reckless, driving, through twenty miles of Los Angeles traffic at high speed. We said few words through the whole race. I was impressed. I slammed the door shut, wearing a huge grin, and told him I would meet him in a couple days, to give him a copy of the self-defence video – and to let him know if I was going to take the gamble and drive a car laden with cocaine to Texas, for $10,000 a pop.

§

I had been without a car since my small hatchback Corolla had been totalled a few weeks after the skiing trip to Tahoe. I had parked it in front of a building on Franklin Ave and gone upstairs to make love to a pretty, older woman I had met at Gio's Restaurant. She had given me a bold smile from across the old-fashioned, glossy wooden bar, and that's all it takes. She had a good-looking intelligent face framed by wispy hair cut short in a modern style. She filled her sweater, a good size 38, and looked at me with a crooked, naughty smile. One thing I had quickly learned about the American woman … when they liked you there was no messing around, they got straight to the point, pretty quickly.

"I love your accent, where are you from?" she purred.

Now there may be many negative things said, even sung, about American women, but when it comes to screwing and romping in bed there is no white woman in the world to beat an American woman. These Californian girls were naturally loose, uninhibited, willing and fun. She hung her sexy head back over the edge of the bed, panting and moaning, squeezing her plump pink nipples on her big ivory tits and letting me do what a man does best. American, particularly Californian, women held nothing back. They are unrestrained, not cursed with the "but I come from a good family" or "I have been well brought up" barrier that men had to contend with in South Africa. Californian girls screwed like there was no tomorrow.

Right at this point I heard the crash. My car was five storeys below, directly under the bedroom window. Just by the sound I knew it was my car that had been hit. Like a good South African lover I carried on regardless through the last minute, as her strong thighs shuddered with pleasure and she howled like a coyote on a rabbit burrow. As soon as she relaxed and sighed, I rudely abandoned the good ship lollipop, ran to the balcony and looked five storeys down, to the street. There was my car in the middle of Franklin Ave, hatchback up, all my tools spread out on the tar. Fucked! Hit and run.

She looked up at me with dreamy eyes.

"Come back to bed, honey."

So I got back into bed.

§

Big Lebanese Mike the Plumber had come to the rescue.

"Jeez, what *kak* luck about your car hey, my china! While you were screwing a bint, hey? Was she *lekker*? Well, like I said, my china, you can buy the old Mustang if you want," Mike offered.

"Don't have the bucks Mike, but I got a boxing fight coming up and I can pay you then."

"Naw, it's cool. Pay me then. Who you fighting this time?"

"Another Mexican."

"*Izit*, my china? You better *moer* him, hey!"[3]

Mike let me drive away in his red 1965 Ford Mustang with a fucked-up door and a huge 350 engine. It was both a beauty and beast. This old muscle car was one of the first and best Mustang models produced, with a distinctly strong design, big front and small rear end, with a small back window. I pulled away and instantly performed some unintentional wheelies in first and second gear, even though it was an automatic. Big Lebanese Mike watched me, nodding and smiling from ear to ear, as I made a U turn on a dime and roared past him, waving.

The Mustang was just as Mike had said, a monster. He had warned me that the passenger door would fly open if I made a fast left turn or hit the brakes hard, and that I would have to lean over and catch it. Apart from this automatic passenger ejector door (which would come in handy later) it was great. This particular Mustang had been around for some years and had been through some rough times; her red paint was badly faded by the strong California sun, her extra fat whitewall Goodyear tyres were smooth and urgently needed replacing, there were a number of deep rusted gashes and some dents on the corners and doors, and the vinyl covered seats and console were cracked and torn – but the engine growled like a fiend. It had a kick radio permanently stuck on 95.5, the classic rock station, which suited me fine. When I stepped on the loose gas pedal the engine growled and then roared, like a hungry lion. I knew that this baby had come through the sixties and seventies in Los Angeles; it was a party animal and had it been able to talk, it would have told more than a few stories of wild times in California. A pure American beauty.

---

3   Afrikaans to English translations: *kak* (shit), *lekker* (good), and *moer* (beat up).

Chapter Fifteen

SUCKER PUNCH

'If You Love Somebody Set Them Free' ~ *Sting*

The 350 engine of Mike's Ford Mustang roared twice as loud in the underground parking of the three level Century City parking lot. The tyres squealed loudly on the smooth concrete as I wound down through the levels, looking for a parking space. I had persuaded everyone to stuff themselves into my new car and the gang giggled and commented as I wove through the covered parking, gunning the engine. But Stephanie LaMotta was upset and scowling at me. She had almost been flung out the passenger door when I turned to the left and now she slammed the faulty door, hard, after climbing out.

"Where did you get this piece of shit anyway?"

The misaligned door bounced back at her, which made her even madder. We had not been getting on well lately. Her New York Italian heritage had given her a way of phrasing things and Jake LaMotta, The Raging Bull, was her father. And the apple had not fallen too far from the tree. For the last few days Stephanie had had it in for me, for some or other reason. I couldn't figure it out. I was beginning to suspect that she had her spies everywhere. Right now a group of us were on our way to see the movie, *Platoon* the new Oliver Stone movie breaking box office records.

It had been Stephanie's idea that we all go see it. Going to the movies in Los Angeles was not at all like going to the movies in South Africa – in LA the patrons chatted loudly to friends a couple of rows away, while waiting for the movie to start; then they cheered and clapped when the good guy came blazing through, kicked the bad guy in the teeth, so he fell over the balcony. In South Africa we whispered in each other's ears and waited for loud music before we opened a packet of crisps or crunched our popcorn.

Platoon started off as a good film. In the American uninhibited style, I crunched my popcorn and chuckled at Darryl's bullshit. He was holding firm to his LA habit, insisting on wearing his sunglasses at all times, even at night or when at the movies. I enjoyed the movie in the beginning, identifying with the actors as they went through training and prepared for patrols into the jungles and rice paddies of Vietnam. I related to the comradeship between the very tired-looking soldiers, casually zig zagging through the thick bush of Vietnam, helicopters flying in at high speed at tree top level, the rotors hammering as the chopper turned. Then something started happening that had never happened to me before. It began to feel as though the movie had been made too close to reality. Scenes had been shot in the new style of fast cuts and extra close

The 1965 Ford Mustang with the 350 engine was pure American beauty with a gas pedal like a snipers trigger.

close-ups. The sharp crack of rifles. A civilian's body collapses, dead. Close up. Clothes tear as bullets rip through them. Dead eyes were staring blankly. Shouting. Halfway through the movie there was a close-up of blood flowing and spraying. Soldiers were shouting at each other … too much! Peasants were screaming … too loud! The camera angles were close up and dramatic … too close. The audience watched and crunched their popcorn. What the fuck? More shouting. Villagers shrieking … pigs squealing. A tall trooper opens up with his automatic, shooting a civilian to pieces. Blood and flesh flying.

I sat forward in my seat.

"They said this is supposed to be a good movie?" I thought to myself.

On the screen a soldier throws down a retarded Vietnamese civilian and batters his head with the butt of his machine gun, until his brains leak out on the floor.

I stood straight up, out of my theatre seat, in genuine reaction. I tossed my popcorn to one side and dropped my Coke on the floor.

"What the fuck bullshit is this?!" I shouted, involuntarily.

I felt lightheaded as I pushed my way out, from the centre of the row of seats, and stumbled into the aisle. Shaking and mumbling as I walked up the aisle, through the doors, out of the movie theatre into the fresh air. I was shocked.

What bullshit is this?

I walked out the cinema and stood at the balcony looking down at the mall below. I thought everyone was raving about this film? Supposed to be a good movie? What the fucking crap is this, blood, shouting, civilians shot, pigs and heads broken open and brains in the dirt. Pigs squealing. How dare they put this shit on the screen and calling it a good film? I fumbled for a cigarette. My hands were shaking … the paper match caught and then sputtered out. I tried another match. No go. What's with the stupid paper matches they have in his country? Where are the Lion wooden matches.

My reaction was very strange, violent, but a genuine experience that had never happened to me before. I leaned over the balcony, looking down on the clothes stores and shoppers walking below. They looked like faraway ghosts … my own memories flashing through my mind, like my own movie.

An overcast day in November 1981. We were on Operation Daisy, about 250 km across the Border, inside Angola. My platoon of paratroopers had been called to order and briefed. Seventy SWAPO terrorists had been seen by the spotter plane. They were making a desperate escape from the back of an abandoned base camp we had just attacked. An officer stabbed his fingers at a map. Our blond lieutenant nodded his head in urgent understanding; his hair was long, having been in the bush for many weeks, in back-to-back operations. He grabbed the map from the senior officer and stuffed it down the front of his shirt, turned to us and waved … and thirty of us ran, hunched up and squinting, through the dust and wind of the prop wash to the two Puma helicopters, their rotors already screaming at take-off speed. We crammed into the well-worn Pumas. I was first in behind the lieutenant and was forced to the back. Now I regretted having put my head under the tap of the water truck, moments before we got the surprise call from the chubby signalman. My wet shirt was cold and clammy on my body, my hair as wet as if I had just climbed out of a swimming pool. The Pumas took off vertically in the thick bush, no space for a forward run. Slowly they lifted above the trees, their noses down, like dragon flies. The pilots expertly turned them on their own axes and the green Angolan bush flashed beneath us as we accelerated, flying fast, at tree top level. We flew for two minutes from the staging post in the deep bush, then banked sharply and landed on a small shona. Our platoon leapt out of the Puma and quickly formed up into a scraggly, widespread battle line.
"Spread out in a line! Move forward!"
The overpowering hammering of the blades of the two helicopters faded quickly in the overcast morning. We were left in the humming silence of the bush, with only the sound of our own laboured breathing and the crunch of our boots in the sand. Suddenly we heard a burst of fire from the 20 mm explosive head cannons of the Alouette gunships ahead of us. They were firing at fifty or more fleeing terrorists, trapped in a small thicket of thin trees.
BOOM BOOM BOOM!!
The sound of the 20 mm shells echoed back from the ridge ahead. Gunships always fired in groups of three.
This would be no lemon! We advanced through the scraggly bush in a raggedy spread out formation, heading towards the small hill ahead of us where the shooting was happening. We could already see a haze of gunsmoke and dust from the battle, hanging above the trees at the top of the small hill.

Lieutenant Du Plessis pointed urgently towards the hill, turned to us and waved his arm. We all picked up the pace, advancing forward towards the noise of battle. I had ended up the last trooper at the end of the sweep line. It was a position I instinctively sought out, from my days of having been an LMG gunner. I moved my eyes from side to side, peering hard through the dry bush. I had learned long ago how to look through the bush and not at it. It was a skill that had taken some time to master, but once learned never forgotten.

Suddenly, just ahead of me, at eleven o'clock, I saw a soldier moving from left to right, coming out of a thicket of shadows into a patch of sunlight. He was dressed in camouflage uniform and was casually crossing my path, not thirty metres away. Because I was at the end of the sweep line I was the only one who had seen him. He hadn't seen me and walked in such a relaxed manner that for a second I thought he must be one of our own troops.

"What the hell is one of our own Koevoet[4] members doing here?"

Seemingly in slow motion I realised that this was not one of our own but a SWAPO guerrilla, right in front of me, making good his escape from the hillside slaughter. For a millisecond I was captivated, watching him, walking in his easy, unsuspecting gait across my path. He had reached about one o'clock, in front of me, when I raised my R4 rifle, already tucked into my shoulder, and shouted at him. But my shout was weak and caught in my throat. Kevin, on my left, had now also seen him and he too shouted. The SWAPO guerrilla heard it, his head spun round to look at me, shocked and surprised. Our eyes locked on each other. In that second I saw the whites of his eyes grow to the size of saucers as he realised he was dead. With my rifle already in my shoulder, both my eyes wide open, I aimed my glare down the barrel, through the sights of my R4, at his mid-section ... just as they had trained us at Airborne. I fired two shots at his midriff and he fell straight down as if he was ducking. Kevin and I both charged forward to where we had seen him drop. We found him lying curled in a foetal position. Kevin fired two shots, taking off the top half of his head. We checked his pockets for documents but found none. I had already taken some photos to document our time in Angola. Now I pulled my cheap instant camera from my side pants pocket and took a photograph of the dead soldier in the perfect afternoon light. I did not realise then that it would be one of many that would haunt me for years to come.

---

4   Koevoet was the counter-insurgency branch of the South West African Police (SWAPOL). See page 19 for more details.

"Korff saw him first Lieutenant," Kevin MacKay said quickly, when our lieutenant, who had halted the platoon sweep line, had run over to see what was going on. Lieutenant Doep looked down at the dead SWAPO man, lying in the Angolan dust. Then he looked at me and nodded, "Mooi, (nice) Korff."

I nodded back.

"I thought he was a Koevoet for a second, Lieutenant," I said.

Our platoon's sweep had hardly paused in the clearing while Kevin and I had shot and searched the terrorist. Now it started forward again. We left the man lying dead on the sand and ran to catch up with the rest of them, moving cautiously closer to the site where the helicopter gunships were still firing. Now the gunships were just one hundred metres away, hovering above the crest of a small steep hill. The sweep line turned into a left wheel now and we gasped for breath, tripping over rocks as we clambered up, using our hands to climb and pull until we came to the top of the small rocky hill. As we breached the top of the hill we came upon a nightmare scene. The gunships were orbiting in a tight low circle thirty metres in front of us. The whine of their turbines and hammering of the rotors was deafening. On top of this their 20 mm explosive head cannons were blasting away.

BOOM BOOM BOOM!!

Tearing off branches, spraying up sand and smoke, the gunships fired into the group of seventy terrorists who had been cornered in a thicket of trees. We had come together in the perfect pincer movement on our enemy, almost like the tyrannical Zulu Monarch King Shaka's bull horn fighting formation, and we were here to finish them off. Ghostly figures stumbled around under the trees in front of us, lurching and falling in the dust and smoke. Immediately I dropped to one knee to fire my R4 at the ghosts in the fog, just as fast as I could pull the trigger. Thirty paratroopers emptied their magazines into the terrible scene. Shadowy forms staggered and crumpled in the chaos, like wraiths caught in a dust storm from hell. I changed magazines as fast as I could and dropped my empties in the sand, nothing taped together this time ... I pulled back the bolt and kept on shooting at the figures ahead of me, caught in a killing zone like no other, consumed in a hell of deadly fire, dust and smoke and rifles and cannons, all at close range. I could now barely see through the smoke, just fired at anything I saw that moved.

They moved and fell without even knowing that we were firing at them from the side.

My old mate, Darryl, came out of the movie theatre and joined me at the balcony rail. He lit a cigarette and asked, "What's cutting bro? Why the freak out in the movie house, hey? Jeez?"

I was quiet, lost in thought and took some time to answer. I didn't know what to say. My reaction while watching the violent war film had caught me by surprise and as hard as a sucker punch.

"Dunno."

For once Darryl was quiet. He said nothing but pulled out his box of Marlboros and offered me another cigarette. I had stomped out the first one half finished.

I looked over the balcony, watching the Century City Mall Christmas shoppers walking in and out of the stores beneath me, shopping bags filled with Christmas gifts and goodies. Everyone was well dressed and seemed to be enjoying themselves. Which life was more real? These shoppers going about their important mission in the mall, searching for the right shoes? Or walking for weeks in the bush, a close, fast, firefight, flashes behind leaves, the smell of gun powder, quickly turning over and searching several dead bodies, the numb feeling of victory ... the vindication of being a soldier, doing what you've been trained to do – kill the enemy.

Which life is the reality? To which world do you commit your loyalty? On which of these realities do we build our future reactions, values and judgements?

"I thought it was supposed to be a good movie ... what's with all the close-up violent scenes?" I said to Darryl "I don't need to see this shit" I grumbled.

We smoked our cigarettes and I began to calm down. Darryl made a couple jokes about how I had tossed my popcorn over the heads of the people seated in front of me.

"Jeez, bru. What a freak-out hey? Come, let's go back in," he chuckled.

Darryl was an old friend, had been since elementary school, we knew and understood each other well. Together we went back inside the movie theatre, squeezed through the rows and sat down in our seats to watch the rest of the film. I had no more popcorn or Coke with me but all the same Stephanie gave me a long, hard look. The soundtrack was loud and everyone was engrossed in *Platoon*, the action magnified on the screen in front of us.

I watched the film but did not see it ... my own movie was playing inside my head, a movie I had seen and replayed many times before.

"*Cease fire! Cease fire!*" *someone shouted. Slowly we stopped shooting, barely able to breathe in the thick gunsmoke. The silence was deafening, then: "Forward!" Our rifles pushed hard into our shoulders we stumbled forward, tripping over rocks, moving in among the trees of the killing ground, still draped in the fog of gunsmoke and dust. I walked fast, as usual, and stumbled again. It was hard to make out what was in front of us. My throat and eyes burned from the cordite and the thick dust, still hanging over the small thicket of trees, like a shroud. The 20 mm cannons had burnt and ploughed up the sand, like the grim reaper's plough. I reached the killing ground and began to make out the bodies of SWAPO terrorists ... in their dirty uniforms, old AK-47s at their sides, behind the trees, under bushes and in the open, their bodies covered in sand and dust scattered throughout the thicket. Some of the bodies had been cut in half, behind the thin tree trunks where they had crawled, making their last stand, trying to take cover from the gunships. The soft sand was torn up like an overcrowded beach after the crowd had left. Chilled, shocked, I began to make out the shapes of women, old and young, and some children, lying on the ground among the dead insurgents, also cut to pieces.*

"*There are children here!*" *shouted John Delaney, the first to enter that ghastly area.*

In front of me lay a San mother, topless as is their custom, on her back, still holding her toddler to her chest with her left arm, her right arm and the top of her chest were missing, the result of a 20 mm round, her ribs shone like a side of beef. The square-headed infant she was holding looked unharmed but as I walked closer I realised the child was dead. Maybe from terror? He had a small turd stuck in his backside but was otherwise unmarked and unhurt, but definitely dead. His dead mother held him to her body with her remaining arm, the other torn away by a 20 mm shell.

We moved through nightmarish scene. In the bushes I saw a group of soldiers, in uniform, with some children, lying in a heap together. To my right a Bushman in uniform lay cut in half, behind a small tree, his guts in the sand next to him. I came across a critically wounded SWAPO guerrilla, lying on his stomach. He moaned, asking for what sounded like water, or help. He still had his old AK-47 half under his elbow, his hand loosely on the old worn grip. The officer at my side gestured to me. Quickly I stepped over him, placed my muzzle on the bump behind his ear and pulled the trigger. His head bounced up, about eight inches. It was the best I could do. There was no other help for him.

I saw an old San woman, possibly a great grandmother, with snow white, peppercorn hair. The matriarch of the Bushman clan lay on her back, her guts and liver lying in the sand next to her, still alive. Five or seven children stood in line nearby, shocked, mute, staring wide-eyed at the terrible scene. I put my rifle on its tripod and knelt down beside her. I signalled for her to relax, that I would get help for her. I pointed to where the helicopter had dropped us, and whirled my hands above my head, indicating that I would get her some help, from the helicopter. We would help her. She seemed to understand what I was trying to say and managed a small smile on her ancient, deeply wrinkled face. Very peacefully she nodded at me through slits for eyes, then she closed her eyes and laid her head back on the sand. I was going to get help. I stood up and started down the slope towards the helicopters, to find someone, to tell them we had to get some help for the old lady. I heard a shot ring out behind me.

Platoon came to an end and we left the movie theatre. I felt utterly drained. Stephanie asked me what had happened, why had I stood up, tossed the popcorn and walked out? I told her that I didn't know and couldn't explain it. Then, for the first time, I told her that a few years ago I had been a South African paratrooper, fighting on the Border and in Angola. We had done much the same as had been portrayed in this film. Those shockingly violent, close-up, scenes, filmed with fake blood … as paratroopers we had performed the same scenes, for real, many times over.

"I just hadn't been prepared to see it all filmed so graphically, so close-up, in this movie, and why" I muttered. She seemed confused. Why had she never heard of this conflict I was talking about? Then she said that sometime later she wanted to hear all about it.

'Everybody Wants to Rule the World' ~ Tears for Fears

I had taken photographs to document our time as soldiers, using a small instamatic camera that I kept always in the side pocket of my pants. This was not your normal photo album, this was my army photograph album … pics which I, and others in my platoon, had snapped, throughout our time in Parachute Battalion.

The grimy faces of long-lost brothers in arms. Young shaven-headed recruits enduring the hardships of airborne training. The mood of the photos changed in the war zone, on the Border with Angola. Uniforms looked more faded, there were fewer smiles, blackened faces, longer unwashed hair and scruffy beards, grim faces, shot and burnt out soviet vehicles, shot and killed terrorists in their uniforms on the ground, burning village huts, crashed jets, marching soldiers, columns of bomb smoke, captured soviet tanks, anti-aircraft guns, filthy drinking waterholes, machine guns, vehicles destroyed by land mines, bomb craters and more killed enemy soldiers.

There were many photos of my smiling, young platoon mates. At one time we had all been as close as brothers, argued amongst ourselves, but without a second thought faced the same danger, always looking out for one another. Then, following a short, final parade we had split up, never to see each other again. What had happened to those guys? Even with our differences we had become close as family. Funny thing … how you can loath or simply detest a fellow soldier, but like it or not, you are cast as brothers in arms, forever linked by your actions, battles, discipline and the pride of having been a member of Parachute Battalion.

§

Darryl and I had met an entertaining fellow South African, from Durban, who seemed to have the run of the Cat and Fiddle, an English pub on Santa Monica Boulevard. Derek was as loud as any American. He shouted and hooted and was able to match the best of them in linguistic skills, talking over anyone, anywhere, exercising considerable volume to overpower them. Also, he was able to slug down beers faster than you can shake a stick. Darryl and I came to the conclusion that, being from Durban it was probably all the time he had spent wearing flip flops and baggy swim suits that had helped him adapt to the California scene more easily than we had done, coming from the East Rand. Also, Derek had been in America for a quite a few years and had clearly picked up and mastered the vibe. Apart from coming from Durban, which was not really his fault, he was a pleasant enough guy.

Fairly soon after meeting him he announced, loudly, that he needed seven or eight guys to do a security gig for Stevie Wonder, who would be playing at the Greek Theatre, as part of an anti-apartheid concert.

"I only want South African guys; I know I can trust them." He lifted his chin to the loud crowd sitting around him. He was putting this security outfit together for a friend in the music industry and was making a big thing of wanting only South Africans, because they had all been 'in the army' and wouldn't fuck around like the Yanks would. He spoke seriously, as though he was putting together a platoon of hardened fighters to fly across the Border and attack a SWAPO base in Angola.

"The only problem is that this is an anti-apartheid gig, but don't worry about it, that's just normal day-to-day stuff here in LA. At least we can make some beer money."

"What do you mean anti-apartheid? We're all South African. That's not going to go down well."

"Doesn't matter. You want to make some easy money?" He grasped his Bass Ale tightly in one hand and looked around.

"They'll stone us if they find out we're all South African."

"No one will know, just keep your mouths shut and look tough."

Derek was going to pay us $300 apiece for the night's work. A snap. All we needed to do was wait for the limousine to arrive, escort Stevie Wonder from his limo to the stage, hang around the stage looking like heavies while he did his thing, and then escort him back to his limo.

After a bit of soul-searching Darryl and I decided to join Derek's 'A team' ... both of us needed the money. A week or so later we were ready. We had corralled together a group of eight South Africans for the security assignment and we all met at the Cat and Fiddle pub, before stuffing ourselves into a couple cars, like policemen, and driving through the busy Hollywood streets to the Greek Theatre. We pulled into the back entrance of the theatre where we had to show our security passes. Most of the SA guys had come overseas as musicians or were in the entertainment industry in some way or another. None of them showed the 'natural South African cunning and aggression' which Derek had asked for on his advertisement for his class A security team. We arrived early and hung out at the back of the stage, watching other performers coming through with their entourage, their bags of stage gear, their equipment. All of them were wearing anti-apartheid shirts.

"Hey, look at all these people here tonight, all to raise awareness about the evils of apartheid ... and we're South African. Isn't it like being a traitor? Maybe we shouldn't be doing this?"

"*Ag*, it's just a job. And we're not joining them, so it's OK."

"Who knows, you might even get the chance to *klap* (smack) one of them, if they come too close to Stevie Wonder."

"Fuck Stevie Wonder ... he's doing this because he was banned from playing in South Africa."

"*Ja*, maybe, but it's Stevie Wonder, bru. He's good, and anyway everyone knows that apartheid is fucked up ... the whole world is against us."

"Well, what other system do you think will work, one man one vote?"

"Why? Don't you think that will work?"

"Why do you think? Because most of the population can't read, never mind never mind vote. Then the ANC takes over and the communists come in. You think you'll ever see a concert like this to raise awareness when they push the whites into the sea?"

"Crap, all that communist stuff ... one man one vote might work, if you give it a chance."

A hushed mini political discussion had erupted amongst us as we watched people going to and fro, proudly flaunting their anti-apartheid banners and T-shirts.

Derek moved quickly to quell the disagreement amongst his troops.

"Hey! Stop it guys, this is not the place to have a *bekgeveg* (debate) about politics. Just focus on the job," Derek chirped, "y'all mercenaries are here just for the money, remember?"

We all laughed and passed our cigarettes around. For the first time I had begun to see South Africa from a different perspective. I was seeing it through different eyes, something like the outside world saw it, I suppose. It seemed it was not such a good thing we had going back home. Yes, I knew the facts, I knew the problems. But it had started looking wrong, a country where a minority of citizens controlled the majority, where everything was based on skin colour? It had seemed OK while I was had lived there, but now, somehow, viewing it through an American lens, it had stopped looking right.

There was an American guy with us who seemed to know the ropes. He was a short athletic guy with long brown hair and beady brown eyes. He had been quiet, watching us closely for the last while, not getting involved in the conversation, but now he offered a keen, matter of fact, observation.

"Why don't you South Africans move your lips and mouth when you speak?"

He mimicked us, talking from the back of the throat, not moving his lips. I didn't find it so amusing until I realised that he was right. When Americans spoke, their whole mouth and lips moved to shape the pronunciation of the words. We South Africans, or those from Benoni, at least, thought it unmanly to have your lips and mouth move too much while speaking – and we really did speak from the back of our throats, like a ventriloquist, in a deep monotone.

"*Izit*, hey?"

The American saw that he had hit a nerve and grinned. He had done a good job of imitating the way South Africans speak and we all cracked up. I had not realised it before, but now I saw the truth of it and made a mental note to start moving my lips when speaking.

We hung backstage as the concert begun. The music was good and I nodded my head to the R&B beat, enjoying the sound. After a few songs a speaker came on and whipped the crowd into a frenzy with a long, screeching monologue on the evils of apartheid and white supremacist South Africans. The crowd shouted a response, chanting "Man-de-la! Man-de-la!" until the next song started. We 'Saffricans' shifted around uncomfortably, looking at one another nervously, as the crowd went wild.

"Don't worry guys, this is normal shit here in LA," Derek spoke quietly, for once, from the side of his mouth, getting us to calm down.

About halfway through the show the white limousine ferrying Stevie Wonder pulled up at the back. We all formed up, wearing our serious, tough, best-not-fuck-with-me expressions. There was some commotion going on inside the vehicle and a few people came and went, after popping their heads through the open door. Finally, Stevie Wonder climbed out but immediately bent back inside, talking loudly. He seemed to be having an argument with someone; then a teary-eyed woman climbed out of the limo and they stood there, arguing in hushed tones. A short man pitched up and seemed to placate them. He started leading Stevie away from her, towards us.

"*Ja!* All right you guys! Here's Stevie … let's go!" Derek gave commands just like a corporal.

Silently we formed a loose half circle around Stevie Wonder. His guide took his arm and he readied himself, straightening out his loose-fitting clothes. We all glanced around us constantly, looking like able, experienced, security personnel, while we all walked slowly towards the stage. The announcer was back on stage and starting up about South Africa again. This was our cue to start walking forward, with Stevie at the centre of our loose half circle. He was led up some stairs and walked onto stage to be greeted by thunderous applause. And then Stevie Wonder immediately broke into a lengthy monologue about the evils of South Africa, apartheid and all white South Africans.

"Free South Africa … free Mandela … boycott Coca Cola!" The chant threatened to raise the roof of the Greek Theatre.

"Boycott Coca Cola? What the fuck's Coke got to do with it?" muttered Darryl loudly.

"Ssshhh! Don't let anyone hear our accents"

Stevie Wonder stood on stage, sporting his famous, big smile, shouting that Nelson Mandela must be released … that the world must unite against the wicked country keeping him in prison, and the majority of its people oppressed. The crowd whistled and shouted its approval. I was beginning to understand what it must have felt like at the Battle of Blood River … our small group of eight shiny white South Africans stood transfixed at the side of the stage, watching the crowd of twenty thousand people baying for the blood of our country, and ourselves, and probably our unborn children.

Finally, Stevie Wonder stopped talking and opened up with his new, award-winning anti-apartheid song, 'It's Wrong', followed by some beautiful keyboard work.

We watched the crowd as he delivered a stellar performance, playing all his hits plus a few numbers I had never heard before. Weird as our presence there may have been, it was great to peep from the side of the stage at Stevie Wonder performing, in the flesh. The crowd seemed to know all his songs and cheered, whistled and clapped, constantly, while he played. At the end of his set Stevie Wonder was led down the stairs to more thunderous applause. And we eight, serious, tough, shiny white South Africans, walked him safely back to his limousine which quickly whisked him away.

"Let's stay and watch the show."

"Fuck that! Let's go! If I hear 'free Mandela' again I am going to fucking freak. Let's head to the Cat and Fiddle for a beer."

We drove off, back to the pub on Santa Monica, where a smiling Derek handed over our mercenary wages and we had a few beers. We laughed, sang some Stevie numbers, and drank a toast to our Stevie who, while seeing no evil, had certainly been unable to see the eight, iniquitous, white South Africans who comprised his entire security detail for tonight's anti-apartheid concert in LA.

Chapter Sixteen

HARDER THAN DIAMONDS, TOUGHER THAN STEEL

'The Power of Love' ~ *Huey Lewis and the News*

On the advice of my new boxing trainer, Ed Wicks, I had tried to extend my time in the USA by acquiring a sports visa.

I had queued in the longest line of people I had ever seen. It extended out the front door of the immigration building in downtown Los Angeles, for about half a big city block. I looked around, noticing that I was one of only a handful of white people standing in a line of roughly seven hundred, and wondered why. Where the fuck are all the white people? Everyone in the line had a healthy mop of black hair. In fact, everyone in the whole of downtown LA seemed to have a healthy mop of black hair. It was quite clear to me, as an outsider, that Los Angeles was being overwhelmed with Latinos. It took three hours to reach the small glass-fronted booth. A Latino woman peered at me from behind the thick glass and told me I was very lucky, there had recently been some changes to the rules for sports visas. She gave me the correct forms and told me I had made it just in time.

I was feeling quite positive about my application. I had included all the right documents, had provided proof of my newly acquired Californian professional boxing license, had shown some of the contracts for my previous boxing fights, all of which proved that I was an actively involved professional boxer. I explained that I would be in the US for another year, so that I could pursue a minimum of five more professional fights before returning to South Africa. I felt confident that the Immigration Department would extend my visa and started telling anyone who would listen that I would soon have my visa extended.

I didn't get much mail so when I saw the envelope from the United States Immigration Department in the mailbox six weeks later I immediately ripped it open. The official letterhead of the Government of the United States of America looked powerful at the top of the crisp white page. In a few formal words the Immigration Department informed me that my application for a sports visa had been denied, and that I must immediately fuck off out of the United States, because I was now considered an Illegal Alien and subject to immediate deportation.

I thought I had misunderstood the short letter and read it again, slowly and carefully.

Subject to immediate deportation. I was deep in thought on my way back to the apartment, ambling slowly over the small bridges and waterways of the big complex. Inside the apartment I decided to follow my mother's remedy for any emergency and immediately made a cup of tea. I had not enjoyed a decent cup of tea for a year and half. There was no decent tea to be found in the American stores – if any existed I hadn't found it yet. We had to settle for using two Lipton tea bags in one cup, to produce a cup of tea which tasted somewhat acceptable.

I sat on the lumpy couch we had found on the sidewalk after being cast out by someone, sipping my lousy tea, pondering my bad situation. Thanks to just one letter I was officially an illegal immigrant and subject to deportation. I was more than disappointed … I had worked so hard to get this right. I wandered around the apartment trying to come up with a plan but soon realised this was not going to be an easy fix. I needed some advice quickly. I pulled out the yellow pages and started flipping through it, looking for an immigration lawyer. I had to speak to someone to see what options I had, what was the next step, apart from an instant flight back to South Africa. I found what seemed to be an inexpensive immigration lawyer, given that the office was in not such a good neighbourhood, across the road from the Hollywood High School. A few days later I pushed past some delinquent Hollywood High School kids, hair dyed blue and red, hanging on the sidewalk. A heavyset, serious Armenian lady, her hair teased into an old-fashioned beehive, slowly read through the official letter from the Immigration Department. She looked at me apologetically and told me sincerely that there was very little she could do to help.

"You are from South Africa?"

"Yes, South Africa".

"Isn't your country in turmoil, with apartheid? Maybe you could plead for political asylum from your country. I think it may be your only choice."

She said it would cost me around $900 to get this second application started, but she could not give any guarantee that it would be accepted.

$900? Political asylum?

I thought about it for the next couple of days and then discussed it with Darryl.

"Hey! She hit the nail on the head bru! That's an easy one … you can say you were forced to fight in the apartheid regime's military forces, to keep the Africans suppressed. Tell them that you don't want to go back because you don't agree with the country's apartheid system and don't want to fight in the army. And look at the *LA Times*, they hate us."

"But I do want to go back to South Africa," I pointed out.

"*Ja*, but then you just go back anyway, whenever you want to…it's just a ploy."

Darryl was right about being hated. Our beloved South Africa was in the news and on TV every couple of days, and it certainly seemed that everyone had turned against our home country.

§

Yes, there was almost always some sort of reaction when I told people that I was South African.(In the mid-80s most Americans knew only what they had seen on the news, about South Africa, and showed a misguided understanding about the complexities of the racial problems back home.) In the beginning of my time in the US I had thought it fun and it didn't bother me, but it soon became unsettling – especially when you were casually trying to blend in … or connect with a girl. Recently, at parties or casual social meetings in bars, I had begun to lie. I mumbled that I was from Zimbabwe or Mozambique, just to avoid having to say the dreaded words 'South Africa' and get the eyes-wide awkward pause response, being shut down or having to go through the whole explanation of no, we don't have slaves, no we don't hate Africans just because they are black.

I had found that there was usually one of three reactions whenever I said I was from South Africa:

(1) Nudge nudge, wink wink. "You guys in South Africa sure know how to handle the blacks in your country, you really hate them that much, eh?" Wink wink.

(2) "Oh, you're from South Africa!?" Silence ... eyes wide while thinking, *Here is a True Racist, standing right in front of me.* Then the questions: "Why do you hate black people? Do you have slaves working in the gold mines? You know, I have many black friends of my own here."

(3) They would quietly stand up, take their things and leave, not wanting even to breathe the same air as your racist self.

I had met a very good-looking blonde girl at a party. She was tall, almost six foot, with big green eyes and a strong pretty face. Her natural blonde hair hung over one eye and she had long legs like the stairway to heaven. She had a strong jaw with a sexy film of fine blonde hair, the same downy hair that covered her forearms. I had watched her dancing in the small living room, moving sexily to the soft jazz which had become one of the new sounds in the mid-eighties. Soft jazz was an annoying, new, 'feel good' jazz derivative, instrumental compilations of soft drums and a smooth, poppy saxophone. It was heard almost everywhere. Black comedians made fun of it on TV. Men joked about it. Women loved it with a passion; they danced to it with their fingers of one hand pointed into the air, a glass of wine in the other. It represented wine and making love in front of a fireplace. The tall blonde moved eloquently to the vibey saxophone, sipping her wine. Despite suffering a hangover from the previous night's activity, I decided it was worth a chance. She had a different look in her eye, not so reserved. I quickly learned that the reason she looked different was that she certainly *was* different. Very neatly she fitted into stereotypical blonde jokes.

She smiled when I introduced myself and commented that I had such a nice Australian accent.

Mistakenly, but honestly, I replied, "No, I'm from South Africa." I should have said I hailed from Zimbabwe.

Her eyes grew big. She couldn't believe her luck, here she was, talking to a real, living, dyed in the wool South African, straight from the dark, racist, bad lands of Africa. I was distracted by her big green eyes and long blonde hair. I should have known ... but I thought it was my charm which had amplified her eyes. Smilingly I ignored her prying questions throughout the evening, as we danced the night away. Early into our second date I realised that she planned to squeeze me into a snare ... not the kind of squeeze I had anticipated. She kept asking pointed questions: Why do South Africans mistreat black people? Do we think whites are superior to blacks? Why were we in Africa?

Having spent half my week's pay cheque at an upscale bar on our drinks and dinner, I drove her through Santa Monica in the old red Mustang and pulled up at the beach to try to make the best of a bad situation. I started kissing her and she didn't seem to object, so I slipped my hand inside her loose blouse while she asked yet more questions about South Africa. The questions became taunts of a certain kind: Did you know that I'm attracted to black men? Why did you whites steal the country from the blacks?

I gave her firm tit a last squeeze, pulled my hand out of her blouse and sat back, having completely lost the moment. I told her that she didn't have any idea what she was talking about. It didn't stop her; her eyes began to glaze over as she continued, finally coming out with what she had wanted to say the whole time. I turned the ignition of the Mustang and the car started with a roar. I accelerated down the busy beach road in Santa Monica, trying to keep my cool while she taunted me with information about her dating history. Did I know how many black men she had dated? Did I know that she was really attracted to black men?

I reached my limit.

I pulled over, standing on the brakes. I knew from past experience that if I jammed on the brakes hard, the broken door lock on the passenger side would ensure that the door flew open as fast as a James Bond ejector seat.

The misaligned locking mechanism did not fail me – as I hit the brakes the door flew open. She was still talking, eyes wide, as I leaned over and pushed her out of the car using both hands. She landed on her ass on the grass sidewalk, her micro mini skirt hiked up, her legs spread wide, flashing a pretty, dark patch. I grabbed her handbag and high heels and tossed them out as far as I could, then pulled off. As I accelerated away, the smooth whitewall tyres screeching, the passenger door swung back automatically – just like 007! I gunned the Mustang into the Saturday night Santa Monica traffic and headed home.

Give me a break with this apartheid stuff already.

§

I spent a week thinking about applying for political asylum from South Africa, as per the suggestion from the Armenian immigration lawyer with the wide, serious eyes. She was right, it was probably the only way possible to become 'legal' in the US – if such an application would be accepted, which I doubted. I was fucked. I came to realise that there was no way I could do it. I would never be able to live with political asylum … I would rather be deported back to South Africa than lie and turn my back on the country I had grown up in, the country I knew and loved. Forget it.

I tore up the rejection letter from the US Immigration Department and threw it in the trash. Fuck that. Now I needed to remove any evidence that I was as illegal as a wetback who had just swum across the Rio Grande. I spread my passport on the kitchen table, intending to remove the small, white, six-month Visa ticket stapled into it. Not only stapled, I discovered, glued as well, to prevent exactly what I hoped to do. I managed to remove the expired visa tag but the process left an obvious mark on the page.

Darryl observed my work with curiosity.

"Hey, that looks fishy… that's not going to work."

"What you mean?"

"It looks like crap; anyone can see you've ripped your visa out."

I felt like I did when I had changed my grades on an early high school report. It was so obvious that I had changed my grades from Es and Fs to Cs, but if my parents suspected something, bless them, they never confronted me about it.

"You going to be pretty fucked, bru. If they catch you, they throw you in the deportation tank with half of Mexico in there. Maybe you should try to get someone to sponsor you."

While I sized up my crude handiwork on my passport, Darryl told me again how he had applied for his green card: "A green card is very difficult to get. First, you have to find a company that will sponsor you, help you, then they have to prove that you have an expertise of some kind that no one else in America has. Your boss will have to do it for you. In my case, we said that I was an expert at recording African drums. My boss worked with me, he placed an advert in the paper looking for an expert in African drum recording ... he had to do this to prove that he had tried, first, to find an American to do the job ... but guess what happened?"

"What?" I asked, as expected, but I was also curious about his story.

"This American guy answers the ad and brings all his recordings of African drums into the studio. Turns out this guy is a genuine expert and had travelled all through Africa, spending *years* recording drums in villages. He has everything on tape, and he comes in with a case full of tape recordings as proof, looking for a job as an African drum expert."

"Did he get your job?" I asked

"No, of course not. That's the whole point. No one will be qualified enough to get my job ... I'm an irreplaceable, one-of-a-kind expert in my field of work. So I'm entitled to get a Green Card. It's a setup, everyone does it."

"So, your boss told this guy that he didn't qualify for the position he had advertised?"

Darryl looked like a mobster, widening his eyes, trying to look innocent but serious.

"Yes, of course. We told him "sorry, he did not have enough experience in African drums". That's how I was able to apply for my Green Card."

I wasn't in the mood for sad stories. This poor guy travels from village to village through Africa to record African drums, is probably one of the most knowledgeable people in the world on African drums, yet he is turned down for the (fake) job that he applies for, because he does not have enough experience in African drums? How defeated the poor guy must have felt, when he was told he had to go back to Africa, to get more experience!

"I can't do that, working as a plumber; there are hundreds of plumbers around."

"I know. But you need to get rid of your passport now. You can see that you ripped the visa out and you *will* get bust."

I argued that I had done a good job but after some days I had to admit that Darryl was right, and that I had to dump my passport. I ripped it up, put all the pages into a cheap, aluminium cooking pot and set them alight. I stood there, watching my photograph and entire identity twisting in the flames, turning to charcoal in the pot. Then I doused the flames with water and threw the whole sorry mess into the trash.

I wore my best sad sack expression, sitting in the offices of the South African Consulate-General on Wilshire Boulevard, Los Angeles, where a wonderfully cheerful South African woman with a beautifully familiar accent asked me how I had lost my passport.

"We were out one night, clubbing on Sunset Boulevard and I needed my passport as proof of identification to get into the clubs. It must have fallen out of my pocket along the way."

"Well yes, that does happen. We will need some details to be checked in South Africa, but I think we should be able to get you a replacement passport."

Her South African accent sounded like music to my ears. It sounded like home. I sat quietly, saying nothing, just listening, as she chatted. I left the consulate office with hope in my heart. All I needed now was to find a fake Green Card – or an alien work permit.

If a million illegal Mexicans can do it, I can do it!

Do You Really Want to Hurt Me? ~ Culture Club

I had changed boxing gyms and now had a somewhat shorter drive through endless shabby black suburbs into the neighbourhood of Watts in South Central Los Angeles. The Broadway Boxing Gym, also known as the 108th Street Gym, was a famous old gym owned at that time by Bill Slayton, who had been Kenny Norton's trainer and manager.

This was a classic boxing gym, located in the black part of town. It was on the second floor of a two-storey old brick building on the corner of Broadway and 108th Street. The wide steps of a short flight of stairs led to a double door which opened into a big hall with a high ceiling. The old yellow wooden floor had long since lost any shine and was especially well worn just in front of a long row of old, heavy, leather punch bags, all down one side of the hall. Two raised boxing rings stood side by side at the far end, their old canvas floors dotted with a thousand small black drops of dried blood. The walls were covered in old fight posters advertising bouts between fighters some I had never ever heard of. Danny Little Red Lopez, Joey Olivo, Carlos Palamino, Scrap iron Johnson. The sirens of fire engines and the sound of heavy traffic wafted up through the open tilt-and-turn windows, mixed with the roar of motor bikes from the black motor cycle gang returning to their headquarters, next door. And, of course, there was the sound of thirty boxers, each one better than the other, pounding away at punch and speed bags, jumping rope, and shadow boxing at a tremendous pace. This was a school of hard knocks boxing factory in the middle of the 'hood' and I had not seen anything like it before.

Life in the big city.

I proudly wore my yellow Sun City T-shirt, acquired at the Gerrie Coetzee vs Greg Page fiasco, while I slowly shadow boxed in front of a long row of mirrors. Looking past my reflection I realised I was one of the very few white guys in the gym, but no one gave me a second glance. The fighters around me pounded and worked out, displaying a much higher level of skill than I had witnessed in South Africa.

Darryl's friend, Thomson, had arranged that I meet a few boxing guys he knew down at the gym. He had told them that he had met a new white guy from South Africa who looked like he could fight a bit. They were interested and had come to the gym to meet me. One of the men was Ed Wicks, a well-known Los Angeles cut-man and coach.

The other man was the boxing promoter at The Fabulous Forum in Inglewood, where a monthly boxing show was held as part of the sponsored Strohs Beer Tournament. The Forum was a big venue in Los Angeles, the home of the LA Lakers, a top professional basketball team, and also 'the' place to fight if you were going to fight.

The promoter, who had introduced himself as Mr Curtis, was dressed in a dark suit with a tie. He had come all the way to the Broadway gym to see me, always on the lookout for fresh meat. He stood to one side, his arms folded, watching me work out.

Ed Wicks seemed impressed enough with my speed. He sweated as he held the pads; I sweated as I slammed them with straight punches. Both Ed and I were performing a kind of audition and we were giving it our best.

"Not bad," called Mr Curtis, "let's see him spar."

I suited up and stood in the corner. My sparring partner was a black kid, a tall, wiry boxer with a smooth complexion and a cool as a cucumber expression. I wasted no time and came out right at him; I drove him back into the ropes then backed off and placed a few hard shots to his head. He kept his hands up, boxed well and caught me with a slick combination. I moved around and threw a fast left in-between his gloves, extending the punch with my shoulder, getting the few extra inches I needed for a solid punch. My strong point was fighting with pressure, and he backed up and couldn't launch his punches. But maybe he wasn't yet under the maximum pressure I could deliver. We did two rounds and I came out on top, even though I had a nick on my eye from a quick left hook.

Back home the punch of choice was the nationally beloved '*Ek slaan jou dood*' (I'll kill you with one punch) blow, a great, big, crashing right, very popular throughout South African boxing gyms. In American boxing gyms it seemed that the left hook was the punch of choice; Mexican fighters also loved the left hook to the liver and called it 'The Gaucho'. Their standard practice was to try and drop an opponent with a hard left hook to the body, or 'liver shot'. I had been felled twice before with a liver shot: once by the South African Light Heavyweight Champion, Sakkie Horn, late at night during a sparring match in Gerrie Coetzee's backyard gym; and once by the 136 kg ex Heavyweight Champion and number 9 in the world, Jimmy Abbot, in a boxing gym in Brixton.

Being hit with a solid punch to the liver is the most debilitating punch in boxing and is certainly no joke, especially when it's delivered by Jimmy Abbot. It takes a second or two for your liver to go into spasm, then a sickening, incapacitating pain rushes through your whole body. You feel as if your liver has been split in two – or three. There is no alternative but to drop to the ground and writhe; you can't 'ride' it out or fake it. Your head is clear and saying "get up, get up" but your body is temporarily paralysed as you struggle on the floor in excruciating pain, for about 10 to 20 seconds. Then it suddenly lifts, without leaving any real after effect. Unfortunately, by that time you have already been counted out on the floor, feeling as if your liver has been removed without an anaesthetic. It has nothing to do with being tough and being able to 'take a punch'. Big Jimmy Abbot was a well-known South African bruiser who didn't give a shit about much, but he was surprisingly friendly as he asked if I was OK, in a strangely high-pitched voice, and extended a huge arm to help me up. Another good lesson from the school of 'never assume or believe that a much bigger man will take it easy on you, just because he is four times your size'.

The promoter seemed pleased with what he saw and gave me a big professional smile.

"Alright, you look OK. I'm going to get you matched up as a middleweight on the next show at the Fabulous Forum. You got about four weeks to get yourself in shape."

I nodded my thanks.

§

I had not heard from Eddie the Stunt Man for nearly three weeks. I had left a few messages for him, telling him I wanted my army photo album back, but still no reply. And now his phone was disconnected. He and I had met up a few times at the West Beach Bar & Grill in Venice, and once at a nightclub in Hollywood. He had told me that someone he knew was interested in marketing the *Self Defence for Housewives* video and had said he would arrange a meeting soon. He had been throwing around big numbers, like $60,000, for signing a deal. Even though I would get only a small portion of the deal it still sounded like a fortune. He had taken his own VHS recording of the tape, said that the guy really liked it and thought it could work if marketed properly, as a South African no-holds-barred form of self-defence. I had thought all of this was just great and had listened eagerly as we downed our rum and cokes.

We had chatted a lot ... I had told him about my time as a South African paratrooper in Angola and had shown him my photograph album. His eyes widened as he flipped through the pages, looking at photos of the Angolan bush and the head count of war; terrorists pulled into rows having been shot to pieces, Soviet BTR armoured vehicles, black smoke billowing from a wrecked T55 Soviet tank, vehicles blown to bits by land mines, bomb smoke, and gritty young South African paratroopers grasping their trusty rifles, their faces smeared with 'black is beautiful' camouflage grease.

Bat Out of Hell

Eddie had been impressed.

"Jeez! This is quite a photo album, hey? Can I borrow this? I want to show my fiancée. I was in the RLI but I don't have any photos. I want to show her what it was really like."

I hesitated. I knew I shouldn't let this photo album out of my hands. But then I relented and told him he could borrow it, on condition that he guard it with his life, because it meant a lot to me. He assured me that he would and that he would call me in a few days to arrange the meeting with the movie guy and to return my photo album. That had been more than three weeks ago, and I hadn't heard from him since.

This was not your normal photo album. This was a pictorial résumé of my past. Horrific to many, maybe difficult to understand, but to me and my friends, whose grimy faces peered at me from the photos, as they stood next to burnt out Soviet military vehicles, dead terrorists, captured Soviet tanks, it had been our reality. Just out of high school we had done our duty for our country, destroying its enemies. Our Paratroop Delta Company had accounted for the deaths of over 200 terrorists, leaving them sprawled in the sand. These armed, communist backed insurgents would no longer be infiltrating through the bush, crossing the Border, to abduct and kill people, to lay land mines. The photo album was my only link to a time long gone.

I had dropped into the swanky West Beach restaurant on Thursday and Friday, but there was no sign of Eddie. Patrons chatted and sweated and mopped their brows; apparently the air conditioner couldn't keep up with the heat wave holding Los Angeles hostage. At the bar I had recognised a curly haired man I had seen with Eddie a few times. He told me he hadn't seen Eddie, but he knew the guy with whom Eddie had shared a condo in Venice. I told him that Eddie had borrowed something of mine that meant a lot to me, asked him to call me if he ran into this ex roommate, and wrote my phone number on a paper napkin. He nodded his agreement. He seemed a straight dude and not cocaine *woes* like a lot of the yuppies who hung out there. The next night I drove to a club in Hollywood that I knew Eddie liked to visit. Country music was making a big comeback in LA, a cowboy line dancing craze had swept through city and quite a few country dancing clubs had opened up.

I was not in a good mood. I leaned against the long bar at In Cahoots, sipping a welcome cold beer. The club was packed. I knew this was one of Eddie's favourite haunts but he was nowhere to be seen. It seemed everyone was trying to escape the heat by visiting an air-conditioned venue. I watched lines of girls with big hair in tight jeans dancing the 'electric slide' under the flashing lights. I didn't like country music and felt as stiff as a Orange Free State farmer at an English tea party in the Devon countryside.

I wondered what Eddie's game was. Maybe he had had to leave for a movie shoot, do some stunts, and would soon be back? He had seemed like an all right guy … although whenever I had asked him about his time in the RLI he always seemed to change the subject. I watched a group of girls at a table, laughing and talking. They were close by and looked friendly, so I walked over and asked one of them if I could buy her a drink. They couldn't hear me over the loud country music, so I asked again. The girl turned her head and sat down. I heard some guy shouting in my ear from the other side.

"Hey dude, they don't want to talk to you."

I turned to look at him. I couldn't hear everything he was saying but I could see his mouth moving a mile a minute, Yank style. He didn't stop talking and moved closer to me, so I could hear him better. What did they teach the kids over here? What do you think happens when you shout into someone's face? The long-haired Californian seemed at ease, unconcerned, and kept flapping his lips at me. I was in no mood for this shit. He had just finished the last of his bullshit when I hit him with a fast one-two-three combination punch that sent him flying back over the chairs, onto the floor and into the corner. My angle was not perfect but the combination had been good enough to lay him out, flat on his back, his eyes huge with shock.

"That's how we do it in Benoni when you chip in pal!"

He stayed down on the red carpet, wide-eyed, as I hovered over him menacingly, my fists clenched.

Why does he seem so surprised? Does he seriously think he can talk to someone like that and nothing will happen?

As with all LA night clubs the security man was on the scene in a few seconds. I had learned this lesson quickly in my short time in the US; I pointed to the wide-eyed irritant on the floor, and announced, with authority, "That's the guy!"

The bouncer took me at my word and reached down to grab the long-haired Californian. It was all the time I needed. I turned on my heel and headed straight for the exit. For once I was not the one being pointed at.

My search for Eddie and my stolen photo album was over for the night.

§

Even though I was enjoying in myself in California I couldn't help feeling like a stranger. Square peg round hole. Luckily I'd planned not to stay in America for long; I would definitely be going back to South Africa in the near future. I'd noticed another strange thing: now that I was in a different country, memories of my home country were becoming more positive … my life in Africa, with family, good friends and good times, was fitting itself into my new memory bank. Trouble was, besides my recollections of *braaivleis*, blue skies and Chevrolet, some of my strongest memories were of my time as a paratrooper, fighting in Angola. Also, I seemed a very different person from the fun-loving, relaxed people I was meeting in LA. They were chilled Californians, who seemed to like living in La La Land … or was I the one living in La La Land? They were relaxed, kicked back, unconcerned about the threat out there. Didn't they know about the beast? Didn't they know they had to be ready, prepared? I was wound up like a spring, primed to hunt down the beast *and* his sidekick, the boogieman, to find them before they found us. I lived permanently in a heightened state of preparedness, ready to spring into action at the first sign of danger. Get them before they get you.

I had heard people in LA talk about their heroes, people who could make touchdowns, or shoot hoops, or were actors in memorable movie scenes. I had even met people who equated movie scenes with real life events and conversations …well, I suppose I was living in Hollywood, after all. But I went quiet when talking to them and couldn't relate to these people. My heroes and role models were Airborne soldiers, men larger than life. Sergeant Majors who shared joint command with God, who could make the ground shake as they brought six hundred paratroopers to attention. Young company commanders, 25 years old, leading paratrooper companies across a country border into Angola, to attack terrorist training base camps deep in the bush. My heroes were hard-faced, 22-year-old lieutenants, who led the platoon from the front into a firefight; unflinchingly loud sergeants, who bullied troops daily, into unquestioning discipline; young recruits who gave the army their all; Special Forces operators – quiet men with deep frowns, steady eyes and old AK-47 wounds in their bodies; the men of 32 Battalion, aka the 'Buffalo Battalion' or 'The Terrible Ones' – foot soldiers who fought year after year, their African faces etched with deep lines, like footpaths in the bush, from years of war. I wondered if I had become one of them?

These were the men that I thought about and looked up to; they were my role models, my heroes; the type of men who didn't fit into the Los Angeles scene too well.

Chapter Seventeen

THE BEST PRICE I CAN GET

'Wanted Dead or Alive' ~ Bon Jovi

I had arrived to collect Stephanie LaMotta from her apartment and could hear her talking loudly the minute I exited the small, old-fashioned cage-style elevator. She had the door open to the hallway, to allow the heat to escape. The City of Angels was still firmly in the grip of a heat wave. She seemed to be coming to the end of a telephone conversation. I made a funny face at her and she smiled then said, "Oh Dad, my friend from South Africa is here, he's fighting at the Forum in a few weeks." She laughed and then handed me the phone.

None other than the Raging Bull, Jake LaMotta himself, was at the other end, in New York.

"How ya' doin? Ya gotta fight comin' up?"

"*Ja,* in a couple weeks. I'm just getting ready."

"What weight you fightin'?"

"Middleweight."

"It's a helluva hard division, ask me, I know! You in shape?"

"I think so."

"Well, good luck!"

"Thanks."

Smiling, a little stunned, I handed the phone back to Stephanie.

Jake LaMotta. The Raging Bull himself. Stephanie and I had recently watched *The Raging Bull* on a rented VHS video. We had driven to a few video stores before we found the movie and I had watched in amusement as Stephanie entered each store in her usual state of emergency manner, enquiring in a voice loud enough for half the store to hear, "Do you have the movie of my dad's life story, *The Raging Bull*?"

Of course, all heads in each of the video stores immediately swivelled in her direction – the desired effect. We finally found a copy at a store off Hollywood Boulevard. Robert De Niro portrayed a portly-looking Jake LaMotta, flying into fits of rage, busting up the kitchen at home, beating up opponents in the ring. Stephanie said De Niro had put on sixty pounds to give the role authenticity and had acted just like her dad. I was not sure I wanted to meet Jake LaMotta. He had been an old school middleweight fighter, tough as old boots, had fought Sugar Ray Robinson six times. Their sixth and last fight, with LaMotta finally world champion Robinson punished LaMotta so badly in the later rounds that the fight became known as boxing's Saint Valentine's Day Massacre. While Robinson had won five of their bouts over a nine-year period, and LaMotta only one, Robinson had never been able to knock LaMotta off his feet.

Stephanie was really excited about my upcoming fight at the Forum. This was 1986 and the Fabulous Forum was the home of the LA Lakers, Magic Johnson, and the sports place To Be in Los Angeles at the time. Even my favourite rocker, Jimmy Hendrix, had played at the Forum.

§

I gunned the Mustang down La Brea. The American beauty was old but the huge 350 engine responded to the slightest touch on its very loose accelerator. We were on our way to meet another well-known person, a movie star, Mickey Rourke. In a strange sort of encounter, I had very recently met Mickey at the Broadway Boxing gym. There were not many white fighters in the Broadway gym and I figured he was just another fighter, although he was a lot more talkative than most fighters. He had come over to make small talk but I had not been responsive – it was not boxing gym etiquette to chit-chat with other fighters. On a recent occasion, after I had finished a particularly hard sparring match with a black kid who had got the better of me, Mickey had come over while I was packing my gear. Wearing a crooked little smile, he asked, "What are you getting ready for, you got a fight coming up?"

"Got a fight at the Forum."

"Hey! The Forum!" he responded enthusiastically. "If you need any boxing gear I have a ton of stuff, gloves, anything you need, you need some boots? I got some great leather boots. What size are you? You look the same as me, I'll bring them over next time I come, I get all the stuff for free."

I thanked him and we shook hands, but I still wasn't quite sure who or what he was. It just so happened that about a week later I went to see a movie called *Year of the Dragon* at the Chinese Mann Theatre on Hollywood Boulevard. In amazement I recognised the lead actor in the movie as the guy with the crooked smile I had been talking to at the gym. *Hey! That's Mickey Rourke – he's the guy in the boxing gym*! It was a great movie and a couple days later, at the gym, I told him I had seen it and asked if that had really been him?

"Yeah, I'm an actor. It's a sissy business but that's what I do."

He immediately launched into a long description of the bullshit one had to endure, working in Hollywood, and said the acting game was full of bullshit. I was quite surprised at his attitude; it sounded like he didn't really enjoy acting. But I thought he had done some great acting in *Year of the Dragon* and told him so. Not everyone can become a Hollywood star actor.

We had chatted more at the gym, whenever we ran into each other, and he told me that he usually hung out at the Improve Comedy Club on Melrose Ave, of a Friday night, and I should swing by and join him in a beer. Mickey had also brought me some boxing kit – white leather boots and gloves. I was really thankful, I was low on money and could never have afforded the quality equipment that he gave me. He said he got it free of charge, from sponsors and friends.

Stephanie told me that the Improve Comedy Club was a fun place, a comedy club as well as a bar and restaurant, so we headed down there at about 21h00 the next Friday. The neon signs sparkled, reflecting off the pack of motorcycles, ape hanger handles and all, parked outside the club. Mickey Rourke was at the bar, surrounded by a group of surly looking, long-haired motorbike boys, who clearly thought they were tough. To me, coming from Benoni, knowing the Boksburg, Edenvale and Jo'burg bikers, they looked like fresh-faced kids dressed up in biker outfits. I ordered drinks for Stephanie and me, then walked through the crowds and said "hi" to Mickey. He turned, smiled at me and then at his group, as he made space for us at the bar.

"Hey! This is my friend from South Africa. He's a boxer ... got a fight coming up at the Forum."

On cue they all grinned and gave us some room.

I think the fact that I had no idea who he was when I met him, and knew little and couldn't have cared less about the movie industry, helped us get along. All I wanted to talk about was boxing. We chatted about the sweet science and its different styles. I liked the killer fighters who put it all on the line, like my heroes: Charlie Weir, Roberto Duran, Papino Cueves. Take no prisoners, destroyers. Mickey laughed and we drank a toast to the fight game. I shouldn't have been going out, having late nights, and definitely not having any beers, but I figured I could run it off the next day, or on Sunday.

It wasn't until midnight that Mickey and his crew left.

"Hey! Good luck, I'll see you in the gym," Mickey waved.

They took off into the hot summer night, hanging on like apes to their high handle bars, their Harleys farting and weaving in and out of the Melrose Ave traffic.

Stephanie and I stayed on, past midnight, and had another drink.

§

It was not long afterwards that I received a typed letter in the mail box from my father. I recognised the South African postage stamps on the envelope before I saw my name. Beautiful birds, with long black tails. It was a short and to the point letter, as was my father's style. He said it all in no more than ten lines:

> *…Your mother and I are getting a divorce, after 30 years of marriage. I will try and sell the plot as soon as possible, for the best price I can get for it. The home as you and your brother knew it, will not be here anymore. The best advice that I can give you is to stay in America if you can. This country is changing and no one knows where it's headed … Love you, Dad.*

It was not often that I received a letter from my father. I missed my parents, my sister, the good friends I had grown up with … I missed my people. I missed the five dogs who ran around the farm. South African girls. I missed South African food. I even missed people that I thought I would never, ever miss. I was ready to go back home. I felt compelled to make a phone call home, just as soon as I could.

So, a few days later, while on my lunch break, covered in construction dust from demolishing a ceiling, I stood in the baking sun at a sidewalk pay phone, and made a call to South Africa, (no cell phones at the time). I was in the busy centre of Korea town, close to downtown Los Angeles. I dropped a handful of quarters into the coin slot and dialled the code for South Africa. I was finally getting the hang of making these overseas calls from a call box. I put a finger in my left ear and shouted into the receiver, over the noise of the traffic. My mother picked up the phone with a casual "hello", sounding as if she was just a block away. I could hear her smiling warmly as she recovered from her surprise and asked me how things were going, and when was I planning to come back home.

It was fantastic to hear my mother's voice on the clear line. She chatted on about this and that, the usual daily goings on. I shoved my finger harder into my ear and just listened, without talking, her voice a tonic to my soul. Finally, I interrupted and asked her about the divorce – what's going on? Are you and Dad OK? She told me yes, they were getting divorced, after all these years, and she would be moving to another house, soon.

I listened as my mother spoke. It was a rare treat. I fumbled desperately with another handful of quarters, pushing them into the pay phone. The line was unusually clear. I was delighted that even over the noisy background of the busy Korea town street, I could hear the wonderful cooing of African doves, behind my mother's voice. I knew exactly where she was sitting while she spoke to me. She was sitting in the back verandah of the big, 70-year-old Cape Dutch style farmhouse. Rows of louvre windows opened onto a dark, wooded section of the garden, next to the wide front lawns where I had played as a kid. There was a huge, beautiful, twisted, seventy-year-old Black Wattle tree that grew out of the ground at an angle, with branches that reached down to the ground, making the giant tree look like a huge spider, its eight legs holding it up.

African turtledoves do not have a soft, sad and lonely voice, like the mourning doves I had heard in California. African doves coo with a loud, satisfied sound of contentment that can be heard easily, from a long pellet gun shot away. They pushed out their beautiful call, sounding like a choir. The tall dark trees behind the farmhouse had been a favourite spot for these peaceful birds, resting, or calling for a mate, or roosting for the night. It was a sound I had grown up with and had become so constant that, as I grew older, I didn't even hear it anymore … like living near running water. Now, on the busy street of Korea town, I could hear the African doves from our garden, over the clear phone line, 10,000 miles away.

"When are you coming back home … to South Africa, darling?" my mother asked.

"Soon Mom; probably see you in a few months."

I felt refreshed and invigorated after talking to my lovely mother. She sounded happy and strong. I wore a broad smile as I hung up the pay phone and squinted into the sun. The fellow on the phone next to me, wearing business slacks and tie, also hung up. He had been looking at me with concern as I shouted, one finger halfway down my Eustachian tubes, on the left, into my family home 10,000 miles away, into the phone receiver there.

The stranger asked if everything was alright, and could he help in any way. I was not dressed in manual working clothes, like a worker would have been; I was wearing an ordinary shirt and jeans, but they were filthy from working. So I must have looked a sight, shouting into the phone.

Bless him.

I smiled and told him that I was just fine, thank you, but thank you for your concern. Americans are a good-hearted people.

'I Can Hear It In The Air Tonight' ~ *Phil Collins*

It was a miserably hot day on which to get a broken nose and it wasn't going to be mine.

The strong South Central Los Angeles boxer down at the Broadway gym had finally got his wish. My trainer, Marty Monroe, who I had recently run into having first met in South Africa announced to his coach that we were ready to spar. A last heat wave of summer had gripped the city and the row of tilted-up open windows had brought the street noise and traffic fumes wafting into the gym. A strong black kid at the gym recently had been given

Bat Out of Hell

his professional boxing license. He and his trainer had been eyeing me, the only white boxer in the gym, for the last couple of weeks. He had heard that I was fighting at The Fabulous Forum in Inglewood and was licking his chops to show me that he should be fighting in my place. The gym confrontation had been brewing for some weeks and today was the day.

"Get your left out fast, like snatching a fly out the air!" Marty snorted.

Marty had been coaching me to use a short, no telegraph, shoulder punch. For three weeks I'd been standing 10 inches from the bag. In the beginning it had been impossible to punch from 10 inches, but by the third week I had got it all together. It felt amazing. Suddenly I had the beginning of a short, ten-inch, solid lightning punch that I had never known existed. It had been impossible to punch from such a short distance, because there was no space in which to extend your arm. Therefore, it all had to come from the shoulder – or the short punch wouldn't work. It's akin to the Bruce Lee six-inch punch theory. It's the torque within the upper body, shoulder and even hips that makes the punch so powerful.

Marty Monroe smeared Vaseline on my hard-as-a-rock, Mexican-made M&M gloves, while I watched the black kid getting ready. He had a glint in his eye as his trainer buckled on his headguard.

"Just go in there and do what we've been working on. Shoot the left hand fast from the shoulder, just like in training – then smash him with the right," Marty whispered, but loudly.

I wondered why it was that American blacks and latinos automatically thought they could beat any white guy in a fight. I must have missed that class when I had grown up in South Africa.

The well-endowed black fighter stood in his corner, bouncing athletically on his toes, flexing his muscles. He seemed excited. He was a new professional boxer and had been licking his chops while watching me work out for my upcoming fight. He wanted to use me, to gauge himself as a newcomer in the professional ranks. He had even come up to me once, after our trainers had exchanged words, and said that he should be fighting me at The Fabulous Forum. I had not answered him.

He was my height but very well built, with thick strong legs and a strong upper body, and a thick boxer's neck. I had been in no doubt that he and I would face off against each other sometime soon, and had planned well for this very day. Over the last few weeks I had watched him from the corner of my eye. He was too slow; he also talked too much to his trainer, in-between throwing a series of combination punches. If he thought I was some white boy who had just walked into the boxing gym, because I recently I had seen a Rocky movie, he had a big fucking surprise coming. I had been knocking out big deals like him since I was in high school. His other big mistake was that he thought he was too tough … which is the biggest mistake you can make in any boxing gym. It's a humble game.

"Do it!" Marty shouted in my ear.

The strong black fighter leapt forward into the middle of the ring, his head tucked in low, his eyes wide. He had been waiting for this for almost a month. My arms felt alive, as if they had volts of electricity flowing through them. Quickly I turned my back to the long row of windows at the Broadway gym, an old gym trick he didn't know, yet, as he squinted, half blinded by the low, late afternoon glare of the sun. I shot my first solid left-hand into his face, as fast as 'Razor' Ruddock. His head snapped back. I did this again, and again, before he could even launch his first punch. His punch became my trigger. I punched as he punched, but I was faster. He tried to throw a few big hooks … I slammed a solid, shoulder-driven, straight left into his mouth and nose, and pulled my punch back before his had even reached me. This was beautiful! My short distance, high-speed training was working like magic.

His expression changed quickly, having tasted a few solid straight lefts with my full shoulder and body weight behind them. A trapped look appeared in his eyes and he tried to change his style. He dropped his left, low, and started doing the boogie-woogie-with-hooks, American style. I was European style. Straight up, chin tucked in, hands high with laser straight punches. We came from two different schools of boxing and, today, mine was the superior school.

I slammed my left as fast as a bullet into his mouth, from my shoulder, again and again. His eyes rolled back in his head from the snap. It felt as if my punches did not belong to me. They were coming out with a timing of their own. Fuck! Marty Monroe was right. My left now snapped out by itself with a shoulder behind it. Thick blood ran from his nose into his mouth. His eyes were watering. Both corners were loudly shouting advice for this long-awaited sparring match, but it was my coach, Marty, who was ecstatic, shouting the loudest, jumping up and down with glee, both feet on the ring apron.

"Knock him out, Boss! Knock him out, knock him out!"

The mainly all black gym had come to a stop. Thirty-odd boxers had stopped hitting the bag, or working out, mesmerised by the sparring match that had immediately morphed into a long time coming fight. People separated into supporters for him, supporters for me.

"C'mon! Get close in Tyrone!"

"Go my man! Keep that left hand going, it working good!"

The gym was hot as a sauna. His trainer wiped blood from his nose and mouth and shouted instructions in his ear. He stood up, looking confused. This sparring session had quickly turned into a full-on fight, which the Broadway gym was famous for. He came out for the third round and tried to keep his hands up high, to block my straight punches. He was now as slow as an ox stuck in mud. I had no mercy. I extended my punches straight down the pipe between his gloves and they landed solidly. Soon the snot and blood was running into his mouth again. Part of me felt like giving him a chance; the other part silently shouted at me to hurt him, destroy him, show him! How dare he challenge me, blatantly, like I was some punk white boy beginner!

"Keep going! Don't stop Boss! Knock him out!" Big Marty shouted, loving it.

My adversary staggered into the middle of the ring, at a loss as to what to do, and lowered his hands for just a second too long. Instantly I loaded up with a straight right cross that came all the way from South Africa. His legs buckled and he dropped, almost to his knees.

"Time! Time!" shouted his corner, jumping into the ring.

"Hey, your man going too hard, this a sparring match man … what's the matter with him … this ain't a fight!"

Marty Monroe also leaped into the ring, ready to do battle. Marty had been a sparring partner for Gerrie Coetzee, and a top ten heavy weight contender. He was well known for his famous fight against Eddy 'The Animal' Lopez.

"Too hard? This is professional boxing, baby. You the one's been asking us to spar … for weeks." Marty stood his ground and shouted, gleefully, "What's wrong now? Your man not ready? This is the pros Daddy! If he can't handle it then maybe your man's not ready for the pros!"

I was fortunate to cross paths again with Marty Monroe at the tough Broadway Gym in Los Angeles after meeting him in Johannesburg. I learned a lot from Marty as a trainer albeit a short reunion.

The strong black kid looked out on his feet. He wanted no more. His corner wiped the snot and blood from his face.

Marty was ecstatic that his training methods for the left hand had worked so well. He wiped me down with a towel.

"You see? I told you that's how to work that left jab, didn't I? See how it worked!"

I had to agree. For three weeks I had been standing ten inches from the bag, working a fast, hard left hand, and it had worked beautifully.

"Yes, Marty, it sure did!"

"I learned that from Earnie Shavers himself, the hardest hitting fighter on the planet!" Marty told me, smiling ear to ear.

I had first met Marty in the boxing gym when he came to South Africa with Jackie McCoy, as one of Gerrie Coetzee's sparring partners for the Greg Page fight at Sun City. He had been the big heavyweight sparring partner who always carried a huge boom box radio on his shoulder; they had trained in the Yeoville gym. By chance they had all attended the boxing event in which I had fought and knocked out my opponent in the first round. Then, to my great good fortune, I had run into Marty again while I was working security in Hollywood. We had chatted and realised we had met each other earlier, in South Africa, and that Marty had been at my fight when I knocked down the feared Willie Nolson, three times in the first round. In LA the delighted Marty had recalled, "I seen you fight in South Africa boss, when you knocked that guy down – three times!" and had immediately made me an offer, "Let me train you, here in the US."

Now, tonight, I was feeling good. I was very nearly the only white fighter in the Broadway gym and the black boxers around me were laughing and chatting about the unexpected street fight and defeat of the young pro.

But my faded T-shirt from the Coetzee vs Page bout was finally no good anymore, soaked with the blood of my opponent.

Following that street fight, for reasons unknown, Marty stopped coming to the gym, so he and I were unable to continue working together as coach and boxer. It was a real pity; Marty Monroe was the only trainer with whom I had bonded, and since then I had been running solo, alone, bouncing from one trainer to another. The kiss of death for a boxer.

§

The swanky new apartment complex Daryl and I were living in was great. It was closer to the beach with a frequent cool, sea breeze, and I had recently discovered a great cycling path that led all the way through to the beach. I had been using this for roadwork while I was getting into shape for an upcoming fight. Also, running to the beach was a lot more enjoyable than running in downtown Hollywood. I sucked the cool marine air deeply through my nose, keeping up a good steady pace, picking my way between the slow coaches walking their dogs, and the cyclists. There was a strong smell of rotten seaweed from the huge concrete storm water channel that washed into the sea. I breathed deeply, ramping up my pace to a three-quarter sprint, getting ready for the last hundred metres of full out sprint to the beach. My arms pumped high at my side, up and down. Don't trip now! I deliberately lifted my knees high, using a choppy style and running dangerously fast, close to a full sprint. People cleared out of my way and I added a little zig-zag, to break my rhythm and make things harder.

In a micro second my mind flashed back to the tall, black FAPLA soldier who leapt from a bunker, thirty feet in front of us …

…He had watched us approaching over the dry field towards the bunker where he had been hiding, holding his position. He had not fled earlier, like the others. We were spread out in battle formation and he had waited too late, and knew a grenade was a minute away from being thrown into the bunker, where he was trapped. At the very last moment he leapt, shirtless, from the bunker, in one fast fluid move and was immediately on his feet running. Like a jack rabbit he took off in a full sprint, racing for his life, zig-zagging to make a harder target for the bullets he knew would come. His elbows pumped high as he ran, like an Olympic athlete, a sprinter, in a run for his life. Had he shed his military camouflage FAPLA shirt in the hope of mercy? He was unusually tall and lean, the bare skin of his sinewy, muscular back shone black as tar. I watched his shoulder blades bulging, his legs driving the huge zig-zag strides. His unarmed hands were open and flat, cutting the air like blades. The image is burned into my brain.

I lifted my rifle. It seemed like slow motion but it took mere seconds.

"There!"

Six of us, paratroopers, recovered from our surprise, slammed our rifles into our shoulders and began firing at him as fast as we could. Swiftly he reached full speed, racing across the open clearing. His big boots kicked up dirt as he dug them into the sand to turn abruptly, to run a sharp zig-zag from side to side in the sprint for his life, avoiding the hail of our bullets as though charmed. Through the gun smoke I saw that we couldn't hit him, that our bullets were kicking up dirt ahead of him. In a second I changed my footing to a better position. I exhaled, aimed between his shoulder blades, squeezed off four or five fast shots. He ran at full speed, dodging our bullets as though his open back was shielded by a hand.

I kept my rifle up but involuntarily stopped shooting, just watched him go.

He was almost at the tree line. I lifted my finger off my trigger and heard myself silently shouting, "Go!Go! You're almost there! Go for it!"

I kept my rifle up so the others couldn't see I had stopped shooting. He kept running. I could hardly breathe amid the thick pall of gun smoke. Barely a few metres from the safety of the tree line the tall youth seemed to trip over his feet. His long legs twisted, his body ploughed into the white sand of Ondjiva. No movement ... no sound. We moved forward cautiously. Someone placed a high velocity shot that took off the top of his head. He lay there, his eyes open.

We moved on.

Out of nowhere I endured this vivid flashback while still running, pumping my elbows in a full speed sprint, getting closer to the beach. *What terror as he ran, like I'm running now.* The next second my body seized up. It felt like my arms, legs and lungs had been thrust into reverse, like a jet engine landing. I moaned as negative chemicals shot through my body, shutting it down. The plug had been pulled on me and my sprint came to an immediate halt, as though I had torn a muscle. My lungs locked themselves in reverse and wouldn't take in air. I had gone from close to a full sprint to a dead stop, within ten metres.

"AAAHH!" I gave an involuntary shout of despair at my mental and physical shut down.

What the fuck!

I stumbled off the busy bicycle path like a race car with a blown engine, sucking hard for air. I leant against the fence to catch my breath, my chest heaving. Other cyclists and joggers went past me; some of them looked at me as if I had hurt myself. I stared towards the beach, up ahead.

Where the hell had that thought come from?

And then I wondered what the FAPLA soldier had thought, watching our weary platoon approaching over the dry field towards the bunker in which he was hiding. He must have watched us approach for about ten minutes while the realisation dawned that he was doomed. Why hadn't he run, escaped, earlier? Was he trying to be brave?

The mental flashback that I had just 'seen' was as vivid as the day of that event. I remembered that day clearly, it had been my twenty-first birthday and the day had started with a bang.

South Africa had sent two battle groups across the Border into Angola, to attack the big military base at Xangongo, and the smaller town of Ondjiva. It had been like viewing a movie. We watched the South African Mirage fighter jets in vertical dives, from miles high, down through the small puffy clouds of flak from Angolan anti-aircraft guns, to deliver their 1,000 pound bombs into the armed positions of the FAPLA base, sending brown columns of bomb smoke thirty stories high, with a sound louder than any thunder clap you have ever heard.

Soon the show was over and it was our turn. Under fire, with bullets zipping and cracking past us our company of paratroopers kicked open the heavy sides of the Buffel troop carriers, leaped leap out and began to advance, firing, towards the still unseen trenches of the big Angolan base camp ahead. We didn't get very far from our vehicles before having to dive close to the ground, as bullets cracked close overhead. Each time we tried to spring up, to dash three steps forward as trained, bullets cracked past, close to our ears. Our advance into the Angolan military base quickly ground to a halt ... we were pinned down on the white sand, under accurate fire.

What strange places one's mind wanders into while pinned down, under fire, unable to move ... time seemed to stand still. In this soul-searching time of 'pondering and observation', we watched as our brave medics came running from behind, twice, to collect Kruger (shot in the hand) and then Fourie (shot in the leg). Finally, the ground under us started shaking – another bomb run had been called for, to free us up. Again we watched as an Impala jet came streaking low over the trees, not far ahead of us, to deliver smaller 250 pound bombs. The fire from ahead of us stopped and finally after maybe close to an hour we could heave ourselves up, to move forward three paces at a time, then dive down, then up again. Not for long. No sooner had we advanced fifty metres closer to the first trench than a Soviet tank came out at us from the tree line to our right, sending the foremost troops scattering for cover, again, as the tank's big diesel engine roared, sounding as if the driver was stuck in first gear or something. Again we dived down flat on the sand; there was very little cover so we had to make ourselves as flat as possible, listening to the tank revving its engine in the tree line. Straight out of a movie, as quick as a blink and coming from behind us, a South African Eland armoured car with a 90 mm cannon darted past, weaving between our staggered lines of troops, to a point thirty feet past me. Then it turned right, spraying sand, stopped to face the tank, aimed and fired a 90 mm shot that blew the turret off the tank. Black smoke billowed from the burning tank.

It was one hell of a way to spend my twenty-first birthday, and it wasn't over yet.

As soon as we advanced past the burning tank the Soviet anti-aircraft guns in the base camp, which had been firing at our Mirage jets, dropped their barrels to ground level and started to shoot brain numbing, terrifying, burps of 23 mm anti-aircraft shells over our heads, bringing the branches of large trees crashing down around and behind us. Again, we dived down and hugged the dirt as tree limbs fell around us. It took us a vulnerable 45 minutes to figure out that the guns were shooting high, about 6 feet above our heads, and could not get any lower. After a good hour of this sporadic but determined 23mm fire, the brave FAPLA anti-aircraft gunner must have run out of ammunition, or left his post, because the anti-aircraft shooting stopped, thankfully.

But the fun wasn't over yet. Just when we thought we had reached the trenches a hidden machine gunner started firing sporadic, but accurate long bursts at us, from a hidden position. He fired erratically, just enough to keep us down and not reveal his location. After perhaps 40 minutes of this cat and mouse game, our sharp-eyed RSM, Sakkie Marais pinpointed his hidden position and ordered Aaron 'Doogy' Green to pour 7.62 machine-gun fire into a distant, semi-concealed sand wall bunker complex. The FAPLA machine gunner stopped firing. All this before 10h00 that morning.

Only then could we enter the massive trench system surrounding the 13 square kilometre MPLA base, to start an exhausting 24 hours of trench and bunker clearing. Many of the Angolan soldiers had escaped through the trenches into the surrounding bush, after the initial early morning attack. But many of them had hidden, or were trapped, and decided to die fighting while waiting for a chance to escape, in a very *eventful night to come.*

The tall Angolan soldier who had jumped from the bunker a few metres in front of us and sprinted for his life, had been a mid-afternoon event in that long, hard day.

This was not the first time that I had experienced flashbacks. Most of them were quite normal, benign, so I thought. Even a simple thing, like the taste of hot, sweet tea, could bring back pleasant memories of scooping up a cup of tea after guard duty, or cooking up a brew out in the bush over a small fuel tablet. Most memories were good. The smell of freshly torn leaves, or freshly dug dirt … in a second could take me back to a deep ambush hide where we had lain for hours. Other flashbacks or memories, on occasions, were utterly debilitating and could be triggered at the strangest times.

Sometimes, while enjoying a simple pleasure, like watching a band play in a nightclub, trying to enjoy the music and have a good time like others around me, would launch me straight back into a fire fight that led to some terrible killing, to terrorists being shot to pieces. As if I was not allowed to enjoy life anymore? Why? What had I done? I quickly learned to switch off and detach my emotions, rather than try and enjoy them like others could, because sometimes they were hijacked by an inner voice shouting, "Killer! Killer!"

Of course, I didn't have bad memories all the time; I reasoned to myself that the bad ones were just memories of my military service, but it was not that simple … there was a price to pay. The spirits of the blood we had spilled in the white sands of Angola and Namibia demanded that they be acknowledged, not forgotten, and had found a way to return. They worked very effectively, manifesting themselves in the most perverse ways, affecting me and those closest to me, robbing me of my most precious memories and loving moments, in the midst of a loving memory of my family, or a close loved one, I would be hijacked by the headless ghosts of SWAPO fighters or shattered FAPLA fighters, their brains on the sand, twisted in death, perverting my memories so that I saw my loved ones shot and broken to pieces, like the men we had left under dry bushes in Angola.

At first these visions were so terrible, so shocking, that I would lose my breath, like a punch to the stomach, and have to pull over to the side of the road in busy LA traffic to recover and gather myself. Any good and precious thought or memory could be ambushed, drowned in the blood of men with their brains blown out, mothers cut in half from 20 mm shells while still clutching their dead children. How could I have these visions! I felt very ashamed and didn't dare tell a soul about them.

Why was I having these involuntary, intrusive thoughts? Associations? Flashbacks? I was far from a superstitious man but perhaps this is what that lunatic street bum had meant, sometime ago, when the ragged filthy man had rushed across the busy street weaving his way through the traffic of West Los Angeles to get to me, as if he knew me, had singled me out, had been waiting for me. He had run across the road then, in mere seconds, and accosted me, stopping a foot in front of me on the sidewalk.

"Satan will get the ones closest to you! He will get the ones closest to you!" he screamed at me, splattering filthy spittle into my face, his insane eyes glittering.

Immediately I shoved the grimy faced street bum backward. He stumbled but then jumped forward in his ragged, torn clothes, filled with manic energy, determined to fight me, his fists held high. I reacted immediately when he came at me again, using a straight left to deter him. Not a damn. He kept on with his crazy assault, unafraid, bobbing and weaving and boxing like Satan himself, fighting at the Grand Olympic Auditorium.

What the fuck!

Realising that he was a nutter I turned serious and I drove some fast, hard punches into his skinny body, trying to stop his attack. Our exchange took longer than expected and progressed from the sidewalk to the street, but finally I sunk a long fast shot into his middle and he folded, in the centre of the road, gasping for breath amongst the backed-up cars. I was beside myself with the shock of his spontaneous attack and kicked furiously at his sack of filthy belongings on the sidewalk.

"He will get the ones closest to you!"

I walked away fast, wanting to get away from the unpleasant scene as quickly as possible.

But I was pretty shaken – and I have never forgotten it.

Chapter Eighteen

ALWAYS FIGHT HARD

'Run to You' ~ Bryan Adams

The bar at the West Beach restaurant in Venice was as busy as usual. I sat and ordered a beer. The guy helping me to try and track down Eddie had told me that Eddie's ex roommate had agreed to meet me. The skinny fellow sniggered when I told him that I had lent Eddie my army photo album, and my (our) self-defence video, and that he had disappeared with them.

"You'll never see that photo album again; Eddie lives out in Florida. This guy is a con and a thief. He talks shit like it's made yesterday, for free."

"What about the movie stuntman stuff?"

"All bullshit, most of it anyway."

"Eddie said that he was meeting with a guy interested in my video?"

"All bullshit, Eddie is a chronic liar; everything he says is bullshit."

I felt numb. I didn't care about the self-defence video that had vanished with Eddie, I could always get another copy. But I couldn't believe that someone would rip off my army photo album. It was pretty low, to steal a photo album from someone, to brag about something you didn't do. The curly haired guy at the Bar gave me a phone number and an address for Eddie, in Florida. I drove home late, through thick Friday night traffic, thinking about my next step. Maybe it was a good thing that the photo album had gone? Maybe it should be gone. Darryl's girlfriend from Texas had even lashed out at me, and called me a murderer, when Darryl made a bad decision and suggested I show her the photos. Then she had burst into tears. Maybe it's best that it's gone, and I shouldn't try to get it back? There were some terrible photos in that album. Who keeps an album like that anyway?

On my drive home I pondered how strange the double standards of life were?

Does God forgive a soldier for some of the dreadful things he does or participates in during combat? That so-called *collateral damage*. When the call came in, that a group of 70 terrorists had been sighted, but no one had known that half the number were women and children? Would God forgive us for the women and children we shot by mistake? The toddler? The ancient old San grandmother, with snow white hair?

Is killing a human the worst sin of all? Or is a sin a sin, and all sins are equal? If so, then there must be worse qualities than someone who kills. A man who kills another person, might be a good and honest man. But someone who is a liar, cheat and a thief, will always be tainted by those loathsome qualities. A puzzling conflict in the balance of values.

"Never think that war, no matter how necessary, nor how justified, is not a sin," wrote Hemingway.

Maybe I should just let the photo album go ... forget about it?

§

I got home at around 22h00 and called the number I had been given for Eddie. It must have been about 02h00 in Florida. There was an answering message with an automated voice. I left a message. I told him that I had his address and that if he didn't return my photo album to me in one week I was going to fly out to his address in Florida and beat him to within an inch of his life – even if it meant going to jail. I didn't care. I told him he could use my message as proof of my threat, if he wanted to, but it would not save him. I put the phone down and wondered how to get the money to fly to Florida, to retrieve my photo album.

I had decided that I couldn't let the photo album go. The grimy faces of my old paratrooper comrades, now phantoms in my memory, along with dead enemies on the ground, was my lifeline to the past. Such as it was.

Also, I hoped that the number on which I had left my threatening message was, in fact, Eddie's number.

§

The Fabulous Forum held a full house for the Heavyweight Stroh Beer boxing tournament. The winner stood to win $200,000, but I was a middleweight so I couldn't participate. Bummer. But I was on the undercard. It was exciting walking through the back entrance and going to the dressing rooms. The Forum was the home of the Los Angeles Lakers and I looked at the lockers of the famous players I had seen on TV – Magic Johnson and Kareem Abdul-Jabbar among them. I moved loosely around the locker room, doing some shadow boxing. I felt good. I was in good enough shape, and I had managed to get in some good sparring. I had been sparring with the Number 1 ranked middleweight in the world, a future middleweight World Champion – Michael Nunn. He was a tall, slick boxer and had bettered me in almost every round that we had sparred, but I had tried to learn from him, to move around, to think and box more, not fight like an African bush animal. I had tried both these styles on Michael and the boxing approach had seemed to work better. With this in mind I walked into the ring at the Forum determined that my game plan was to try and box smart.

The Fabulous Forum was a high modern stadium which imitated the round Roman style of a Forum, with huge pillars surrounding the big building. Very different from the haunting, old Grand Olympic Auditorium, built in 1925. The rows of modern orange seats went up at a gentle angle, the place was brightly lit and even the ring looked colourful and modern. I was introduced as coming from South Africa and once again the full house crowd booed. I had been expecting this but was a bit disappointed when the boos were less than usual; there were even a few claps and cheers in between. I looked around the crowd and from the corner of my eye saw Stefanie who, just as she had said, was sitting next to an older man close to the front row who I assumed was Jerry Buss, the owner of the Forum, or the Lakers that she had spoken about. I never did find out which.

While the announcer, Jimmy Lennon Jr, was wrapping up his introduction I eyed my opponent, warming up in his corner. He seemed smaller than me and seemed to have a bit of a belly. Instantly my fighting lust and bush animal instinct got the better of me.

Go for him! Kick his ass quick! Get it done and go home.

The bell rang and I came out fast. I moved straight out of my corner and met the shorter fighter in the centre of the ring. He threw a left that went over my shoulder. I saw an opening and drove straightforward into him with a fast, eight or ten punch combination. The last three punches caught him solidly and he twisted and went down on the canvas. I stood over him ready to give him more, but the ref pushed me towards the neutral corner and started to take the count. It felt good to have put him on his ass in less than 10 seconds of the first round, felt like old times again! The crowd cheered, this time some on my side shouting for blood, and I watched as the ref counted over him. It looked like he was going to get up. Instinctively I wanted to rush him again, attack with both hands and get it finished. And then, as I watched him get off the canvas and rub his gloves on his boxing shorts, I reminded myself: *Don't screw this up. Box like Michael Nunn. Box smart! You're fighting on TV. This is a good chance to show yourself. Box and look good!*

I watched him get up at the count of seven. I came out with my hands high, started moving around, boxing smart.

Box like Mike, box like Mike, I kept chanting to myself.

Instead of advancing with an assault I jabbed out a pawing left and moved around. He shot his left and moved around. We moved around each other waiting for an opening. When I saw a gap my instinct was to jump right on him, hard, but I was forcing myself to move around, flicking out the left hand, boxing smart.

By the end of the second round the three-times-stitched scar above my eye had re opened and I had a deep cut with blood running into my eye. I was no stranger to fighting with a bad cut and just kept calm, moving around, not wanting to attack too hard, staying focused on boxing well.

In the fourth round I realised he was out-boxing me. Every time I threw a punch he moved his head just an inch, left or right, and I missed him. I heard my old Scottish trainer Johnny Hogg's voice: "Ya have to always fight hard son. Attack, it's the way that works for you, it's your style, always fight hard!"

Fighting hard was the only way I knew. Forget this boxing!

But I realised this too late. Into the fourth round I tried to change my style and jumped in and attacked. I backed him up into the ropes but he caught me with some solid punches as he tried to bob and weave. The crowd went wild, but it was too late, my gas tank was running low and when I did give my four punch combinations my needle sank deep into the danger zone of an empty gas tank. I was mad as hell when the young Jimmy Lennon Jr raised the hand of the Mexican fighter, declaring that he had won on points.

Stephanie LeMotta was pissed at me and drove her VW bug more aggressively than usual, as we headed to the Cat and Fiddle.

"You should have beaten him. You had him knocked senseless in the first round!"

The English pub smelled of sour beer and cigarettes. I sat at the table and sipped a cold Bass Lager. Darryl was going on about how I should have finished him in the first round when I had the chance and had dropped him.

"You knocked him down in the first round… you should have stuffed him up then and there, he didn't know where he was."

"I was trying to box, and to look good for TV," I muttered.

I looked around at the patrons in the bar – they were having a blast.

I couldn't close my jaw properly but tried to explain that I had wanted to finish him, but at the last second I had decided to try and box instead, to try and show that I could *box*. I had wanted to look like Michael Nunn, the Number 1 middleweight in the world. He was a very slick boxer and perhaps I had been badly influenced by his smooth stick-and-move style.

Darryl thought I was stupid. "Well, you not Michael Nunn, and you can't box like him. You should have stayed with your rough style and you would have finished him. You get one shot at this, only one shot! Either you make it or you don't!"

Darryl's words echoed in my mind, "One shot at this, either you make it or you don't!"

I was disappointed … my jaw hurt … the deep cut above my eye ached. In the dressing room a ring doctor had pulled the gash together with butterfly strips. He had said it would be fine but do not remove the tape for three days. I was surprised; in South Africa it would have been off to the hospital for more late-night stitches.

I acted like I didn't care but inside I was deeply disappointed. It wasn't in the plan to lose these fights. Wasn't my style.

§

I didn't go straight home after work for the next week or so. I felt like a bum after losing the fight on points but forced myself not to think about it. Instead I roared around LA in the faded red Mustang. There was a very welcome crisp autumn chill in the air and the afternoons were getting dark at five o'clock, ever since they changed the clocks back an hour, for daylight saving. Who's ever heard of them changing time? How can you change time? It was new to me.

Hollywood was gearing up for Christmas. The traffic was really bad and when gridlocked the tail lights blurred with the brightly coloured Christmas lights, flickering in store fronts, on trees and on the porches of the old Hollywood houses.

I had recently discovered a great place off Sunset Boulevard, with great hamburgers and ice-cold pitchers – Barnies Beanery – where I sat the bar with a string of loud patrons. These Yanks sure had the gift of the gab, knew how to chew the fat. They sat at the bar with not a care in the world, free and easy, light hearted, laughing loudly. I sat quietly, with nothing to say. They would crack up laughing about something that I found humourless. I had tried, earlier, to get in on the conversation but came to understand that there was a gap between me and them the size of the Atlantic Ocean. Lately I had almost given up trying to fit in with the folk in my new country. I just sat quietly, sipping my beer.

I was thankful to see a girl I knew enter the busy bar. She was tall and cute in a gawkish kind of way. I had spoken to her, casually, a few times before, but now she stood looking at me, curiously, clearly interested in my yellowing blue eye and the deep cut above my eyebrow.

"Oh! I thought you were faking when you said you were a boxer, in training for a fight! In LA everyone says they're something that they're not. I think it's so cool that you really are a boxer."

She inspected the deep cut above my eye.

"Didn't that cut need stitches?"

"Why? Does it look like it needed stitches?"

"Yeah, it's growing together with a kind of bump in the middle."

"Yeah, I know, I thought so too."

I was glad someone agreed with me that the deep cut should have been stitched. Like when I was cut twice in South Africa, although, looking back, I suspect that no one took me for stitches in the US, because no one wanted to pay for them, which my father had done in South Africa.

She told me she was from the Midwest somewhere, St Louis or something, and hadn't seen her family for five years. I thought it strange for someone not to see their family for five years when all they needed to do is jump on a plane and take a short flight. I had been missing my own family lately; but they were 10,000 miles away and, being 'an illegal', I was unable to travel. I had spent a lot of time wondering when I would see them again.

She had come to Los Angeles to pursue an acting career, like half the people in this town. She went on about how hard it was to work and get time off to attend auditions during the day and looked sad when she said that LA was a cold and lonely city. But you couldn't blame that on California, really. Most of the residents here were not native to this metropolis; they had come from all over America, and the world, for some reason or other, business, to be an actor, or a musician, or a comedian or a screenwriter. Millions of people bustled about the city together, yet everyone was set on their own chaotic path, too busy to make friends. Passing each other without a wave, she told me, like ships in the night. People were very diverse, had little in common, and it was hard to find someone that you could be with ... a cold, lonely city.

I took a big bite of my hamburger as I listened to her chatter about Los Angeles and now remembered that my jaw still hurt. I prodded the side of my jaw bone with my fingertips, pushing hard against the bone to find out exactly where the shooting pain was coming from. I couldn't feel anything unusual, but it hurt. A lot. I pushed the bone harder, wondering if the bone was cracked.

Instantly my mind flashed back to the dead SWAPO terrorist with his chin blown off ...

> *... I saw his grey face as plain as yesterday. We had come into the camp in the late afternoon and John Delaney had taken me to see the seven or eight SWAPO terrorists that Delta Company had killed in their first contact with the elusive enemy. This SWAPO soldier had a grey face, relaxed in death. A bullet had entered his head through the front of his jaw and had exited from the side of his neck. His shattered and exposed chinbone was white against the ashen skin of his face. His eyes were closed and apart from his fragmented chin, he looked peaceful and relaxed, as though asleep.*

What a place to get hit with a bullet – in the jaw!

John's eyes were a vivid, excited blue as he jumped around the place, demonstrating the action in the fire fight.

"Me and Lieutenant Doep and a tracker are running up in front, following the terrorist spoor with Koevoet behind us, in Casspirs, (mine-resistant ambush protected vehicles). As we get to the middle of the mango field – Whooosh!! – *fucking RPG-7 rockets fly right past my head*. All hell breaks loose – we've walked into an L-shaped ambush."

John's eyes were wide as saucers as he told me how he and Lieutenant Doep had dropped down for cover, the instant the ambush had been sprung. Koevoet, in their Casspirs, had immediately charged forward into the ambush as they always did. (Military wisdom prescribes that opposing forces always charge or attack an ambush.) They passed John and Lieutenant Doep as they headed straight towards the 50-man SWAPO ambush, firing from the trees ahead. John and Lieutenant Doep were lucky not to be run over by our own vehicles.

The vehicles stopped amongst the ambushers and the contact quickly had become almost hand-to-hand close combat. In the end, Koevoet had killed the seven or eight men John was showing me, now. Clearly, these SWAPO insurgents had fought bravely, but had died nevertheless.

Most of the other terrorists had managed to escape into the thick bush. Our company, back together now, would track down and kill a number of these survivors a couple of days later, also in thick bush.

Quickly I dropped my hand from my aching jaw and stopped chewing. I was ashamed that I had been so caught up in thoughts about the ambush, so clear in my mind, while she had been chatting to me. With an effort I pushed the memory away.

"Is your jaw hurting? You should take small bites."

It felt good to have someone concerned about me. I smiled at her, reached out and touched her hand.

She carried on, happily nattering, none the wiser, while I finished the hamburger, taking smaller bites, as she had suggested. She told me she had been in a few TV commercials and that I should look out for them. One of the commercials had advertised a wristwatch and she had been featured riding a scooter while wearing a mini skirt. I didn't really watch much TV but I told her I would look out for it.

She lived in a house behind a store front, hidden from the street, which she shared with another older woman.

"Sshhh! Come on in."

Once inside she quietly put down her handbag and made no bones about what she wanted from me, turning and supporting herself against the wood panelled wall as I hitched up her skirt.

§

I tore open the package – from Florida – at the door of our apartment. I ripped it apart and found my old, brown, army photo album nestling inside. I thumbed through it, checking to see that all the photos were still in their places. There were the grinning faces of my old comrades in arms; there were the faces of our dead enemies, not grinning. All of them in place, none were missing.

It had been over a week since I had spoken to Eddie, in person, about the photo album. I had called every day and left the same threatening message. A few days into this repeat exercise he picked up the phone but kept silent while I explained his options. I was relieved he had answered, partly because I hadn't been sure that I was leaving these threatening messages on the right number. What if it was someone else's phone number? I repeated that I was ready to buy a ticket to fly to Florida if I didn't get the album in the mail right away. He was quiet on the other end, which was unusual; generally, he would have been the one doing all the talking, American style. But I felt relieved for many other reasons: I was protective over these pictures, and they were mine. These were my brothers in arms, with whom I had experienced maybe the best and worst times of our lives, pride and dedication, acceptance, humility, bloodshed, fear and courage, young men grinning at the camera, full of defiance.

The other reason was that I didn't have the money to buy a ticket to fly to Florida – as I had threatened to do.

Chapter Nineteen

FACES LIKE FLINT, EYES LIKE FIRE

'All She Wants To Do Is Dance' ~ *Don Henley*

"Korff! Granger! You made bail… c'mon."

The West Hollywood Sheriff dressed in brown noisily swung his big set of jailer's keys as he started to open the big cell door. I stood up stiffly from the corner that I had claimed as my own. It was not the first time that I had landed up in the klink for the night or two. I had learned my lesson from times before and had found a place in the holding tank furthest from the open toilet and close to the open bars. It paid off when drunks and heroin addicts puked and shit themselves after the night on the town. I had been forced to go head to head with a red-haired monkey who had quickly taken my spot when we all stood up to collect our couple bologna sandwiches and kool aid, the standard lunch and dinner in these Los Angeles places of leisure. The dim-witted red head was chomping open mouthed on the dry bologna sandwich as if he was eating delicious hot pastrami. I had also learned from times before that you have to talk up quickly when in these situations, don't let things fester.

I was thankful to follow the sheriff with his swinging keys down the hallway leaving the Saturday night haul behind me in the holding cell. Another thing I was learning was that the American cops were very fast onto the scene and you could find yourself in the back seat of a black and white LAPD cruiser before you could say *howzit*. I walked down the long hallway through to the front of the Police station. I had a dull head ache and a bruised eye brow from the night before.

I had played the scene through my mind the whole morning and was convinced that I had been right to punch the six ft 5 in bouncer at the famous Rainbow on Sunset Boulevard. He had no respect. Who did he think that he was talking to! Some rock and roll punk? The Rainbow was a famous rock club on the Sunset strip and well known for having bands like Led Zeppelin, the Doors etc. playing there. We entered the club, bought a whisky, and stood against a wall to observe the busy dance floor when the big security man hollered something at us indicating with his arm. Maybe I didn't understand his American accent, or he didn't understand mine, as I asked the big bouncer what he wanted from us? Immediately, displaying a major attitude and serious disrespect, he had shouted loudly in my ear, telling me we should move to the side from where we were standing.

Who the hell do you think you're talking to, buddy?

I was standing square as the big guy leaned forward, off balance, to shout at me, his wide mouth against my ear. It was irresistible … instantly I shifted my weight and threw a solid (and justified) short left hook and right-hand combination that felled him like a tree struck by lightning. It was a punch I had practiced more than 20,000 times, in sweaty gyms and dusty backyards, ever since I was a kid, and I don't think he had ever been hit by a professional boxer before, albeit one having lost a couple fights.

But now after almost 24 hours in the police station, I was thinking that maybe it had not been such a good idea, after all.

"Sign here. Where in England are you from?" The young officer asked, being surprisingly pleasant as I started to walk away.

"I'm not from England, I'm from Johannesburg, South Africa," I mumbled, walking out of the police station.

Darryl was standing outside, smoking. He had come through and paid the three hundred dollars for my bail.

My old school friend also looked down in the dumps as we drove down Santa Monica Boulevard, weaving through the afternoon traffic. Everyone seemed to be driving like maniacs on that windy afternoon. Perhaps it was true that strong winds delivered negative ions that made everyone irritable.

"So what the hell happened with you?"

"The bouncer was disrespectful; I'll tell you about it later" I answered.

"At least you still have a punch … looks like your boxing days aren't over yet, hey?" Darryl laughed.

I was embarrassed at having to be picked up from the sheriff's office, again, and I wasn't feeling talkative. My throat and neck still hurt from when the almost 6' 8 ft tall famous bouncer, Lenny, had grabbed me from behind, in a huge arm lock around my neck, while I stood there looking at his partner lying flat on his back.

"How did the cops treat you?"

"They were OK, they're pretty professional these Yank cops."

What I didn't tell my old friend Darryl was how foolish and embarrassed I felt about having verbally abused the LAPD officers who had arrested me, just as I was making my forced exit from the nightclub. I had literally run slap bang into the LAPD Saturday night Sunset Boulevard foot patrol. And very quickly they had me sitting on the sidewalk with my hands handcuffed behind my back. Full of adrenaline and whiskey, I had asked the fresh-faced LAPD officer if they had ever heard of the Border War in Angola; had he ever attacked a terrorist base with 23mm ripping over his head; how many fire fights had he ever been in? And more. Thankfully the LAPD officers had been professional and hadn't overreacted. Now I felt like a real fool.

Darryl and I pulled into a burger joint for some lunch. I hadn't eaten anything other than bologna sandwiches in two days. The tall palm trees leaves slapped in the wind and people scuttled past, heads held low, holding onto their collars. The gusty Santa Ana wind had been blowing for a few days now and while the wind had cleared away the usual LA smog and dust and pollution, which was great, the harsh sunlight had the unfortunate effect of making everything look like an over exposed photo. Which was making my headache worse. I very much regretted having lost my shades. The unceasing wind charged the air with electricity, making everyone irritable. Drivers changed lanes impatiently, at speed; pedestrians strode by, heads down, unsmiling.

I sat quietly and let Darryl do the talking. He too was down in the mouth, having been dumped by his girlfriend; said he was sick of America, was thinking about going home, back to South Africa; he had lived in LA for five years now, it was enough.

I let him ramble on but I was only half listening; I was doing some deep reflection of my own. I was still embarrassed about my behaviour, two nights before, was wondering if I should try and talk to someone, someone professional. A counsellor, or a psychologist, or something. I had developed a hair trigger reaction to life's problems, there was no in-between, no wait and see, my fight or flight mechanism was in permanent overdrive. It was always about respect or the lack thereof, or a tough attitude. Maybe I was the problem? I wasn't certain, but I did know that this was no way to start my American adventure.

I thought about the pretty Italian girl I had been seeing for a while. Recently she had gently put her hand on mine, told me that I was in a new country now, and should try to forget the past. She told me about an uncle of hers who had returned from Vietnam a troubled man; he was constantly getting into fights in bars and had ended up doing a stretch in prison. I listened, nodding, I could easily see how that could happen. But I did not want to be like her uncle. I had no malice in me and I wished only good things for people, well, most people, most of the time. Maybe she was right, maybe I should try to put my past behind me.

But why should I forget the biggest adventure of my life?

It seemed that being in a foreign country was bringing out, or highlighting, my thoughts and emotions and memories of my life in my old country. Actually, what was filling my head, then, had less to do with memory and more to do with reactions and day-to-day associations, feelings, thought processes and judgements. The events in my past were still too recent, too close to me, to have become memories.

South Africa seemed so far away ... but I couldn't help wondering, as I had many times before, if there were other South Africans who were having trouble processing their experiences in the Border War.

Or was it only me?

'I Want to Know What Love Is' ~ Foreigner

It wasn't long before I was down at the Broadway gym again in the tough black area of south central LA. The boxing gym is a magical place. A place of refuge from the world, a place where nothing else matters except trying to throw the perfect left hook combination with perfect balance and others are doing the same It was a place where you left your troubles as the door. But it was a tough gym and you had to shit or get off the pot. No time for posers at this gym. Jamaican-born heavyweight, Donovan 'Razor' Ruddock, was holding court, sparring every afternoon. The whole gym would come to a standstill to watch the famous big Jamaican. Although his big mouth dropped open, his body barely moved when he jolted out his left arm, his entire shoulder behind it. That lightning fast straight left snapped back his opponent's head before he had even launched a punch. I was dead impressed. I had never seen such a big guy punch so fast, and I had started trying to emulate him with my left hand.

I wasn't supposed to spar so I kept to myself and spent a week or so shadow boxing and working the bag. Ed Wicks had not been happy that I had lost the fight at The Forum and had not come to the gym since then, so I was looking after myself. He said he was busy making boxing shorts and gowns but it sounded like he and I were coming to the end of our association. I was aware of an old black guy who had been hanging around the gym, giving pointers to a few fighters. I hadn't given him a second thought, thinking that he was just one of the old street cronies that hung out in the gym every day, wearing their shabby old clothes.

"You gotta keep your legs closer together … and don't reach out," the old fellow said to me when he stopped near where I was working the bag. Even though I thought that he was a walk-in guy off the street, I heard a certain knowledgeable authority in his voice and instinctively obeyed. I closed my stance and he came up close, pushed my hands up, higher, in front of my face.

"Keep your hands up, like you holding a basketball in front of your face, right here," he lifted my hands higher, holding each one next to the temple. I moved around, keeping my hands high, as he watched me.

"Yeah that it… fight low … now roll your shoulder with your punch as you snap it out…keep it short."

I did as he said, and it felt good.

I mentioned to James Weir that the old 'street guy' walking around the gym seemed to know what he was talking about. James's face, troubled from worry and damaged from years of professional boxing, lit up. Grinning hugely he said, "Oh no, oh no no. He's no street guy and he knows what he's talking about for sure. Do you know who he is?"

"No, I don't, who is he?"

"That man fought Rocky Marciano and Muhammad Ali. He got over 200 professional fights and about 130 knockouts…that's Archie Moore … 'The Mongoose'."

Archie Moore – The Mongoose. Boy! Had I misjudged the man, thinking he was some old fellow that had wandered in off the street.

§

In 1988 the 10,000 plus miles between South Africa and Los Angeles was a lot farther than it is today. I had been an illegal alien in the US, with false paperwork, since my six-month tourist visa had expired in 1986, felt like decades ago. I sat at the small reception desk in the high-rise condominium, in the exclusive Wilshire Corridor, close to UCLA. It was late and most of the retired wealthy residents living in the twenty-storey building had retired for the evening; by now they were watching the late-night show with Johnny Carson. The expansive tiled reception area was empty and quiet. I preferred it this way. I sat back in the uncomfortable chair in reception and prepared for the quiet graveyard shift.

Someone had left a *New York Times* on the desk. It had been well-fingered by the day-shift security guards, before me, but a front-page sub-headline jumped out: *South Africa threatens to use its nuclear capability if necessary*. I snatched up the paper and slowly read the long column, which explained that South Africa had threatened to use its tactical nuclear capability – if the Cubans used poison gas.

What the hell!

It told of a fierce tank-to-tank battle in thick bush, an artillery battle that had been going on for many long weeks deep into Angola, as the South Africans took on a concentrated, combined Cuban and Angolan force, driving down towards South Africa.

It told of South African Mirage fighter jets flying at tree top level under the Cuban manned radar systems, roaring 100 feet above the Angolan savannah to blast Angolan convoys, seeking to break a siege that the South Africans were maintaining over a huge Cuban fighting force.

A Namibian farmer was quoted as saying that it had taken a full week for convoys of South African military vehicles, rushing up from South Africa, to pass his farm, on their way north to engage the Cubans.

Bat Out of Hell

What all-out conflict had this been? A week of long and constant military convoys?

In the last few years, living in America I had heard next to nothing about the South African-Angolan Border War. But, for some reason, I had always assumed that the fighting had died down and indeed had come to an end, in about 1982–1983.

I went on to read the strangest thing: the paper said that in this battle the Cubans were close to the Namibian border, that Soviet MIGs were flying sorties against the South African troops, that they had air superiority, and that the SADF heavy tanks were in Angola, engaging Cuban tanks.

Cuban flown MIG's with air superiority? I thought this might be a typo or, perhaps, mis-information. These Yank newspapers get stuff wrong all the time.

What the fuck?

If there had been an SADF tank battle in Angola, there was some big shit going down. But there was no real way of finding out what was going on! (No internet back then.)

I sat back and thought about what I had just read in the *New York Times*. I felt a rush of loyalty to a legion of soldiers I had thought were dead and gone. No, they were not gone, they were still in the bush, still fighting with faces like flint and eyes like fire, they were still digging fox hole scrapes, loading fuel and ammo onto choppers, checking their magazines, flying mere feet above tree top level into combat. I could hear the shouts and the orders in Afrikaans. It sounded like an all-out offensive against the Cubans.

Lucky for me I had picked up the newspaper; otherwise I would never have known about all these goings on. I felt a bolt of energy jolt through me and decided to do a security walk-through, to get away from the front desk. I got out at the twentieth floor. The elevator smelled like old people and the stairwells smelled like dog piss.

I ran into the old Iranian fellow who was always out late, walking his little, white, insolent dog. He had told me he had brought the dog with him from Iran. He was a nice guy but I barely understood a word he said; he probably said the same about my thick South African accent. I also suspected that it was his dog pissing in the stairwell. I exited through the service door to the roof top and lit a cigarette.

Smoking, standing quietly in the open air I looked out and over the endless mass of the lights of the city. I could see the tall skyscrapers of downtown Los Angeles, almost over to Santa Monica Pier on the opposite side. I heard a crowd cheering and the sound of a brass band coming from the UCLA sports stadium, close by. The university campus was spread out below me, tall buildings with the traditional ivy-covered walls. The blinking lights gave the view the merry feeling of a medieval Italian town.

"There must be a football match going on," I thought.

Life was easy in America. Nothing to worry about here.

I looked out over the horizon and thought of my own small country at the tip of Africa. Probably, somewhere out there, right now, young South African conscripts were fighting like lions on the ground, in a close-up tank battle in the thick bush of Angola. It sounded as if all the Cubans and the entire Angolan army had combined their strength, were making a push south to engage the small South African army in an all-out offensive to drive us out of Southern Angola. But, judging from the article in the *New York Times*, the Cubans were being chewed up by the South African-made long range G5 artillery.

My mind flashed back to being in an operation in Angola, loading shiny bright new bullets into magazines, writing your blood group in big letters above your left pocket and on your web belt and jump helmet, don't want the medics to miss that important fact … pulling boot laces tight three times over, stuffing extra battle wound dressings in pockets, just in case, surrounded by smelly, unwashed sleeping bags, wearing filthy brown uniforms hard as cardboard from a month of adrenalin-filled sweat and black camouflage grease, and boots scuffed white from the soft sand. Then being pervaded by a quiet acceptance – "If today's the day I die then let it be so and let's get on with it."

I wondered if any of my old mates were there, right now, while I was doing fucking, boring security duty in this fucking reception office in America. I felt I should get on a plane and fly back to South Africa, to do my bit.

Later that night I showed the newspaper article to an older security guard who shared the graveyard shift with me, an Ethiopian man. He was a pleasant fellow, wore his hair, flecked with grey, in a semi Afro hairstyle. We had shared many jokes together and there was a definite bond between us, both being *uitlanders* (foreigners) in the US, both from Africa, albeit north and south. I told him I had also fought with the South African army, in Angola in 1981. He smiled his big gentle grin.

"My friend, why do you think that a communist is the devil himself? Why do you think that Cubans are such terrible people? I am a communist myself. It is a better way of living, especially in Africa." He gazed at me steadily, expecting an answer.

I had known he was from Ethiopia, but we had never discussed the communist part. I was a bit taken aback. I had never had a discussion with a real, live communist before, not knowingly.

"Look," he said quietly, "it's a way of life that provides better living for the masses, who don't have the opportunities that richer people have, especially for education. With capitalism, poor people stay poor, rich people stay rich, generation after generation."

He spoke all the time with a warm, disarming smile, something that all Africans did so well.

I responded tersely: "I'm not rich, my man, nobody has ever given me any advantages."

I was beginning to get annoyed.

"You wrong. Even though you may have nothing, you are rich. You have been educated, you learned how to fit into working society. You have been exposed to a way of thinking. Your upbringing means you can fit in, understand and take advantage of opportunities that may come your way. Why should only a small few have the chance to have such things?"

"We're both sitting here in the same security guard uniform, so we are equal, you and I."

"Yes, my friend, but you have the capability to leave this security job tomorrow and get accepted in a better position, go as high as you can in working society. A poor peasant will not ever have that chance, nor will his children."

I didn't quite get his drift, except that he was telling me I could be whatever I wanted to be because of my apparently 'privileged' upbringing. I'd always thought I'd had just a normal upbringing. I supposed he might be right, I'd never thought of it like that before. All relevant, I suppose, but I didn't bother putting up a decent argument. First, I liked and respected him; secondly, we still had an all-night shift to share, until 07h00, and maybe more to come. I picked up the newspaper again, and soon my mind was back in the Angolan bush.

§

There was no way of finding out what was going on, on the Border. A week or so later I called home from a call box, but my mom said she hadn't heard anything about a Cuban attack on the border, that as far as she knew everything was quiet.

Years later I learned that the *New York Times* article had been referring to the battle of Cuito Cuanavale, an offensive mounted by eight FAPLA brigades, trying to bring an end to their struggle against the South African backed UNITA forces. The FAPLA brigades, with help from Cuban armoured and motorised units, and support from the Soviets, including one hundred T-62 tanks, had made their way south, towards the South African border. But, in planning their offensive they had failed to plan for a South African intervention. This intervention resulted in a series of pitched artillery and tank battles in the thick bush, from long and close range, comprising the biggest tank battle in Africa since World War II.

The battle for Cuito Cuanavale had taken place on the banks of the Lomba River late 1987, close to the town and air force base of the same name (Cuito Cuanavale), between UNITA (supported by the SADF) and FAPLA (supported by Cuba and the Soviet Union). It was a series of battles over some months. Since then, contradictory opinions about the decision by the SADF to launch the attack have emerged.

One opinion is that the SADF was influenced by its intention to rescue the UNITA forces under siege in Cuito Cuanavale, and by its need to capture the FAPLA air force base there. The SADF forces attacked the town in assault after assault, with massive 155 mm G-5 guns, led by its crack, mechanised 61st Battalion, the 32 Buffalo Battalion, and, towards the end of the battle, the 4th SA Infantry group. Colonel Jan Breytenbach, commander of 32 Battalion, has written: "the UNITA soldiers did a lot of dying that day" and "the full weight of FAPLA's defensive fire was brought down on the heads of [SADF] Regiment President Steyn and the already bleeding UNITA".

According to this perspective (supported by Horace Campbell, Hasu Patel, P. Gleijeses, Ronnie Kasrils and others), the SADF failed in its intention and was overcome by the combined Cuban and Angolan forces.

Contradictory opinion maintains that the SADF had only a limited objective for the battle; that it wanted to halt the enemy at Cuito, to prevent the airstrip from being used, and then retreat. Any action beyond this would have interfered with negotiations between Cuba, Angola and South Africa, which had begun in London earlier that year, as a result of the South African government having acknowledged the political change in Russia and the end of the cold war. General Jannie Geldenhuys, Chief of the SADF at the time, claimed that the most important battle in the campaign had been the defeat of the Cubans at the Lomba River, and that Cuito Cuanavale was merely part of a mopping up exercise after that battle.

At the time this claim was supported by the South African Minister of Defence, General Magnus Malan. Since then it has received (ongoing) support by the SADF and several historians, including Fred Bridgeland, W.M. James and others. In addition, statistics regarding the losses (of both life and military resources, sustained during battle, prepared by both the SADF and independent military analysts, contradict claims of a victory by the SADF.

In the end, whether the battle of Cuito Cuanavale is seen as a tactical retreat by the SADF or a victory for the Angolan forces, there can be no dispute that it was the turning point which brought the Border War to an end. It led directly to peace negotiations, the withdrawal of the SADF and Cuban forces from Angola and Namibia and, ultimately to the independence of Namibia.

For anyone wanting to read about the battle of Cuito Cuanavale I can recommend two books: *Battle on the Lomba 1987* by David Mannall, and *At Thy Call We Did Not Falter* by Clive Holt.

§

Some days later, after a long night at my security shift, I walked into the apartment to find a message on our answering machine – a long message from Alex Hatten, a new trainer with whom I had been working, on and off, at the gym. He said he hoped I was keeping myself in shape because he was working on getting me a fight on a show at the Reseda Country Club in four weeks time, if I could get my weight down to middleweight. The fight would be six rounds, against a fighter who had been on the 'reserve list' of the US Olympic team as an amateur, who had come off a win two weeks previously in Las Vegas. I lay awake that night, unable to make a decision: take the fight or not?

I wished that my old trainer, Johnny Hogg, was around … he would know what to do. Johnny had always known which fights to take and which ones to sidestep. Me? I had always wanted to take every fight that came my way. But Johnny had known better.

"Ye gotta pick and choose ye fights son, this a hard game." Fondly I remembered Johnny cautioning against my gung-ho attitude, in his soft Scottish burr.

But, yet again, I needed the money, so I started scheming. If I could negotiate $1,000 for the fight, I could use some of the money and send the rest straight home to South Africa. With the favourable exchange rate that would be about nine thousand rand to add to the pot. I had begun to send money home, a bit at a time, and had started building up a good stash, to have something waiting for me when I returned to SA. Which I was definitely going to do, sometime soon.

OK, I hadn't fought for over five months, and I was certainly not in top fighting shape, but in four weeks I could still get on that bucking bronco and ride it. Hopefully I could catch the guy with a good punch and it wouldn't go the full six.

Also, I really needed something to stop my mind from fixating on the tank battle raging between South Africa and the combined Cuban and Angolan forces. Apparently Cuban Migs were flying sorties across the Angolan border and even bombing the South African troops. But news about the war in southern Africa was still patchy and hard to find. I needed something else to concentrate on.

The next day I called Alex and told him, yes, I would take the fight.

I started my week with running in the morning and going to the gym at night. By the weekend I was feeling pretty good and agreed to spar with a black Englishman who was getting ready for a fight. I hadn't sparred for a couple months and decided to start slowly – a big mistake in professional boxing.

Bat Out of Hell

The bleary-eyed, broken-nosed Englishman took me by surprise. He jumped me cold, came at me full steam as if I had robbed his mother. He caught me with a big solid left hook that landed high on the side of my head and made my knees buckle. My brain exploded into a black cloud and I tried to defend myself against the following right hand that was sure to come next.

Mother fucker! What's your problem!?

He had caught me cold with a super hard punch. Immediately I started to box defensively, knowing I would not be able to handle another big punch like that. The English fighter was a hooker … throwing sweeping full force left and right hooks from his shoulder with all his might. I boxed defensively, not my style, but I was able to keep him at bay for the next three rounds with my straight punches. Still, I could not lay a good one on him, and I never recovered from that crashing left hook in the first seconds of the first round. I climbed out the ropes on wobbly knees. My feet felt like lead weights. I walked carefully, in measured steps, to the heavy bag, pretending that nothing was wrong. I was able to fake it while working the bag, but in truth I could barely see straight. Alex, my new manager-trainer, was nowhere to be seen.

I drove home carefully, struggling to focus on the road from my blurry daze. I had never been hit so hard before … I could hardly focus on the red tail lights of the evening traffic.

At home I pulled all the ice there was out of the refrigerator, shoved it into a plastic shopping bag and flopped onto the couch, the homemade ice pack clutched to my head. I lay there, groaning, hoping like hell I didn't have a fucking swollen brain.

Heavy blows to the head can also cause whiplash injuries; the fast backward-and-forward movement also strains the neck muscles and can stretch and tear tendons and ligaments in the neck.

I knew I would feel even worse in a few days' time and that I would have a stiff neck for at least a week. The pain, faulty judgement, forgetfulness and disconnected feeling that comes with a good concussion can set in and stay for a few weeks or more, so it takes a few days before the damage from a solid punch can be really felt and realistically assessed.

I fell into a fragmented, disconnected sleep and when I woke the next morning my first thought was of the English fighter, his bleary, groggy eyes and broken nose ... then the crashing hook that had caught me by surprise.

The following morning was the same.

"Mother fucker!" I shouted out loud, sitting on the side of the bed. I was mad as hell that I had let it happen.

Like most boxers I had become an expert at hiding any damage, but inside I felt fucked up. I could barely remember my name. I thought about the fighters I had knocked cold in my time. Now, for the first time, I felt empathy for them. Some of them may have been badly hurt, and I had never known.

Also, in the game of boxing, which isn't a game at all, there is always that terrible feeling of being a loser, being no good, the moment a boxer gets the better of you in a fight, or even in a hard sparring match. It wasn't like losing at tennis.

I went to work and drove my work van slowly around Hollywood, disguising my disorientation by smiling and humming tunes. I had to concentrate hard to perform simple, easy tasks and even then my mind would shut off halfway, just stop working. I was struggling to connect thoughts and felt disconnected from my daily interactions with the world. In the afternoons, when I was tired, everything was worse; it was hard to function. I decided not to go to the gym for a week.

All I could think of, all day long, was the bleary-eyed Englishman with the broken nose.

I thought about him first thing in the morning when I opened my eyes; I thought about him when I was trying to work; I thought about him when I was eating lunch or dinner. Everyone started to look just like him. The black guy wearing a beanie, riding past me on his bicycle, looked like him. The fellow waiting at the light to cross the road looked like him. The waiter serving coffee looked like him.

What the fuck, I couldn't get him out of my mind!

I decided I was going to fuck up this Englishman if it was the last thing I ever did. I had been pretty much out of fighting shape when I had climbed into that ring to spar with him – a cardinal sin in professional boxing – and I had paid the price. As a pro you *have* to be in shape, *always*.

I decided not to go to the gym until I was in proper fighting shape. After a few days I started running wind sprints in the morning before work and then again at night. Sprinting always worked and soon I was sprinting as fast as I ever had. Quickly I felt my wind coming back to me. On top of this, I worked my left hand in my bedroom, until late, and must have thrown 500 quality jabs a day, I went back to my roots and moved from side to side, like I had learned from Brian Mitchell, and put my hips into it, like I had learned from Harold Volbrecht. Pretty soon my left was shooting out like a kick from a colt and it wasn't long before I felt ready to Take Care of Business

So I drove down to the gym.

I strolled into the club and saw that the English fighter was indeed still around. Good. He had just finishing jumping rope, was ready to spar.

His manager approached me, smiling, and asked if I wanted to join in, to move around a little, for a few rounds with the Englishman. I remembered that phrase, "move around a little", from the previous time, when I had been cold-cocked early on in our sparring match.

I looked all relaxed, cold and half asleep, as if I had just woken up … an old boxer's trick.

Only 45 minutes ago I had been drenched in sweat, having just finished in my room at home a full one-hour workout that had built up to *full on, real time speed* shadow boxing, for six rounds. Afterwards I had blow-dried my wet hair, patted my flushed face with a cold cloth and then driven to the gym with the air conditioner full on. Casually I had sauntered into the gym eyes half closed looking as though I had just climbed out of bed. But I was well warmed up, primed for the occasion.

I nodded, said, "Sure, I'll move around with him a few rounds. When's his fight?"

"In a week, this is almost his last sparring match."

"Mother fucker! Have I got something for you!" I thought to myself.

The black Englishman came out of his corner just as he'd done last time. Full steam ahead. Bobbing from side to side. His face looked exactly as I had been seeing it, first thing every morning and last thing every night, before falling asleep. His small eyes looked bleary, punch-drunk, his nose was still broken – and his hands were held low! Or was it just that mine were held high, this time?

Sure enough, early on he threw that same big hook … but this time, because of my high-speed training, he seemed as slow as an English ox on the moors. Instantly I smashed a jackhammer solid left, deep between his gloves into his face, and felt my hard fist make contact, right through the padded glove. I did it again and again, and again and again. I was counter punching. The split second he moved to throw his hook, I smashed a swift, straight, shoulder-driven left between his gloves and into his mouth and nose. I wasn't holding back. I was putting my shoulder behind the left jab which turned it into a power punch. Very soon he started bleeding, but I kept at it.

Fuck you!

The second round was even easier; his hands were lower, his hooks seemed slower and the blood ran from his nose. His move was my trigger, my straight punches were faster than his hooks, so even though he started his punch before me, I landed my straight, solid punch before he could land his. I got the better of every exchange. I didn't give him a break and his corner finally called it off after round three. Revenge was sweet! I felt great inside but acted all nonchalant as I took off my gloves and worked the speed bag. My head was clear, untouched.

Finally, he ambled over to me.

"Boy! Good one mate ... man, I couldn't do a fing, could I? You 'ad that left in me face all night long. Good job!"he said, in a thick English accent.

I nodded and thanked him for the sparring.

"I hope you have a two-week headache, like I did, mother fucker," I thought.

I was relieved not to see his face anymore when I woke in the mornings.

§

I had been overjoyed when, round about this time, (1988) my brother, Murray, had arrived in LA on a tourist visa for a 'walkabout' as the Australians call it. He arrived with the news that a friend of ours, Lance, also from Benoni, would join us soon after. I had been delighted to welcome Murray to the US, to Los Angeles specifically. We had spent a hectic time together, running around the city, showing him the ropes, out until the early hours of the mornings. He had moved in with us in the apartment Culver City, close to LAX, the Los Angeles international airport and soon Lance was to follow. It had made a huge difference to my life, to have one of my own family members living with me in this huge, impersonal country – made home feel slightly less far away.

But, in what seemed a very short space of time, Murray's, then Lance's tourist visa expired – join the club – and so all of us were illegal aliens in the USA. We managed to buy ourselves fake 'Green Cards' at the notorious MacArthur Park in downtown LA, with which we were able to score temporary jobs, off and on, here and there. We were living a more or less 'fugitive' sort of life, with the threat of deportation always around the corner … but at least we were doing it together

§

Fight night at the Reseda Country Club. There was a different face in front of me … this one was named Wilfred. He also had small, squinty eyes but he didn't stay in one place for a single second. I threw left hooks and right-hand combinations, fast, but he was too slippery to land a blow. Wearing crazy multi-coloured shorts (which he tailored himself) Wilfred bobbed and weaved, his legs in a wide untidy stance, moving his body from his waist to his knees in a wild, awkward style, not caring that he looked like a runaway windmill – but one in very good physical condition.

My girlfriend had seen him prior to the fight and had rushed over to me, deeply concerned.

"I know this guy," she'd said, wide-eyed. "I see him running, on my way to work every morning at 05h00; he runs up the hills on the way to the beach."

My heart sank. Oh boy! All I needed was to get into a fight with a super fit boxer who runs up hills, several hills, before breakfast every morning. I had seen him a few times in the gym; he didn't seem to have much style, just punched the air non-stop, workout after workout. I had never seen him spar.

When the bell rang I found I could hardy touch Wilfred. He bobbed and weaved and ducked and dived; he was here, then there, then back again. Thanks to his jitterbug behaviour he couldn't settle down to land a solid punch, but he was able to land a bunch of untidy, light punches.

"I can't tag the guy, he's moving all over," I grumbled to Murray, sitting in my corner with Alex.

"Don't try knock him out, just work the left jab, and forget about power ... just speed, he's a spoiler, so watch it," Murray advised.

In the third round I stood fast, stopped chasing him, waited for him to come to me, and as he crossed the border into my territory, I shot out a solid double left. This seemed to work and I had him back-pedalling. I wasn't getting suckered into his wild style.

The fight continued. Wilfred was a local fighter and a favourite at the Reseda Country Club, with a large following who hooted and hollered at his wild antics.

"For fuck's sake stand still!" I yelled at him, silently.

I was getting frustrated and started dropping into Wilfred's style. It didn't work. No one could catch this guy. Now I understood why he had been an alternate on the 1984 US Olympic team. As a professional boxer Wilfred was fighting every two weeks and had just come off a win in Las Vegas. He was what is known as a spoiler; a fighter with a very awkward style, who makes everyone he fights against look bad, as though they can't do a thing against him.

Wilfred turned cartwheels when the ref lifted his hand at the end of the fight.

He went on to have a close, split decision loss against James 'The Heat' Kinchen, a few fights later. The Heat was a well-known bad-ass.

'I Still Haven't Found What I'm Looking For' ~ U2

Darryl had called me to say that he was leaving Los Angeles, to go back to South Africa. This would have been a real blow, had Murray and Lance not been with me in LA, but it was a blow, nonetheless. I had suggested a few farewell drinks at Nicky Blair's, an upscale Italian restaurant and bar on Sunset, not far from the 100ft high sign of the Marlboro man, and the Whiskey A GoGo and Rainbow nightclubs.

The Hollywood night life on Sunset Boulevard in the late 80's was slick – Sylvester Stallone was one of the regulars, standing at the bar with his entourage, just a few feet away, sporting his long haired Rambo look. Beautiful girls with big hair sat at the long, granite bar counter, laughing and chatting to each other. Black was *the* colour in Los Angeles in the 80s. Most guys wore a black turtle neck sweater with an expensive black leather jacket or black sports coat, and slicked-back, greased hair, ala the LA Laker's coach, Pat Riley. That was The Look.

I stood at the bar, waiting for our order of Long Island Iced Teas, our drink of choice. Can't go wrong with six different alcohols mixed in one glass.

I had butted into conversation with an extraordinarily lovely brunette, whom I had met before. Once again I was instantly depressed that she wasn't mine. She was a high calibre natural beauty with a face that in ancient times certainly could have sparked a war. Clearly, she had enjoyed her natural beauty most of her life and was well used to having men struggling not to drop their eyes while chatting to her, to get a good look at her entire body. After a minute of repartee she broke eye contact with me – bless her heart – and pretended to look away, across the bar, allowing me a good, long opportunity to peer down her loose sweater. How thoughtful. I loved these American girls.

"You not going to miss this? Look at these girls," I said to Darryl.

He shrugged, "The girls are better in South Africa, and I can enjoy a good rum in Johannesburg just as well as here."

"You won't have Sylvester Stallone standing in the corner though," I teased him.

"Who cares?"

It was our last night out on the town in Los Angeles and Darryl sat sipping his strong drink, telling me his plans to pack his bags and fly back to South Africa. He had recorded and worked with famous musicians in his 5 years in Los Angeles but he was done. Going home.

I almost choked on my drink when he explained that he planned to drop into Israel on his way back to South Africa, to pick up Lee-Anne, his South African long-time ex-girlfriend, who had now converted to Judaism. Lee-Anne had been living in Israel for the last five years and had even joined the Israeli army. I had known that she was in Israel, but I had no idea that Darryl and Lee Anne had recently started talking again, after a silence of five years.

That night, our last night out in LA together, Darryl and I discussed the highs and lows of having lived in LA for the past few years. We agreed that it had been a worthwhile adventure. I was sad to see him go but told him that I would probably see him soon, when I too returned to SA. I just wanted to stay a bit longer, maybe make a bit of money, come home with a nest egg.

A week later I saw Darryl off at LAX International airport. We shook hands, then slapped each other's back. "I'll see you soon bud. I'll probably also be heading home to SA in a few months, so get things ready. I'm also sick of this place … say hi to everybody!"

I drove home from the airport in the Mustang, in solid, bumper-to-bumper traffic and felt a pang of jealousy when I saw Darryl's big 747 airplane take off over the Pacific Ocean, turn its huge wings around to set its course, and disappear into the setting sun.

I too was planning to leave this place, soon, probably in six months' time, also take a Jumbo home to South Africa, to see my family and good friends again.

Chapter Twenty
RUN ALL YOU CAN

'Time' ~ *Pink Floyd*

Ten years later

Almost everyone has heard of Odysseus, the Greek warrior, whose story begins in Homer's epic poem *The Iliad*, all about the Trojan War, and continues in his second epic poem, *The Odyssey*, which describes how Odysseus wandered the seas for ten years, attempting to return home after the Trojan War.

In Greek mythology, the Trojan War was waged between the Greeks and the people of Troy. It began after the Trojan prince, Paris, abducted Helen, the wife of Menelaus of Sparta. Menelaus persuaded his brother, Agamemnon, to lead an army against Troy. For nine years the Greeks ravaged Troy's surrounding cities and countryside, but the city endured. Finally, the Greeks built a large hollow wooden horse (the Trojan Horse) and concealed a small group of warriors inside it. The Greeks pretended to sail for home, leaving behind Sinon and the horse. Sinon persuaded the Trojans to take the horse inside the city walls. That night the Greeks returned, their companions crept out of the horse, opened the city gates, and Troy was destroyed. The Greek victory marks the end of the Trojan War.

However, the end of the Trojan War was just the beginning of a gruelling decade for Odysseus, who led what remained of his men in various failed attempts to return to their homeland (Greece) and their families.

While Odysseus battles mystical creatures, suffers shipwrecks and other disasters, and pacifies the angry gods, his wife Penelope and his son Telemachus successfully stave off 'the suitors' (a band of vulgar men who are vying for Penelope's hand and the throne of Ithaca) long enough for Odysseus to return. *The Odyssey* ends with Odysseus winning a contest to prove his identity, slaughtering the suitors, and reoccupying the throne of Ithaca (an island in the Ionian Sea).

Given the time it had taken Odysseus to return home, he had completely forgotten what his mother, father and family looked like.

I was no Odysseus and I had not been in a great Trojan war, but I had done my two years of service in our Border War, and in just 11 months of operational service our Company of Paratroopers had left some 200 enemies dead in the sand during that war. Now, years later, I understood that there was a price to pay, in some shape or form, for these acts. It's like a law of life. I wondered how many other South African unintended warriors, or heroes, perhaps, were out there, spread around the world, or stuck in a shack in South Africa, paying the price in many different ways. And I empathised with this Greek warrior who, after 10 years away, had been unable to remember the faces of his family members. I, too, now, after 10 years of having lived away from home, retained only flimsy memories of my parents and sister.

Ten years! A decade had flown by and I never had stepped onto that big South African Airways 747 and returned to my country, as I said that I would, as I had always believed I would do. Plans had changed, always; a new smiling girl had come around, or a new money making idea to pursue, always something. For years I had kept the expired return ticket in my drawer, as a keepsake, long after it had faded and curled at the edges. Months had turned into years and years into a decade – of blind headaches, daydreams, victories and losses, hopes, longing, laughing and chasing sweet American pie, just as Roger Waters of Pink Floyd had lamented … years flashing past in the blink of an eye, waking too late to hear the shout to GO, running to catch up, never quite making it.

While rushing through daily life in LA I was always aware of the Jumbo jet staking off from the LA international airport, close to where I lived. They would make their usual powerful climb and then tauntingly swing their huge wings around into a wide turn over the ocean, to head somewhere far away, far across the world.

When I had left South Africa I had been in such a hurry that I had barely had time to think about what I was doing, or say goodbye to friends. My three-month visit to America had turned into three years, then seven years and then a decade. I still didn't know where I was going – but what a ride!

Much had changed in this time. Nelson Mandela had been released after spending 27 years in prison … and was now President of South Africa after the country's first true democratic elections. America was at war in the Persian Gulf; Russia had invaded Chechnya; and even Israel and the IRA had both finally signed peace accords.

Frequently I would sit in my car at an intersection, bemused, doing a two-minute evaluation of my life while waiting for a long, red light to change, watching a group of Los Angeles pedestrians dragging their asses in the crosswalk in front of me, wondering: *What the fuck? How the hell did I get here … stay for so long?*

I tried to figure out how it had happened. Here I was, still running around the streets of LA, a lone wolf, half of me still at war, half of me captivated with the huge city and enjoying my new world, both halves longing for Africa. If I returned home to South Africa, just for a visit, after having lived illegally in America, I would not be permitted to return. Something about living in this huge metropolis had grabbed me and I had stayed on in the vibrant, fascinating city. The anonymity, the diversity, the fast pace, the new culture, the fiercely positive attitude of people on the west coast of America was addictive, and I was determined to find my niche amongst it all.

But, through much of this I still felt like I was carrying the weight of a dead man over my shoulder. Americans are good people but as much as I led a very social life, still carousing in hot spots and clubs, I continued to feel detached. There was a wall around me, maybe a self-made wall, maybe I had built the wall myself … brick by brick … but I was unable to connect with most of the laidback, easy going Californians in the city – apart from the occasional Vietnam veteran that I ran into, now and then. Every time that I made a social breakthrough with personal growth I would soon default and go back to what I was – still half at war, still a paratrooper. A lone wolf behind the lines, far from home, surrounded by strangers, out of touch with my past. My short walkabout in the US had turned into my new life.

I had not seen, touched or held my mother, father and sister in ten years. I had not seen an old friend, an acquaintance, old classmate or even just someone whom I recognised from the old times. I felt disturbed when I struggled to visualise the faces of my parents, family and friends. In all this time I had not possessed any photos of them. No internet back then; no Facebook in those days. Just the ol' landline. For some strange reason the face of some old friends, including my old girlfriend had been almost totally erased from my memory.

The west coast of America was literally the furthest place on earth I could be from my homeland, and my old life in South Africa had started to seem like a long-ago dream. It weighed heavily on me that I had not seen my parents and sister for so long and I prayed to God that nothing bad would befall any of them before I was able to see and hold them once more.

Our family home and 13-acre farm in South Africa was gone, sold and sub-divided. All the old farm workers had died in a relatively short space of time, from illness or car accidents, so my father had told me. All except Alec, who had gone from being a farm worker to moving into a house in town with my father as his Man Friday, but Alec too would soon die from AIDS, the dread 'new' disease that ravaged both Africa and America in the late 1980s and 1990s.

All this time Murray and I had been illegal immigrants in America. Our only documentation was the fake green cards we had bought on the street, at Macarthur Park, in downtown Los Angeles. We moved around and worked as illegal aliens, with the constant threat of being discovered and deported hanging over us. Our long-time friend, Lance, had taken his chances and upped and moved to Boston in pursuit of a girlfriend. As much as I was enjoying myself in this wild American adventure, I often questioned just what I was doing, and sometimes I longed to be caught, busted, deported as an illegal immigrant, sent home courtesy of a free ticket on a jet plane to South Africa, to land at the Johannesburg international airport in Kempton Park, walk or hitchhike the few short miles to my mother's home, knock on the door, walk into her house and lift her off her feet in a great big bear hug.

Hollywood. The hustling tinsel town of werewolves and film stars, nuts, dreamers, movie studios, limousines, Capitol Records, Chinese tourists, idle rich, nightclubs, fancy restaurants alongside trashy diners, and long-haired runaway kids from the mid-west of America sleeping in groups in alleys at night. A transient place. A place where I had started, ten years ago, when I first arrived in America.

I hadn't planned on coming back to live in Hollywood, but then beggars can't be choosers. My brother and I had recently and luckily landed jobs, in the nick of time, as apartment building managers in Hollywood. Life throws its curve balls.

Just a few weeks earlier we had made an emergency, midnight exit from our digs, a small house in Culver City when, after a month of wishing and dreaming, I had finally caught up with the muscle-bound son of our neighbour, recently out of prison, who had repaid our kindness, (helping him and his mother with cash, giving them lifts, that sort of thing), by kicking in our back door and robbing our house, in search of our new computer equipment and a printer, which we had planned to use in our budding children's bookstore.

It had taken me a month to catch up with Jerry, the long-haired muscle-bound ex-felon, but around noon on New Year's Day, 1994, I had seen his car outside our house. He had thought it safe to return and visit his mother for the holidays. I had tricked him, talking with him through the window, in a soft reasonable tone, coaxing him to come outside and talk to me about the robbery – maybe it hadn't been him – let's talk about it, let bygones be bygones. Foolishly he fell for my 'truth and reconciliation' plea and came out of their house, all muscles and bravado … and I proceeded to give him the mother and father of all hidings; a beating that even Roberto Duran would have stopped, had he been the ref. It did not go well for Jerry. After an ass kicking he would never forget I had dragged him to the peach tree between our two houses and dumped him there, like a sack of shit, where he lay unmoving, but moaning.

His people did not call the police, because he was a low-down thief and out of prison on parole, but we watched him being helped into a car and taken to hospital.

I had only ever kicked one man before, while he was down; and that had been in the army – the man who had killed my cats. Now I had done it again, maybe I had gone too far, this time.

At 23h00 that night Murray and I decided it was time to make an emergency exit. Can't take a chance. After all this was America, where bush justice was frowned upon, plus both Murray and I were illegal immigrants. We had taken our faithful cat, Major Jannie, everything we could fit into the back of our pickup truck, and abandoned the rest – beds, cupboards, chests of drawers, a couch. All cheap stuff. We could buy more later.

We had driven to our friend, Steven Oliver, the manager of an apartment building in the heart of Hollywood. Steve had been a well-known TV and film actor in the 60s and 70s. We had met him at the famous Formosa bar on Melrose Avenue and had become good friends. Steve had never really made much money from acting but was an old fashioned down to earth, gutsy guy with a gravelly voice, who had lived a very interesting life. He loved the fact that we were from South Africa and we had become firm friends. We explained our present predicament to Steve and he immediately offered to put us up in an empty unit in the apartment building he was managing.

"Good to have you boys around. Listen, you boys lay low and try not let the other tenants see you. The owners come every Thursday to walk the building, so make yourselves scarce on that day, OK?"

So we settled in, living a 'camping' kind of life, scans furniture, and spent sundry companionable evenings in Steve's small living room while he regaled us with stories of his bad boy Hollywood actor days.

"You know my friend, Grizzly Adams, he could piss right over a parked car," Steve told us in his gruff voice, many, many times.

Steve told us about his years as a leading man in the TV series, *Peyton Place*, and acting in movies like *Werewolves on Wheels*, and the cowboy movie, *Tom Horn*, in which Steve McQueen had played the title role. McQueen had recognised Steve on set as the youngster who had punched him in a gas station years before, when he had driven over Steve Oliver's foot while he had been working as a gas jockey – as lots of young, unknown actors had done, still did. He told us stories about himself and William Smith, the actor who played Anthony Falconetti in *Rich Man Poor Man;* they had been room mates for years and had enjoyed many riotous parties in Mexico. Steve seemed to have met all the big names. He also explained why his acting career had come to a sudden end.

"I was blackballed from acting in Hollywood when I said President Johnson was behind the assassination of JFK, and then I punched a senator's son ... all this happened at a music concert in the mid-west. The promoter of the concert was a friend of mine, a crazy guy, but a good guy. He had me come on stage to say a couple words to the audience ... this was sometime after President Kennedy had been shot and killed. I didn't know what to say, so I told them that in my view President Johnson was behind the assassination of John F. Kennedy …. then I punched that punk, backstage … the senator's son … and that sealed it. My contribution to the concert was aired on TV and that was it, I was fired from *Peyton Place* the next day … I haven't worked in Hollywood since."

Several nights later Steve started talking about another film, *Malibu Beach*, in which he had played the leading role. I remembered this film clearly and stopped him in mid-sentence.

"You were Doogin, the bad guy, the lead actor with all the tattoos, in the film *Malibu Beach*?" I asked, eyebrows raised.

"Yes, I played Doogin in the film – why?" Steve asked, in that gravelly voice.

"Well! That is just too much of a coincidence!" I said, astonished.

"Why so?"

I explained. When I had been in the Airborne, in South Africa, we often requested the movie *Malibu Beach* for our Wednesday night film, because of its bikini-clad girls. We had come to know the script off by heart and knew exactly when the girls would make their appearance. All the troops had grown to love the swaggering, tattooed, bad guy who bullied the young beach boys, so he could get to the bikini girls. The character's name was Doogin and for some reason we had given our friend, Aaron Green, the LMG gunner in our platoon, the nickname of 'Doogy'. The name had stuck and he had been known as Doogy ever since.

"I saw you in that movie years ago, in South Africa, when I was in the army. We all loved that film … we named our friend, our platoon gunner, after your character in that movie," I told Steve.

He was as amazed as me.

"Was he a good machine gunner?" he asked.

"Doogy was the best," I said thinking back to Doogy next to a trench, standing legs spread next to his spotter RSM Sakkie Marais shooting out 2 x 50 round belts on 7.62 to eliminate the hidden FAPLA machine gunner that had kept us pinned down.

After a week or so of hanging out with Steve he gave us some sound advice.

"Listen, you guys had better go check if you can see that neighbour of yours," he growled at us, "you need to know if he's alive or not."

So, for a few days in a row, we drove down to our old neighbourhood, parked down the block from our old house and sat there, waiting and watching. After a few days we saw our house robber, now an honest man (?!), all hunched over, slowly walking to his car, his entire head wrapped up like the Elephant Man.

"There! That's him. So… he's walking slowly … but if he can drive then he's fine," Murray said coldly. No sympathy there.

But I had been feeling bad, for days, about the severe beating I had laid on Jerry the Thief.

"Don't feel sorry for him, he's a thief and a house breaker. He robbed us after we helped him and his mother, for months. Don't worry bru, don't feel bad. Look, there he goes."

Murray was wholly indifferent to Jerry's problems. We watched him drive off, his swollen head looking double its normal size. But maybe some of that was due to the wrapping. Personally, I was thankful to see him alive and now regretted having trashed my new work boots (possible evidence) in a dumpster in Hollywood, later that night.

Even though it may have been a righteous beating, I felt that in future I should try to handle situations like this in different way.

Oh well, next time. Maybe.

§

As fortune would have it, a month later our good friend Steve Oliver, the rugged old Hollywood actor, upped and left, as was his impulsive way. Steve had always grumbled about "getting out of Hollywood" and heading up to Northern California, to walk the hills and smell the fresh air. One morning he packed his equally rugged old car with his meagre belongings, some movie posters with his name on them, his sawn-off shotgun, and took off for the north.

"I've put in a good word for you boys with the owners, they might approach you to manage this building. Good people are hard to find around here," Steve had said, with a nod and a wave.

Steve Oliver was one of a kind.

Within days Murray and I had taken over Steve's job and became the new apartment managers of the building. What a luck! Not much of a job, but free rent and few responsibilities, and minimal tasks to do around the building. A good opportunity to regroup in the low point that we were in and lick our wounds after the past few years of long, 13-hour days in our swimming pool relining business, then working nights on our plans and preparations for a children's bookstore. The small book store had barely got off the ground when we were forced to throw in the towel, thanks to our status as illegal aliens; and Jerry's theft of our equipment.

§

THE WALL

He had moved around the room, sorting some papers and pushing me towards a chair, gesturing to me to sit down. It was one of those chairs that you would never buy for yourself, a modern wide, flat, with folded layers of leather, like padded pancakes stacked on each other, the edges of the pancakes hanging down over the pancake below, and a back rest that would probably tilt too far back if you leaned into it. He walked around the table and settled down in a matching chair, facing me. He leaned way back in the chair. Nothing happened.

I started to speak, slowly at first, not sure what to say or where to begin. And I kept peering into his eyes as I spoke, wanting to make sure that I did not see signs of 'this is bullshit' in his eyes, any sign that he thought me some sort of dingbat off the street, some lout trying his luck at stolen valour. He was sitting back, relaxed, his eyes fixed on me. I was aware of a strong, pleasant scent in the room. I couldn't put my finger on it; at first I thought it was wintergreen, but then I decided it wasn't. It was something like motorcar oil, maybe gun oil.

It was strange talking to someone who seemed to have some knowledge of, and even some interest in, what had been on my mind for so many years. I had met many other people in this huge, diverse city, but their eyes had glazed over and they had peered at me disbelievingly, as if I was bullshitting, whenever I spoke about fighting communist fighters with RPGs, tanks and ZU 23 mm AAA, in the bush in Angola. (The ZU 23 mm AAA is a Soviet towed 23 mm anti-aircraft twin-barreled auto cannon whose barrels can also be adjusted down to be used as an anti-tank and anti-personal weapon that numbed your brain as the huge rounds split the air over your head with a sound that you had never in your life heard before.) No one had a clue.

"Communist tanks in Africa?" I could see their minds registering a blank as they searched their memory banks, trying to retrieve some information about the dark continent. Then, usually, it would become clear that their mental filing cabinets, reserved for the storage of knowledge about Africa, were pretty much empty – except for stuff about lions and elephants. I could see this written on their faces before they changed the subject and asked questions like, "Are there lions close to the towns in South Africa?" Of course, I always told them yes there were, and they roamed the streets, roaring, outside our houses at night.

Although I did have one fellow tell me that his great-grandfather had left America for South Africa, to fight for the Boers in the Anglo Boer War … and another who said he knew a guy from school who went to fight in Angola and had been killed there. I always wished I'd been able to ask him a few more questions, but the conversation had taken place on a construction site with everyone arses up and elbows down, working. For some reason I had always thought he had probably meant Rhodesia, because he looked a bit older than me. Not that many Yanks had come to fight in Angola, except a few dozen Vietnam Veterans who became pathfinders in 44 Brigade. They had done a good job helping our small war.

Now the roles had changed. I peered into the brown eyes of the man in front of me, trying to detect any of the customary glazed eye reception. I could see none. He gazed at me, non-judgementally, from behind an impressive American Indian hawk nose. His face was angular, with high cheek bones and lines running down from the corners of his eyes, mapping his face like footpaths in a Vietnam jungle. He looked about ten years older than me, although his long, straight, black hair hung past his shoulders, so that he looked like an Apache warrior. Suddenly I had a clear vision of this man as a slender 19-year-old, in camouflage fatigues of a US soldier in the dense jungle of Vietnam, close to the action ... closer than others. I could see him seeking out danger, silently pointing ahead to an enemy close by. He was not a man to be left behind in base camp, organising stores or driving a water truck. He continued gazing at me, calmly, intently, honestly ... then he asked a question, to which I replied:

"Yes, we were on the Border with many others. In South Africa everyone had to do their two years national service, either with the army or the police. You spent six months in training and then, maybe, you were shipped up to the Border, the Angolan border with Namibia, to an area called Ovamboland. It's a small region on the Angolan border, where South Africa has been fighting an ongoing bush war against SWAPO insurgents, or terrorists, that's what we called them. They were trained inside Marxist Angola where they had their base camps. SWAPO was fighting for the independence of Namibia, from South Africa."

"They wanted independence for Namibia, from South Africa? Was it their land?"

I paused, not liking his question. I looked around the small office for the first time, trying to locate the source of the strange scent pervading the room. I saw no flowers, no incense burning. What could be causing this strong, pleasing aroma? Something like motorcar oil, or rifle parts he had been busy oiling ... I looked on the floor to see if there were some used motorcar parts stashed somewhere but found nothing of the sort. I was forced to come back to his question, and realised it was not the question I disliked, but the probable answer.

I had often paused to ponder this same question lodged in my own head, but this was a first, having to answer the question because it had been asked by someone else. I knew that Namibia did not belong to South Africa – we all knew that. We all knew that the United Nations, through its Security Council Resolution 435, had granted Namibia its independence from South Africa in September 1978. Even earlier, in 1971, the International Court of Justice had stated that South Africa's possession of Namibia was illegal. We all knew that. Now, for me, thinking about all this, after having lived on the other side of the world for a couple of years, my perspective was different. The fact that

SWAPO had wanted independence for a country that did not even belong to South Africa carried some weight. I fumbled for words and leaned back – and the pancake chair tilted too far back, just as I had suspected it would. Awkwardly I tried to sit forward again, feeling foolish.

"Yes, actually, I suppose it was their land." I gave the only answer I knew, which was the reason given to all South Africans by the nationalist government for its army's intervention on the Border and what we had seen first-hand evidence of in the bush with Soviet and Chinese weapons and equipment. "So, yes, maybe it wasn't actually land belonging to South Africa … but the SWAPO fighters were backed and supported by the Soviets, and communism. You couldn't just hand over the country to the communists. What then? The Soviets would move in next door? Communist neighbours?" My answer made sense to me.

"Yes," he nodded his head in agreement, "I can see that would be a problem, to have communist neighbours."

I was thankful to see that this man understood my point of view; understood the world the same way I did. Even though he seemed only about ten years or so older than me, he seemed much wiser, more knowledgeable, than me. Already I felt he had experienced life changing events, had encountered crossroads in his life which had altered his course, motivated him to lift himself up, to arrive at this place where he could help others with his hard-earned knowledge and wisdom.

Chapter Twenty-one

AMBUSH

'Bat Out Of Hell' ~ *Meat Loaf*

I had hung up the gloves years before, when I realised that I was not putting in the dedication required to box as a professional. I had not set foot into a boxing gym since. Professional boxing could be a deadly game – it required 100% dedication and focus on your goal. In America I had soon discovered how difficult it was to survive in boxing, at the pro level with no finances and no support team for encouragement, motivation and guidance, as I had enjoyed in South Africa. Which had kept me in line. In the US I had jumped from trainer to trainer, making my own decisions about fights and how much they paid. The lure of Los Angeles night life had also been overwhelming, again with no one to keep me in line. The kiss of death for a boxer.

After I had quit boxing I had made a conscious decision not to walk into a gym again, or not for a long time. Much like an alcoholic, one whiff of the boxing gym and you'll find yourself back at it, gloved up, hands high, building the rage that would get you through the fight. I had enjoyed the boxing, all of it, win and lose, and regretted nothing about it. I had caught a fleeting glance of what it had been like to be a fighter amongst professional fighters. I had caught a taste of how it felt to be in top physical shape and to face professional boxers, on a daily basis, in tough gyms in Los Angeles and Johannesburg. No, I would never be a South African middleweight champion, as had been my dream, one that I thought I had pursued really hard.

Maybe I could have been if I had returned to South Africa at the right time? Or maybe I had never been good enough? I would never know. The dream was over. It had all been a great experience and I had met and rubbed shoulders with men about whom I would only have read, otherwise. And I had learned a lot in those five years as a boxer. You learn many things about yourself when you get into the ring and fight, or spar, against tough professionals.

The gym wars were worse than the fighting. Most of the damage suffered by fighters happens away from the brightly lit fight nights. Gym wars could go on for weeks, trying to get the better of one another every day in the boxing gym. You got me today, I'll get you tomorrow, and so on. This is where a fighter gets hurt, in gym wars and hard sparring, not so much in the actual contests. One thing I had found out for sure that was that I could take a damn good punch and keep on fighting!

Inexplicably, now that I had finally stopped boxing, a strange and disturbing thing had started up, something far worse than the headaches. Now that the hard, daily training routine of running and workouts, which I had conducted for many years was over, my channel and outlet for tension had gone. Now that I was trying to live a normal casual life, like other people, relaxed, staying out late, drinking more than I should, I had more time to reflect. And my past had caught up with me. I found that my bid to be a normal, relaxed person had been ambushed. Ambushed by scores of dead 'freedom fighters', in blood-soaked, filthy uniforms, with their rusty, old AK-47s. Scores of men we had killed. Ambushed by the spirits of determined dead men, and the women and children who had been caught in the crossfire, their blood spilled on the white sands of Angola and Namibia. The dead had gathered their strength and were finally having their say.

These surprise attacks came in the form of intrusive thoughts or visions, manifested in perverse, clever ways, and they always took me by surprise. Sometimes they grabbed me just when I was enjoying my happiest or most tender thoughts, maybe of a loved one or family member, or any good and precious memory. Suddenly I would be hijacked from a comfortable mental space and flung into the recollection of blood soaked, dead men, their brains shot out, teenage freedom fighters dead at our feet, mothers and grandmothers cut in half, still clutching their dead children. I would be dancing in a nightclub, enjoying myself, laughing with a pretty girl … having a tender moment thinking… and I would be surrounded by dead SWAPO fighters in dirty blood-spattered uniforms, curled in the foetal position or spread-eagled on the sand, with mask-like rubbery faces and empty heads, dead from the hail of our undiscriminating bullets. These flashbacks came from nowhere, and so suddenly that sometimes I lost my breath.

I was ashamed that I was capable of having thoughts like this. I dared not tell anyone about these alarming memories and flash backs. Why did they appear so suddenly? Frequently I wondered about the many thousands of troops that had served in the SADF. Did other troopers have trouble forgetting these things or was it only me? What had become of my old paratrooper friends who once had been as close as brothers, from Parachute Battalion, for which I still felt such a powerful loyalty? Glover, Stan, Delaney, Doogy, Barnes and the others? Our platoon lieutenant, Lieutenant Du Plessis (Doep), who had always led us from the front into a fire fight, his cheeks flushed, his baby face carved from rock, his rifle in his shoulder. Our quiet and calculating company commander, Captain Leipoldt … all of us would have followed him anywhere. Where were they now?

These men appeared now, in my memory, as faded ghosts from the past. Even though all this had happened so long ago, and 10,000 miles away, I still felt an attachment, a profound loyalty to this legion of ghosts and memories, walking the sands of a continent that I had not walked, now, for a decade.

§

It was 1994 and times had changed. Crack cocaine was on the city streets, everywhere in LA. Our apartment building was packed with musicians and actors who had come from all over America, chasing their American dream. My own dream was over.

I had packed on weight and needed to carve another hole in my belt. I used a steak knife for this task and then adjusted my favourite belt, with the big Iranian belt buckle, to allow the .45 pistol to sit snugly in my waistband, in the small of my back. I had hardly done any working out for about two years and had put on thirty pounds. I was not the beanpole middleweight contender I used to be, and I could feel the difference when I puffed up the stairs that I used to take two at a time. I had been meaning to get back into running again but always had some injury that took months to heal. I had never, in ten years of living in America, had medical insurance. I would just wait for any injury to heal – my twice broken hand, a cracked foot, broken shoulder, a cut-to-the-bone knee, and a seriously strained back which had taken two years to heal.

Most of these injuries had come from fighting, a few from my work.

In Hollywood I had taken to walking with my .45 pistol stuck into my waistband, ever since Edward had been shot on the corner, outside the apartment building. Ed was a young black kid who had moved into the building six months before, a good kid, happy with his new life ... until one night when he fell through my office door onto the floor, rolling in pain, shot through the knee by a gang member.

Hollywood had changed.

Crack cocaine had taken the City of Angels by storm. By 1994 some of the city streets had become bloody war zones and there were almost daily drive-by shootings, as gangs and dealers fought for turf throughout the huge city. The 18th Street gang had recently staked their claim and achieved an elevated status in Hollywood, after some well publicised shootings. It was a Salvadoran street gang, run by 'senior' members from within prison. At that time the 18th Street gang was still a fledgling operation. Decades later, after the LAPD had deported thousands of its gang members back to El Salvador, and the gang had grown in strength, had multiplied like street dogs, it virtually held the country of El Salvador to ransom. Eventually, in 2013, the gang declared peace with the government. But in 1994 the 18th Street gang had the courage to call Hollywood nights their own; they stood on our street corners in twos and threes, scowls on their ugly faces, glaring at the world from beneath their 90s mullet hairstyles.

Ever seen an ugly Salvadorian drug dealer with a 90s mullet? Each gang member looked nastier than the one next to him; all of them openly made various hand signals that advertised the sale of crack cocaine. I wasn't going to take any chances while walking through Hollywood at night; I planned to put a bullet through one of these Salvadoran mother fuckers if he even looked at me wrong.

But I had adapted to the big city and it was not all bad. Hollywood was filled with artists of all kinds; they thrived on the performing arts and made it a city in which enchantingly creative and bewitching people lived alongside the deranged and decidedly degraded. Living in the midst of all this creativity had inspired me to buy a small keyboard. Many nights I sat up until late in our small apartment, trying to teach myself to play blues piano. I had also started to frequent a modest blues piano bar, just off Hollywood Boulevard.

It was here that I watched Lilly playing a late-night set of smoky piano blues. She was very pretty in an Owl'ish eccentric way. I sipped my beer and thought it strange to see a woman in a Hollywood dive like this, at midnight, playing such passionate blues, her wild hair almost reaching the keyboard, silhouetted by the neon lights behind her. The small group of patrons in the bar shouted requests and for the first time I heard Howlin' Wolf's ' Red Rooster' played on the piano.

I watched as Lilly packed her equipment at the end of her long set and realised she was alone. I offered to buy her a drink which she declined. Then I asked her if she gave lessons.

"Lessons in what?"

"Piano."

She eyed me suspiciously as she packed.

"Do you play piano?"

"I've just started playing, I have a key board," I answered.

She still looked suspicious, after all this was Hollywood.

"I used to teach, but I don't anymore, "she said, packing her sheet music.

"Oh, that's a pity, I would sure love to learn a few of those blues riffs I heard you play," I said, being completely honest.

"Do you play the blues?"

"Well, I'm just starting."

It was the truth. I had bought a Casio keyboard and was spending long, frustrating evenings, my fingers feeling as if they were made of stone, trying to learn the blues scale in C, on the small keys of the keyboard. Many a time I had felt like throwing it across the room, giving up, but so far I had stuck with it, for about six months.

"I just need a few lessons ... maybe one or two."

"Are you from Australia?"

"No, Johannesburg South Africa."

Her eyes lit up and suddenly the quiet suspicious apprehension was gone.

"My best friend at school was from South Africa," she smiled openly, the memory making her look suddenly younger.

At last I was getting a good reaction for being a South African.

"Sure, why not? Here's my number. Call me and we can do a few lessons."

At my first lesson Lilly peered, like a wide-eyed, pretty owl, at my hands. They looked like clubs with knobs for knuckles, as I tried stiffly to follow the blues riff she was showing me, on her old, baby grand piano.

"Your hands look broken," she said, matter of factly.

"Yes, they are," I replied, matter of factly.

"You're going to have problems playing piano with those," she frowned, looking concerned, "you're going to have to do a lot of exercise to get your hands loosened up."

"Ok, I'll try," I promised.

Not long after my first piano lesson Lilly and I found ourselves rolling around on her puffy feather bed, in her small house, tucked away in the Hollywood Hills just above Sunset Boulevard. She was an interesting woman, a few years older than me, and had been playing jazz and blues piano from a young age. She introduced me to old blues musicians like Pinetop Perkins, Herman 'Junior' Parker, Howlin Wolf and some newer performers – George 'Buddy'Guy and Stevie Ray Vaughan. Until then I had never heard of them.

Lilly had come to Los Angeles, from Kansas, years ago, for a short stint in the music world. Like many people who came to Los Angeles she had put down roots and stayed. She said this was who she was and she could never go back to Kansas. She was a night owl and stayed up into the early hours after playing at late-night gigs. I would meet her at different venues in Hollywood and gradually came to realise just how talented she really was.

One night while we were having a post-midnight glass of wine, Lilly told me, "You need to get a piano, I'll show you where you can rent one."

"I don't have room for a piano," I argued.

"Not true, there's always room for a piano," she smiled.

And so, within a short space of time I was helping the movers to manoeuvre an upright piano into our tiny apartment living room. What a difference from the small Casio keyboard!

"You need to practice at least two hours a day, or more. It's the only way that you'll become proficient," Lilly ordered.

Frequently she encouraged me to spend every spare moment practicing the scales and the riffs she had taught me. I was a willing student and did as I was told, which almost drove Murray through the roof. I played the same scales and the same run over and over, for hours on end. I was going to get these piano scales down pat if it was the last thing I did – if other people can do it then I can do it!

"Are you ever going to learn something other than that scale?" Murray grumbled.

"Well, I have to listen to you and your country music, all the time," I defended.

As the apartment managers of a small 32-unit building, Murray and I had a lot of spare time on our hands. This was a new experience for us and we were using the free time to get back into music. Murray was a great country music songwriter, with an equally good singing voice. Recently it seemed that his own music ambitions were working out for him – he was never at home, was always away at a home music studio in the Hollywood Hills, right next to the 1960s home of Jim Morrison of the band, The Doors.

Murray had met someone who was enthusiastically helping him to produce the country songs that he had written and played and now they were full time busy with recording a demo tape. My brother's songs were great. I thought he had a really good chance at getting some serious attention. He had even played a set at the famous Palomino nightclub in North Hollywood. They had rustled up three female background singers for his hastily put together band, and soon after that Murray was never at home at all; he was always at Cheyanne's place, one of the lovely background singers who just happened to have a penthouse suite above Sunset Boulevard.

§

THE WALL

"What was the terrain like in that area?"

His interest in what I had to say made me feel at ease, accepted … finally I was being acknowledged by someone. His question about the terrain in our war zone didn't feel strange to me. It would have been one of my first questions to anyone telling me about their military conflict in another country. I felt he was looking at my story through the eyes of a soldier.

"Dry and hot, with thick bush in clumps, all joined together, hard to see through ... flat open areas called *shonas*. It's a region called Ovamboland, just south of the Angolan border. It's beautiful. The whole region was white sand, almost like a dry river bed, with high palm trees and open flat areas in amongst the bush. All the large and small open flat areas would flood in the rainy season ... six inches of water. Really beautiful. All in the middle of nowhere, a thousand miles of bush on all sides ... the stars at night are amazing."

"So how did young high school students in South Africa feel about having to do two years of compulsory military service, and maybe go into the fighting zone?"

I tried to think back to what we had felt about it while still at school. I pictured my last small high school building, an upstairs office block off Voortrekker Street in Benoni. A small, new 'college' type of school, probably only 70 students, where you could wear your hair long, where you could smoke. I wondered if it was still there and if the same group of teachers was still teaching there. I recalled that the prospect of having to go to the army was hardly spoken about, hardly discussed amongst the boys. Just an unpleasant two-year period that you wanted to get behind you as soon as possible ... it had not even warranted talking about. Almost, like, talking about it would have made it worse.

"We all knew that there was no way out of it, we had all resigned ourselves to having to do it, just as our brothers and neighbours had done. It was almost a rite of passage for us. Of course, you dream of ways to get out of it, but not too seriously. You knew that it was going to be dangerous. In fact, from my own small high school, one of the boys in the year ahead of me, Donald Brooks, was killed on the Border. A really nice guy, always with a smile on his face, we would see him every day at school ... he was one of the guys who came to our parties ... it was a strange turn of events; on the first day of my arrival at the Border we walked into the operational paratrooper camp and a siren started wailing loudly. We watched our senior parabats, the fireforce, whom we had come to relieve, charge towards the helicopters, some still putting on their shirts, strapping their kit to their backs, R4s in hand – "

"What is a 'fire force' and what are 'parabats'?" he asked.

"Parabats is the name for South African paratroopers. Fireforce is the name for a quick reaction force of two helicopters and two platoons of paratroopers. They – we – were always on standby, 24/7, at our airborne base camp, ready to react to any enemy contact that was called in within the red area. Fireforce was the ultimate duty; no one could mess with you, no exercise, no getting fucked around, no cleaning the base or training, just two weeks of hanging around in our tents, ready and waiting for action, three days of kit packed, boots and pants to be worn at all times, ready to run for the helicopters when the siren sounded the alert."

"The helicopters were close to you troops?"

My mind flashed back to the familiar sight of the two Puma helicopters, their blades drooping and strapped, always on standby on the chopper pad, just 70 metres, if that, from our tents. They were always parked there, every day and every night. The only time they were absent was when the loud siren on the tall pole outside the small armoury wailed its eerie alarm. That meant action, enemy sighted, someone had made contact with SWAPO terrorists within the area. The standby paratroopers, resting on their beds, writing letters, playing pool, washing clothes, grabbed their packed kit and raced to the choppers, just 70 metres from our tents, ready to fly, ready to go. Anyway, that day, a couple of hours later, they returned and unloaded four dead terrorists. They had been part of a larger group who had ambushed a vehicle convoy, school buses, travelling between Ondangwa air force base and Oshakati town, being escorted by military vehicles. Sometime later I was told that my school mate, Donald Brooks, had been one of our army guys killed in that ambush ... but I'd had the satisfaction of seeing his killers brought in, riddled with bullets.

"You say that you were a paratrooper, was that a volunteer?"

"Yes, I volunteered for the Airborne. I figured that if I was going to spend two years in the army I might as well get into the action and make it worthwhile. Not everyone made it into the parabats, it was a pretty tough selection course to get in."

"What was it like when you all first arrived on the Border?"

"Well ... it's a war zone, and being the reaction paratroops in the area, there was always something going on. In the first couple weeks we were called out to a village close by where an individual from the 'home guard', a local civilian force of men from surrounding villages, had gone off his rocker, shot and killed 13 people at a Sunday afternoon party. He had just strolled through the village of ten, maybe fifteen shacks, and shot at the partygoers, children, old women, anyone who crossed his path, killing 13 of them. We arrested him when we got there, then we loaded the 13 dead people onto a trailer and tied them down, with rope. Then we returned to base and changed back into shorts to continue the braai we'd been having. The others had saved some pork chops for us … I didn't eat any of the big army pork chops they had kept for us, that day."

Chapter Twenty-two
TEN THOUSAND MILES

'Every Breath You Take' ~ Sting

I could hear the kraal (enclosure of huts) mutts barking. The barking grew louder. There were a few of them, surly, with long, curled-up, pointed tails. As they all had. They were not far off, barking in the kraal we were passing in the dark. First, a lazy, don't-disturb-me sort of bark. Now they were barking incessantly, in a committed kind of way. Everyone on our line was quiet. I could see the round helmet of the troop in front of me as he turned around and put his finger to his lips.
"Shhhh."

For some reason we had stopped, no one was moving forward. Now we seemed to be stuck in one place, as you are sometimes in dreams. We could not move but I had a feeling of warm security with my armed, airborne comrades in front and behind me. I felt safe. I could trust them with my life. We had been walking for hours through the dark night in the soft sand and our shirts were damp with sweat, even in the cold Angolan night. Our platoon was on a deadly mission to spring an attack on a small group of SWAPO terrorists in the Angolan bush. We were being led by none other than one of their comrades, a skinny Judas who had turned on them, who was leading us to where his former friends lay sleeping. We had stopped, cautioned by the barking dogs, as we prepared to cross the big open shona (clearing) next to the kraal. The white sand of Angola was lit by a bright, almost full moon, but for some reason we sat listening to the barking dogs and could not move forward. They barked and barked, the intensity increasing.

In my mind's eye I could see them: their floppy ears, wrinkled foreheads, noses against the wooden branches that made up the kraal fence, barking at something they had heard passing by in the dark night of the vast Angolan bush. Their barks would warn their African masters, lying in a grass hut, that someone was approaching the family kraal.

In war torn Southern Angola it was a sure bet that no one would come out to investigate the barking dogs. Terrorists and soldiers alike used the darkness to outsmart, hunt and kill each other ... in the vast empty ocean of the green bush of southern Angola, an area the size of the Mediterranean Sea. The barking felt comfortable and familiar. It grew louder. We stayed hidden in the shadows, as the dogs barked incessantly, on and on, even louder, and would not stop.

Slowly I emerged from a deep sleep, very disoriented. Where am I? I lay there, confused.

Had they seen us? The dogs were warning someone. Everyone knows that we're here. Let's go! The terrorists will have heard the noise by now, they can't miss it.

Awake now, my eyes open, I could still hear the barking dogs.

The kraal ... where am I? How can I be in a bed?

I was surfacing from a deep, hypnotic sleep. It was taking long confused minutes to gather my thoughts, piece by piece ... to trace my steps ... to work out where I was.

Fuck ...I'm in America! Ten thousand miles from Africa. I'm ten thousand miles from hiding in the shadows, under the thorn trees in Angola.

I lay there quietly, feeling small, disturbed by the deep, hypnotic dream that had held me in its thrall. In the near distance I could hear the neighbourhood dogs, barking incessantly. They must have been the trigger for my dream.

But what a strange and powerful dream ... how vivid and real it had been. All triggered by the barking neighbourhood dogs. I lay there for a while, trying to separate my reality from my dream. The powerful feeling of comradeship and safety I had felt in the dream, as we had knelt in the shadows, a helmeted soldier in front and behind me, lingered with me. How real it had been, and what a different world I had woken up in. As reality took hold, I began feeling thankful that I was in a bed in Los Angeles, and not in the middle of Angola, creeping through the night and the Angolan bush with fresh intelligence, intending to kill terrorists who lay sleeping close by.

I continued lying in bed, continued listening to the neighbourhood dogs, still barking in the distance. They must have trapped a creature, a possum or a raccoon. Strange how their barking had stirred such a powerful dream in me. I tried to go back to sleep but I had been ambushed, again, by regret and anxiety. I spent the rest of the night tossing and turning in almost unbearable turmoil, a stream of endless regrets and disappointments whirling through my mind, waxing and waning, some deeper than others.

Why? When? What if?

I struggled to remember the faces of my parents and sister.

Will I ever see them again?

It had all passed so fast, like the blink of an eye.

In the early morning, just before the sun rose, I fell asleep again, to be rescued, thank God, by a dozen hopes and dreams for the future, and a list of victories I had already recorded. I snapped awake to the sound of my father's voice, plain as day, from his seat in the crowd at my long-ago boxing matches, spurring me on: GO *Grey* GO!

§

Homer tells us that when Odysseus was washed ashore on his island home, Ithaca, ten years after the Trojan War had ended, ragged and broken, he was unrecognisable to people who had known him before he left to fight in the Trojan War. Equally, his homeland is almost unrecognisable to him; much has changed during his long years away, as a soldier. In his absence, those who had not gone to war had made great social and economic advances. Odysseus himself had changed so much that no one recognised him, apart from his nurse who had cared for him as a very young child. She remembered the scar on his foot, the result of having been gored by a wild boar while hunting with his grandfather as a young boy.

Homer also tells us that Odysseus has changed from the man he had been before leaving for the Trojan war. He is now aloof and cold and cruel, even with those whom he loves, for whom he had travelled for so long, and so far, to see again. The people closest to him suffered the most from his cruelty. Odysseus was still in combat mode years after the war, was still living on the plains of Troy.

Odysseus learns that his father, Laertes, now an old man, is coping with his sorrow and grief at the loss of his son, by engaging in the constant and backbreaking work of clearing the land and planting orchards and vineyards. Odysseus approaches him dressed as a beggar; his father does not recognise him and does not believe that the man standing in front of him is his son. Only when Odysseus tells him the exact amount and kinds of fruit trees that were in the first orchard, which Laertes had given to Odysseus as a child, does the father realise that this is his son, returned, not dead and lost, as everyone had thought.

Frequently I would slip away into my own world, thinking about anecdotes I had heard of soldiers who returned home from some or other war. They had all changed, somehow. How many South African warriors were still out there, fighting a silent battle, trying to fit in to daily civilian life as husbands and fathers, teachers, salesmen, businessmen, who had also left part of their souls in Angola, like Odysseus, on the plains of Troy?

And what about our 'enemy', SWAPO? Earlier I had not given much thought to our enemies, the men we had fought during our small war. Now, on reflection, I considered them to have been brave and worthy foes. Communist backed SWAPO guerrillas had crossed the border from their rough base camps in Angola to engage their 'enemy' – us. They travelled long distances on foot, no helicopter gunships for support, no helicopter CASEVAC for the wounded, no supplies of food and water. By contrast, we had attacked their base camps in Angola with fighter jets and mechanised ground troops. Whole battalions of SWAPO men had been decimated, had died in the bush, to win their new country ... and they'd had no 'rotation' system, like ours, for rest and recuperation.

Now that their bush war was over, how was their return to civilian life? What had become of the remaining SWAPO soldiers when the Bush War ended? After years in the bush, fighting South Africans, had they returned to their villages and towns as heroes? And then resumed their normal lives? Or were they also constantly travelling back in time, to when they were at their finest, remembering the smell of the bush and the clatter of their AK-47s? How many SWAPO warrior/heroes, like Odysseus, were still out there, now, ten years later?

When a soldier returns from a war he is expected to be the same son, brother or father he had been before the war. But, for many returning soldiers, this is just not possible. Part of them has been changed by their experience of war. No one knows about their actions during the war, except their brothers in arms. So they keep quiet and tell very few people about what they have done, fearing that they may be, looked down upon, perhaps even jailed.

I wondered why the authorities had not made more of an effort to de-brief our South African soldiers when they returned from border duty. I had read a book by Dr Jonathan Shay who claimed that, in ancient times, 'de-briefing' had been almost the norm for returning warriors. And in medieval times the church required that everyone who had shed blood, during a war, had to do penance; if you had committed atrocities, then you had to do more penance. Even non-combatant personnel had to do penance.

Most warrior societies, as well as many that were not dominated by warfare, had insisted on communal rites of purification for their returning soldiers.

In the Bible (Numbers 31: 19) Moses demanded a seven-day purification process for "... whosoever hath killed any person or whosoever hath touched any slain" when the Israelite army returned from attacking the Midianites, having killed everyone, male and female, including children.

Ancient Athenians required all returning soldiers to undergo a unique therapy of purification, healing and reintegration, to facilitate their re-entry into the social sphere as 'citizens'.

The early Romans (apparently) applied a ceremony of purification for their returning armies, which required returning combatants to pass under an arch or beam with their heads covered and bowed.

While all these approaches were only symbolic acts, they were clearly powerful medicine for returning soldiers, through which they received society's recognition and acceptance of their service to their country.

At the end of our time at 1 Parachute Battalion all we had done was stand in a big circle, for ten minutes on the day before we *'klaared* out' (completed duty), and each of us took his turn to describe what he planned to do in Civvy life, now that military service was over.

I had said I was going to 'live life', whatever that had meant.

...But all was not right with the spirit of the man who came back. Something was wrong. They put on civilian clothes again, looked to their mothers and wives very much like the young men who had gone. ... But they had not come back the same men. Something had altered in them. They were

subject to queer moods, queer tempers, and fits of profound depression alternating with a restless desire for pleasure. Many of them were easily moved to passion when they lost control of themselves. Many were bitter in their speech, violent in opinion, fighting. Young men who had been very skilled with machine-guns, mortars and hand grenades found that they were classed with the ranks of the unskilled labour in civil life.
Philip Gibbs, British, 1920

§

Hollywood was a town full of strange and colourful characters; some you stayed away from, but others you couldn't help getting involved with. One such character was Vance.

I had been waiting to meet Lilly at a small bar in the Hollywood Holiday Inn when I first met Vance. He had been living on the 13th floor of the Holiday Inn for the past eight months. I had overheard him talking to a porter about his last amateur boxing fight, as a youngster, when he and another small-town favourite had beaten each other to a pulp for bragging rights. I had told him that I used to box as a pro and of course we became instant mates.

Lilly was not so sure and gazed at him with her big owl eyes.

Vance was insane, no doubt about it, but what a character. He was about 65 years old, had long, thin, wispy hair, half way down his back. The only clothes worn by Vance were shiny, glittering, matching shirt and pants, something like a clown outfit, or perhaps a stage outfit, with big French Louis 16 thruffles around the collar, down the shirt front and at the cuffs. He wore these outrageous outfits day in and day out and had 20 different such costumes in his closet. Red, white, gold, blue. Not one normal shirt, pair of jeans or chinos hung in his closet. With his fog horn voice and his extreme outfits, he turned heads everywhere that he went.

Vance was a musician, promoter, bullshitter and con artist of note. He claimed to have made and lost millions, and displayed a long list of accomplishments: he had been the drummer for Jimi Hendrix, before Jimi became famous; then he was a big-time music concert promoter, across America; then he was a music producer, writer, etc. We could never determine which of these claims were true or false. But, apparently, it was true that Vance now had a Christmas record album, almost complete, which he had written and produced, and was trying to have released.

Vance claimed he was getting huge investment funding from big spenders like Coca Cola and Chrysler, amongst others. He was a small man, obviously had never done a lick of exercise, but demonstrated the inner physical strength of an insane man – with a bull horn voice always at volume 10, constantly announcing to anyone within 20 paces that he would be receiving $2 or $5 million, the following Tuesday or Wednesday.

Of course, something always got in the way of the money arriving on that day … so it would be coming in the following Tuesday, by 17h15 – of course and so on. And naturally this was just the first tranche …the next $30 million would be coming soon, from Sony records, supplemented by the still wealthy 'House of Hapsburg', the old German royal family to whom Vance regularly spoke on the phone.

He claimed that the 'Hapsburg' children were singing on his Christmas album. He said that as soon as the album was released sales would reach $100 million, worldwide, and then more. Soon we would all be rich and of course he would give Murray and me a cool million or two – just because we were such good guys. Vance did not think, ever, in small chunks of bullshit!

Bullshit, of course – or was it? Just as you were about to write him off as the Total Bullshitter of All Time, Vance would come through with proof of his background. Like the time he came rapping on our apartment front door, late one afternoon, and then walked in with music legend Ike Turner in tow.

"Ike, these are the South Africans I was telling you about. Guys, this is Ike Turner, of Ike and Tina Turner fame."

Ike Turner walked into our shabby, old apartment with a jail house strut. His eyes lit up when he saw my old Yamaha acoustic guitar, propped against the wall. He snatched it up and sat on the arm of the old blue couch.

"You mind I play this here guitar?" asked Ike Turner.

"*Ja*, no …go ahead, please play … it's out of tune."

Ike Turner pulled the old guitar into his lap, bent his head, and expertly tweaked the old, cracked knobs. Soon he had the instrument tuned and began a fast, open hand, strumming version of 'Rocket 88'. His hands slid up and down the neck of the guitar and he sang from the back of his throat, thumping the side of the guitar with an open hand, maintaining a drum rhythm.

Vance smiled like a Cheshire cat, from ear to ear, nodding his head up and down to the beat, keeping his eyes on me to make sure that I wasn't missing any of it. The big hands of the music legend flew, in a blur, as he easily contorted and stretched his long fingers, pressing down on a string to reach a note.

I was fascinated, watching his hands as he did small lead breaks between chords. His hands were big, wide; he could easily have been a motor mechanic or a construction worker. I watched him bend those big hands into an especially difficult chord and couldn't help feeling a twinge of sympathy for poor Tina Turner who, if the newspapers were to be believed, had been on the receiving end of more than a few hard *klaps* from these same hands.

Ike's eyes were alive as he pushed through to the second verse, and then abruptly stopped.

"That's 'Rocket 88'; the first rock and roll song ever written – by me, in 1958. It's in the music hall of fame. This guitar got a good sound," Ike Turner said, leaning it back against the wall.

"I got it years ago," I said, "it's got a big sound."

And then Ike Turner gave me a lesson about guitars: "Yeah, it's the wood you see, got to be dry when they make the guitar. New guitars they dry them with machines. These Yamahas, like this one, they're unvarnished, they don't sound so good when they new, but they improve with age ... the playing changes the shape of the wood over the years, so the sound gets better."

It sounded sensible ... I supposed if sound could shape and bend water then it could shape soft wood as well. And this wisdom was straight from the mouth of Ike Turner, the guy who had written the first rock and roll song ever. Who was I to disagree?

For years I had been telling anyone who would listen that this guitar had a special sound, and now the music legend Ike Turner had agreed with me. I felt vindicated. Then Ike noticed the piano in the corner.

"Who's playing piano?" he asked.

"Me, I'm just learning ... some blues, some rock and roll."

Ike's eyes lit up. "Let's hear you, man."

I sat down and started thumping out a Howlin Wolf number, 'Little Red

Rooster'. I didn't think I was particularly good, but Ike Turner smiled.

"Sounds good, my man, nothing like the blues, keep practicing. We goin' down to the grocery store to get some supplies – you cats wanna come?"

So we all piled into Ike Turner's Cadillac and roared off to do some grocery shopping. Evidently he had just been released from prison, where he had been doing time for cocaine possession. Again.

§

THE WALL

"When did you first see the Travelling Wall, the Vietnam memorial wall that you mentioned to me, and what did it mean to you?"

I had first seen the Travelling Wall when it was set up in a park, close by to where I lived, and had been deeply affected by it. I had pulled over in my car and walked across the park to scrutinise it. It was an exact replica of the Vietnam Memorial in Washington DC, except that it was only three-fifths the size of the permanent memorial. Nevertheless, it was a very impressive structure of interlocking metal panels, six feet tall at their centre, with a span of almost 300 feet, side to side. Its most commanding feature was the 5,800 names engraved on it – names of all the US soldiers who died during the Vietnam War. The Travelling Wall moves throughout the US, from city to city, to allow people who cannot get to Washington DC the opportunity to remember and pay tribute to their fallen veterans, family members and loved ones.

I was awestruck as I scrutinised panel after panel of names. It seemed that no one was immune to getting killed in a war. All the different names, from the grandest sounding name, like Brand Preston Sawyer, to the simplest name, George Jones Jr, no one was immune from dying in a war. No matter what a good family, how well-mannered, what a nice a guy, how good looking, how athletic and how promising the life of each soldier, everyone is the same when it comes to catching a bullet, or a land mine, or a rollover in a vehicle, or an accidental discharge or friendly fire accident.

When you first walk up to the Travelling Wall it has the feel of hallowed ground, like walking into a shrine or a temple, then when you are close enough, you see the engravings, the name of each individual soldier. It's just a name, but each name has a family, mother and father, sister and brother, maybe some of them were an only child. Each one had their own story, growing up, their family, going to school, first loves … maybe, at 19 years old, some were so young that they died never having had a girlfriend, never having made love to a woman, ever. Each name had nourished hopes and dreams and promise for the future, plans the person had hoped to achieve. Now they were only a name on a Wall, but a name that living people came to see and touch, mourn and honour.

Strange as it may seem, I had always easily accepted soldiers from *other wars* as veterans, for the time they had served, but for some reason it had taken years before I considered myself and my comrades as veterans. And even then I didn't feel like a proud veteran. Why was that, I wondered? Was it because in South Africa we had no choice and had all done our military service … it was just a normal part of our lives … but I felt I had been used in a way, used to do somebody else's dirty work. But – I had volunteered for the sharp tip of the spear, so I was not entitled to gripe. Nevertheless, I never thought of myself with the same esteem as other veterans I had met or read about. I felt that Americans, or the British, or others, were entitled to march as veterans, flags flying, all dressed up, wearing their medals with pride and dignity. But this did not apply to me, as a South African veteran of the Border War.

Not that I had ever wanted anyone to thank me for my service, as the Americans do. South Africans don't talk about the Border War much, even the men who completed their service. It was an experience that almost everyone just pushed away, almost like forgotten soldiers from a secret war, a conflict that even our own government kept playing down. They told us our experiences had been quite normal, go home now, you've done your time, no need to talk about it, don't call us we'll call you. But remember, you have to do it again in a year or so.

I felt it had been a great idea for America to create the Vietnam Veterans Memorial Wall, and the smaller replica, the Travelling Wall, in remembrance of the all the guys who had lost their lives while fighting for their country.

"In South Africa, is there a place of memorial, or a monument, for the soldiers who died in your Border War, like the Vietnam Wall here?"

"No," I answered, "not that I know of. When I left the country the Border War was still going on, it wasn't over yet, and I've never heard of such a memorial. Maybe it'll come later ... I suppose they'll have to create something, some kind of memorial to recognise the service and sacrifice of South African men, black and white, who were killed on the Border. Maybe there's one already, and it's just that I haven't seen it."

I thought of the 50 or so paratroopers from my own Battalion who had been killed in action ... and wondered why there was no plaque, or a memorial bearing their names, somewhere at 1 Parachute Battalion, so that other paratroopers could see and honour these dead veterans. But then it struck me that maybe this was not a good thing to have inside a military base camp, maybe it's not the sort of thing you want young recruits to see. I thought about how I would have reacted as a raw recruit, on seeing a memorial bearing the names of 50 paratroopers killed in action.

Maybe it wasn't such a good idea.

"How would you describe your time in the army as a paratrooper?"

"Well, looking back, it was one hell of an experience! It was like a love-hate thing, doing national service, going through training and base life, defiantly hellish. It was not a fun time, but we knew that we were doing something important for our country, and, as paratroopers, we knew that soon we would be heading up to the Border, or the bush, as we called it, where we would definitely see some action.

Of course, we were kept in the dark during training, although we heard rumours about what was going on ... and while we were rookies, doing our training, our senior paratrooper companies, older than us would come back to South Africa, tanned to a crisp, with long hair, after big cross-border operations into Angola. They raided our bungalows for kit that they needed and harassed us ... and they told us stories about how they had hit the base camps in early morning attacks ... how the Mirage and Impala fighter jets dropped their bombs on the terrorist base camps. Of course, we all knew about the attack on the SWAPO base at Cassinga, in 1978, when paratroopers from 1 Parachute Battalion did an airborne drop into the base camp."

"There are strong bonds between comrades who were with you during these times?"

I looked at the man in front of me, thinking about what he had asked, wondering how to answer. It was clear to see that he was a man of honour. Honour, I knew, came with attributes such as discipline and even bravery. His face showed a strength that was different from, say, a successful sportsman, satisfied with what he had achieved on the sports field, or a wealthy business man, confident about his investments. His expression spoke of insights born of experience and, to those who could read such things unsaid, a code of honour.

I was certain his experiences had included having to survive in the jungle in Vietnam, having to dive for cover under the crack of enemy fire, chasing and hunting the enemy through swamps and jungles, thinking that any minute you could be as dead as the enemy body sprawled in front of you, twisted in the mud, pants half down, shirt half off.

It's strange to relive the physics and dynamics of what can happen around you in the heat of even just a minute or two of an adrenaline-filled fire fight, two groups of people trying their utmost to kill each other. The body responds and moves with an untapped energy reserved only for just this moment of life and death. In the insane whirl of a close quarters fire fight, your mind fixed on nothing but getting the enemy in your sights and pulling the trigger, amazing things happen around you. Your pants might split, boot laces miraculously come undone, kit straps tear, kit bags and webbing twist around to the other side of your body. In the middle of a fire fight one moves with a force that are simply not available in normal life.

Yes, there was something about going through this together that created a bond between men that is hard to find anywhere else. I looked at him and was certain he already knew the answer to the question he had asked me.

I looked up and answered simply, "Yes, there are strong bonds between military comrades."

My interest in the man listening to me was growing. I wondered what his story was. An American Indian … where and in what town or city had he been raised? Was it maybe on a desolate Indian reservation? What had motivated him to sign up for Vietnam, or was he drafted and forced to go, like we had been. How much of his family history did he know? As a boy I had been fascinated by books and stories of the fighting prowess of Native American Indians but, coming from Africa, I had not met many.

Except, of course, the American Indian I had knocked out with a long overhand right, not too long ago, and then dumped under the peach tree in the backyard, in the pouring rain. He had been the first American Indian I had ever met. In fact, he had also been a paratrooper in Vietnam, or so he had told me before our conversation had gone south. I believed him, that he had been a paratrooper in Vietnam, not that we had ever had much time to talk about it.

I wondered if, perhaps, the only two American Indians I had ever met, had also known one another. Los Angeles is a huge city, but they may have met along the way.

There were framed certificates on the wall behind him, but I didn't see any photographs of Vietnam. I didn't see any bits of memorabilia – like an enemy camouflage cap with old, black blood stains, like mine; the one which John the Fox had picked up and flung at me seconds after we had charged from our ambush position and finished off those who had been left stunned by our surprise attack. I didn't see a bayonet on his desk, like the one I had twisted and bent off an SKS 7.62 Chinese carbine, when we threw 29 shattered, blood splattered SWAPO weapons on a heap, after having caught a large group of SWAPO insurgents in a pincer movement. His office was neat and sparse, just a few pens and books on his simple desk.

Slowly the feeling came over me that I didn't want to be here; part of me wanted to make an excuse and leave, tell him I had to be somewhere else, walk out to the busy sidewalk full of pedestrians, cross the street and keep walking. Light a cigarette, buy a Coke from the corner store, drive into the traffic and get lost in the crowd. I could go down to Gladstone's at the beach and have a few Long Island iced teas.

Part of me regretted coming in here – what was I going to say to him? Maybe it had been a mistake, to come here.

I had never heard of any South Africans doing anything like this. But then again, I had not met more than a couple dozen South Africans in the ten years I had been living in the US.

The time had flown past in the blink of an eye.

Chapter Twenty-three

RIDE THE SAME TRAIN

'Little Red Rooster' ~ *Howlin' Wolf*

Lilly had packed up and returned to Kansas. She told me she'd had enough of Hollywood and California, things had changed, the blues music scene was bigger in Kansas than here in California, and anyway she wanted to be close to her family. I said I understood, I too had not seen my family, back home, for many years. I was sad to see Lilly leave with her wild hair and small hands that played the piano like a blues king. We had enjoyed a strange relationship – I had told her nothing about my past in South Africa and she had told me nothing about her own life, growing up in Kansas and then coming to Los Angeles. Just two strangers bonding in this huge city. I also had been getting sick of Hollywood and all the problems that came with living in the place.

It never rains in Southern California but when it does, man it pours. Rain was pelting into the courtyard; the gutters gurgled, spewing water into deep puddles on the uneven surface of the apartment walkways. I woke up instantly. I had always been a light sleeper and a faint thump had alerted me. I had known the thieves would come back. An apartment next to our office had been robbed a few nights before, when the intruders had taken a few guitars and some equipment. But they had not touched the heap of musical equipment in the back room, so I had expected their return – and I had laid an ambush for them. I had arranged to sleep on the floor of the office, my face against the window. Slowly I pulled the vertical blinds apart, to gain a full view of the door into the apartment.

A crook always returns to the scene of the crime.

I was right. Through the blinds I saw two figures in black leather jackets, hunched over in the rain, working at the lock of the door to the apartment. Salvadorean 18th Street gangsters.

"Mother fuckers!" I looked around me, wondering, "Do I take the .45 pistol or the club?"

Both weapons were close by, one on either side of me on the floor. I had the pistol, with a short magazine and a Billy club (baton) that I had made out of hedgerow wood.

Take the .45!

I snatched up the pistol, softly pulled back the breech and pushed a round into the snout.

They hadn't seen me peering through the blinds and I watched them for a minute. The man working the door was small, with a hoodie, and seemed to know what he was doing as he worked the lock. A bigger guy was standing behind him; he had dark hair and was looking around while his partner worked at the lock.

I had slept with my shoes on, as I had years ago in the bush. I took a deep breath then turned the lock and yanked the door open all in one movement, then leapt out into the rain

"Freeze motherfucker! Stand still!"

The two gangsters were as fast as the sheet lightning that crossed the dark Los Angeles sky. They dropped everything, bolted around the small garden and through a closed corridor, towards the garage of the apartment building. I was just as fast. I leaped the big puddle in the courtyard, took a short cut through the garden and turned, catching up to them, only metres behind them.

"Stop or I'll shoot!" I shouted as loudly as I could. It was all I could think of and it came from a radio programme 'Squad Cars', popular forty years ago in SA.

I was right behind them as they jumped the small wall into the parking lot. I leapt over, almost close enough to grab one by his long hair but slipped in a puddle. I went sprawling and fell hard against a pillar, keeping the pistol pointing up. My MC Hammer 'parachute' pants were soaked but I was up again. The two robbers had gained fifteen metres on me, had made it to the steel gate, the short leader was opening the gate to make good their escape.

In a millisecond I decided to shoot past them. I would at least scare the mother fuckers. Still in a full sprint I pointed and pulled the trigger. I heard windows shatter and an alarm start shrieking. The .45 is a hell of a loud report at 02h00 in a semi-covered garage in an apartment block. In the middle of built up Hollywood it sounded like a cannon echoing amongst the old buildings.

Beyond the gun smoke I saw them escaping like greased lightning down the sidewalk, past the Magic Castle, long hair flowing behind them.

The car alarm was wailing. Out of breath I reached the gate and stopped. I looked down the short road and at the van.

What the fuck! Why did I shoot?

My bullet had missed them by inches, but it had ploughed through the middle of the side door of a Ford panel van parked at the gate. The bullet hole in the van door was as thick as my thumb. Both the passenger and driver side windows had shattered. It was the car alarm howling. I looked up and down the dark, deserted, wet road. Then, quickly, I turned and headed back into the property, my head held low. I tucked the pistol into my wide Hammer pants. Half the balconies of the building looked over the garage area and before I could reach the shelter of the covered building a few tenants had come outside.

"Get back inside," I waved at them, "18th Street gangs are shooting outside here."

The big 135 kg tenant with whom I was always arguing – he played his guitar way too loudly and too late – looked at me sceptically. We'd had a few run-ins and he'd accused Murray and me of managing the building like some foreign army camp.

The owner of the Ford panel van came out, having recognised the sound of his car alarm. He had been visiting the pretty singer on the third floor.

"You better get out of here, buddy! Look! The gangsters shot up your van."

He came hustling down the dimly lit stairs and was shocked to see the bullet hole and the shattered windows.

"Get out of here pal, these gangs are no good."

I walked fast back into the office where I removed the bullets from the magazine of the pistol. I was disgusted with myself. If that bullet had hit one of the gangsters in the back, I would be spending the next ten years in jail.

I decided that this was the last time I had carried a loaded pistol on me. Pulling the trigger came too easily for me.

§

As they say, it's very hard to get Africa out of your blood. While napping one afternoon I heard the familiar *koo, kooroo* of an African dove. It went on and on. How could this be? I lay listening, enjoying the familiar sound. How strange I thought still half asleep. Finally, I got up to investigate. I was disappointed to find that all I had heard, from a distance, had been the hum of the noisy old refrigerator.

Forgetting Africa is not that easy, as anyone who has Africa in their blood will know. I was concerned that I did not want to die here and be buried in American soil. I wanted to be buried in African soil with the *koo, kooroo* of African doves in the tall black wattle trees, or the soothing *Piet-my-Vrou* call of the red-chested cuckoo in a thorn tree, or the high-pitched song of the cicadas on a hot, slow afternoon. I wanted to pick up a shiny black *shongololo* (millipede) from the red dirt and watch it curl, or see a Kudu lookup and take off at a run. I wanted to hear the raucous, ridiculously loud call of the big hadeda ibis, warning that the big black rain clouds were bringing the afternoon rain – at exactly the same time as the day before.

I was always aware of a disconnect, no matter how hard I tried to join in with my American friends. *The wall ... the wall.* I felt I was always holding something back, unable to let go, holding my loyalty reserved for a finer group of men, a legion of men in maroon berets that were now just memories, or a legion of ghosts. Sometimes I felt that maybe I had left part of myself in the battle field bush, in Africa, and I was trying to make up for the missing bit with parties and running wild and fighting. As if part of my soul lingered, frozen in time, over the ambush where we had crept silently through the small enemy camp, a dozen metres from the terrorists ... and slaughtered them at their breakfast fire ... or over the rocky hill where we had wiped out the Bushman clan, and their families.

What does a Bushman know about communism, or being a terrorist? The San Bushmen were the soul of southern Africa, an ancient people imbued with spiritual meaning derived from their nomadic lives, moving with the great wild herds as they migrated, leaving behind them the rock and cave art that celebrated their hunts. Why had this clan, maybe 70 San, half of them had been armed with soviet weapons, worn SWAPO uniforms?

After a decade of being away from home I yearned for my people. What had

I done in my life, to have to spend these years rambling around this strange country like a fucking nomad, secretly journeying back to my past, reaching out for lost ghosts and spirits? Was I trying to get back to years gone by?

How long can this guy last? Let's see...let's push him for another five years, away from his homeland and family and friends. Let's dangle another carrot in front of him and let him chase this one for the next five years, then test him again. Let's keep lining up idiots that he'll have to deal with and see how long he keeps knocking them down. It's a test to see how long broken hands ... hearts ... souls will last.

I looked at the almost full moon, hiding behind some clouds; same gleaming moon I had looked at as a child, same impartial, bright moon that had lit up a hiding place in the Angolan bush, like daylight. I felt like stripping off my shirt and running into the big Santa Barbara mountains, until I was drenched with sweat. Then I would keep walking, for days. Sleep on the ground under the stars. Not wash. Grow a beard. Cook small food on a fire and keep walking for a month or more. Maybe walk 600 miles like the Spanish missionaries.

Maybe I'll follow their trail and walk all the fucking way up to San Francisco.

§

THE WALL

I didn't think that killing enemy soldiers had bothered me or affected me in any way ... but I wasn't sure. I knew that killing the children and old people had disturbed me. And some of the insurgents who had been in uniform ... like the terribly wounded SWAPO man in his tiger stripe uniform, lying on his stomach, who had turned his head and moaned, asking either for water or help. I had known immediately that there was no helping this poor man, not here, so far into the Angolan bush. Without thinking twice, I had placed the hot barrel of my 5.62 R4 a few inches from the hump behind his ear and pulled the trigger. It was all the help I could give him. The adrenaline still raced through me in the midst of the smoky carnage. I had not felt I was doing any wrong. Throughout most of our contacts I had felt no emotion. It came on afterwards. Maybe I would have asked or expected the same treatment from him, if I had been as badly wounded, most of my intestines lying in the sand.

Should I have just left him to die by himself, without shooting him?

Or the incredible dawn ambush where miraculously 16 of us had crept unheard through a terrorist position, to within thirty metres of a group of SWAPO enemy, standing and sitting around their breakfast fire. Could there ever have been a more perfect ambush? We were so close we could have stoned them. We opened fire all together in a barrage of bullets and RPG7s, and in seconds we had killed or grievously wounded, all of them, plus the stragglers we had found hiding in the bush, armed, wearing their SWAPO uniforms. Prior to this small night operation we had been ordered *not* to take any prisoners. There were other, similar incidents I had almost forgotten about.

But something else was de-railing me, not allowing me into the same room of life as others. I couldn't put my finger on it. It stopped me buying a ticket, to ride in the same train as other people … it seemed I had to ride in a separate train. Or I couldn't even find the door to get into the room, to mingle and play pleasantly with the others. There was an invisible wall around me, a wall that had probably been built, block by block, probably starting from the first day we had all lined up for arms issue. Surly, I thought, there must be other South Africans, border veterans, that felt the same as me? The store man in the armoury had roughly pushed at me a well-used Israeli Galil, an R4 rifle, with the words, "three dead" crudely scratched into the worn camouflage paint. Unknowingly, other blocks were added, continually, as we became the senior paratroopers in the operational red area in 1981. More and more blocks in place, and the wall became impenetrable. The kill rate of Delta company rapidly reached three figures … as the young hesitant recruits, first time on the border, rapidly changed into a hardened, seasoned, well-oiled, close knit fighting machine – the parabats.

"Were you were doing a good thing in your role as a soldier?" the calm, quietly spoken, former warrior asked.

My instinct was to answer with a nod, to tell him, yes, indeed, we were the forces of good in Ovamboland and Angola. But then I remembered 1981 and the people of Ovamboland …

… We had gone through many villages or *kraals* in Ovamboland, searching, talking to the inhabitants, hoping to gain some intelligence. Not once were we greeted by the locals with smiles or cheers; always their responses were scowls of non-committal, or blank stares. Maybe the headman would come out, unenthusiastically, rubbing the back of his head. He would talk in a soft, low voice and point vaguely in the direction of a place where, he thought, SWAPO might have passed by. As in any guerrilla war the locals were stuck between the security forces and the local insurgents. We had been told that most of the SWAPO soldiers we had killed were Ovambos, from Ovamboland. That was odd; they were the people who lived in the area where we were fighting. Maybe the local Ovambos were considered heroes for having taken up arms, fighting for the independence of the land which, from all accounts, did not even belong to South Africa? Maybe some of these fighters had been filled with deep ideals and commitment, had hoped to free their country from the control of South Africa; had intended establishing their own country, with new laws, new hopes and dreams.

As SADF troops we had known nothing about them. We had only ever seen SWAPO fighters as a blur in our sights, as wraiths in the gun smoke from our R4 barrels ... and afterwards as bodies, lifeless in the sand, in dirty, ripped uniforms, old AK-47s at their sides.

Despite these memories I answered in the affirmative: "Yes, I think we were a force for good," I said, hesitantly.

He looked at me knowingly, as if he had once thought the same thing about himself. What had he done when he came back from Vietnam? Had he found a job and settled down, lived a normal life? I had heard that a lot of returning Vietnam vets in Los Angeles had joined the LAPD, had become policemen on their return from South East Asia. He didn't seem to fit the part of a policeman, didn't seem a violent man ... actually seemed like the kind of person who never wanted to pick up a weapon, ever again.

I felt the same. I had conducted a love affair with weapons before my time in the army; and, when I turned 18 years of age I couldn't wait to purchase my own hand gun. (A right I had later been denied, as a civilian, through my own doing.) Now, years after active duty in Angola, I found I had grown to dislike weapons, would avoid even touching one.

"So, tell me about this wall?" prompted the calm man in the pancake chair.

What could I tell him? About the children we had shot by mistake? About the old people? The terrible flashes of unwanted thoughts that took me by such surprise that I would lose my breath, and have to pull over to the side of the road in busy traffic? The horrific visions of many of the dead people we had left in the sand ... visions which had grown, over the years, which intruded into personal, private thoughts and moments. The headless, or brainless, bodies of SWAPO soldiers left in the dirt had morphed into larger-than-life apparitions that sometimes left me reeling, dumb and senseless.

I had stopped boxing and had tried to live a normal life. I had also stopped the disciplined, daily physical training I had done for years, ever since leaving the army. Now I tried to live an ordinary life but at times I was ambushed by what felt like a battalion of demons. Should I tell him what I had never told anyone else, not even my closest friends? When these horrid attacks took control of me I would try to blank my mind, to think of something, anything, else. I tried to think of an open field of grain, endless husks of wheat swaying gently in a breeze. I pictured shifting sand dunes in a desert ... a forest of tall trees in the Transkei, green moss softening their trunks, ribbons of trailing vines, like in the Tarzan books. I recalled the long dirt roads around the plots in South Africa, where I had grown up. I imagined the sound of our horses' hooves as we rode home, hard and fast as a freight train at midnight, holding on for dear life to saddles and manes, the horses' necks stretched ahead, ears flattened, bits in their mouths, at full gallop along the straight dirt road that led back to our old farm house ...

"No, I meant the wall that you told me about ... you feel there is a wall between you and other people, since you finished your military service on the South African border."

"Yes, I do feel that way ... and I think sometimes it comes from the contrast between all that training, all those resources, just so that we could become skilled at hunting and killing, and getting a pat on the back when the bodies piled up ... but if you did the same thing, as a civilian, you would be executed, hanged, life in prison, labelled a serial killer, a sick man and a disgrace to society."

"Yes. But isn't the hunting and killing part of your duty as a soldier?" he asked.

I was silent for a moment, reviewing the scattered dead bodies. An achievement? I thought about the SWAPO man who had died while showing me an obscene hand gesture. There were many others, but just then I remembered him. Shot through the throat, he had lived just long enough to run twenty metres from our attack at their cooking fire, to die in a small clearing, lying on his back sending us his last message – an obscene gesture for whoever found him. My eyes burned like coals at the sight. Only seconds before we had charged through our own gun smoke, thirty metres into and through the area of our ambush, where enemy soldiers lay dead and dying around their dawn cooking fire – the result of our perfect attack. What a feeling. What a pure high – emotionless life and death, close quarters, action. Nothing could ever compare.

Surely this scene is as old as man, has been played out over and over, from the beginning of time. Creeping stealthily, in the dark, into an enemy position, moving silently through their sleeping area, to find them standing and sitting, totally unawares, in the open, like targets, not thirty metres in front of you, with their rifles, swords and stones, their weapons, propped against nearby trees, cooking breakfast, making plans for the day. A scenario as old as mankind. A whole night of long silent walking and then a devastatingly close quarters attack. I was locked into a surreal state of efficient clarity, calm and cold, no mind chatter, no fear. No thought of dying, just an enhanced, simple and emotionless effective state of kill-or-be-killed. The smell of gun smoke still hung thick amongst the trees as my eyes locked on him. I walked purposefully towards him, lying in the small *shona*, my rifle fixed on him, my finger on the trigger. But there was no need to shoot, his hard face was just relaxing into death, looking peaceful … contradicting his last message to me. His right hand rested on his chest, his fingers locked in the well-known gesture, thumb pushed between index and middle fingers – the 'fuck you' gesture.

His wounded comrade did not make such a peaceful end. I had looked up and spotted him right away, twenty metres away, lying on his side, he was wounded and was using his arms to pull himself towards his AK-47. I lifted my rifle, aimed, but shot short, spraying sand onto him. I corrected and shot again, low, maybe hitting him in the hips. He buckled but stayed up, supporting himself with his arms. I strode forward, determined to finish him off, my rifle still firm against my shoulder. I aimed at his head, pulled the

With zero connection with old military comrades for well over a decade I thought that I alone struggled with the past.

trigger, and heard the hollow click of an empty magazine. Sensing John the Fox close by I barked his name, standing with my legs wide, still holding my empty rifle in my shoulder, pointing at the insurgent's face. John the Fox, his blue eyes glittering like a serpent's, broke from the bush and walked towards us, cool as ice. The insurgent saw his end coming towards him. His mouth opened and, still holding himself up with both arms he wailed, a long, urgent cry. It sounded as though he was calling for his mother – then The Fox fired into his head.

In the cold dawn 98 degrees of body heat caused a cloud of steam to rise, as if someone had emptied a bucket of hot water on the cold ground.

"Yes, I believe it was my duty, as a soldier, to do this," I answered.

Suddenly my thoughts shifted to the poor FAPLA soldier who would not die, a scene too terrible for words. Like the last bird I ever shot, as a schoolboy with a BB gun, a tough-looking, old yellow Finch with a black face, who just would not die … and I ran out of pellets and in desperation had to cut off its head with a kitchen knife. My avid bird hunting days ended that morning; the old Finch was the last bird I ever killed. The FAPLA soldier also would not die. He had lain, partly hidden by branches, on a raised sandbank, next to a bunker. I had shot him twice, so had Botha, just seconds before me. Half his head blown away, the soldier carried on thrashing and heaving for breath. We watched, mesmerised, suddenly childlike again, our rifles still smoking in our hands. John the Fox finally broke the terrible spell. Leaning forward over the small ditch, his R4 extended, he placed the muzzle point blank against the man's heart and pulled the trigger. The thrashing stopped. We turned and left … walked back to the staging point.

"Yes, I suppose it was our duty, as soldiers," I repeated, looking at him

I wondered if any of my paratrooper comrades thought about those times, those deaths. Or was I the only one?

Chapter Twenty-four

A LIGHT CLOAK OF RELIEF

'Do You Really Want to Hurt Me?' ~ Culture Club

"What is that cap on your TV, my friend?" I asked.

I was working on a plumbing job near downtown Los Angeles and had recognised the unmistakable, ridiculously high crown of a Russian officer's cap, carefully wrapped in plastic and set in a place of honour on top of the TV set in the small living room. The cap looked in pristine condition, with the band and insignia (the red star surrounding the hammer and sickle) below the crown and above the peak, as usual. The walls of the cramped apartment were filled with assorted framed photos from the tenant's former life, in Russia.

"What? This one?" the Russian replied, pointing to the cap.

"Yes, the cap," I said.

"Oh, this," he said in his thick accent, "this is the cap of my best friend from Russia, he was killed ... and his mother sent me his cap. We were best friends from when we were small children in Russia."

He thrust out his arm to indicate the height they had been as children; his hand was not high from the ground.

"What happened to him?" I asked, interested.

"He was killed, in Angola. Have you heard of Angola?"

I looked at him, my hands still full of work tools.

"He was my best friend, we were like brothers and grow up together, and he was helicopter pilot, and they shoot him down ...and killed," he explained.

"When was this?" I asked, startled.

"This happened in 1981, in the south of Angola."

I paused, taken aback by the coincidence of working in this complex, in this apartment, for this Russian man, whose childhood friend had been shot down and killed in southern Angola. What were the odds?

"My friend," I said, putting my tools down, "I know about Angola well. I am from South Africa, I was in southern Angola in 1981 and may have been within a few hundred kilometres of where you friend was shot down."

The pleasant Russian seemed lost for words; he looked confused, digesting what I had just told him. Then he smiled, "Aha! You are from South Africa, yes, I know about South Africa."

I told him that our military had been fighting against SWAPO insurgents and the Angolan army, and that the Soviets had been supporting and training Angolans, when I had been in Angola.

"We are two immigrants, from different countries, with a strange connection in common," he said, smiling at me.

I nodded, picked up my tools and headed downstairs to work. Yes, he was right, what a strange connection.

As it happened, it was a few days before my birthday. Birthdays, of course were good days, but I had also had some crappy birthdays. I don't believe in astrology, but my birthday had often been a significant life-changing day for me. As a youngster I had been arrested for possession of marijuana on two consecutive birthdays, my 19th and 20th birthdays. Then, on my 21st birthday, we had been in the front line of an attack on a military base at Xangongo and the town of Ondjiva, some 80 km inside Angola. We had crawled forward on our bellies with bullets, RPG rockets and ZU-23 mm rounds tearing the air apart feet above our heads. Not a great way to celebrate a 21st. So, three bad birthdays in a row – what are the chances of that happening in one lifetime?

Later, when I left South Africa it was on my birthday and when I arrived in America the next day, it was still on my birthday – thanks to having crossed the international date line somewhere along the way. Another life-changing experience.

Often when I was fully engrossed in hard physical work of plumbing, carrying, cutting, climbing crawling, drilling, jack hammering my mind would easily slip back to the bush and even lift my head to any sound of a jet plane or helicopter flying over head in the city half expecting to see a Puma or Mirage streak by. As well as on and around my birthday when I couldn't help to reflect back on that action packed, three-day, clearing trench-to-trench attack in Angola. Today, working under the apartment building in LA was no exception. Even though the plumbing work was hard, cutting out old pipes and piling them to the side, drilling new holes through the wooden sub floor to run new lines up into the building, I had been transported back, to another world and time. While I worked I heard the sounds of the Angolan early dawn …

> *We sat in an armoured vehicle, waiting to attack, listening to the thunderous explosions of the 1,000 lb bombs being dropped by South African Mirage jets, onto the deep defensive trenches of Xangongo. In the gaps between explosions we were aware of the frantic beating of the wings of wild birds, escaping like bats out of hell from their dawn perches. We waited for the bombardment to end so that we could advance towards the trenches.*
>
> *"Deploy Deploy!" I heard Lieutenant Doep shouting, at the top of his voice, ordering us to deploy from the safety of the Buffel armoured vehicle. I heard the clang as we kicked open the heavy metal side panel and jumped down to the ground, bullets cracking and zipping past our heads and pinging against the vehicle. I smelled the cold fresh dawn and the peppery smell of Angolan sand.*

My head was filled with shouts, the whine of heavy diesel motors, gun shots in the early morning dawn, while I drilled holes and sawdust fell in my face.

"Donde es mas pipa?" (Where are more pipes?) the Mexican labourer shouted.

"*La pipaesta arriba! Traega me mastres cuatosy mas soldadura!*" (The pipe is above! Bring me more three-quarter pipe and solder!) I shouted in Spanish to my Mexican workers, annoyed that they were bothering me in the middle of my daydream.

In my well over ten years in Los Angeles I had never once had the chance to speak Afrikaans; now I struggled to string together five words or more. My Spanish was now better than my Afrikaans had been (almost), and I was especially fluent in street Spanish.

I lay in the small basement surrounded by tools, trash and extension cords, working like a demon, pushing away trash, cutting pipe, drilling holes, kicking away debris, crawling forward on my belly, dragging a mountain of tools with me. The faster I worked the more the sounds of war reverberated in my head ... long bursts of machine gun fire echoed in the early dawn ... the shouting of orders. Advance! The feeling of being pinned down, unable to move, bullets zipping through the air inches over your head, breath draining, the unforgettable sound of 23 mm AAA shells, fifty in five seconds, ripping through the air above us, the big shells bringing heavy tree limbs crashing down behind us.

"*Hey senor! Hey senor! Luncha es aqiu ... es luncha amigo ... toma vescanso!*" (Hey sir! Lunch is here ... it's lunchtime, friend ... take a rest!" My workers were calling me for lunch.

I ate lunch outside with Mexican workers, listening to them joking, fooling around. The Russian from upstairs walked out of the building and I waved to him. He waved back. I was the first South African my Mexican workers had ever met (all they knew about South Africa was 'Mandela!') and they constantly asked me questions about South Africa.

"*Hay muchas animales en Sud Africa?*" (Are there many animals in South Africa?)

"*Si claro ... Sud Africa es un pais bonita ... pais de los Dioses, muchas animales y mucho mas tranquilo de aqui.En Los angeles es la vida loca!*" (South Africa is a beautiful country, the land of god and not a crazy life like Los Angeles.) I frequently joked with them and in the comradeship of hard work they were also my willing audience, listening to my stories about my days in the bush. I told them about *La geurra contra terroristas en Angola.* (The war against terrorists in Angola.) Some of them had heard my stories before but they were always eager to listen again. They munched their *burrito's asada*, listening, smiling hugely as I told them stories about our small war in Angola, unaware that I was a ticking time bomb.

My judgements were too harsh. The lines I drew in the sand were too rigid. I was instantly responsive when startled; as a result I had been involved in more fights in the last ten years, in America, than I could remember. Something was not right.

§

THE WALL

"How old were most of the troops that you were with?" he asked me.

"I suppose most of us were around 19 or 20 years old at the time, in the second year of our operational duty on the Border. Our platoon lieutenants were probably about 21 or 22, our company captain was probably about 26 years old."

I pictured our company commander, Captain Leipoldt. A tall, quiet man, with an impartial mind. We all respected him and would have followed him anywhere he led us. To us, he carried absolute authority and although he seemed many years older than us troopers, in reality he was only about five years older. The only time that I heard Captain Leipoldt raise his voice, shout loudly, was the afternoon that I kicked fifty shades of shit out of a staff sergeant who was acting camp sergeant major, from an infantry unit. It's a long story but this man had killed two of our pet cats by stomping on them and slamming them against the mess wall. So I desperately tried to do the same to him, with my boots worn white from having walked for a month inside Angola. I had almost succeeded. We were all shocked to hear Captain Leipoldt yelling, from across the small parade ground, as he strode towards me, past the crumpled sergeant major, shouting at me in Afrikaans, demanding to know, "Do you think you're the god of Ovamboland?"

He was furious that one of his paratroopers had delivered instant and severe 'bush justice' to the cat killer, but I believe that he understood, and perhaps even sympathised with, my reason for doing so.

Later Captain Leipoldt wrote a letter in my favour which was read at my court martial hearing. I believe that his strongly worded letter of reference was my saving grace, at the time, and that it served to get me off with a suspended sentence instead of a stint in DB. That and the fact that they needed every paratrooper available for the biggest ever South African cross-border operation, which was being planned at that time. By the end of that day I had rejoined my Company; before dawn the following morning we crossed the border into Angola, at the start of Operation Protea.

Our Delta Company spearheaded the Operation, running alongside and sometimes in front of a mechanised attack group, fighting against a large, well-entrenched and defended Angolan regular military base camp. Operation Protea marked a new phase in the Border War.

"Did you and your fellow paratroopers receive any debriefing, after you had finished your service?" he asked.

I didn't have to think long about this question. I remembered my last day in the army: our Delta Company, now one hundred well-seasoned veterans, who, just a few days ago, had been up in the operational area, had transformed themselves back into happy youngsters. We stood around in a circle, kicking stones, smoking and joking, big smiles confirming that finally our last day had arrived – our two years of military service was over.

Our commanding officer told us each to take a turn to describe what plans we had for our futures. We all laughed and heckled each person who stepped forward, into the circle, to say that he was going to, "pursue a teaching career" … "go to university" or "a trade technician" … or "work in my father's business", etc.

I remember thinking it was a shame to let us all go, that they should have kept us in service for another six months. Over the last two years of constant training and back-to-back cross-border operations, we had become such a well-oiled machine, a family that knew everyone's strengths and weaknesses, a large and effective fighting unit; each one knew his role, exactly. And now all this training and expertise would disappear, on the day we walked through the big iron battalion gates for the last time.

"Not really, we all just stood around on the last day, in a circle, and described what we wanted to do with our lives, now that it was all over. This person wanted to be a teacher, another wanted to go to university, or college, and so on."

"What did you say you wanted to do?"

I paused, remembering what I had said when it was my turn to speak.

"I said, 'I was going to live life', whatever that might have meant."

He smiled at me, intrigued by my answer: "And are you doing what you said, 'living life'?"

I sat and thought of the last ten years, gone in a flash of sweat, boxing gyms, hard punches, blue eyes, concussions, victories and defeats, street fights, beer and shooters, the last call, waking in strange apartments, women I had loved, achievements, self-acceptance, persistence, making a life in a new land, without a single helping hand. On the one hand I suffered regrets that affected me on a daily basis – what if I had chosen a different path, and so on; on the other, I had no regrets at all, and would happily do all the same things all over again.

"Yes, I am doing what I said I would do; I am living my life with no regrets."

The American Indian wise man smiled at me, leaning far back in his modern arm chair, the kind of chair you would never buy for yourself.

§

I knew that my response and answer to life issues needed attention. My reactions had become too harsh and severe. In recent years I had become a ticking time bomb. Only recently I had knocked out an Apache Indian paratrooper. He was a Vietnam veteran friend of an ex neighbour, with whom I had met a few times. He knocked on our door late one night, during a storm, drunk, walked in mumbling, glaring at me past his long-ago broken nose, clearly expressing some sort of smouldering American Indian antipathy. He had no business standing in my doorway so late. In a second, without a word, I had leapt from the couch and decked him with a long right hand. Then I had dragged him outside by his long Apache warrior hair, in the pouring rain, and dumped him half unconscious under the peach tree. I had not paused to think that maybe this Vietnam veteran paratrooper might have had his own problems, from his soldiering past. Maybe he was simply looking for shelter from the storm? All I knew was that he was glaring at me, right in *my* living room. Two vets with bad recollections meet?

Soon after that I had finally caught up with our big, muscle-bound, ex-convict and another neighbour. I had given him a brutal New Year's Day thrashing, to teach him that it was not good manners to kick in our door and rob our home. But I had gone too far ... I had beaten him really badly, then kicked him with my heavy work boots ... and then dumped him close to the same peach tree as the Vietnam paratrooper. The ex-convict had been taken off to hospital and had apparently been in a bad way for some time. But he may have learned a lesson about respect ... and breaking and entering and stealing from your neighbour.

Then there was the insolent idiot at the park who came towards me on his rollerblades, talking smack … as if I was going to just stand there and let him insult me. Challenging me while he was on roller blades! What a surprise he got.

Then the knock-down-drag-out in a narrow walkway with a Brazilian *capoeira* enthusiast, with him performing his spinning kicks and me boxing. It turned out a hell of a fight and I broke my shoulder, had to slouch around in a homemade sling for over a month.

Then the unarmed 18th Street gang members I had ambushed and chased through the Hollywood apartment building, firing a shot from my .45 as they got away. Luckily it missed them by inches. But it hit a parked van and left a thumb-sized bullet hole, having gone through both front doors and exploded both side windows.

The list went on. And on.

My hands ached, permanently, and were now misshapen – the result of badly healed broken bones, from constantly dishing out what I believed was justice. I had become a lone wolf, with hardly any family or friends or culture, to guide and push me back into line. Like a dog running the plains, I ran where I wanted, did what I wanted. The big city did not care how you behaved and would invite you back night after night. I had broken my hands, shoulder and feet in altercations over respect, personal space, or simply a tough look. I had lost some fights but had won most of them. But, in a way, I always came off second best, relentless feelings of guilt, incessantly questioning my own behaviour, and, of course, long lasting physical injuries. It had become too much.

§

It had been a long time coming. I had driven past the building that housed the Vietnam Veterans counselling centre for years. The simple single-storey building, with its murals of Huey helicopters and US soldiers in Vietnam era uniforms, turned my head every time I drove by. *The Vietnam Veterans Counselling Centre.* It was hallowed ground for only a few, yet I felt drawn to the place, as a boxer is to a gym. Inexplicably, I had only recently come to the realisation that

I too was a combat veteran, just like the soldiers I saw in parades, with medals and flags. Young South African men, just out of high school, had trained hard and had become one of the best western armies of the time. Some of them had volunteered to fight at the tip of our nation's sword. Many had not come home. Our small Delta Company, under 80 men, had put a large dent in our nation's' threat', had left the bodies of over 200 so-called terrorists scattered in the bush in southern Angola, never to infiltrate our borders again. I visualised 200 men lined up, shoulder to shoulder. It seemed like a lot of souls.

I walked into the office of the Vietnam Veterans Counselling Centre and asked if I could speak to a counsellor. War was war, and although this was American hallowed ground I didn't feel like an imposter. The office clerk asked me where I was from, and did I have an appointment? I told him no, I did not, but wanted to make one. He told me to take a seat and while I sat, waiting, I was aware of a small feeling of ... progress?

I sat in the small lobby and looked at the Civil Rights posters on the wall, stating that every American had the right to free speech, privacy, religion, assembly, a fair trial, and freedom of thought ... the guarantee that regardless of gender, skin colour, religion, nationality, age, disability, or religion, a person should not be discriminated against.

Well, we may not have been in Vietnam but we too had memories, and had paid the price of training, tracking, ambushing, attacking and killing communist enemies, in the last proxy conflict of the cold war, in a faraway corner of Africa that the Portuguese named *O fim do mundo* (the end of the world).

§

"Granger Korff? Come in."
The long haired American Indian counsellor led me into a small room.
"Where are you from ... you have an accent?"
"I'm from South Africa."
"South Africa?"
We sat down he looked at me sceptically. He paused and for a moment I thought perhaps that he, like so many others in America, might not know of South Africa. Then he nodded his head, indicating that he did.

"What brings you in here today, and how can I help you?"

"Well, it's quite a long story. I'm not American and I've never been in the United States military. I didn't fight in Vietnam, or anywhere else for America. But I was a combat soldier. I'm from South Africa."

"What was going on in South Africa?" he asked.

"For more than a decade we had a Border War going on, up in the bush on the Angolan and Namibian borders. It was a small, low intensity war, compared with your Vietnam war, but by the end of 1978 it had escalated. South Africa doing frequent cross-border attacks on terrorist training base camps across the border, in the north, up on the Angolan border. Do you know anything about it?"

He nodded again, but hesitantly. I wasn't sure he knew anything about the Angolan bush war.

"Do you perhaps have some time, so that we can talk?"

"Sure, I have time," he smiled.

"In South Africa, after high school, we were all conscripted to do national military service. I volunteered for the Airborne. It was a small hide-and-seek bush war in southern Angola and Ovamboland. Patrols, following spoor, ambushes, and attacking terrorist base camps in Angola. I was a paratrooper and there was quite a lot of action. We used to fly across the Border and hit them in their base camps where they were training – "

"Who is 'they'?"

"SWAPO terrorists … communist trained terrorists who would cross the Border into South Africa."

"Communists?"

"Yes, communist backed and trained."

"In Africa?" he asked, mystified, as everyone always was when they heard this for the first time.

He sat back in his chair to listen.

I didn't spend much time talking about the Bush War. Quickly I got to the point. I opened my mouth and told this long-haired stranger stuff that I had never dared tell another living soul. I told him about my hair trigger aggression, my detachment, being hyper-vigilant, always ready to end a threat in seconds, sometimes even pre-empt it before it started. Of the soul crushing flashbacks or intrusive thoughts that sometimes took my breath away, how they had over the years assumed some sort of control over my present life.

He was a stranger ... so I could tell him. He would not judge me.

I told him how our Delta Company had seen enough contact in the dry bush in Angola, had killed well over 200 guerrilla fighters. Any soldier who had been in combat would know what the KIA can look like. Some of these we had even had to tie to the bumpers of our vehicles, drive for a day or two, to bring them back to Oshakati for finger printing. Cook our food with these day-old, dead enemies a metre away, like deer tied to the bumper.

I told him how thoughts that I held dear, loving, priceless memories of my loved ones, friends often were hijacked by half headless men we had shot and left on the sand, their brains on the sand next to them. Young, old, mothers cut in half, holding dead babies. The blood of dead terrorists, empty eyes, empty heads, curled in foetal positions in their last moments, an enemy soldier calling for his mother with his last breath in the last second of his life. A terrorist, mortally wounded, shot through the throat, running thirty yards then dying on his back with his thumb pushed through his fingers in a final, obscene 'fuck you' gesture, his hand on his chest for us to see, as John the Fox and I reached him, our still smoking barrels pointed at him.

The Bushman clan of terrorists, escaping together with their families, women, grandmothers, children ... killed with their men folk, uniformed and armed. A mother with half her chest gone from a direct 20 mm gunship hit, still holding her dead baby in her other arm ... the baby looked unharmed, but it was dead. Maybe dead from fright at the awful sound of fifty weapons? A terrible mistake ... not one of us had spoken about it, even once, afterwards ... no one had said a word about it, not even amongst ourselves. As if it all had to be buried and forgotten, never to be spoken about, a terrible mistake, part of the cost of war. Was all this to be forgotten, like it never happened?

Placing my still smoking barrel, burning hot from having shot four magazines, just inches behind the ear of a mortally wounded terrorist, groaning for help, and pulling the trigger, thinking it was the best I could do for him.

Atrocities? Yes, both sides had committed them. Well brought up youngsters, alone or on Civvy street, would not dream of taking part in acts so callous, so shocking ... yet they could easily be caught up in the loose rules of war, the dehumanisation of the enemy. Us or them. Communists! Shoot fast, shoot first, shoot anything that moved, or shoot until it moved and ask questions later. Yes, I had seen troops take fingers and ears and more, as trophies. Yes, I had seen bodies propped in trees deep in Angola, after attacking a lone enemy base camp, left as a crude and terrible message to the comrades of our enemies that they were within our reach.

Comrades who had been reached in their own backyards, deep across the Border, where they had thought they were safe. The same attack where the feral pigs had come out of the bush alerted by our dawn gun fire, crazed by the smell of the blood of thirteen men, as the sun rose, pushed their way into the killing zone, unafraid … and had eaten the brains of some of the dead terrorists. Maybe these pigs belonged to the terrorists, and they had planned to eat them? To pot them first? We threw clods at the pigs to chase them away, but they stubbornly refused to go, maddened by their sick meal. A hellish scene.

The wounded terrorist who had reached for his weapon and called for his mother, when he realised it was too late. His brains had steamed in the cold sand, like throwing a pot of hot water into the cold dawn. The pigs were close.

Many times over the years I had thought about sudden death. We had seen and caused so much of it. A human being with hopes, dreams, aspirations, a sense of humour, happiness, likes and dislikes, fears and memories, then – one second of pulling a trigger – nothing, no life, no hope, just nothing. Empty, same as a rock or an old car tyre

Which paratrooper hadn't seen terrorist corpses with fresh Marlboro cigarettes stuck in their mouths? Young men, alone in the deep bush of Angola, coming away victorious from a fire fight, they alone had done it, they alone had waited, walked for a month through the bush, tracking the enemy. They alone had killed them. No one there closer than 100 miles, only them and the dead enemy.

The well-defined muscles of that extraordinarily tall, shirtless FAPLA soldier who leaped with no weapon, unarmed from a bunker, just yards from us, and ran for his life but didn't make it. Why had he run, why didn't he try to surrender?

Were these memories or visions classified secrets – that we had to keep and never talk about? Had we joined that club of former combatants who were silent about these things until their dying day – when old men cried on their deathbeds?

The brave sniper who lay in hiding in the grass, just thirty yards away from us as we took a smoke break; for five minutes he waited then he took his last shot at Lt du Plessis and missed (although he might have died thinking that he had hit Lt Doep because of the way that Doep fell from the near miss with the bullet passing through his hair) then, knowing he had no escape, did not even try to lift his head as the three of us charged at him through our gun smoke, shooting as we ran forward.

I could still see the wide white eyes of the terrorist who came out from the thicket, thinking that he had successfully escaped the fire fight, but then turned to look me in the eyes as I pulled the trigger.

The FAPLA soldier who lay hidden, no more than eight metres away from me, when I bent over to puke and didn't even see him. A couple seconds later he would have shot me, but my comrades, John the Fox and Paul Greef, were faster than he was, cracking their bullets inches past me to get him.

Does war steal your soul?

The white-haired grandmother, her stomach and liver on the sand next to her, who smiled at me when I said I would find help for her. But there was no help for anyone so deep in the Angolan bush.

The South African government had labelled them terrorists and we had fought them as terrorists, with little quarter given on either side. They were certainly backed and trained by the Soviets, under the name of communism. But how many of them had been hard core terrorists? How many were no more than young tribal men with nothing better to do in the bush than join a struggle to liberate a land.

When you end someone's life does your life end too?

The solemn American Indian counsellor, with the long black hair of an Indian warrior, sat back, relaxed, in the simple chair, supporting his chin on his hands.

I sat on the edge of my chair, my back as stiff as a board. But as I spoke to this stranger, a comrade in arms, a man that I knew had seen the same things I had, I felt the decade-old grip of the spirits of death weaken, as my words reached this wise man's ears and he nodded, slowly. Already I felt a flutter of freedom in my gut, as I told him my worst visions and flashbacks, that rolled like a super-fast movie through my mind during what should be my happiest most cherished moments, like with a girl, laughing, enjoying lunch at a café, or making love … hijacking my loving memories of family and loved ones. The more I spoke the more I felt new life flooding through my veins.

Then I told him how hard I had tried to forget these memories.

"You should not try to forget these memories. Your memories, good and bad, are part of who you are. You should learn to live with your bad memories, alongside your good memories. You have every right to be here and to have your happiest memories and happiest moments, you have every right to be here and live a full productive life and thrive, and live everyday on this earth, just as the trees have every right to be on this earth and the birds and the animals and the mountain, so do you."

I told him I had left my country ten years ago, left all my friends, family and comrades.

You can travel the world a hundred times you will carry your demons with you.

"Have you ever been back to your homeland, since then?"

"No, not in more than ten years."

"You should try to go back, to see your people again and see your land. I think that will be a great help for you. The people that you left behind and try to forget, are the people who can help you. It's your community that can help you. You have no community here. You know that the American Indian tribes would care for their own warriors when they returned, the people would hold celebrations and comfort them in ritual, knowing that they would bring back dead spirits with them from war. They would wash them and everyone, young and old, had to listen to their stories of battle, because they were also part of it, because it was their warriors who had endured and fought for them, they were together. You need your own people from your own land, to talk to, they will understand you, wash you."

The older American Indian Vietnam Veteran-turned-counsellor spoke slowly and I started to see just how insightful he was. He spoke quietly from a place of inner peace. I knew, certainly, that he too had seen such actions. The fog of battle … all wars were the same … from the time of creation. The Bible tells of situations in which men, women, children, and dogs and chickens had been slain, leaving not a living soul, human or animal.

I left that counselling session feeling the beginnings of a new man. My terrible secret was out … my spoken words were setting me free.

'Fly Like An Eagle' ~ Seal

Living in Hollywood, surrounded by creative people and their art, and with some spare time on my hands, I developed the notion that I should try to write a book about my experiences as a South African paratrooper in the Bush War. I knew there was a story to tell about our small war in Angola, a place that seemed so far away, and in such a different world, but I could still remember most of it, like yesterday. I'd had very little contact with South Africans for the past ten years, in which time I had become convinced that I was the only one who couldn't forget about the Border War. Maybe there was something wrong with me? Maybe it shouldn't be like this?

I decided to start writing as soon as possible and bought myself several writing pads with yellow, lined pages. Instead of the seemingly impossible job of trying to ignore and push away my memories of lost lives, fast brutal fire fights and long, boring days spent doing patrols, I would invite the (previously unwelcome) memories into the forefront of my mind. At night I started making notes and planning the shape of my book.

The South African Defence Force had done such a good job of normalising everything we had done that until now I had not even considered myself a war veteran, it had just been something that we had to do. Unlike the Americans. The US military and public alike, thanked their veterans, with medals and memorials, flags and parades. But I was not one of them … I was not one of their veterans. I was … well, I was no one. I had never had anyone thank me, had never even thought of it. Why would they? I had never ever thought of putting on my uniform, to march in a parade, so that the South African public could smile and wave and say, "Thank you, for fighting for us."

I sat and smoked a Marlboro, watching the moon rise. I had spent an enjoyable afternoon watching, for the first time ever, a Memorial Day parade – usually I maintained a cool distance from such festivities. But this had been a long parade for the soldiers returning from Operation Desert Storm; it had included a number of military vehicles and several companies of big burly American troops, holding their banners and company flags, marching down Sunset Boulevard in Hollywood.

Toast of the army, favourite son! Hail to the brave Big Red One!

They were the 1st Infantry Division, the 'Big Red One' with a fighting history that went as far back as the Great War. I had watched from the knoll on the corner of Vine Street, standing next to a tall American soldier dressed in civvies. He told me he had been with these same marching troops in Iraq, but for some reason he was not participating in the parade. He was an easy going, big, blond guy from somewhere in Middle America. With time to kill and not wanting to lose our spots on the grass, we stood side by side in the hot sun, waiting for the parade to reach us. It felt good to be talking to another soldier and I started telling him about having been a South African paratrooper in the Bush War in Angola.

He was a nice guy and he could see that I was really getting into the subject, so he listened and let me talk. When I finally left the parade I realised he probably hadn't believed a word I'd said.

Some years ago, during a late-night phone call with a bad connection, my father had told me that he'd received a medal, sent in the mail, for my service 'In the suppression of terrorism'. It was in a box somewhere in my mother's house and I had never seen it. I thought about all this as I drove home from the military parade, musing about my own status as a war veteran. It may sound strange that it had taken me so many years to think of my own national service in the same terms as a veteran from a different war, but that's how it had been for me.

The South African Bush War had been a conflict that was fought almost in secret. And the SADF had done such a good job of downplaying and normalising the Border War – just a normal experience for all young men, nothing out of the ordinary, nothing worth talking about, Civvy street doesn't owe you anything – these were their last words to many as they walked out the gate of 1 Parachute Battalion after two action-packed years.

The South African culture then was accepting and unquestioning; SA citizens asked little and were told less about what was happening on the Border, and they accepted it. On top of that, we were naturally conservative young men and hardly spoke about our experiences. It had taken me many years to realise that I was the same as the American military veterans marching in the parade that day.

I had learned some valuable lessons in the last few years. I had become quieter and, by and large, I had stopped talking about my army experience in Angola. No one knew what I was talking about, and reliving those events always made me feel unsettled. I was not so brash; I was humbler, more forgiving, and I was working to ingrain in myself a kinder outlook on life. I had consciously tried to shut down my memories of brothers in arms, flashing muzzles in the bush, the smell of gun powder, shouts of triumph, and a hundred worse visions. I was trying to focus on fitting into day-to-day society in my new country.

Years of trial and error had brought me some success at banishing these dark memories, but they were double-sided entities and had merely slid into the shadows, where they watched and waited – just like the Vietnam counsellor had said. Like a two-headed dog, one good, one bad, the one I fed became stronger. Some of my worst experiences were joined at the neck to some of my best, most meaningful, memories. I had never been able to cast them far enough from my everyday thoughts, because they were my history, they were part of me. Like someone in an abusive relationship I needed them, even though I knew they would do me damage. When these memories were cast out they left reluctantly, like rejected pets, but they did not go far. They perched, silently and stubbornly, like flocks of black birds in trees close to a camp site, day after day, year after year, a familiar everyday sight. They had been chased away but they refused to leave, because they had nowhere to go. They were nothing without me …they would die, alone. And I was just as empty without them, they provided meaning and I could not banish them entirely.

The beginning of my book about my time as a South African paratrooper in 1 Parachute Battalion was slowly taking form. I had endless points and notes on what I remembered clearly. Much of it had been burnt into my brain. The jokes, the gruelling training, strangers who became comrades and brothers, hardened instructors, seasoned leaders, first blood, the smell and sound of battle in the bush, the change from boy to man.

I tried to imagine the number of SWAPO, FAPLA and Cuban enemies who had been killed, throughout the entire Bush War, surely ten thousand? Maybe more. I tried to imagine them all standing together, brigade after brigade, standing at attention on a huge parade ground in the bush. And the South Africans killed in the bushwar all standing together on another parade ground. A battalion of South African heroes who would never grow old, like the rest of us.

I continued making short notes on my military time in my yellow writing pads. I had started on my first day of the army when my shoulder length hair had been cut, first, and then shaved, right down to a number four. Then I recorded the events that had followed training, one by one. I began slowly, writing down one memory, followed by another. I kept the note book next to my bed and often times I would jump up and write down a memory in the middle of the night.

The flock of stubborn, silent black birds slowly returned, circling and flapping their wings, not sure if they were welcome ... then they saw that the gates were open. They had been invited in, finally, called back home where they belonged.

Memories I had tried really hard to forget soon came flooding back, home to roost, but this time I was ready. Unbeknown to the birds I had set a trap, an ambush; I let them in and caught them, in an ambush of pen and paper, for everyone to see.

I captured them in untidy notes in the middle of the day or the middle of the night, I caught them while driving, pulling over to write them down; I caught them while eating, while showering, while listening to music.

I thought perhaps I'd give my book the same title as a song I had sung, frequently, while on the dusty border – *19 with a Bullet*.

Like the Gods of war, the fearsome NCO's of Parachute Battalion hammered recruits into an iron hard fighting force, a cycle repeated ever since man first took to the field to slay his enemy.

Chapter Twenty-five
CITY OF ANGELS ON FIRE

'Nutbush City Limits' ~ Ike and Tina Turner

We had met Ike and Vance at the top of the Hollywood Holiday Inn, to meet Ike's new protégé. Ike Turner, as well known for his libido as his famous rock and roll numbers, did not hide the fact that he approved enormously of my girlfriend's full figure. Not that I could blame him; besides being a tall, strong girl she was blessed with the firm, round backside of a sprinter.

The band played soft jazz with a poppy saxophone in the revolving penthouse restaurant of the Hollywood Holiday Inn. Ike Turner nodded and winked at me as he handed us our tall cocktails and introduced us to his new blonde partner. I had heard Ike talk about her but had not met her before. She was a seriously good-looking blonde who could apparently sing and dance and was destined to be part of Ike's new act.

"Ya gotta hear this girl sing, she's amazin', gonna have a number one hit soon."

Every time we went out with Ike I couldn't help thinking back to my time as a young teenager, spending Friday afternoons in my bedroom back home, listening to 'Gruesome Gresh' (David Gresham), counting down the SA Top 20. I remembered that, sometime in this period Ike and Tina Turner had scored a hit with 'Nutbush City Limits'. It was the last hit single the two of them produced together.

"Have you been in the studio Ike?" I asked.

"Yessir, already got some tracks down. Ya gonna hear about this here girl real soon. Watch the headlines, she can dance even better than Tina." And Ike winked at my date, again.

Ike's new partner did not say much ... she smiled at us and quietly sipped her drink; there was a sober look about her. She seemed to be serious about her future and I thought she certainly looked like she could become the new (white) Tina Turner.

Vance stood close by, talking loudly about the well-publicised court case of our LAPD police officers on trial for the horrendous beating we had all seen countless times on television. A black motorist, Rodney King, had led the police on a long, high-speed chase and when he finally pulled over he was beaten for three minutes solid, by four policemen with batons, as he tried to get up. The entire episode had been filmed by a man standing on his apartment balcony. In a strange coincidence, the man who had filmed the beating, George Holliday, became my boss when I joined his plumbing company, a few months later.

"There's going to be a riot in this city, you watch and see," Vance predicted, sipping his coffee, no alcohol for Vance, "these cats are not gonna give up until this city is burning, they gonna riot for real this time, if those cops get off with a light sentence for that beating."

"But he wouldn't summit to the cops," I said, arguing as the devil's advocate.

"Hell no! Would you stay down? There were six or seven policeman on top of him when he was down on the ground; he had to keep movin' – to save his own life. There's definitely gonna be a riot, "Vance glared at me.

Even Ike had tuned into the conversation and was nodding his agreement with Vance.

Dressed as per usual in his shiny, glitter covered outfit, Vance soon steered the subject away from the trial and the upcoming verdict for the LAPD officers, back to the topic of the millions of dollars in funding that he was about to score from Coca Cola … or Chrysler … or Sony … for his Christmas album. This information was broadcast, confidently, to the entire bar while Vance sipped his coffee, topped with whipped cream, from a tall glass with a handle.

Vance had moved from Canada to Los Angeles in the 60s; he was an eccentric, possibly a madman, who drank no alcohol and survived on a Spartan diet of mostly coffee, bread and bologna. He had been living on the 10th floor of the Holiday Inn for a year, (we suspected he had conned the hotel manager with a percentage of the coming of multi millions in lieu of room payment) and never wore anything other than his shiny Las Vegas outfit, with his gnarled hands appearing from puffy lace cuffs – like the penguin in the batman movies. Vance didn't drive, had no car and found his way about town in taxi cabs. No one could write a character like Vance and be believed. I had once seen him without his shirt and had glimpsed about 30 faded, old, scars, cut across his veins all the way down the inside of *both* his arms.

Vance had been a concert promoter in the heyday of music festivals and had told us how he had walked away with shopping bags full of money. He had made and lost several fortunes from the music and Hollywood scene in the 60s and 70s, and often reminisced about the free love floating around at the time.

"Munchkins, I'm going to need your help," Vance had sidled up to us and was speaking as quietly as possible. "The cat I told you about, who's been keeping my coins, he's coming to town soon and I'm going to need help keeping them in a safe place for a while."

"The coins?"

"Yeah, the silver dollars! I've got a suitcase full of them, worth millions. Ya gotta help! I don't trust anyone here, you South African kids are not like these other germs around here."

('Germ' was Vance's favourite term for anyone he didn't like, or with whom he didn't agree, and that was most people.)

I remembered Vance talking about these coins, ever since I had met him, a year ago, but he had delivered so many tall stories that I had learned to take all of them with a pinch of salt.

"I'll let you know when … I'll give you cats a few coins and that'll set you up for a while, get you out of this shit hole. They're worth 20k or 30k apiece and I've got hundreds of them in that suitcase … hundreds of them."

(He had also signed a paper saying that Murray and I would get 2% of his Christmas album when it hit the market, for having helped him out of some sticky situations; but I wasn't holding my breath about that, either.)

He beamed at us, from ear to ear. I'd believe the coins when I saw them, but I nodded and returned the smile, "Surething. No problem. You just let us know."

The band leader called Ike Turner onto the stage to introduce him as being in the house. Ike had a spring in his step and jitterbugged a little as he waved to the patrons. Vance's Cheshire Cat smile grew even bigger and he pointed to Ike on the stage, "Watch this cat, he's going to be right on top again."

Lately Vance and Ike were inseparable (I had even heard them spoken about on a morning radio station) and together they were a force to be reckoned with; Ike had played a major part in the legendary story of American rock n' roll, and Vance was full of indomitable confidence in the hundreds of millions of dollars he was (always) *just* about to make. They were both trying to find a way to break back into the music biz; both were very experienced and neither of them ever thought small. Vance had his tapes for the album stashed at the studio and was getting ready to mix as soon as the alleged sponsor money arrived ... maybe next week. Ike was about to take on the world with his new blonde Tina Turner.

I had always been heavy-handed at both pouring and drinking: my cocktails and drinks were knocked back in a few sips. No one in Hollywood woke up early and my easy apartment manager job with its flexible hours lent itself to long nights out on the town. Too much booze, too many late nights and one-night stands. I had met some good people but as much as I enjoyed musicians and music, I was worn out and needed a change.

Change was a comin'.

The 'Rodney King' riots in Los Angeles were soon in full swing, just as our eccentric friend Vance had predicted. This was rioting on a scale we thought we had left behind in South Africa in the 70s and 80s. However, this was not South Africa but America. The metropolis of Los Angeles quickly had been brought to a standstill, for over a week between 29 April and 04 May, by rampaging, mainly black and Latino mobs, looting and pillaging until the city of Los Angeles looked like Beirut. Hundreds of columns of black smoke rose into the air from the plundered city; thousands of buildings and businesses were looted and/or burnt to the ground; 3,000 people were injured, 12,000 people were arrested, 63 people were killed; and a billion dollars of damage were recorded – in six days of rioting. Order was reinstated, finally, when the California Army National Guard and federal troops from the 7th Infantry Division and 1st Marine Division were brought in, to implement a dusk-to-dawn curfew, quell the riots, and patrol the streets of Los Angeles and Hollywood in Humvees fitted with 50 calibre machine guns.

April is a special month in Los Angeles. There is still a last hint of crisp winter chill coming from the melting snow in the mountains, but fruit trees and roadside blossoms are already in bloom, heralding the coming spring. But the 29th April 1992 became a day that Los Angeles would not forget. The fires in the city had started late in the afternoon just hours after the acquittal of the four LAPD police officers for the assault on Rodney King. At first there had been only a few isolated columns of smoke rising into the sunset over downtown and south LA. But the next day, after a restless night of watching the growing violence on television, we woke to see tall black columns of smoke rising straight into the clear sky, from hundreds of fires. They made the cityscape of Los Angeles look like Rome burning. By late afternoon another 1,000 fires were burning: shops, restaurants, strip malls, cars and dumpsters had been set alight and burnt by angry, out of control hordes. The fires raged, uncontrolled, and the fire department was unable to reach them, due to the mobs rampaging through the streets. All the smoke columns seemed to rise to the same height and then flatten out in the high air current, mingling with each other and making an ugly smudge in the sky that covered Los Angles like a black shroud.

Murray and I had climbed the Hollywood hills behind our building to get a better look from a higher vantage point. Los Angeles looked more and more like Beirut.

"Those rioters are going to be here by this afternoon. You'd better get to the bank to cash those checks. I'll get chains and locks, you get the .45 pistol from the pawn shop."

I had bought a temporary, small, pickup truck after we'd lost everything in the pool business, including an almost new Ford 250 truck. But the replacement piece-of-junk truck was quite cool – every inch of it was covered in graffiti, a head turner even in Hollywood. It was a junk bucket that kept us on our toes; it was anyone's guess, all the time, as to whether it would start, or not.

I drove to the bank amid the wild feeling that had taken over the streets. People ran across intersections against red lights; cars zipped between the lanes, racing to get out of Hollywood before the coming rioters and fires, getting closer all the time.

Bat Out of Hell

"Geez Louise!" My heart sank when I saw the line at the bank, almost out the door. Everybody must have had the same idea of drawing cash and the ATM machines had been emptied. Everyone was aggravated, waiting in the long line, but there was also a feeling of pulling together, and people spoke to each other in hushed tones. Even the financial managers were acting as tellers, calling out loudly that they were only doing cash withdrawals, no deposits.

Finally, I reached the front of the queue and cashed a couple of cheques from having done some construction work on the side. I stuffed the few hundred dollars into my pocket and prayed that the Graffiti All Over pickup would start. It did. I headed down to the pawnshop to withdraw the .45 pistol I had pawned, not wanting to have it immediately to hand, wanting it in safekeeping, but close to our apartment.

"Aw c'mon!" I exclaimed. The line of people at the pawn shop was as bad as the one in the bank had been. Again, everyone had arrived at the same idea; everyone was pulling out firearms from the hock shop. I took my place in line, on the side walk, and watched as customers walked briskly out of the shop, firearms held in their hands, out in the open.

"Did you see those shopkeepers in Korea Town open fire on the looters, on TV? Man, they were shooting full out," said someone in the line.

I didn't feel like talking but I had also watched the scene on TV. Anticipating the arrival of an angry mob the Korean shopkeepers had armed themselves and climbed onto the roofs of their shops. As the rioters came into sight the shopkeepers had shot down, into the lawless crowd, defending their property with deadly force, emptying ten round magazines into the oncoming crowd. Those Koreans knew how to do it right. I paid up the money, stuffed the .45 into my waistband and walked out to the pickup.

I turned the key and the engine gave an empty click.

"Aw fuck! Not now!"

I tried again but got the same dead click. I slammed the dashboard with my hand.

"Piece of crap!"

I tried a few more times then got out and slammed the door.

"Fuck that. I'll leave the fucking thing here if I have to," I slammed the door, cursing and looking around. With any luck some rioter will put a match to the damn thing! I pushed the pistol snug and started to walk quickly along the couple big city blocks to La Brea. I saw a bus head past me and ran for the bus stop, holding the pistol under my shirt. The bus driver waited for me to reach the bus stop, which was unusual. Probably the last bus, I thought, as I jumped onto the almost empty bus. But the driver said he was changing his route and heading away from the violence, so I soon jumped off and jogged the rest of the way clutching the pistol stuffed hidden inside my waistband. I was surprised at how quickly the situation had escalated in our area; already there were some creeps out on the street, kicking and breaking windows and stuff.

I made it just in time. Murray closed the gates behind me and wrapped them in chains and padlocks. We had slipped into South African riot police mode and we were taking no shit. The building we managed had 32 units, occupied, mostly, by long haired musicians who attended the Musicians Institute (MI), some Mexican artists and some long-time, weird residents.

Looters were rushing past the building, pushing shopping carts full of loot from the stores on Hollywood Boulevard; several shopping carts were loaded with TV's and other big electronic items, looted from the nearby Radio Shack store.

I watched as Rioter A approached Rioter B, punched him, hard, and took off with his cart. I saw people running into the buildings across the road, carrying small TVs and electronic equipment. The streets all around the building were littered with trash, loot, boxes and carts and people running. In our ground floor apartment I stood with my arms crossed, my .45 pistol strapped to my belt, alternately looking out the window and watching the news on TV. There were now three thousand fires burning in the city. Then I heard a rustling noise in the hedge next to my apartment.

"What the hell? Sounds like someone hiding in the hedge outside."

I unlocked the padlock and stepped through the gate onto the street. Carefully I walked around the corner to the hedge ... where I found an Hispanic-looking man, his arms full of looted clothes and more. He was trying to hide his spoils in the hedge. He wasn't surprised to see me and probably incorrectly assumed I was just another looter.

"Hey Homey! You got a car?" he demanded.

I thought quickly.

"Yes, I do ... follow me."

He hefted his loot and followed me to my car, grinning. He had found someone to help him. He carried a pile of Hollywood T-shirts and stolen electronics in both arms, as if carrying a heavy load of laundry. I walked fast, making sure he was following close behind me. At the front gate of the building I spun around on my heel and threw the hardest right hand I had thrown in a long time. He was trotting towards me, from behind me, and my punch caught him right between the eyes. He dropped as though he'd been shot, with all his stolen loot on top of him. I shouted for Murray to open the gate and dragged the looter unceremoniously inside, to the pool. My brother threw the handcuffs to me and I cuffed the looter's hands tightly behind his back.

The Mexican singer who lived in apartment 102 had started screaming, as if an atrocity was being committed. The thug sat there, dazed, looking around him, trying to focus. Murray roared at her to back off and she went off on a tirade.

"This is America! You can't do this ... why is he bleeding? You can't do this."

The rioter had now come to and was staring at me, wide eyed, blood running from his nose. I dragged him to the utility cupboard, fumbled with the keys and pushed him into the small closet, along with all the brooms, rakes, buckets and cans of paint, and locked the door.

I was back in southern Africa, back in Angola. Fuck them all! The only way is to fight terrorism is to fight back, hard. Who's next?

The TV news showed us stuff we couldn't see around us. Walmart and many other large chain stores, big and small, being totally plundered by thousands of black rioters, who were casually pushing shopping carts out of the stores, loaded with stolen goods. They were even being interviewed by various reporters and, clearly, they felt quite good about themselves. Cars were burning, liquor stores were burning, the strip mall was burnt to the ground. No police to be seen. Everyone asking, "Where are the police?" No police to be seen. Talking heads on the TV spoke of the National Guard coming to the rescue, to restore order. The police were outnumbered and overwhelmed and had been ordered to stand down, ordered not to engage with the rioting, looting crowd.

"Stand down?! The police should be engaging with this crowd, shot guns blazing!"

After about four hours I decided what to do with the rioter in the closet. It didn't look as if the LAPD was about to pick up the phone or respond in any other way. Murray suggested leaving him in the closet until the morning. I disagreed. If the police don't care, then who was I to keep him locked up in the closet for hours. At about 02h00, when all the residents had gone to bed, I went out to the back of the building. His eyes lit up. I made him turn around and unlocked his handcuffs. He looked around, full of new life and energy, filled with excitement at his second chance to live and loot again. He took off like a wild dog, his head darting from side to side, looking for a new pack to join and run with. But he was too late – all the stores in the area had been cleaned out and burnt down, and probably he would only have been beaten up and robbed himself. Ironically, I was left in charge of his loot – cheap T-shirts, Hollywood memorabilia, some electronic items. There was nowhere to return it to, all the shops had been burnt and were closed for months to come.

Oh well.

The state of emergency and three-day around the clock curfew, enforced by the US military, was unprecedented in Los Angeles and Hollywood. For once the bustling city was as quiet as a one-horse town: no pedestrians, not a car on the roads. What a sight, like a scene from a movie. The only periodic break in the eerie silence was the low hum of a diesel engine, as a military Humvee, complete with an infantryman manning the 50 calibre machinegun on its roof, moved slowly past our building and then turned down the litter-filled, dark Hollywood Boulevard, followed by a platoon of armed marines in full fighting gear. After three days of anarchy the California Army National Guard and federal troops from the 7th Infantry Division and 1st Marine Division from the 29 Palms Marine base had finally been called in, to restore law and order to the City of Angels. Due to some minor setbacks, i.e. having no weapons, it had taken three days to get boots onto the sidewalk of the stars.

The around the clock curfew had been announced via TV news.

"Looks like The Rapture has taken place, streets empty and we're the only ones left."

Murray laughed, "No, if The Rapture had taken place these Hollywood streets would still be full of people going about their business, believe me. What food do we have left? Any more pasta?"

"No, just mealie meal and canned butter beans."

"Aw c'mon, man. Open the cans of spaghetti sauce."

"There's only one left."

Surprisingly quickly, in three days we had gone through the few cans of food and most of the vegetables that had been in our kitchen cupboards. The only items left were a big box of maize meal and a can of spaghetti sauce. Normally, we cooked the maize meal with salt and water to make mealie meal, a traditional African staple eaten throughout the continent.

"Back to plain old mealie meal again ... can't you mix the spaghetti sauce onto the mealie meal, to make a sauce?"

"You mean on top of it?"

"Yip, but let's cut up that old onion too – but cut it fine, not in chunks."

My brother was fussy about his food, even in times of emergency.

We sat together, eating the mostly dry mealie meal.

"Maybe we should just fuck off back to South Africa?" I suggested.

My brother didn't lift his head as he ate.

"What? You want to go home, after ten years, and start over again? And besides," he added "if you leave America after living here illegally, they will never let you back in again."

I calculated what Murray had said. Yes I had never planned to leave South Africa for good. Had always planned to return yet hadn't. If I did leave America now, return to South Africa even for a vacation to see family I could not return. The new immigration law was well known among immigrants. If you over stay your visa you are automatically barred from re-entering the United States for ten years.

He drank plain tap water from a cup. The Coke was finished and some looters had burnt down the corner store

I pondered: Here we are in the middle of a race riot in America. Seems that South Africa isn't the only country to have its race problems. My mind drifted...

... strange how life works. I sat and thought about how lucky our platoon lieutenant had been that time when we stopped for a smoke break and an enemy lay in the grass ... after ten hours of trench clearing ... and the end of a very long first day of the attack against a 13 km spread-out base camp in Angola, during Operation Protea. Lieutenant Doep called for the platoon to take its first official break in an action filled day. No one had even thought of eating through that day. With the first small smiles of the day we took off our helmets for the first time since 05h00.

We took out crumpled, sweat-drenched boxes of Marlboro cigarettes, and relaxed for a minute, talking in low, strained voices as we eyed the last large ominous field we were preparing to sweep through next, as the sun dropped midway down the afternoon. Unbeknown to us, for five minutes while we laughed and smoked, a FAPLA soldier had lain a stone's throw from us, in the grass, not twenty paces. He must have known that he had no chance as he lay hidden and watched our platoon approach his hidden position. Then, to his horror we had made a right wheel turn and stopped right in front of him, lined up, started getting ready to sweep across the field where he lay.

It had been a long intense day, sweeping the huge enemy base with its miles of trenches. During the two cigarettes that I smoked the stout-hearted Angolan soldier must have had each one of us in his sights, as he decided who he was going to take with him. He decided on our blond-haired lieutenant, the only one standing, talking on the radio with his helmet off, his long blond hair wet with the day's sweat. After five minutes of aiming, the FAPLA soldier finally took his shot. Lieutenant Du Plessis, the only one standing up at the time, fell over backwards, his boot coming up in front of him. The brave MPLA soldier had made the mistake of aiming for the head; his bullet had cracked through the lieutenant's hair, missing his skull by a millimetre. A few of us who were closest snatched up our rifles in a second and, our helmets still off and rifle tripods still out, charged forward, shooting at his hidden position in the grass, his gun smoke hanging in the air above him as a marker. The MPLA soldier must have died thinking that he had taken Lieutenant Doep with him, because he had fallen back so violently. The sniper died, unmoving, on his belly, in his shooting position, in a hail of South African bullets.

The unprecedented state of emergency, 24 hour a day curfew had been in place for some days. The silence of zero traffic made the great city of Los

Angeles seem as quiet as a one-horse town on a Sunday afternoon. The curfew had created a sombre mood: millions of Los Angelinos were locked down in their own houses, big and small, with nothing to do but watch the 24-hour news coverage of the LA riots on TV. Hollywood was filled with creative artists of all kinds and the sound of musical instruments and laughter could be heard from small apartment building windows, lit up late into the night – because no one was allowed to go to work the next day. Long-time residents in buildings who had never given each other more than a passing nod as a greeting, now came out and spent time talking with each other about the current events. Some brave apartment dwellers could be seen defying the curfew and darting across the road to visit a friend in the building next door.

There was nothing to do, nothing could be done so I spent my nights tinkering on some blues songs on my piano and the days writing my manuscript for *19 with a Bullet*. I sat on my mattress, my back against the wall, and cast my mind back in time to the Angolan bush, continuing the writing I had begun earlier, about my time as a paratrooper in South Africa's Border War. I was writing in longhand and had already filled three of my yellow writing pads. I sat there, spinning the pen slowly in my fingers, staring blankly at the wall in front of me, retrieving memories of my years in the bush of Namibia and Angola. Police sirens in the city faded away as I journeyed back to the Border. I had spent months deep in thought, writing down hundreds of details I remembered from my action-packed time, serving with the SADF. It had only been eight years since I had been in the army so some names and memories were hazier than others but most of them were as clear as yesterday. I could remember the gist of many conversations, arguments and jokes, even some actual words we paratroopers had used …

Now that I was actively inviting these recollections to return to the forefront of my mind, memories that I had tried so hard to forget, that I had banished like black Crows to sit in distant trees in the wilderness, to languish in dark discontent, disregarded, abandoned, staring at me from the far side of the sandy *shona*, constantly trying to reclaim their original roosts, sneaking back whenever they could, to cause disconnection, destruction, another broken hand, another lost job, remorse and shame … only to be banished again … now that they had been invited, they returned in flocks, in droves, having spread the word that they were welcome once more. Like big black birds happily migrating home, my exiled memories returned home to roost.

This time my pen and paper were waiting to capture them.

'Dangerous' ~ Busta Rhymes

Nine days later the Los Angeles riots came to an end. The final reckoning of the damages showed that 63 people had been killed and thousands more injured; 3,600 fires had been set, and 1,100 buildings had been destroyed, resulting in one billion dollars of property damage. For some months after, the burnt-out shells of shops and building stood silently, amid heaps of rubble on the streets, stark reminders of what had taken place a short time before. It took a while before life returned to normal. People hustled along, heads down, not sure if the person walking in front, or behind, or to their side was a Former Rioter, had been engaged in stealing, burning and stabbing. Everyone's nerves were on edge.

Sadly enough, our friend Vance had become one of the riot statistics: he had been savagely attacked and stabbed multiple times on the first day on the riots. The hospital had opened him up from chest to groin to save him. Murray and I had helped him when he was released from hospital, after a three-week long stay and a $2,000,000 hospital bill. He went back to his suite on the 10th floor of the Holiday Inn and slowly returned to his old self. It was a relief to see Vance on his feet again, lifting the shirt of his shiny, glitter-covered outfits, to show anyone who was interested (or not) the grotesque, purple scars from both his stabbing and lifesaving surgery. His standard opening line was, "The germs stabbed me in the riots" followed by a torrent of racist adjectives.

It was around July, just a few months after the riots, when our good friend, Steve Oliver, came back on the scene, having been gone for a year. Steve had made his escape from Hollywood but dreams are made to fail ... and he was back in Tinsel Town, where he had previously enjoyed an acting career and some degree of fame, having been a well-known actor in the 60s and 70. He was a big-hearted, generous man in his late fifties, a straight talker who looked you in the eye while delivering a strong opinion on whatever subject was being discussed. He was also gruff, short tempered and quick to take things the wrong way, which had led to many confrontations and bad turns in his life. But it was great to see him swagger into the apartment, announcing that he was back in town.

Steve had played the tough guy in a well-known American TV series, *Peyton Place,* for years; he had also played the lead in movies like *Werewolves on Wheels* and *Cycle Psycho,* amongst others. And he had been married, briefly, to the famous actress, Lana Wood, sister of the more famous Natalie Wood.

Murray and I had first thought that we would have to prevent Steve and Vance from meeting. We suspected they would definitely not get along and a two-way encounter could easily become a bloodbath – they were both eccentric individuals, loud and unreasonable, who could fly off the handle at the slightest provocation. We knew that Steve had little patience with oddballs, freaks and hairies, and Vance was all of those things ... plus being volatile and had little to no patience. We had accepted that keeping the two of them from meeting was going to be difficult; especially as Vance was recently out of hospital, hobbling around, leaning on a cane, and relying on us for odd bits of help, here and there.

A few days later Vance walked into our apartment unannounced, hollering and hooting. He was recovering well and although weak was almost back to his old self, cursing everything that moved and making long phone calls to sponsors about his Christmas album. He was especially on form that day, louder than ever.

Half an hour later there was a surprisingly hard knock at our door. I opened it, cautiously, expecting trouble of some kind, and was taken aback to see Steve Oliver on our doormat, swaggering and scowling.

His scowl deepened as he cocked his ears, listening to Vance's fog horn voice wafting through from the living room, making some point, loudly, to Murray.

"Oh boy, here we go," I thought.

We had done what we could to prevent the two of them from meeting, but Steve and Vance were about to run into one another, in our living room, and there was no way to avoid it. Oh well ... let the teeth fall where they may. This was going to be a clash of titans, personalities, and Hollywood eccentrics.

Steve's face tightened and he braced himself, a steely look in his eyes, as we both listened to Vance speaking loudly.

"Steve, c'mon in, I want to introduce you to a friend of ours."

Like a good actor Steve 'slipped into character' and swaggered into the living room, an eyebrow raised at Vance, who sat there clutching a sandwich, clearly intending to use it as a club. The two of them glared at one another, with intent, for a few long seconds, long enough for me to think it was going to be worse than we had anticipated. They glowered at each other, gazes locked, not saying a word … then –

"Steven Oliver!" exclaimed Vance, his whole face lighting up.

"You look familiar; I know you from somewhere," Steve responded, gruffly.

"Yes, I organised that music concert in Kansas, when you punched the senator's son backstage, I was the promoter … I remember you well! You were The Actor back then, how're you doing?" Vance shouted excitedly.

"Still breathing, so I can't complain. Haven't seen you since '69 or so … what you doin' these days?"

Vance immediately flashed his shiny silver shirt, revealing the gory scars from his stabbing and lifesaving surgery.

"The germs stabbed me in the Los Angeles riots! I died! Surgeons brought me back to life! By Gad, it's good to see a face from the past. You used to have that big house on Laurel Canyon, always full of people and parties."

Steve had a smile on his face that I hadn't seen before.

Murray and I breathed sighs of relief and settled down to watch Steve and Vance getting on like a house on fire, talking about old times. Vance looked like his old self, moving around with ease, his injuries forgotten.

"Yeah, yeah. Parties all the time, went on for days … I remember you and Grizzly Adams and William Smith, I remember, good to see you, are you still acting?"

"God no, haven't acted in years, no one will hire me. I was blackballed from Hollywood after that comment about President Johnson being behind the Kennedy assassination."

Steve turned to us, smiling, "This guy was one of the biggest music promoters around, back in the day, always saw him in a Rolls Royce."

Vance beamed, the usual, ear to ear, while Steve filled us in about Vern's life as a music producer and well-known concert promoter in the 60s and 70s.

"This is the guy that organised that concert, when I punched the senator's son!" Steve gestured at Vance, both of them smiling and chortling, remembering the good old days.

Murray and I shook our heads and chuckled while the four of us sauntered down to Hollywood Boulevard for a bite to eat, Vance and Steve leading, chatting and laughing like long lost friends. It was great that Steve and Vance had known each other in their previous lives, when they were young, in their prime, when things were good.

Murray and I cast a sidelong glance at one another, smiling about how we had expected them to fly at each other's throats.

Also, because of this meeting, Vance, with all his bullshit and hot air, was somewhat vindicated. The never-ending stories of his past life, as a concert promoter, drummer, writer, producer and friend of the stars must have had some truth to them – although the more than 500 old silver dollar coins stuffed into a small suitcase which we had helped Vance to collect were definitely fake.

It was both comical and a relief to see them getting along, after all our trepidation … but inside I was thinking that I had to get out of Hollywood, had to get away from all these dysfunctional hagglers and hucksters.

Chapter Twenty-six

FINLANDIA[5]

'Two Step' ~ *Dave Mathews Band*

An enticing aroma permeated the kitchen of the vegetarian restaurant, a heavenly combination of vegetables, garlic and cilantro. The tall, slender blonde with hair that reached halfway down her back was multi-tasking, expertly chopping vegetables in measured heaps, mixing spices, tossing stuff into three huge pots on the stove, glancing at me over her shoulder with big blue hazel eyes and a smile, while watching over the four-gallon pots of soup. Eventually I finished answering the annoying questions from the restaurant manager, about the leaking faucet I had been called to fix. Only then could I move across the busy kitchen and chat with the blonde girl, while packing my tools. I insisted that she give me her phone number, or I wouldn't leave the kitchen.

"South Africa? You a long way from home."

"Yes."

"What brought you to LA ... not acting?" she asked, looking stern.

"No."

"I'll give you my number as long as you swear to me that you're not an actor."

I assured her that I had not come to LA to be an actor and couldn't act even if I was paid to perform. Los Angeles was filled with waiters, taxi drivers, cooks, security guards, couriers, all of whom had come to LA to fulfil their dreams of acting in Hollywood. I was not one of them. I was a hardworking plumber.

Satisfied with my guarantees she smiled and slipped me her phone number, written on a soup recipe.

---

5 *Finlandia* is a symphonic poem by Jean Sibelius, the Finnish composer. It was first written in 1899 and then revised, in 1900.

God bless women. Loving and nurturing, seeing the world through kinder eyes. A smile and touch that puts a man's soul at rest, enabling him to peel away the hard layers of armour donned against the world. Not seeing or knowing the invisible foes which men see while going about their daily lives, not hearing the shout, not seeing the threat, not knowing the obedience to *Ex alto vincimus* or seeing danger around every corner. Women turn a house into a home, a place for rest, and men always seeking a pillow from their women, on which to rest their heads. Liisa was a truly nurturing soul. When I visited her I found that I didn't want to leave, that I missed her when I drove back to my Hollywood apartment. I did not want to get up from lying in her bedroom amid the scent of lit candles and incense, thick drapes blocking out the summer sun. I wanted to stay there and rest. I wanted someone to care for and look after, I wanted to love someone. I wanted to talk to someone, to hear all about them and tell about my life, my family, the place in which I had been raised.

Liisa's blue eyes shone when she spoke about making dinners or going on outings. She found value in and could get excited about the small things in life, relished working in her backyard, watching old time black-and-white movies. I felt relaxed in her company and we spent many hot California summer nights cooking, laughing and chilling in her backyard until the early hours, watching meteor showers and shooting stars. She had a circle of good friends who frequently came over for barbecues, and I introduced them to the good old South African style *braai*, with *boerewors* – which could be found in LA. I was working full-time for a large plumbing company on the late-night shift and when work ended I visited Liisa, at her home, to enjoy a good home-cooked meal and a glass of wine. Just one of the benefits of having a top restaurant cook as a girlfriend.

I enjoyed the stability, felt more settled and began keeping regular contact with my family in South Africa, via more frequent phone calls. Also, I started reaching out, trying to find old friends back home. (The internet had just come into being but was not yet freely available.) For the first time I began leaving LA city to explore California. We would head out of town to her family's beach house in Ventura … or go camping in the pine forests alongside the Kern River. We drove through small oil towns on our way to the Mojave Desert, to see the flowers in springtime. I was surprised to find just how fulfilling it felt to be part of a solid relationship.

During this time Murray, my older brother, married Cheyanne, whom he had met when she sang background on his country music recording. The two of them had left California for Texas, wanting to get out of Hollywood and make a clean start to married life.

About a year later Liisa and I found ourselves standing in a small chapel, just off the flashing lights strip in Las Vegas, being married in the same venue in which Elvis Presley had been married – or so we were told.

I enjoyed being married; I relished having someone else to care for and someone to come home to. I felt like a genuine member of society, a solid citizen, and took great pleasure at being welcomed into Liisa'a family who were proud of their Finnish heritage. For the first time in years I participated in good, old-fashioned Thanksgiving turkey dinners, and family Christmas dinners, the first family interactions for me since I had left South Africa. I particularly enjoyed Liisa's father, Ed, a very pleasant World War II navy veteran and a savvy, big building construction man, easy to respect. Ed was always tinkering in his huge tool room, either building or fixing something, with the right tool for every project.

Of course, it wasn't long after the Las Vegas wedding bells that, to everyone's delight, Liisa announced that she was pregnant – our baby, a little girl, was on the way. It was a very special time, watching Liisa and her big belly making ready for our daughter. Clothes, toys and a cot were bought, a room was painted and kitted out, a new carpet was laid, throughout the house, for our baby girl to crawl on. A book listing 10,000 names for girls was purchased, but Liisa and I couldn't agree on any one of them. On 25th November, a gusty, blustery day with trees toppling over on every other block, we rushed to the nearby hospital where Liisa gave birth to a healthy, beautiful baby girl. I was thrilled to hold the exquisite, crying child in my arms. Suddenly she stopped wailing and gazed at me … a long serious look, as though inspecting me. I felt the connection. It was the happiest day of our lives, Liisa's and mine. My cheeks hurt for a whole week from my constant, huge smile. God is great. And Liisa and I finally settled on a name for Natalie, the name of an aunt that I had loved. Natalie who had arrived on the windiest day of the year with trees coming down in her honour.

§

I was told by one of the assembled guests, all dressed up for a sumptuous Thanksgiving lunch, that the host, along-haired Englishman with a concert grand piano in his living room, was a member of the English rock band, Supertramp. He and I sat at the lavish, long table, with place settings for 20 people, while I wrote out my invoice … a double overtime charge for having repaired the leaking kitchen sink on Thanksgiving Day. As he wrote the cheque the well-mannered English super star thanked me for having saved the day, just prior to the arrival of his guests. Extraordinary. You never knew who you would run into in Los Angeles. I told him that I loved his piano playing in Supertramp and I was also rushing off to my own family Thanksgiving dinner. He made out the cheque in my name.

Yes, finally, I had my own plumbing business *and* a family to go home to after work. This time I had a necessary and practical plumbing business that was bound to work. No more embarking on strange, risky business ideas. In the first flush of early marriage, with some help from my father-in-law, I had started my own plumbing business. There had been a few beginner's bumps, but now I was getting busy and decent money was coming in. This time it was going not to A Boss, but to me! And I loved coming home to Liisa and baby Natalie, who had started crawling on the new carpets, talking in her own gibberish language, pointing to the noisy crows. Married life was good. I felt settled, but I still had a hard outlook on life.

Sadly however it wasn't long before the differences in our cultures, humour, outlooks and values began to make themselves felt in our relationship.

Our relationship had taken a bad turn and it had begun to look as though our marriage would not survive. Our differences in outlook were too great for our relationship to last. It had taken more than a year for Liisa and I to get to stand in the long line in the downtown immigration building, queuing for the final 'interview' for my resident alien status in the United States, the coveted Green Card. The Nigerian interviewer with a thick accent smiled with an openness that could only have come from Africa, when we showed him our wedding photos taken in Las Vegas and assured him that our marriage was legitimate.

But, by this time, our new marriage had started to show irreparable cracks. Different culture, different humour, different outlook. Although my twitchiness had improved in the last few years, I was still moving to internal commands which only I could hear; steely-eyed paratrooper heroes were still my role models in life. I was still jumping out of bed to investigate every small sound in the night; still viewing life through the eyes of soldier, a warrior.

The friendly Nigerian immigration interviewer smiled broadly when Liisa and I started an argument in front of him, over some small detail of the photos and how to answer his questions. He nodded, amused, clearly accepting that this marriage was not a fake union. There were no further trick questions, designed to trip us up. Swiftly he signed and stamped a few documents and that, as they say in the classics, was that.

Not long afterwards I moved out of the house where Liisa, Natalie and I had lived together. I rented a small room in the backyard of a house in a neighbourhood close by, until Liisa and I had 'sorted out our differences'. It didn't look like as though this was going to happen any time soon. I was both angry and sad about splitting with Liisa; but I still had Natalie in my life … and I intended having her in my life for the whole of my life.

Around this time I ripped open an envelope from the Immigration Services and first held my longed-for Green Card in my hand. Not the MacArthur Park version which I kept in a drawer just in case; this was the real thing. What an important little card! A great day. At long last I was a legal resident in the USA, able to travel, leave the country and, more importantly, able – legally – to return.

I had been in regular contact with my family and immediately started planning a visit to South Africa. Together we fixed the dates and I bought a return ticket on South African Airways. On top of this excitement, I had heard from Leighton, my childhood friend, who was trying to arrange for me to attend, with troops from 1 Parachute Battalion, their annual water jump from a C-130. Imagine that!

It was 1998, thirteen years after arriving in the US, and finally it was my turn to step onto the South African Airways 747. The flag on its huge tail was not the same as the one that had delivered me to the USA thirteen years before. I sat in the window seat just forward of the wing of the huge Jumbo

Bat Out of Hell

Jet. Into the early hours of the morning, with the cabin lights off and most of the passengers fast asleep, I gazed out the window. It was hard to believe that a few hours from now this plane would land in South Africa, my home. Tears trickled down my face as I sat quietly in the middle of the night, wide awake, watching the big red light flashing at the wing tip, lighting up the inky black, moonless night, with nothing but darkest Africa beneath us. The powerful 747 engines sounded beautiful, roaring with a high-pitched urgency, taking me home at 500 mph, each minute bringing me closer to stepping onto African soil.

It seemed like a lifetime since I had left South Africa on my supposed three-month vacation in America. It was a lifetime. South Africa had turned around completely, from white minority rule to black majority rule, with Nelson Mandela as its president, having spent 27 years in prison. Not even Hollywood could have produced a more dramatic turnaround, in a fabricated movie. The Border War was long finished, national service a thing of the past. What a trip the next six weeks was going to be! Tracy, my little sister was getting married and I would be at the wedding. *And* I was going to do a trip to the bush. *And* Leighton had arranged, through a mutual paratrooper friend, Richard Dawson, for me to participate in the annual 1 Parachute Battalion water jump, from a C-130 aircraft.

At sunrise, to my amazement, we flew over Angola and crossed the border into Namibian air space.

The Border ...

The live flight path map in front of me indicated, according to my memories, that we were flying almost directly over Ondjiva, Xangongo and Ondangwa, where we young South Africans had fought our Bush War. As the sun peeped over the horizon I could see clearly the endless green bush which, years ago, had been the war zone. I thought I could see *Oom Willie se wit pad*, a long, straight, white, dirt road that cut through the green bush in a straight line for maybe 100 miles or more. I saw the white open sand *shonas* that we used to cross so cautiously, exposing ourselves to enemy mortars. This is exactly where our war had taken place. This sea of green bush below us had been the operational area where the memories of so many young South Africans had been made. Far from any sign of civilisation ... literally, in the middle of nowhere; well named by the Portuguese (who had fought to occupy the territory until 1975) as *O fim do Mundo* (The End of the World).

Two hours later I was craning my neck, watching the Jumbo dip its wings, to circle far around the west side of the metropolis of Johannesburg, with its gold mine dumps and freeways, the city skyline and the unmistakable Hillbrow tower. An country steeped in history. Vast African townships, dams, smoky veld fires, and beautiful, dark, summer storm clouds in the distance ... everything just as I had remembered. The plane came around low over Boksburg, flaps down like an eagle, and landed on the runway just a few miles from my childhood home. I walked out of customs into the waiting crowd ... friends and family, smiling and waving ... laughing when I dropped my bags, bent down and kissed the cold airport floor.

I hugged them all. Mother, father, sister and friends. Mentally I had prepared myself for the worst. I had not been able to imagine how my parents might have aged; would I even recognise them? I was overjoyed to see my mother looking as beautiful and glamorous as when last I had seen her, my father just the same. How reassuring ... how uplifting! What a feeling it was to be back, the smell of the Highveld, driving the freeway past Kempton Park into Benoni along the route I remembered so well that I could have climbed out of the car and walked home.

Old friends dropped by and stayed late, yards of *boerewors* were cooked on the braai at the side of the pool. Summer storms washed us out, Hadedas shouted with excitement in the backyard, African Doves cooed in the trees when I woke in the morning. African *ousies* (black domestic workers) chatted on street corners, TV news reporters sounded strange, reporting in thick South African accents. I found I could barely speak a few words in Afrikaans and could not recognise the voices of my friends over the phone – all the South African accents sounded the same.

Wearing a coat and tails I witnessed my beautiful sister and her new husband say, "I do,"; heard my father, a good few whiskeys later, give a long, rambling speech, as he was wont to do; danced jubilantly with my mother while the champagne and Old Brown sherry flowed. Tracy's wedding was attended by well-loved family friends, amongst them many faces I had thought I would never see again, or even recognise, but I had instantly recognised them all.

(Tracy's husband, David Kruger, had also seen a lot of action on the Border in the famous Koevoet police unit. At the time of their marriage he was working as an undercover policeman in organised crime. David would be shot and killed a few years later in an assassination hit outside his mother's home, while returning home late one night.)

I don't think I stopped smiling, not even once, during that first visit home. I thought I was in dreamland, every night, when I lay down to sleep. Twelve years is a very long time to spend away from home.

§

"Standup! Hookup!"

The African parachute dispatcher shouted at the top of his voice over the noise of the engines as the South African Air Force C-130 cargo plane began levelling out over Hartebeestpoort Dam. We stood up, fumbling to hook our parachute static lines onto the steel cable.

"Check equipment!"

We shouted as loudly as we could, going through the check list, checking ourselves and the paratrooper in front of us. I had forgotten most of the drills but they all came back quickly, as I shouted with the rest of the men. The C-130 lurched down and levelled out, locking onto the correct jumping altitude of only 1,000 ft above the huge dam. The Legion I had thought dead and gone was very present. They were standing with me, their parachutes hooked up, ready and able, and I was one of them.

We had done our refresher training the day before at the old Voortrekkerhoogte military base just outside Pretoria. After so many years away from South Africa it had felt quite unreal, standing in line in the SADF military base, giving my force number, watching the officials search through the 'big book' of qualified paratroopers, and then issue each of us with a jump number.

My name was there, with my force number, in the big 7-inch thick book of that listed all South African paratroopers. It had not been a dream. I was standing in line, bullshitting along with other paratroopers, old and young, some with scars on their hard faces from fist fights over who knows what.

These were men just like me, a tough bunch. I was not alone. I was not the only one who had spent years thinking about our small war. I was not the only one who still heard the shout of the dispatcher, the shout of the lieutenant ordering us forward under fire … not the only one whose life had been altered, re-shaped … constantly harking back, often reliving the most exciting, horrifying and character-shaping couple of years of our lives.

"Stand in the door – GO!"

We shuffle-ran out the door of the noisy C-130, dropping like stones, to be sucked upside down by the slip stream of the great propellers. I felt the jerk as the parachute popped open. It had been many years since I had jumped but now I remembered my jump drills like yesterday.

'Look up and check chute … kick out of twists …push down leg harness … good parachute position.' Then there was silence as our parachutes floated down to the water, some faster than others. We hit the cold water with a splash, welcome after an hour of waiting, chuted up, in the sun at the military airport; then being squashed into the hot C-130. Finally, we were pulled out of the cold water by helping hands in fast Zodiac rubber boats.

Afterwards, back on terra firma, the beer flowed – as did the stories. This one had been shot, that one survived a close call; some of these men walked with a limp and had old wounds to show – and goose bumps when they described them. I listened to them say it had been the best time of their lives – but they would never want to do it again.

I scanned the faces of hundreds of paratroopers, looking for my comrades from Delta Company. Around midday from afar I recognised one of mine, Paul Greef from behind, walking away from me. I had not even seen his face but instantly I knew it was him, by the back of his head, the slope of his shoulders and his peculiar gait. Paul had saved my life when he and John the Fox had shot a terrorist hiding under a tree, while I was bent over, retching, right in front of him.

Paul was amazed to see me, said he had always thought that I was "long dead" from the wild lifestyle for which I had been known, years ago. I told him I was alive and well and kicking arse. He immediately told me how he had struggled, for years, to 'settle down', after the Bush War. I ran into Blaine Oslo, a pathfinder, and Dudley Grant, Owen Croft, officers and men of steel who had ruled with an iron hand, men we had all looked up to, veterans of action in the Bush War.

With their help I was able later, to track down my old friend, John Delaney and arranged to meet him at a shopping mall, for breakfast and a catch-up session. John and I had been side by side for a lot of the same actions and fire fights and we shared the many of the same memories.

On reuniting John immediately started talking about his experiences in our small war – and couldn't stop. His breakfast grew cold in front of him while he talked, lost in his own world, reliving some of the haunting action we had seen.

"Remember the Soviet tank that came out at us … the South African armoured car that blew up the tank right in front of our eyes … remember when we were pinned down, unable to move until the Impala jet was called and came in low over the trees with a 250-pound bomb run, to free us up … remember when so and so shot this guy … remember when the FAPLA truck came through our platoon in the middle of the night and we had to dive to get out its way … remember anti air craft guns shooting just feet over our heads as we advanced to the trenches … remember the 1,000 pound bombs exploding … remember when we escaped through the night with almost no ammunition while being tracked by a soviet BTR, whose engine we could hear roaring like a dragon behind us."

Two things happened.

First, I knew, again, that I was not alone with my memories. My paratrooper brothers, whom I thought I had lost, were just like me; they also could not forget our small war, and never would. I had spoken to only a handful of my old comrades, so there must be thousands of South African war veterans, who, like *Odysseus* were still fighting to get 'home'; still fighting a war within themselves that felt just like yesterday. Thousands who were immobilised by remembering when they had been at their finest, whose lives had been touched and altered by their actions and memories of the Bush War.

Secondly, it was a complete overload for me. Raw footage flashed through my mind's eye, scenes that I had cut from the sanitised version of my memory bank. They came at once, each one hard on the heels of the one before. Fleeing figures, gun fire, shouts, gunshot wounds, dead enemy soldiers I had forgotten about. At the breakfast table in the busy shopping mall I struggled to breathe and wanted to retch. I was having some sort of asthma or panic attack.

"Must I stop talking about it? Are you OK?" John asked, coming back to reality.

"No, I'm not OK – let's talk about something else," I mumbled.

It was very strange to hear myself say this – I was always the one who wanted to talk about it.

We sat quietly for a few minutes as I gathered myself, took some deep breaths. John looked down, quietly picking at his cold breakfast. How strange ... did I just have a panic attack? My chest had closed just as it had done in front of the unseen, hiding terrorist, an asthma attack, out of the blue.

John changed the subject and told me what he had been doing, as a minister, going back into Angola to preach the gospel.

"John! You! A minister!"

He said he had been a minister for the last decade, while I was running wild in America. He had been preaching the word of God in most countries in Africa and had established his own ministry. He told me how, for years after the army, he had been a wild man, unable to settle down. Then he had joined a seminary and given his life to the service of the Lord. He had burnt all his photographs of the war, along with all the memorabilia he owned, including his uniform and his maroon Airborne beret. He said that God had set him free and he had married a girl he had met in the seminary. I was astounded.

Then I told John that I was experiencing similar problems; that I was plagued by frequent flashbacks, thoughts and visions, which many a time got the better of me; that I was unable to settle down, to be at peace in the world.

Without hesitation my old partner put down his knife and fork and, in the middle of that busy restaurant in the middle of that busy mall, reached across the table, put his hand on my arm, and prayed in the name of the Lord.

I felt a gate open as John prayed to God to release me from bondage to the spirits of death, the spirits of those whom we had killed, to forgive us for the things we had done as immature young soldiers. Tears rolled down my cheeks as my brother in arms prayed for me. He prayed that God look down on all of us soldiers who had done that which we had been asked – or ordered – to do, defend our country against an enemy that threatened our own people.

Afterwards I smiled through tears, finished my breakfast – and ordered some more.

I almost choked on my toast when John told me that our friend, Antony Stander, aka 'Stan the Man', was also a minister, preaching the word of God from his very own church.

"Stan a minister as well? Cold as ice and hard as nails Anthony Stander is a minister?!"

"Yes," John smiled, "he robbed five banks soon after leaving 1 Parachute Battalion and spent seven years of a 30-year sentence in prison, where he became a strong Christian believer. Ever since his release, which he calls a 'miracle pardon', Stan has worked in the ministry and now has his own church."

It was hard enough to think of John as a minister, but it was well-nigh impossible to imagine my old comrade Anthony Stander as a preacher! The mind boggled.

(To this day Stan is active in the running of his church and is as hard a man of God as he was a young paratrooper, fighting on the Border.) Stan had endured a rough upbringing as a youngster, had become a good soldier, and had been well known for his steely, ice cold outlook.

So, both John and Stan were ministers of God? It was hard to believe … then I remembered that transforming the experience of war into the service of God is an old, old story. Prior to his spiritual conversion St Ignatius of Loyola, founder of the Society of Jesus (Jesuits), had been a combat veteran; and St Francis of Assisi was a veteran of two different wars, before he founded the Franciscan Order.

It was becoming clear to me that, for even the first few of the friends with whom I had made contact, their lives had been changed, in a big way, by the experience of the fighting and killing during our Border War.

John told me that Aaron 'Doogy' Green, our platoon machine gunner, was living in the UK after having had to leave South Africa in a hurry. A few years later Doogy became a security contractor for an English security company, for whom he worked for 14 years, in Iraq, Afghanistan, Sudan and other hotspots around the world.

It was fantastic to see and hear about my old comrades and I was beginning to feel a sense of belonging again. Living in another country, with no contact with my roots, had made it all seem like a dream. They were not all dead and gone. They were not a legion lost in the realm of my memory, not a list of ghosts from the past. They were here, in South Africa where I had left them, they were strong, and they were men of God. They were on their feet, still swinging.

Back at my mother's house I sat beside the sparkling pool, feeling whole. I felt like before, like I had felt as a youngster. The country had changed. The system of apartheid was dead and gone. And a good thing too, as I was discovering.

The people of South Africa seemed resilient and strong, full of life and hope for the future of their new country. It was marvellous to be back. I began to feel that I could stay exactly where I was, back home in South Africa where I belonged, with my people – my family and friends – who came to visit and stayed the whole day. People whom I knew and understood. I should stay right here in this beautiful country with its new all-inclusive democracy.

There was not much waiting for me in America, and I could write off the last twelve years as experience. I had lived overseas, successfully, against the odds, and I could start over in South Africa.

Not a lone wolf any more, I'll find a job, start my own plumbing company, find a good South African woman, settle down.

An easy thing to do, with so many friends around me. I would go back to the US to settle things, then return to South Africa and start afresh.

A dream?

Chapter Twenty-seven
RICH AS A KING

'Cross Road Blues' ~ Robert Johnson

I relished each hour in South Africa but all too soon I found myself packing my bags for the long flight back to the US. The night before my departure twenty of my friends came to bid me farewell at the English pub in Benoni. I was truly privileged to have such great friends; it felt really good to shake their hands and clink our glasses together, to toast our good health and good fortune. It turned into a long, long night of leave-taking.

The next morning, while packing, I felt clammy and cold, as if I was coming down with flu' or a bad head cold. Maybe it was alcohol poisoning from the farewell party the night before, and the one before that, and the one before that ... I had forgotten how South Africans can drink alcohol! By the time we were on our way to the airport for another sad goodbye I was shivering and definitely feeling unwell. I hugged my parents and a group of my friends and sadly waved cheerio. I cried inside as the Jumbo Jet lurched up into the night, its powerful engines roaring. Once again I craned my neck, turning to look back at the twinkling lights of the houses in which I was leaving all my loved ones behind, once more. My home town, my neighbourhood, was close by and all around the international airport ... too quickly the lights were left far behind as the big plane turned, setting its course for America.

By the time the Jumbo levelled out at 23,000 ft I was shaking with cold and feeling sicker than I could remember ever having felt in my life. Luckily (and this good fortune has not happened again, since then, on any overseas flight) there were no passengers on the four seats next to me, so I was able to lie down and sleep, albeit fitfully, all the way to the States. At customs clearance in New York I had a headache so blinding that I could hardly lift my head. I shuffled through the process, showed them my newly attained Green Card, shaking with fever all the while. When I reached Los Angeles my recently estranged wife, Liisa, collected me from the airport, alone, without my baby daughter. Despite being concerned for me, she said that if I was sick with some African disease she didn't want me seeing Natalie until I had recovered. Can't say I blame her. I had called her from New York and told her just how sick I was feeling ... but then again, my daughter was the only reason I had returned from South Africa.

Liisa was the only person in LA whom I knew, who was close to me, at that time. She was kind enough to fetch me from the airport and take me to the small room, not much bigger than a postage stamp, which I was renting in someone's backyard. I pulled off my sweat-soaked clothes and fell straight into bed, without unpacking. More fitful sleep. When a section of the sheet was soaked with sweat I rolled across to the dry section on the other side, and back again, and so on. Maybe this was some kind of African disease?

For the next three days I lay in bed, racked with fever and nightmares. I had never felt so alone in my life; there was not a soul within 10,000 miles who I could ask for help. A black and bitter depression set in and devoured every bit of my reserves ... all the hope and light that I had so recently discovered.

Drenched in sweat I moaned aloud in the small room, tormented by isolation and the feeling that I had been totally abandoned. The shabby walls of the small room seemed to close in on me like a makeshift coffin. What was wrong with me? There was some instinct within me to try to get up, and run, and keep running, but I was too sick to move an inch.

I dreamt of my home in South Africa, about going back for good ... then I woke and, still consumed by fever, planned how I would buy a ticket as soon as possible and leave America. I would return to South Africa soon as I could. Just a few days ago I had been the richest man in the world, rich with family and friends, people who chose to visit me and didn't want to leave, rich with people I had known throughout my childhood and ever since. People who cared... friends I could count on and who could count on me. Now, lying in this postage stamp dump of a room in America, amid 320 million people, I was as alone as a leper, just another immigrant from a strange country, with not even one good friend to think of coming by to help.

After a few days the fever broke and with it came some sanity. The crippling headache had eased enough that I could lift my head. While sitting weakly on the side of the bed I discovered, one behind my knee and one under my crotch, two big, bright red, 'bulls eyes' – inflamed circles the size of a dollar coin, each with a black dot at its centre. I realised I did not have malaria or some other strange disease but probably had been bitten by a tick on our 'lost in the bush" adventure. The weird African malady I had been suffering was in fact tick bite fever.(Anyone who has gone through the experience of untreated tick bite fever will understand just how sick one feels for four to five days ... utterly wretched, from the high fever and the blinding headache that comes with the illness. Welcome back to Africa!)

I had lost weight. I had hardly eaten in four days, there being no one to make and bring me a meal. I was consumed with longing to return to South Africa, for once and for all. My head was still swimming with memories of my comrades, friends and family. I discovered that my little plumbing business had survived my having been away for six weeks; my one employee had been reasonably busy and had done a good job. So there was enough money to buy a ticket back to South Africa.

I was torn between my two worlds ... but there was one vitally important thing I had planned, while lying in bed, something I needed to do as soon as I could get out of bed.

I dragged myself upright and searched through various boxes for my old army photograph album. Then I sat on the still damp bed and slowly picked my way through the well-worn photos of my time as a paratrooper on the Border; images that had meant so much to me for so many years. One by one I pulled out a selection of photos and placed them in a pile on the bed. The terrorist with the top of his head blown off, whose wide eyes I remembered so well, as he turned to look at me as I pulled the trigger. I took out perhaps a dozen similar photos of our brave and worthy foe, the enemy we had fought in rapid firefights in a long-drawn-out bush war, who had paid a heavy price for the independence of their land. Men who were the heroes of their own struggle. Dead heroes whose youngsters would sing songs at parades, who would honour them in poems.

I found an old shovel with a broken handle behind the shed, piled the photos onto it, walked slowly into the overgrown and unkempt backyard, littered with scraps of wood. I dug a shallow hole in the sand, piling the sand in a neat heap next to it. Using my lighter, one by one I set fire to the photos of 'my' dead SWAPO fighters, and watched the terrible images burn ... and quietly I asked for their forgiveness, and asked for absolution from God.

The images I knew so well twisted, turned and burned to wispy grey ash, until I dropped them into the hole. Unexpectedly my stomach cramped, and tears came in a flood. I did not try to stop them, or wipe them, they rolled down my face and fell onto the ashes in the hole. I heaved and sobbed like a child, for quite some time, and then I felt a miraculous thing ... truthfully, literally, I felt a physical burden lift off my body and soul. And so I knelt, and covered, buried, the smouldering ashes of my old African enemies in American soil.

I had felt the weight lift off me. I was forgiven. I was free.

I walked back inside my room, my face wet with tears, exhausted by the bewildering emotion – but liberated and free. I made a cup of the *rooibos* tea my mother had packed for me and sat on the bed to drink it. I thought about my family, good friends and army brothers. The people I had met in South Africa were steadfast, resilient and strong; they had re-vitalised me. I had felt their energy. I had seen and held my family; I had prayed with my old comrades, men who were just like me. I was not alone, as I had thought for so many years. I was not the only one who remembered the birds erupting from the trees, like bats out of hell, as the bombs dropped and the shooting started, when, as youngsters just out of high school, we had fought like lions, and spilled blood at the tip of our spears, for our country. There were legions of us.

Sitting on the side of my bed I decided then and there that I could not go back to South Africa, where I would be rich as a king in terms of friends, family and comrades in arms; where I knew people from all corners of the country and all walks of life. I could not leave the US, now.

I decided to stay, thrive and succeed, for myself and for others who would not grow old like us ... even those we had left behind in the sand.

Just as the Native American counsellor had told me, my own people had prayed with me, washed me and healed me. I would stay in America and I would work to develop the best parts of me, find some more.

I would stay in the big city of Los Angeles, the furthest point on the globe from South Africa. If I died in the US I would be buried in American soil.

I would dismantle the thick walls I had built around me and I would finish the book I had started writing, earlier.

Most importantly, I would be a father to my daughter and make a success of parenthood.

I could not, would not, leave my baby daughter with the big smile and serious eyes. The baby girl pointing at the noisy crows in the trees, smiling, mocking their calls ... who listens to dogs barking in the distance, a block away, with a concerned and frightened look on her face ... who tells me long stories in her own nonsense language about the wind that blows Winnie the Pooh away ... the baby girl who leaps into my arms when she sees me and points to her books and wants me to read her a story, *now*! ... who goes into fits of laughter when I stuff as many coins as will fit in-between her stubby little toes.

No, I would not leave. I would commit to staying and thriving here in America, with Natalie, to be her father, at her side, always. In this huge country with all its assets and drawbacks, my little girl with the serious eyes would need her father, for as long as God willed it.

I would accept my past, present and future. I would do as I had said, all those years ago: I would live life.

> But will those warriors lay down, together with the iron in which they are covered, their spirit, nourished since childhood by familiarity with danger? Will they don, together with civilian dress, that veneration for the laws and respect for protective forms, those tutelary deities of human associations? To them the unarmed class appears vulgar and ignoble, laws are superfluous subtleties, the forms of social life just so many insupportable delays.

Benjamin Constant, Swiss writer and political theorist, 1767–1830

[The quotation above is an extract from *The Spirit of Conquest*, published in 1814.]

The End

GLOSSARY

Apartheid   The policy and system in South Africa, of institutionalised racial segregation and discrimination, was applied in 1948 and enforced until 1991. Apartheid is an Afrikaans word meaning apart-ness or separate-ness.

Border War   The South African **Border War** is also known as the Angolan **Bush War** (and sometimes the Namibian War of Independence). It was fought in South West Africa (now Namibia), Zambia and Angola, from August 1966 to March 1990, between the South African Defence Force (SADF) and the armed wing of the South West African People's Organisation (SWAPO). Main activities took place near and across the border between SWA and Angola. The South African Border War/Bush War involved some of the largest battles in Africa since World War II and was strongly entangled with the Angolan Civil War (1975–2002).

FAPLA   The People's Armed Forces of Liberation of Angola. In the early 1960s the People's Movement for the Liberation of Angola (MPLA) named its guerrilla forces the People's Army for the Liberation of Angola (EPLA). In 1974 the MPLA announced the formation of FAPLA (to replace EPLA). In 1975, when the MPLA took control of the government, FAPLA became Angola's national army.

KOEVOET   Koevoet (crowbar in Afrikaans) was the counter-insurgency branch of the South West African Police (SWAPOL). (The name refers to 'prising' insurgents out of the civilian population.) It included white South African police officers, usually seconded from the South African Security Branch or Special Task Force, and black volunteers from Ovamboland. Koevoet was modelled on the Selous Scouts, a multiracial Rhodesian military unit which specialized in counter-insurgency operations.

SWAPO The South West African People's Organisation. A political party and former independence movement. It was founded in Windhoek, South West Africa (now Namibia) on 19 April 1960, to advocate for immediate Namibian independence from South Africa. It has been the governing party in that country since it achieved independence in 1990.

UNITA The National Union for the Total Independence of Angola is the second-largest political party in Angola. Founded in 1966, UNITA fought alongside the MPLA in the Angolan War for Independence (1961–1975), and then against the MPLA in the ensuing civil war (1975–2002), during which UNITA received military aid from South Africa and the United States, while the MPLA was supported by the Soviet Union and its allies.

Made in the USA
Monee, IL
28 April 2026